N

Pacific Ocean

RALIA

Brisbane

BLUE MTNS.

Bathurst   Newcastle
            Sydney

delaide

ALPS

Bendigo
Ballarat   Melbourne
Geelong

BASS   STRAIT

TASMANIA

Launceston

Hobart

AUSTRALIANS
AND THE
GOLD RUSH

Other Books by Jay Monaghan

BIBLIOGRAPHY OF LINCOLNIANA, 1839-1939

DIPLOMAT IN CARPET SLIPPERS:
LINCOLN DEALS WITH FOREIGN AFFAIRS

LAST OF THE BAD MEN:
THE LEGEND OF TOM HORN

THE OVERLAND TRAIL

THIS IS ILLINOIS

THE GREAT RASCAL:
THE LIFE AND ADVENTURES OF NED BUNTLINE

CIVIL WAR ON THE WESTERN BORDER

THE MAN WHO ELECTED LINCOLN

SWAMP FOX OF THE CONFEDERACY:
THE LIFE AND MILITARY SERVICES OF M. JEFF THOMPSON

CUSTER: THE LIFE OF GENERAL GEORGE ARMSTRONG CUSTER

THE BOOK OF THE AMERICAN WEST

Vessel Capable of Carrying 100 to 175 Gold Seekers on the Three- to
Four-Month Voyage from Australia to California

Courtesy San Francisco Maritime Museum

Jay Monaghan

AUSTRALIANS
AND THE
GOLD RUSH

❀❀❀

California and Down Under
1849-1854

UNIVERSITY OF CALIFORNIA PRESS
Berkeley and Los Angeles 1966

UNIVERSITY OF CALIFORNIA PRESS
BERKELEY AND LOS ANGELES, CALIFORNIA
CAMBRIDGE UNIVERSITY PRESS, LONDON, ENGLAND
© 1966 BY THE REGENTS OF THE UNIVERSITY OF CALIFORNIA
Library of Congress Catalog Card Number: 66-23182
DESIGNED BY DAVID PAULY
PRINTED IN THE UNITED STATES OF AMERICA

to Mildred

who adds to this writer's aspirations,
subtracts from his frustrations,
and multiplies the joy of culminations.

Contents

Contents

Illustrations

1

Where Is California?

"Where in the world is California?" John Fairfax, editor of the *Sydney Morning Herald*, must have asked himself when the first news of the discovery of gold reached Australia in December, 1848. He was a ruddy-faced man, aged forty-four, with firm, piercing eyes, a mouth straight as a line, bushy white hair and a white beard. An important person in Australia, he stood habitually with his feet apart and his stomach out—an aggressive John Bull, accustomed to command but unaccustomed to being struck.[1]

December was midsummer down under and from his office window, on lower George Street, editor Fairfax looked out at the omnibuses, gigs, hansom cabs, and tandems of spirited horses kicking up hot Christmas dust on the paved thoroughfare. Liveried footmen sprang from their lofty perches to open carriage doors, and many of the "gentlemen" who emerged were ex-convicts, emancipists who, having served their terms and succeeded in business, were now wealthy. John Fairfax knew that these emancipists were courted in counting rooms, toadied to in the best business establishments, and welcomed by governors, but were absolutely excluded from many "fashionable parlours." A gold rush might do odd and upsetting things to Sydney's segregated society.

John Fairfax looked at his map of the world. "Where indeed is California?" Finally he located it and saw that the new goldfield must be in a country as remote as any place on the globe. The Sandwich Islands, later renamed Hawaii, were well known to him. Alaska appeared reasonably close to the Russian ports, and its coast was familiar to all fur traders, but California seemed to be one of the least known and most inaccessible parts of the world;[2] the gazetteer on his desk described it as a "peninsula at the extremity of N. America."

Mystery and intrigue permeate John Fairfax's original announcement of the California gold discovery. The first report of the event came to him in newspapers brought by the *Plymouth*, a little schooner from the Sandwich Islands which anchored at Sydney on Wednesday, December 20. He immediately noted the vessel's arrival in his *Herald*, but for some reason did not mention the gold discovery until Saturday, December 23. Several explanations may account for this delay.

Perhaps the *Plymouth*'s captain, George H. Gould, withheld the news in order to negotiate secretly with certain local merchants for a cargo at bargain prices and thus beat potential rival shippers to the California market. His crew were South Sea Islanders who talked little English, so the secret could be kept. Certainly the firm of Montefiore, Graham & Company immediately consigned a cargo on the *Plymouth* and chartered a much larger schooner, the *Despatch*, to follow her. However, such a secret could not have been kept long, because a vessel from New Zealand arrived on either the same or the next day. (The records on this point are conflicting.) The second craft brought Hawaiian newspapers as well as some sixty people, counting the crew, and the discovery of gold must have been common talk among them all. Yet John Fairfax, when he printed a detailed account of this second ship's voyage, once more failed to report any discovery of gold.[3]

Was the captain of this second vessel also withholding the news, which could no longer have been a secret, or was John Fairfax withholding it for some reason of his own? His *Herald* was a four-page sheet, with two pages devoted to local news as well as items clipped from other journals. The balance of the paper carried advertisements, mainly of goods brought by the latest ships. It is possible that he considered the discovery too far away and too trivial for notice, but he actually had other, better reasons for wanting to suppress the news.

John Fairfax was a man to reckon with. The Fairfaxes had been landowners in Yorkshire, England, for three hundred years.

Some of the family emigrated to colonial Virginia, where they were intimate with a man named Washington who turned traitor to the Crown. John, a bankrupt, moved to Australia with his wife and three children in 1838. As editor of the Leamington *Chronicle and Warwickshire Reporter,* he had been sued for libel and ruined by prolonged lawsuits. In Sydney, New South Wales, adjoining an area the Australians called New England, he began life afresh. The settlement had been founded as a penal colony shortly after the American Revolution, when Britain could no longer send convicts to Georgia. This traffic, still practiced in neighboring Van Diemen's Land, had ceased to exist in Sydney by 1841. Here John Fairfax had become a power in the land by publishing a newspaper that catered to the great livestock-station owners, the big city merchants, and the shipping interests. His paper molded public opinion.

John Fairfax had little acquaintance with, and less respect for, Americans. His knowledge of them had been colored by Cooper's Leatherstocking Tales and Lord Byron's poems about Daniel Boone. Australia had comparable characters and an outback as large as any in the United States. Only the preceding month, November, 1848, an explorer named Edmund Kennedy had been killed by spear-throwing natives while charting Cape York, about as far from Sydney as California was from the Missouri River outfitting points.

The only Americans whom John Fairfax had known were whalemen; every year some twenty or twenty-five of their ships dropped anchor at Sydney.[4] The town was located twelve miles from the sea on the south side of Port Jackson, a magnificent inlet with many deep coves stretching out like the fingers of a hand. Narrow promontories, called the Heads, and a lighthouse marked the ocean entrance to this maze of inland waterways. The hardy American whalemen, who had sailed from North Atlantic ports in quest of blubber, seemed like odd fellows to John Fairfax. When told to "seek a ostler at the mew" they might look blankly at their Sydney informant and with a nasal drawl reply, "Sorry, pardner, I don't speak Spanish."

Such bizarre characters amused John Fairfax, but he shuddered at the possible effect a gold rush from Sydney to America might have on Australia. As an upper-middle-class Englishman, he was steeped in the prejudices of Harriet Martineau and Frances Trollope, who feared the success of American democracy lest it ruin the British social order. Sydney, like England, had several propagandists who preached constantly about the horrors of American government, pointing to Herman Melville and Charles Wilkes, who had recently sailed the South Pacific, as disseminators of half-truths, like all Americans. Wilkes's uncle, the notorious Whig, John Wilkes, had made much trouble for George III during the Revolution. The anti-American prejudice had undoubtedly increased since workmen in the United States were striving to form a strong nativist American party to persecute British immigrants. Relations between the two English-speaking countries thus were already at an ugly low, and this gold discovery might push them lower still.[5]

For John Fairfax an annoying phase of the news about California was the date of its arrival. During Christmas season every conservative Englishman should remain at home and celebrate with his family. Sydney, with a population of 60,000, resembled the English town of Chester, or Scotland's Edinburgh; travelers pronounced it more British than London.[6] Some said the odd accent and the peculiar rhythm of speech heard on Sydney streets reminded them of the Irish, a traditionally turbulent element in the population which could be expected to make trouble whenever exciting news was printed.

Business in Sydney this December differed from other yuletide seasons John Fairfax remembered, for the merchants were worrying about a surplus of goods. Stores along George Street overflowed with supplies which people seemed reluctant to purchase. Show windows displayed handsome vases, hats, wigs, ladies' slippers, and editions of the best English classics which had arrived on recent ships. Shelves behind the counters were piled high with newly imported bolts of cotton cloth. Sporting-goods shops advertised English fishing tackle which wives might buy husbands: silk lines, gut-snelled hooks, sinkers, reels, and shark gaffs. They also offered selections of a recent shipment of Wellington boots, swords, tennis balls, horsewhips, and "percussion guns"—flintlocks were already dated. Shopkeepers pointed to gifts for children. They offered a new stock of rocking horses, Noah's arks, dollhouses, spinning tops, magic lanterns, and tool chests. David Jones's large store opposite the post office specialized in supplies for graziers, the well-to-do stockmen who lived in manorial fashion on stations back in the bush. David Jones sold them "Scotch woolens," blankets, jackets, red and blue shirts made from their own fleeces shipped halfway around the world to be manufactured in British mills, then shipped back again.

In spite of the depression, Christmas decorations ornamented all the shops. Even the stalls where beef was sold had been draped with green eucalyptus boughs.[7] Yet to John Fairfax all the gaiety seemed counterfeit—a kind of mockery. The people were unhappy, and they might respond unpredictably to news of a gold discovery. Always at Christmastime the upperclasses admitted a homesickness for Old England. December was the hottest month of the year down under, and Australians felt a melancholia for a white Christmas, with villagers stamping in out of the bracing air to hobnob with cronies around a snug fire. They also felt a vague nostalgia when they read in Shakespeare and other English classics about the sweet birth of spring in May and the soft, warm winds from the South. In Australia, May marked the beginning of winter, and winds from the South came straight from icy polar regions.

An Australian could never forget that the English moon stood on its head south of the equator, that trees shed their bark instead of their leaves, that wood in their country—some of it at least—did not float, and that two of their quadrupeds had birds' bills and laid eggs. Yes, and Australian birds squawked, even laughed, but did not sing, and a few of them wore hair.

Perhaps John Fairfax realized that the feeling of being far from home might make the people unusually vulnerable to the exciting reports about California gold printed in the Hawaiian papers. Perhaps he suspected that the reports might be a hoax, or at least an exaggeration. The news had reached Hawaii on the American lumber-carrying freighter, the *Euphemia*,[8] and John Fairfax questioned the reliability of "Americans." He also deplored the fact that lower-class Australians showed signs of becoming like the Americans, instead of developing like true Britishers. Many of the Sydney rascals were the sons of criminals or of the lesser order of civil servants; England held no memories of a cherished "home" for them. Instead, they reveled in lawless independence, liked to think themselves "wild colonial boys," and often wore cabbage-tree hats—the cheapest kind of headgear, handmade in the outback. Such rowdies scoffed at English manners, English dress, English gentlemen. Indeed, well-dressed men at the theater complained that unseen hands might tip a patron's fine beaver hat forward over his eyes, or, with a quick, insulting blow, tap the expensive felt down over a wearer's ears.

A recent depression in the price of wool had reduced wages, and graziers, desperate for help, hoped to revive the transportation of criminals from England or even to import coolies from the Orient. City workers, especially the cabbage-tree-hat boys, objected to both proposals: they did not want to compete with either convict or yellow labor. This rowdy element worried John Fairfax, and he knew that republican America set a bad precedent for them to follow. The disturbances sure to accompany this gold discovery might foment an outbreak of lawlessness such as the Australians had never seen. God forbid! Yet, almost immediately after the disturbing news had arrived laborers held a mass meeting to discuss forcing wages up to five shillings, sixpence a day. In vain the employers' representatives told the crowd that a week's food for one of the laboring class could be purchased for three shillings. The workers replied that they must also rent houses from the landlord class and had no hope of independence for themselves. Told to go to the country and work as stockmen where their found was supplied free, they said that they were mechanics and must not infringe on the shepherds' trade. They wanted higher wages here in Sydney, and they would organize to get them. Labor leaders promised to establish a newspaper devoted to their rights, championing manhood suffrage and all the reforms that Chartists had rioted for "back home"; it was to be called the *People's Advocate*.

Certainly, a gold rush to California boded infinite troubles for John Fairfax's wealthy readers, but he prided himself on honest reporting. He decided to print only cuttings from the Honolulu newspapers concerning the gold discovery—news items too fantastic to be believed. From these, his readers learned that gold was being picked up under trees and shoveled out of dry creek beds in California. San Francisco's newspaper, the *Star*, had ceased to twinkle since editor and typesetters had gone to the diggings. Indeed, all but eighty of the town's thousand residents seemed to have joined a rush to the mountains a hundred miles east from the coast. Another thousand, from God knew where, were already at the goldfields under the leadership of one Sam Brannan, a Mormon. (Just what was a Mormon? Fairfax would have to find out and inform the public.)

Then a startling idea illuminated Fairfax's mind: Why not urge other shippers to follow the example of Montefiore, Graham & Company? Beat the Yankees to their own market! Not only would gold seekers from the United States require three months to cross the Plains and the mountains to the Pacific Coast, but they could not start until grass grew next spring. They might save a little time by crossing the Isthmus of Panama, but the danger of fever on that passage would deter them. The third possible route, around the Horn, sometimes required six months. Supplies for the miners would have to go that way. Therefore, Australia was the closest "civilized" country to the goldfields. What an opportunity to liquidate the surplus goods glutting the Sydney market and profit mightily while doing so! Fairfax also reminded those of his readers who had mechanical ability that they might invent and manufacture gold-washing machines. Then, to discourage honest laborers from emigrating, he warned that the diggings would attract the worst class of adventurers.[9]

This was editor Fairfax's Christmas message to his townsmen in 1848, but their response fulfilled his hopes only in part. To be sure, wholesalers called at his office to place advertisements in the *Herald* offering their surplus goods. They itemized supplies of ready-made clothing, slops (overalls), shoes, nails, axes, gelatin, preserved meat, soups, oatmeal, potatoes, flour, and bread; even books might be shipped to California and sold there. Speculators were urged to buy tinned meats especially suitable for "the starvation districts of California." Gunsmiths advertised carbines for the goldfields. Stationers wanted to sell charts of the North Pacific.

To make the business transactions safe, shipmasters announced that their vessels would be armed. This seemed sensible to John Fairfax and his merchant readers, but the next action of the shipowners displeased him. Advertisements appealed for passengers as well as freight. Great broadsides on walls along Market, George, and Pitt streets all the way to Circular Wharf screamed: "GOLD, GOLD, CALIFORNIA." Cheap passage was offered, thus threatening to draw off the scarce supply of labor and make it easier for mechanics to organize and insist on higher pay.[10]

One of the leaders among these shipowners urging passengers to embark was canny, English-born Robert Towns. A practical sea captain, he had traded, in his youth, from Britain to the East Indies, accumulating enough capital to buy one vessel. Eventually becoming the owner of several ships, he visited Sydney first in 1827 and settled there permanently in 1842 after having married the half sister of William Charles Wentworth, a wealthy pastoralist and powerful politican who lived in a magnificent manor at Vaucluse Bay, a cove between Sydney and the Heads. Wentworth's extensive formal gardens sloped from the house to the water's edge, where he had built a pier. Many well-kept paths, bordered with boxwood hedges, crossed and recrossed the brook that babbled from a natural fountain down to the bay. Convict-gardeners cultivated the flowers and shrubs, and those who committed minor offenses while serving Wentworth lolled in his private "gaol"—a stone dungeon among other outhouses behind the mansion.

Wentworth had been schooled in England and on the backs of his rich father's thoroughbreds, which the boy raced with skill. Now, when he had reached middle age, his grazing interests were so extensive that he worried constantly about an adequate supply of labor.

With all his wealth, Wentworth inherited a handicap which might have crushed a man of less spirit. He was twenty-nine years old before he learned that his father, D'Arcy Wentworth, who posed in Britain as an Irish gentleman, had been twice arrested for highway robbery. The records did not show a conviction, but it was whispered that D'Arcy saved himself by volunteering to leave the country. However that may have been, D'Arcy came to Australia as surgeon on a prison ship, meeting on board a girl convicted of some minor crime. She lived with him in common-law marriage, bearing three children before she died in 1799. D'Arcy Wentworth was once court-martialed by Captain William Bligh, of *Bounty* fame, but London disallowed the decree. D'Arcy died in 1827, the biggest landholder in Australia. According to some gossips his eldest son, the tall and brilliant William, had hoped to marry into the socially prominent McArthur family, but was turned down because of his questionable ancestry; others said there had been a quarrel over money. At any rate, young Wentworth pulled the props from under the old social structure of segregation by organizing the emancipists and insisting on their equal rights. Now, in the 1840's, he had become a political power in the land.

The bitter social and political division in the upper classes and the bubbling discontent among laborers made Australians peculiarly susceptible to news of a gold rush that might depopulate some of the feuding factions. Wealthy W. C. Wentworth, having used his great political influence to induce the government to furnish workers free passage from England to Australia, watched with dismay as thousands went to the United States instead. Now his brother-in-law, Robert Towns, was advertising cheap rates to move Australia's precious labor out of the country. Here was seed for a family row, but Robert Towns, the hardheaded sea captain, said frankly: "In trade there are no friendships!"[11]

Unlike Wentworth, Robert Towns did not live on a country estate. His residence was in town near his warehouses. From the windows, as from the poop deck of one of his own ships, he could survey the full crescent of Circular Wharf, later called Circular Quay, where his vessels tied up to load and unload. Towns was one of those well-to-do men who watched every penny, and complained openly that he was losing money every year. No matter how prosperous his trade, he might say to an acquaintance, "Last night I balanced my year's operations and, considering wear and tear on sails and rope, depreciation on vessels, I lost just about £1,000." Towns had been "losing £1,000 annually" for the last twenty years! Prior to that, not having £1,000, he probably "lost" only £100 each year.

Towns usually kept one or two vessels at sea whaling, but he considered sandalwood trading his principal business. Knowing the chiefs of several South Pacific islands, he sent them trinkets in exchange for the fragrant wood that was prized by the Chinese for coffins and cabinets. His vessels also carried to China quantities of the black sea slugs dried into what was known as bêche-de-mer, a highly prized delicacy. In addition, Towns shipped horses to British army officers in Calcutta. New South Wales had proved an excellent range for saddle mounts, and "Walers" brought top prices in the Indian service. As much as £25 would be paid for a thoroughbred raised outback on free grass. The McArthurs, most prominent of all the grazier barons, shipped horses and wool in Towns's vessels. So did Thomas Icely, from his station west of the Blue Mountains—an area that would loom large in the gold-rush story. Towns's marriage to W. C. Wentworth's half sister, combined with his big shipping interests, made him the "uncle" of the Wentworth clan. Whenever one of the younger ne'er-do-wells needed a situation, Towns was called on to supply it, and this, no doubt, kept many of them from objecting to his self-interest in urging emigration to California.

Robert Towns and John Fairfax, both destined to be giants in gold-rush history, were opposites in many ways. Towns, with all his wealth, wore rough boots, a frayed stock, and rusty black frockcoat. Fairfax catered to wealth and considered appearances important. On the day after Christmas, while Towns devised plans to take advantage of the startling news, Fairfax printed a long, critical editorial. He told his readers that the California climate was unhealthy, sickness was prevalent, and famine likely. He stressed once more that the rush would attract the worst scoundrels in the Pacific. And, as he had also done previously, he pointed to the great opportunity for the sale of

Sydney's excess goods.[12] Four days later (note again the suspicious delay in reporting the news), he announced that a keg of gold, some lumps larger than peas, had arrived in the *Plymouth*.

Robert Towns, the cautious businessman, realized that passengers promised the surest profit: they paid in advance. No speculation there! His first step was typical of his business methods. On January 5, 1849, as agent for London owners, he laid on the 480-ton bark *Eleanor Lancaster*, advertised for emigrants, and began loading the holds with bricks—good ballast that might be salable in a pioneer community such as California. Next, he urged others to ship their goods on his bark; let them speculate, pay the freight, cover expenses, and render him a meager profit. With this assured, he himself speculated, in a small way, loading on his own account 10 hogsheads of rum, 1 of loaf sugar, 19 bags of salt, 6 bundles of spades. Towns noted in his journal that the lot amounted to only £188 3s. 5d. As a sixpence was a common coin, most merchants would have been content to estimate the worth of the goods to within a penny, but not Towns.[13]

Towns's problem with passengers was more complex. He advertised fares at £30 for cabin class, £10 for steerage, and immediately had more applicants for jobs on the ship—not cash customers—than he could employ. Cabbage-tree-hat boys who did not know the main-truck from a buntline claimed to be able seamen, but passengers with money were slow to appear. The law required Towns to employ a surgeon for so extended a voyage. This seemed a needless expense to him, but he found a Dr. Silver who would pay £10 for a round-trip passage, cabin class, and act as surgeon while on board. For the ship's captain, Towns engaged Francis Lodge, a retired mariner, who seems to have been operating some business, perhaps a pub. Lodge was a man-about-town with a piano-playing wife, and he insisted on taking her on the cruise. Towns agreed to assume Lodge's obligations and liquidate his business profitably after the ship sailed. For the important position of supercargo, Towns hired J. C. Catton and instructed him to report market conditions in San Francisco as soon after his arrival as possible. Towns told speculators who might entrust goods to Catton that he spoke Spanish and was, therefore, highly qualified for trade in California.[14]

In addition to Towns and Montefiore, Graham & Company, many others laid on vessels for California and advertised their services. A rush had started to send goods, not emigrants, to San Francisco. Circular Wharf became a beehive of bustling men and popping whips as horse-drawn drays unloaded at ships' sides. Stevedores were getting work again; ship chandlers were doing business. Taverns would sell grog once more, and groceries would be purchased. Good times, in a minor way, returned. In the midst of this new activity, the first issue of the much-heralded workers' newspaper, the *People's Advocate*, appeared.[15] A twelve-page weekly, it sold for sixpence—too dear for a laborer's wages, but copies would undoubtedly be read in taprooms and coffee houses. The *Advocate*'s editor opposed emigration to California, as John Fairfax did, but, unlike Fairfax, he opposed immigration to Australia of skilled workers from England, both convict and free. However, the *Advocate* did approve of importing a limited number of unskilled Englishmen for employment on the outback stations. Such fellows, the editor said, would not take jobs from skilled city laborers.

The *Advocate* bitterly opposed wealthy woolgrowers, many of whom happened to be going bankrupt because of the drop in wool prices. Its editor attacked John Fairfax and his *Morning Herald* as the mouthpiece of these plutocrats, pointing out that workingmen had no representation in Parliament. The *Advocate* said that it did not oppose a master class, did not want to overturn it, but was interested only in bettering the workman's standard of living. Obviously the new paper's editor had the un-American idea that labor was a fixed class. It never seemed to have occurred to him that laborers might eventually become employers and capitalists. Readers who disregarded his advice and went to California were due for an eye-opening experience in the New World. It is noticeable, too, that the *Advocate* tried to interest its readers in local athletic contests, horse races, and ball games, in fact anything to keep them happy at home[16]—the ancient palliative of bread and circuses.

On January 8, 1849, while the big vessels were still loading cargo and prospective passengers were haggling over fares, the little *Plymouth*, carrying the Montefiore consignment of cargo, slipped her cables, floated down the bay and out between the Heads—the first to leave for the American goldfields. Passengers who had engaged berths on the *Eleanor Lancaster* fumed at Towns's delay. They had paid good money and were in a hurry to get to California.

The rush from Australia—if sending shiploads of goods without passengers could be called a rush—started with the *Plymouth*, and on January 9, 1849, John Fairfax devoted another editorial to the goldfields. In a lengthy column, he admitted that the discovery might make the United States one of the leading countries of the world. Certainly, England and the United States would soon be the two great powers, and Fairfax feared that the reckless and excitable Americans might declare war on some country in order to expand their national boundary across the Pacific.

Six days later Fairfax printed a description of San Francisco copied from the London *Times* of September 16, 1848. The *Times* article, in turn, had made use of a report by Charles Wilkes, the American naval commander who had visited the port in 1841. In this report Wilkes described San Francisco as "a large frame house occupied by an agent of the Hudson's Bay Company; a store kept by an American; a billiard-room and bar; a poop-cabin of a ship, occupied as a dwelling by an Anglo-American captain; a blacksmith shop, and some outbuildings."[17] Fairfax should have realized that this was not the San Francisco of 1849, but he failed to note the distinction.

Six vessels now lay along Circular Wharf outfitting for California, and all advertised for both freight and passengers. Most of them promised to sail "immediately," one within "eight days." All hoped to beat deliberate and conservative Towns's *Eleanor Lancaster*. Among these competing vessels, tugging at their hawsers, stood Sheppard & Alger's old bark, the *Lindsays*, Captain W. Mackenzie commanding. This ancient tub had been condemned in a Bermuda prize court in 1833.[18] She offered the cheapest fare, a tariff that would be dear at any price because the dilapidated craft might never complete her voyage. She was advertised, however, as being the next to sail, and her agents touted Captain Mackenzie as "late of the *Heroine* and *Sir John Byng.*"

This business competition prompted owners of the *William Hill,* now loading rum, tobacco, paint, nails, and clothing, to announce that their vessel might not be first to leave but would be first to arrive in San Francisco.[19] Undaunted by such salesmanship, agents for the *Lindsays* advertised in the morning paper of January 15 that she would sail that day, stating that berths were still available. They remained unsold, however, and the bark stayed at her moorings.

Next day the agents for both the *Lindsays* and the *William Hill* found themselves outwitted. The 138-ton schooner *Despatch,* chartered by Montefiore, Graham & Company, upped anchor and sailed down the bay. She carried only one passenger, Mr. F. Montefiore of the big mercantile firm that had chartered her. He was following the *Plymouth* with an assorted cargo including beer, spirits, and hardware. The wealthy Jewish family of Montefiore might establish a bank in San Francisco. In any event, they hoped to have the *Despatch* back in Sydney by July 1 with a complete report.

With two ships ahead of them now, the *William Hill,* the *Lindsays,* and Towns's *Eleanor Lancaster* renewed their appeals for passengers. The *Lindsays'* owners assured prospective emigrants that she would sail on January 17 "positively," but she was still tied to the dock on January 20 when the *William Hill* cast off with only three passengers, all of them Sydney merchants interested in the ship as well as her freight. Their vessel was ballasted with brick and carried a cargo of clothes, guns, meat, tools, wine, rum, iron, and tobacco—all surplus stock that had been advertised by Sydney merchants.

A little English brig, the *Deborah,* was warped into the *William Hill's* vacated berth. She advertised for passengers and freight which, her agents said, would be sold by "an old California trader." Next day the *Lindsays* cast off. After an entire fortnight of advertising for passengers she had succeeded in booking only three men willing to brave a voyage on the old tub, one of whom owned the entire cargo and may also have had an interest in the vessel itself.* His name was J. H. Levien, and he was taking to California a supply of cigars, candles, kegs of brandy, tins of lemon syrup, men's shirts, carriage harness, and haberdashery—in short, more surplus goods bought at reduced prices in Sydney. Levien had an eye for bargains and a respect for property which would be notable when the vigilantes assumed control in San Francisco.

While the *Lindsays* drifted toward the Heads, Towns's *Eleanor Lancaster* cleared at last. She carried fifty-two passengers, the first legitimate gold seekers to leave Australia. Cabbage-tree-hat boys and sunbonneted women with clay pipes in their mouths stood in her waist packed like sheep in a pen. Fifty of the fifty-two travelers would arrive in San Francisco seventy-one days later.[20] Towns admitted that some, even those traveling cabin class, were the worst rascals in Sydney, but they had the money for their passage. Good riddance! His man Catton was on board as supercargo, and Towns's last word to Captain Lodge was, "Be first in San Francisco!"—surely an order for the benefit of shippers only.

In spite of all the advertisements for passengers, few had gone. John Fairfax's *Herald* and the *People's Advocate* seemed to have succeeded in preventing a popular rush to California, but a deceptive lull often precedes a storm.

* Charles Bateson, *Gold Fleet for California: Forty-Niners from Australia and New Zealand* (Sydney, 1963), p. 156; *Alta California*, Aug. 4, 1849. Records in San Francisco show that the *Lindsays* arrived with twenty-eight passengers. If both figures are correct, the additional passengers could have been picked up in Honolulu.

2

Be First in San Francisco!

The *Eleanor Lancaster* slipped away from Circular Wharf on January 21, 1849. The *Lindsays* was only a few miles ahead of her down the long inlet. Both were barks, three-masted craft that should sail well in the steady trade winds. As the *Lancaster* rounded Bennelong Point, just below Circular Wharf, Sydney Town disappeared from view. Looking forward, her passengers, eager to be first in California, could see the *Lindsays* coasting along under jib and topsails. The *Eleanor Lancaster* followed her, passing tiny Pinchgut Island close enough for the passengers to wave at artillerymen manning the guns there. Beyond, voyagers on the starboard deck recognized other landmarks as they slipped by: Government House, built in Elizabethan style; Farm Cove and its botanical gardens, fashionable Woolloomooloo Bay, dotted with yachts and sailboats;[1] Potts Point, Rushcutter Bay, and Vaucluse—all sites of little villages or large estates. On the hills stood towering, lemon-scented eucalyptus trees with naked, mauve-pink trunks.

Passengers on the port side watched water churn around a group of small islands, the Sow and Pigs, and break in a thin white line on the distant north shore, dark with Norfolk Island pines—spectacular trees whose horizontal limbs supported needle clusters in inverted pyramids. Behind the vessel's bubbling wake, passengers could see Cockatoo Island, where convicts were detained. Sydney boys called themselves cockatoos in fun. California might see nothing funny in that name. Ahead of the *Lancaster*, partly hidden from her deck passengers by the jib on her bowsprit, lay the Sydney Heads, a gap in the long, flat-topped eastern rim of Jackson Bay.

The Heads did not appear lofty from a distance, but when the

Eleanor Lancaster's passengers saw, from far behind, the *Lindsays* enter the gap, they noticed that the 240-foot sandstone bluffs towered at least five times higher than the old bark's tallest masts. A few minutes later the *Lindsays* reached the sea. Her dingy sails fluttered down from their yards, bellied out in a fresh breeze, and under a cloud of grimy canvas she disappeared around the north Head, bound north-northeast for California.

From the *Eleanor Lancaster*, Captain Lodge watched her go. As a merchant returning to a seafaring life, it behooved him to demonstrate his sailing ability. Already he had sent crewmen aloft. They perched like starlings along the yardarms, waiting for his order to "make sail." As the bark entered the narrows her tall masts began to rock, but she churned ahead. A quarter of a mile farther she wallowed into the ocean, and her sailors felt the long, steady roll they knew so well. The first mate shouted through his megaphone. Sail after sail billowed down. The hull jerked forward in a southeast wind, making spray fly from the bark's prow. The *Lindsays*' sails appeared far to the north, and the *Lancaster*'s helmsman swung his wheel. The bowsprit circled until it pointed straight for the rival vessel, then dipped below the horizon as the bark raced toward it. Be first in California! Aye, aye, Sir!

A shrill pipe called the cabin passengers to mess. Robert Towns had watched for every economy and, to make room for extra berths, had reduced his dining saloon by half. Meals were served in two sittings.* Those traveling in steerage cooked "tucker" issued to them and complained later that their rations were worse than those served common sailors, which were notoriously bad. However, the excitement of the race on this first day spiced all meals, and by the time the passengers finished eating and were back on deck, the *Eleanor Lancaster* had crept up to windward of the big, laboring *Lindsays*.

It is easy to picture the scene that might well have followed,

---

* Towns could have made this alteration for the *Eleanor Lancaster*'s second voyage in 1850. William Jackson Barry, *Past & Present and Men of the Times* (Wellington, N.Z., 1897), p. 80, notes the alteration when describing his voyage, which he claimed was the vessel's first trip. Barry says, however, that they stopped at Honolulu, and the records show the *Lancaster* to have stopped there on her second, not her first, voyage.

with the two barks close enough for the travelers to see each other: Captain Lodge offering Supercargo Catton a pinch of snuff as they watched from the quarterdeck of the *Lancaster*, feeling a trifle superior, and Captain Mackenzie, who had been first out of port, standing in philosophical resignation. An old salt, loudly advertised by his vessel's agents as "late of the *Heroine* and *Sir John Byng*,"[2] but hired at a low figure to sail a worn-out tub, we can believe the fellow to have been unkempt, shaggy-bearded, wearing rough, seagoing clothes with suspenders holding up his pantaloons, and carpet slippers easing tired feet which had suffered on Sydney's hot sidewalks (called "futpaaths" by Australians).

As the *Eleanor Lancaster*'s canvas stole wind from the *Lindsays*, little trembling wrinkles appeared on the latter's sails. "Look! We've got the weather gauge," some passenger probably shouted, to gain the admiration of less traveled companions.

"We'll pass her now like she's at anchor," another may have answered.

All watched the *Lindsays*' deck come broadside and slip to the rear—the captain's cabin, the main companionway, the fo'c'sle, and finally the jibboom, martingale, and bowsprit. Captain Lodge must have snapped his snuffbox with satisfaction: he was succeeding, and victory would make his passengers, some of them at least, forget the weevily hardtack they had been served and the rationed sugar for their tea—forget even that two or three months of such fare lay ahead of them.

By sundown the *Lindsays* had been left far behind. Passengers on the *Lancaster* could distinguish her only as a blur on the southern horizon. They did not notice that the daylight was fading until a seaman opened the fo'c'sle hatch. The dull yellow light within, invisible in daytime, could now be seen even from the stern. Overhead, stars rocked to and fro between the sails. The big bark, with every rope taut and true, cantered into the night.

At dawn the *Lindsays* had disappeared, and the *Eleanor Lancaster* sailed alone in the blue saucer of the sea. The *William Hill* was one day ahead of her, the *Despatch* had five days' start, and the little *Plymouth*, thirteen. Let the devil, or Davy Jones, catch the hindmost!

Every day the heat seemed more intense as the *Eleanor Lancaster* sailed north. Now and again, gigantic, misty mountain peaks thrust out of the ocean beyond the port bow, twenty or thirty miles away. The captain, pointing to his chart, might have said: "Fiji, Viti Levu. I know it well! Wallace Island! Not so good!"*

After passing the last of the islands, travelers saw no more schools of white flying fish which had skittered alongside the bark and plunged into the sea like whiffs of grapeshot. Even the South Pacific black-backed gulls that followed vessels for refuse disappeared. Grumbling passengers could say, "No wonder! Old Towns throws no tucker overboard. He feeds garbage to the steerage."

Day after day the voyagers saw nothing above the vast waste of waters except their own sails and little glimpses of blue sky and fluffy white clouds. Finally the trade winds quit. The vessel floundered near the equator, stewing in the sun. Tar dripped from ropes, seeped between the deck boards. Worst of all, as the ocean heat increased, myriads of cockroaches crept up from the bilge. Sometimes the sails hung limp all day long. A half-dozen rainstorms could be seen on different sectors of the horizon. Magnificent tropical rainbows arched under threatening gunmetal clouds. An occasional deluge swept across the *Lancaster's* deck, bringing refreshing coolness for a moment, steamy heat the next.

At last the bark picked up the northern trade winds, and all sails were reset. Men would not have to go aloft again now for days. However, the lack of activity tried everybody's nerves. Steerage passengers congregated in ugly little knots, complaining about the food, the heat, the cockroaches—seagoing routine when men have little else to do.

On April 2, 1849,[3] after seventy-one days at sea, the passengers discerned the Golden Gate behind a veil of gray rain. The *Eleanor Lancaster* had set a record. None of the forty-eight vessels that left Sydney for San Francisco that year beat her time. The California coast differed greatly from eastern Aus-

* I have no proof that these islands were sighted, but the *Eleanor Lancaster* made a record trip and vessels making fast time took this more northerly route. Note the Hobart *Colonial Times*, Dec. 25, 1849.

tralia. Here mountains stood up from the ocean for 2,000 or more feet, bare ridges, bony as an old cow's back, with occasional trees like warts. The Golden Gate was two miles wide and, as the *Eleanor Lancaster* sailed through, her passengers saw no habitations. Ahead of them the bay opened into a new sea, with more bare mountains ten miles beyond.

The *Lancaster* shortened sail, and skirted around a bluff at the south. There, near the coast where broad, dry valleys came together, lay San Francisco—a miserable and dilapidated collection of tents and shanties scattered around an adobe customhouse and one, big, brand-new brick store.[4] The beach was shallow and the tide was out. Several keelboats lay on their sides in the sand flats. Seagoing vessels had anchored offshore. Clustered together, their sailless masts resembled bristles on a brush. The *Plymouth*, the *William Hill*, and the *Despatch* were not among them. Towns's bark had won the race!

Supercargo Catton hired a waterman to row him ashore, the fare $5.00. Catton found the streets running down to the bay littered with flotsam left by the receding tide. Picking his way through stinking, waterlogged debris, he came to dry land. The people he met were mostly Latin Americans in embroidered costumes, some in the steeple sombreros of Mexico, others in the flat-crowned hats of South America. Few of them talked English, so Catton's knowledge of Spanish served him well. These men were almost as new to California as was Catton, having come overland from Sonora, Mexico, or by ship from Chile and Peru.

Catton walked with wobbly sea legs up the street between slab housefronts. Coming to a canvas-roofed store kept by native Americans, he inquired about those people called Mormons, who were reputed to have usurped the mines, and about that man, Sam Brannan. He learned that Brannan owned one store in town and another at Sutter's Fort, had published the San Francisco *Star*, and was well known as an auctioneer.[5] Mormons, Catton was told, were white people from a religious settlement in the desert. He heard, too, that San Francisco's cash customers, the miners, had gone to the diggings, a hundred and fifty miles farther east. They were not expected back for six months. As yet no overland gold seekers had arrived from "the States," but thousands were known to be crossing the Plains. Four hundred had taken the shortcut by way of the Isthmus of Panama, arriving last month. At least a thousand had come down from Oregon, a country settled jointly by Britishers and Americans before the boundary between the United States and Canada was drawn in 1846.

Catton noticed the lack of trees on California's coastal range. If cities mushroomed here, Australia might furnish the necessary lumber from her bounteous forests. Talking with local merchants, he soon discovered that the prices of tea, sugar, pickled beef, and "hardbread" were being quoted differently in the city and at the mines. Moreover, the price at one place might be stated in English shillings or American dollars and at the other in guineas, Spanish bits, and American cents. Being familiar with foreign exchange, Catton calculated that most goods fetched three or four times their San Francisco value at the diggings.[6] Certainly Towns's rum, loaf sugar, and salt should do well farther east. Catton decided to float his cargo closer to the better market, so he employed a pilot for the inland passage. Some of the *Lancaster's* passengers went ashore with their sea chests and sailor sacks. They had had enough of the ship, and were sure that *they* could live by their wits here, if anybody could.

Free of these disgruntled travelers, Captain Lodge ordered up the anchor and sailed eastward, past Alcatraz and Yerba Buena Island, into the open bay. Passengers who stayed on board noticed that the water extended south to the horizon, but the pilot steered north toward a red, volcanic rock protruding through the blue waters. Passing it and two small islands, white with guano, the vessel entered a new sea with hazy mountains on all sides looming into the sky. Twenty miles up this inland bay the pilot turned the *Eleanor Lancaster* straight toward bare hills on the right. As the bark approached them, an opening appeared and she entered it. The channel was deep and almost a mile wide at the narrowest places. Catton, on the quarterdeck, watched treeless ridges slip by, green with spring grass and so steep that the live oaks dotting the crests cast long shadows down the slopes even at noon.

Finally, after sailing ten miles in this crooked channel, Catton spied another inland sea ahead—Suisun Bay—edged with vast spits of tules or bulrushes. On a low ridge at the left he saw a cluster of twenty or more huts and tents. That's Benicia!

A boatman came out—predecessor of today's Chamber of Commerce secretary. He urged the captain to anchor at the town. Harbor as good as Hong Kong, Valparaiso, Sydney, yes siree. You bet! He explained that the San Joaquin River "dreened" southern California, and that the Sacramento River "dreened" the north; they joined in the tules twenty miles ahead. Small vessels might go up the latter to Sutter's Fort and Sacramento, up the former to Stockton, but a seagoing boat was sure to stick in the mud. At Benicia a vessel drawing eighteen feet of water could be moored to the shore. You can't beat it, pardner!

Five other vessels lined the Benicia anchorage and the *Eleanor Lancaster* joined them.[7] Catton decided to hurry back to San Francisco and prepare his market report for Robert Towns. Captain Lodge, who had left a business in Sydney to take this trip with his wife, could stay with the ship, sell the goods, and make additional money converting the hull into a combined hospital and grogshop. Months later, when Robert Towns heard about this arrangement, he wrote Lodge: "My only pain in your case, is poor Mrs. Lodge. Now don't you wish she had a piano? I am aware you are the very fellow to manage the thing if you only know where to stop."[8]

On April 18 and 25, respectively, the *William Hill* and the *Despatch* arrived in San Francisco. The *Eleanor Lancaster* had beaten their time by a wide margin, but the losers profited by the delay. During the critical interval the market in San Francisco had changed and Catton learned that both vessels sold some, though not all, of their goods at a fine profit. Builders paid a fabulous price for the *Hill's* brick ballast,[9] but without it she dared not venture back into the open sea. When the *Despatch's* crew deserted, scampering away to the diggings, both vessels stood helpless in San Francisco Bay. Catton, eager to return to Australia and report, was stranded!

Meanwhile, back in Sydney, Robert Towns waited for Catton's report before continuing his operations. A rival shipper, John MacNamara, decided that delays were dangerous. He operated a few vessels in the Australian coastal trade, was a devoted Irish nationalist, and would later help convicted traitors escape to California. Now he confidently nosed a fast sailing brig, the *Louisa*, into the berth vacated by the *Eleanor Lancaster*, next to the little *Deborah*, began advertising California as "that delightful country,"[10] and offered to take people there. The *Herald*, even as it printed MacNamara's tempting advertisements, poured cold water on his enthusiastic assertions. In a long editorial, John Fairfax rejoiced that the excitement was ended, the rush terminated, but he admitted that during the first days many more might have gone had they possessed the £10 passage money. As it was, the withdrawal of accounts had caused the savings banks to suspend payments, thus fortunately preventing latecomers from losing their hard-earned cash on a foolhardy trip. Fairfax also warned would-be emigrants that, by the time they could reach California, the United States government would take over the goldfields and discriminate against foreigners. These discouraging editorial comments were copied by newspapers in other Australian colonies.[11]

Such remarks made no impression on MacNamara. He had tried, and failed, to prevent passengers from booking on Towns's *Eleanor Lancaster*, warning them that the meals Towns served on shipboard were notoriously mean. Now MacNamara promised more amenities as well as better food on his *Louisa* and announced, day after day, that she would sail "tomorrow." A few berths were yet "available." On January 26, five days after the *Eleanor Lancaster* had gone, the *Louisa* cast off—a fine gesture, but MacNamara held her in Port Jackson, still hoping for more passengers. Three days later he advertised again that she would sail next day for sure and that two cabins and two steerage berths were still "disengaged."[12] Again MacNamara equivocated. The *Louisa* did not leave until January 31. She did, however, have thirty-four passengers, the second-largest contingent yet to leave Sydney. Perhaps the effort to prevent emigration was beginning to fail.

Then a strange bit of news in the Melbourne *Argus* definitely promised to check a rush. Gold had been discovered in Australia, gold in a quantity reported to "completely throw California in the shade." The strike had been made in the Pyrenees beyond Melbourne. One editor said the cry, "Off to California!" would change to "Hey for Buninyong, and the bonny Pyrenees!"[13] Sydney crowds could go there on foot although it was at least 500 miles away, a long walk, but gold seekers who lacked passenger fare to San Francisco might attempt it.

Another paper, the Melbourne *Herald*, questioned the authenticity of the discovery, declared it could not be verified, and reported that police had dispersed prospectors trespassing on neighboring sheep runs (a British word for pasture). Most Australian newspapers agreed with the *Herald*: gold, in non-paying quantities, had been found in Australia for years. To discourage renewed prospecting for it, the papers printed lists of these futile discoveries. Thus, the excitement over gold at home and abroad seemed to die. By February 1, 1849, only about a hundred people had left Sydney since the news came, a mere handful among the 4,961 who would go to San Francisco from Central and South America before the *Eleanor Lancaster* or any other Sydney vessel could arrive.[14] Yet emigrants from Sydney were to earn more notoriety in California than all the others. So far, the interest of Australians in the California gold rush had been largely artificial, a contest between shipowners seeking business and newspapers discouraging emigration. Apparently, the first bout had been won by the press. Many people still questioned the rumors of gold in California,[15] and the newspapers were trying to enhance their temporary victory by urging everyone to wait until one of the ships returned from San Francisco with firsthand information. The *Advocate* even took a fresh poke at the upper classes by warning workers against the greed of "pinchbeck aristocrats." Christopher Pinchbeck, a London watchmaker, was said to have made imitation gold out of copper and zinc in the early eighteenth century.[16]

Almost three weeks passed after the *Louisa's* departure before another vessel set sail for California. The English brig *Deborah* despaired of getting passengers, upped anchor and sailed to New Zealand, 1,200 miles eastward, hoping to find more venturesome colonists there. For the first time since the news of gold in California had arrived in December, 1848, no vessel for the diggings was advertised in Sydney newspapers. Finally an American whaleman, Captain William L. Jackson, who was in port refitting his ship-rigged *Inez*, decided to join the race. He had failed to interest emigrants back in early January[17] when the others left, but now with blubber scrubbed from his holds and decks holystoned, he tried again for passengers and also began purchasing freight. The *Louisa* had a three-week start, but that did not daunt Jackson. He ballasted with bricks and took on all the supplies he could carry, including watches, cutlery, spoons, shirts, shovels, brandy, blankets, and boots, even office furniture and brass-mounted harness[18]— fine stuff, indeed, for a pioneer gold camp. "Oh, these spendthrift Amerricans!"

Then, to gild the Yankee recklessness, Captain Jackson bought two horses, at £20 each, and loaded them on his ship. Horses to California, like coals to Newcastle, eh what! Perhaps he'd fetch back a cargo of kangaroos!

The American announced that he would sail on February 17. He waited two additional days, however, hoping for some last-minute passenger. Finally he slipped away with only eighteen and arrived in San Francisco with thirteen—a heavy loss if due to death at sea, even in the days of sail. The *Inez* anchored in San Francisco three days ahead of the *Louisa*, which had consumed ninety-six days on the trip.[19] Those American whalemen were past masters in the sailor's trade. Both vessels were unable to return to Australia because their crews deserted for the mines. Meanwhile, Robert Towns and other shippers back in Sydney waited for direct reports that failed to come.

Early in March an English brig, the *Spencer*, entered the Heads and cruised the long inlet toward Sydney. She rode high in the water. Small boats rowed out to learn her business and were told that she had come from the Sandwich Islands in ballast, to get freight and passengers for fabulous California. The *Spencer*'s captain maintained there was no mistake about the magnitude of the gold discoveries; as proof, he sent newspapers ashore. Admittedly almost three months old, all the accounts printed in December stated that more and more goldfields were being discovered. They also described San Francisco, in midwinter, as short of provisions.[20] Shippers should make a fortune!

Sydney merchants read the papers, looked at calendars, and speculated on the market their last shipments would find when they arrived in California sometime next month. On March 12 the Sydney port authorities reported another vessel, an American brig, the *Sabine*, first to arrive from San Francisco. She had made the voyage in seventy-two days* and, having stopped at the Sandwich Islands to enlist a new crew, her actual sailing time must have beaten the *Eleanor Lancaster*'s record run. Newspapers on board the *Sabine* were more recent than those brought by the *Spencer*, and the supercargo of the American vessel confirmed all the stories about California. Five thousand miners idled by the winter weather, he related, were streaming into San Francisco when the *Sabine* left in December. All came loaded with gold dust, which they seemed eager to spend before returning to the diggings come spring. Housing conditions for the mob were bad, and the climate was foggy, cold, and wet. There was much sickness. Of course, these were the conditions more than two months earlier. By now, March, the diggers must be going back to the creeks. At the time the *Sabine* left California, everybody's pockets were so full of money that the captain had great difficulty engaging a crew. He finally managed to employ five men, at the incredible figure of $80 each, for the nine-day run from San Francisco to Honolulu. There he hired a crew of Kanakas for the voyage to Sydney.[21]

The *Sabine*'s master announced that he planned returning to America within ten days, and hoped to carry both freight and passengers. Robert Towns thought this renewal of the rush an unwarranted speculation and hesitated to reenter the trade, but John MacNamara ventured another vessel. MacNamara's *Emma* was regularly employed in the coastal trade, but he ad-

---

* According to the *Alta California* (Jan. 4, 1849), the *Sabine* left San Francisco for Sydney on December 29, 1848. The *Sydney Morning Herald* (March 13, 1849) reported that she arrived on March 12, after a run of seventy days. There are, however, seventy-two calendar days between these two dates, minus one for the international dateline.

vertised her as a fast-sailing brig which would be ready to book passengers and freight within twelve hours. Up to his old tricks again, he imitated his successful rivals who had claimed so much for their vessels in the past. His captain, MacNamara said, had been employed by the Hudson's Bay Company, and spoke Spanish fluently. MacNamara extolled "the New Gold Country of California, of the great wealth of which there can now be no longer any doubt, common labourers collecting upwards of £40 worth of gold per day."[22] Next, MacNamara used another sales approach, claiming he had fewer berths than applications. He seemed to think the public would forget that the *Louisa* had lain at anchor for days trying to fill her berths, and he dared say, now, that he had laid on this new vessel to serve applicants whom he had been unable to accommodate previously.[23]

Thus a second effort to start a "gold rush" began. Immediately, the *People's Advocate* shouted for more social legislation to satisfy workers in Australia. Labor, the editor proclaimed, must form clubs to build houses, to purchase blocks of land from the graziers and divide it into homesteads. In the *Herald*, John Fairfax wrote a long editorial. A man of probity, he faced the facts and admitted: "If only one-half of the extraordinary reports we have received from California are to be taken as truth—and it seems impossible to refuse credence to them—the effects on the civilized world—on all results from industrial operations—on all funded property, and indeed on *all* transactions of the present time, will be most extraordinary."[24]

Fairfax believed that three-quarters of the gold would go to England for goods, the remainder to the United States. The British colonists would undoubtedly get their share of this vast trade, and an economic revolution faced the world.

On April 4, 1849, the *Sabine* left with twenty-four passengers and arrived in San Francisco with twenty-three. Her booking had been small, but people were showing a renewed interest in California, although there was, as yet, no stampede. After the *Sabine*, only two vessels a month left Sydney for San Francisco during April, May and June. To attract passengers, owners and agents began to advertise better accommodations and to promise voyagers a reasonable time on board in California prior to disembarkation. Fairfax printed information on American import duties. A Sydney cartographer published maps of California which showed the location of San Francisco, the inland seas, and the gold-bearing mountains beyond them.[25] Now Australians could locate places mentioned in the California newspapers and sketch in "the fields" or Mother Lode, which stretched north and south for more than three hundred miles.*

In June a ship from Britain brought magazines and newspapers. People back "home" seemed much excited about California. That was enough to convince any loyal Australian. Editor Fairfax learned from *Blackwood's Magazine* that Sam Brannan and his religious group were reported to be monopolizing the goldfields. The "Mormons," Fairfax quoted for his *Herald* readers, "were originally of the sect known as 'Latter-day Saints,' which sect flourishes wherever Anglo-Saxon gulls are found in sufficient numbers to swallow the egregious nonsense of fanatic humbugs who fatten upon their credulity"[26]—and so on for half a column.

John Fairfax seemed impressed by an article in *Punch* titled the "Goldseeker's Manual." He reprinted the following from it with evident relish:

"What Class ought to go to the Diggins? Persons who have nothing to lose except their lives.

"Things you should not take with you to the Diggins. A love of comforts, a taste for civilization, a respect for other people's throats, and a value for your own.

"Things you will find useful at the Diggins. A revolving pistol, some knowledge of treating gun-shot wounds, a toleration of strange bedfellows.

---

* The boundaries of the Mother Lode are indefinite. Rodman W. Paul, *Mining Frontiers of the Far West, 1848-1880* (New York, 1963), p. 20, correctly states that an area 120 miles long "came to be known as the 'Mother Lode.' " Thomas Archer, *Recollections of a Rambling Life* (Yokohama, 1897), p. 185, says that the Australians were told that the gold country "extended for more than a hundred miles." Joseph Henry Jackson, *Anybody's Gold: The Story of California's Mining Towns* (New York, 1941), p. vii, defines the Mother Lode as an area some 350 miles long. The *Columbia Encyclopedia* (New York, 1956), says the term is sometimes limited to a strip about 70 miles long, but is popularly used to mean a region more than 300 miles in length. Approximately the same distance is accepted by the California Division of Mines in Olaf P. Jenkins (ed.), *The Mother Lode Country* (San Francisco, 1948).

"The Sort of Society you will meet with at the Diggins. Those for whom the United States are not big enough; those for whom England is too hot; those who came to clean out the gold, and those who came to clean out the gold finders.

"What is the best thing to do when you get to the Diggins? Go back home.

"How Gold may be best extracted. By supplying, at exorbitant prices, the wants of those who gather it.

"What will be the ultimate effect of the discovery of the Diggins? To raise prices, to ruin fools, to demoralize a new country first, and settle it afterwards."

Obviously, the Australian press still hoped to prevent emigration to California—and was succeeding. Only 395 people had left Sydney in the first six months of 1849; one-fourth of them went with the first flurry, in January.[27] For Australians, the best prospects in California still seemed to be in trade, not emigration, but Robert Towns continued to complain about the unwarranted speculation. As he watched others send their goods, however, his professed resolutions dissolved.

Having no ship he could spare just then, Towns decided to send some sale goods through MacNamara. However, that rival tradesman played what Towns called "a very shabby trick." He quoted Towns a freight rate that was much too dear. Towns was sure that MacNamara could not fill his vessel's hold at such a figure and would eventually cut the price. Waiting for this to happen, Towns kept his freight loaded on a truck where his big draft horse, Duke, could haul it to the waiting vessel's side at a moment's notice. Towns also bribed the ship's captain to notify him if the hold was filling, or if orders to sail were received. At the last moment, Towns would pay MacNamara's price, rather than lose the chance of shipping.

But Towns's scheme failed. He could not believe his eyes when he saw the vessel floating away, without a word of warning to him, and all his goods waiting on the truck—a shabby trick, indeed! People said the Old Man "did his block"—a phrase Americans could not understand.

Towns immediately decided to send his assembled goods, and more, on his *Inchinnan* as soon as she came in from New

Zealand. A bigger craft than any that had gone, she carried great square sails which, in the trade winds, should pull her to San Francisco ahead of other vessels. In addition to the usual California cargo, Towns planned to send drugs for the sick people up there. He'd show John MacNamara a thing or two![28]

3

Tasmania Hears about the Rush

News of the gold discovery aroused settlers in Australia's second-largest city more slowly than it did in Sydney. The town of Hobart was the capital of Van Diemen's Land (named Tasmania in 1853), an island separated from the great landmass of the Australian continent by Bass Strait. This colony, far to the south, had forest trees of giant size which grew almost to the water's edge. Some of them stood more than three hundred feet tall, and Hobart shipwrights claimed to have built a 90-ton schooner from one eucalyptus tree.[1] Australian woodchoppers were world famous.

The governor of Van Diemen's Land, Sir William Denison, hoped to develop this natural resource for Her Majesty's Navy. A gold rush would probably interfere with his ultimate objective, but he was more disturbed by an immediate problem. Queen Victoria had just sent him seven notorious prisoners—Irish "patriots"—convicted of various forms of treason. Three of them came with terms of imprisonment ranging from ten to fourteen years. The other four had been sentenced to be hanged until dead. Then, as though that were insufficient punishment, the judge, in his powdered wig, had told each condemned man "that afterwards your head shall be severed from your body, and your body divided into four quarters, to be disposed of as Her Majesty may think fit. And may the Almighty God have mercy on your soul."[2]

Her Majesty had commuted this barbaric sentence to life imprisonment on Van Diemen's Land. Thus her "Chief Gaoler,"[3] Sir William Denison, became the Irish rebels' custodian. A sudden exodus to California—which might follow news of

the gold discovery—could open a way for his prisoners to escape.

As capital of Britain's largest penal colony, Hobart Town
swarmed with ex-convicts, men and women who had already
served their terms. Many of them were Irish, in sympathy with
the seven famous rebels. Thus, when the ships carrying these
traitors cast anchor in Hobart Harbor, they were greeted with
welcome cheers and merry Irish tunes—very embarrassing for
Governor Denison, who pondered where to place his distinguished prisoners. All but one of them had been men of property
back home, so certain amenities were their due.

Tasmania had two principal towns, one on each side of the island: Launceston stood at the north on the Tamor River, which
flowed into Bass Strait, Hobart on the Derwent which flowed
south. Tasmania's southern coast, with a latitude similar to
that of Oregon and Nova Scotia, was precipitous and rockbound, the home of screaming gulls. But when an incoming
vessel rounded the basalt pillars of Cape Raoul, which towered
into the sky like fluted palisades, it sailed north into an inland
sea with distant mountains, east and west. Forty miles farther
north this vast inlet narrowed into the Derwent estuary—a
harbor wider than the Hudson River and capable of sheltering
the entire British Navy. Twelve miles above the estuary
entrance Hobart nestled in hills on the west shore, at the head
of deep-sea navigation. The long, deep channel between the
open sea and the harbor, common to so many Australian coast
towns, would give escaped convicts in small boats an unusual
opportunity to board California-bound vessels after they had
been cleared by port authorities.

Down near Cape Raoul stood the Port Arthur jail—a penitentiary too horrible for Sir William to consider as a proper
place to incarcerate Irish "gentlemen." Crime or no crime, a
man's class must be considered. In fact, by English law, a peer
might be hanged, but he could demand a rope of silk. The Port
Arthur jail had been built on a peninsula connected to the mainland by Eaglehawk Neck, a sandspit scarcely two hundred yards
wide. Any prisoner who escaped the jail and was lucky enough
to make his way up the peninsula for twelve miles through the

forested mountains would be stopped on the Neck by guards and fourteen vicious dogs chained to barrel kennels placed at proper intervals to prevent passage.[4] The only other way to reach the mainland was to swim. Sharks were not so vicious in these cold waters as in those back at Sydney. A man fortunate enough to swim across, however, still had only a slim chance of survival, for he could not hope to live alone in the forest, and without identification papers he would be rearrested at the first village.

Some men took these chances, because life at Port Arthur was unspeakably grim. Yet, ironically, the convict settlement appeared as beautiful as an English village in the Lake District. The exquisite granite church with spires and Gothic windows might have stood at Grasmere. The roads and hedges, a picturesque stone bridge, and the beds of larkspur, delphinium, and hollyhock were as English as could be—Little England on the bottom of the globe, far from Britain. Lush meadows and green hillsides sloped toward a gloomy forest wall. Here Little England stopped and Australia began, a foreign, eerie land of noisy cockatoos and parrots, of eucalyptus trees, their trunks ragged and tattered with curled sheets of flaking bark, pendulous branches sweeping the ground, always faded and droopy. No fresh green tints in spring, no autumnal coloring.

Most of the Port Arthur prisoners were lodged in a vast stone barracks where discipline was maintained by flogging. A hundred lashes, well laid on, were not unusual; sometimes three hundred were prescribed if the culprit lived that long. Often, it was said, a man's best friend was required to administer the beating, and woe to him if the blows lacked severity. Life was so hideous that victims sometimes craved death and drew lots to determine who should murder whom, so that they both might die. And of all the horrors, the worst occurred at night, when lights were out and perverts crept from their bunks for beastly orgies in the dark. No wonder Governor Denison decided to hold his Irish rebels elsewhere, although he found it necessary to send two of them to the notorious jail when the gold rush began.

A prisoner at Port Arthur with a record for good behavior

might either be paroled or get a ticket-of-leave, to work in Hobart Town. The trip by water through a chain of inlets to Hobart was almost a hundred miles long, each mile one of sylvan beauty. Gliding across still waters boats passed charming coves floored with golden sand, islands wooded to the water's edge, deep gulches filled with gigantic tree ferns, hillsides glowing red and gold with blossoms of acacias and flaming gum trees. Thousands of waterfowl—ducks, teal, and black swans with brilliant red faces and a white bar on their wings—followed this same route up the Derwent to the marshes above Hobart. Thus criminals and wildfowl went to Hobart together, and the former soon earned the name "Derwent Ducks"—a name that would be oddly distorted in California.

The promontory below Hobart was named Wrest Point. On it stood a gallows, and condemned men's bodies were left swinging there as a warning to all prisoners on incoming ships. Across a crescent bay Hobart's shingle roofs huddled below the steeple of St. George's Church. Ships could anchor along a quay in front of warehouses equipped with derricks for hoisting cargo from their holds to large doorways into second and third-floor storerooms. Formal government buildings of smoothly cut, buff-colored sandstone stood three stories high with porticoes supported by fluted columns under Doric capitals. Some convict laborers were craftsmen of great skill and they had carved exquisite royal crests above doorways. The same smooth sandstone had also been used by wealthy residents for their homes, substantial mansions with English ridged roofs and double chimneys at the gables. Highly polished brass doorknobs, knockers, and nameplates adorned entryways. Cast-iron fences enclosed English gardens. English ivy grew more luxuriously here than in Sydney.

Among the frock-coated and top-hatted gentry in the hilly, cobblestoned streets, convicts could be recognized by their cropped hair, leather caps, and canary-yellow uniforms. Men on probation wore equally distinctive suits of blue-gray. Female prisoners, dressed in white mobcaps and gray duffel, were required to curtsy before all freemen on the street.[5] Careful observers could detect a man's past in the manner of his walking.

A plowman from the country placed one foot ahead of the other. A sailor walked with his feet apart. An ex-convict displayed a gait all his own. To prevent leg-irons from striking his shins and anklebones, the convict had acquired a peculiar swinging stride. People said, too, that these fellows could not look an honest man in the eyes. Rough, savage chaps were referred to as "regular Norfolk Islanders," regardless of whether they had ever been confined on that outpost for new and incorrigible criminals. On Battery Point, local offenders were confined in stocks. Ragged urchins enjoyed pelting them with refuse.[6]

Freemen in Hobart—most of them civil servants, soldiers, and merchants—led a life of renowned gaiety. They seemed much too comfortably established to be intrigued by the hardships inherent in a gold rush. Social functions centered on the vessels, often as many as forty, which lay in the harbor. Among them were British naval frigates escorting convict ships or on duty patrolling the far-flung Empire. Several hundred guests were sometimes invited to dine on one vessel, then were rowed to another for dancing until dawn. On such occasions decks and cabins were decorated elaborately with scarlet geraniums, hawthorn, sweetbrier, and starry fuchsias from townsmen's gardens. Skillful ships' mechanics fashioned glittering chandeliers out of cutlasses and the countless little mirrors used for trade with natives on South Pacific islands.[7] For these functions the wives and daughters of the leading merchants and government officials donned their best brocades, silks, and crinolines. Chaise carts with wheels five feet high brought the ladies to launches at the dock.

As in Sydney, ex-convicts and their descendants were deemed unacceptable by high society and church alike, even if they had become wealthy. The best people would trade with them, but refused to eat, drink, or pray with them.[8] Also, as in Sydney, everyone who was anybody had been "home" to England. Placards pasted on walls announced that passage first-class could be had to Britain for only 100 guineas.

The newspapers in Tasmania—sure to be important in a gold rush—differed greatly from those in Sydney. Instead of two journals, procapital and prolabor, Hobart and Launceston had a total of eight papers, all of which prided themselves on their independence of opinion. Two were edited by men who had lost government positions and hence dared criticize the administration. One, which claimed the largest circulation, was edited by a devout former Church of England clergyman, now a convict. Another appealed to intellectual religious dissenters. Still another, a scurrilous sheet, delighted in personalities and circulated among "licensed victuallers."

Visitors to Hobart Town who brought their families, "if respectable," could find all the comforts of a "First Rate English Home" at Mrs. Mills's Devonshire House, according to her advertisement. Sailors on shore leave relaxed along Cat & Fiddle Alley. On Liverpool Street drinks were served in the Spotted Cow, and on Campbell Street, at the Bird-in-Hand, the Generous Whale, or the Jolly Sailor. A packhorse brought ice daily from Mount Wellington to cool champagne, refrigerate butter, and make ice cream. Coffee houses and the Friends' Meeting on Murray Street—the largest in Australia[9]—attracted Quaker whalemen from Nantucket who stopped here regularly to purchase whale-oil casks made of fine-grained wattle. These casks were considered the best in the world. Nantucketers also filled their ships' kegs with water from a creek in town which was reputed to be the best in the South Pacific because it didn't generate a green scum. Water on incoming English vessels was often so vile that a man had to hold his nose while drinking it.

The possibility that a gold rush might upset Hobart's established way of life seemed remote. The people cared too much for good racehorses, fast sailboats, regattas, and theatrical performances. Circus troupes and acrobats with trained horses "played" the town while their ships unloaded cargo. Farm workers enjoyed traditional English plowing contests. Hobart's gentry in scarlet coats, black velvet caps, and doeskin breeches rode to hounds.[10] A macadamized highway built by convicts led up the Derwent to New Norfolk, skirting the great swamp where black swan nested. At New Norfolk, a pack of beagles were kenneled behind the Bush Hotel. Here riders met for a stirrup-cup and hunt breakfast. Bush kangaroos took the place of foxes. The runs were short and fast, often in the woods with jumps four and five feet high over walls, farmers' sweetbrier hedges, down-timber, or the "snake-fence of Canada."[11]

The leader in this sport was Governor Denison, who was also an accomplished administrator interested in promoting education, charity, and public works. He had served with distinction in Canada and could expect backing from his brother, who sat in the Speaker's chair of the British House of Commons.[12] A true Tory or "redcoat," Sir William hoped "to check the development of the democratic spirit." He believed that intelligent gentry were best qualified to serve the country, and he favored continuing the importation of convicts for manual labor—an ideal combination for expanding the Tasmanian lumber industry for the benefit of Her Majesty's Navy. A ship's keel that required the splicing of three English oak timbers could be made from a single stick of Australian blue gum. Ship siding sawed from eucalypti was impervious to sea borers and dry rot. Moreover, when oak hit a coral reef the wood broke like a carrot. Blue gum crushed without breaking and could be pressed into shape again. Already Lloyd's of London ranked some Australian timber with English oak for constructing seagoing vessels. To publicize the colony's magnificent forests, Sir William once invited seventy-six legislators to dine with him in the hollow of a giant gum that stood within five miles of Hobart*—cafeteria-style surely! A governor with such comprehensive plans for Tasmania's future was sure to thwart, if possible, a gold rush to California.

Several immediate obstacles, foremost among them a persistent business recession, delayed all Sir William's projects. As in Sydney, there was little money to buy the accumulating surplus of goods cluttering merchants' storerooms. Native-grown wheat was not worth the cost of bullock drayage to the wharves, let alone the price of warehouse storage. There was an excess of imported spirits and also of that usually coveted delicacy

---

* Contemporary descriptions of the size of Australian trees at that time may be found in Captain Harry O'May's manuscript notes (Hobart) and in the *Hobart Daily Courier*, May 8, 1852. [J. R. Godley (ed.)], "Extracts from the Journal of a Visit to New South Wales in 1855" (Mitchell Library, Sydney), notes a stump 42 feet in circumference, 3 feet from the ground.

from Java, rich yellow sugar. Some merchants were bartering their supplies for sufficient farm produce to feed their families.[13]

The first report of the discovery of gold was treated by knowing skeptics as a hoax, a grand scheme on the part of shipowners to get business for their empty vessels. This may explain why Hobart was slower than Sydney to respond to news of the gold rush. It should be noted, however, that when Hobart and the island did become interested, Tasmania sent more valuable cargoes per ship than did her sister colony to the north. Whereas the total exports from New South Wales during the first year were valued at £55,611, those from Tasmania, in almost one-third the number of ships, amounted to a tidy £34,183.[14]

The first men in conservative Hobart who encouraged people to go to the goldfields were two hairbrained individualists: Captain Andrew Haig and John Thomas Waterhouse. These rival promoters pasted placards around town which screamed: "GOLD! GOLD!!" and "WHO'S FOR CALIFORNIA?" Both men advertised in the newspapers, appealing for emigrants, using as bait a quotation from the *Sydney Morning Herald* describing the discovery.

Haig recommended himself as an experienced seaman with a "perfect knowledge" of the Spanish language. He said he proposed to charter a vessel and book passengers in steerage for £25 and in cabin class for £50,[15] high charges considering that Captain Towns in Sydney asked only £10 and £30, respectively. Captain Haig, in his advertisement, extolled the California climate as the finest in the world, said the soil there was suitable for corn, wine grapes, and livestock pasture. Obviously, he was selling more than a chance to find gold. The trip, according to Haig's advertisements, would take only seven weeks.

Haig's competitor, John Thomas Waterhouse, lacked practical knowledge of the sea. He was a minister's son, a ne'er-do-well with a reputation for big ideas and small accomplishments. Like Captain Haig, he had no vessel, but he advertised twenty-five vacancies for passengers on the little *John Bull,* a 71-ton brigantine he hoped to charter. He received no encouragement, however, from either passengers or mercantile speculators. Business, indeed, was so depressed that when the 81-ton schooner

Martha and Elizabeth came in from China, her owner, Edward Gilbert of the Liverpool Tea Warehouse, had difficulty disposing of her cargo, even at low prices on short-term credit or in exchange for colonial produce.[16] Yet it never seemed to occur to Gilbert, until weeks after the discovery had been announcd, to put her in the California trade. Apparently, there was no demand for either passenger or cargo service at that time.

Later, as the rush developed, Edward Gilbert would curse Waterhouse for competing with him, and they would quarrel as bitterly as Towns and MacNamara were doing up in Sydney. To call a rival names was part of being a rugged individualist, but in January, 1849, the gold rush caused no excitement in Hobart. One shipment of goods destined for the goldfields left port on the twenty-first aboard the schooner *Eliza*, to be transshipped at Sydney onto some California-bound vessel—a plan that changed with the changing times, for the *Eliza* carried her freight all the way to San Francisco, spending 103 days on the voyage. Certainly most citizens in Hobart showed little interest in digging gold. Their newspapers devoted more space to accounts of the divorce of Fanny Kemble, an English actress who had married a prominent, though ungodly, American.

Interest in California began to grow early in February, when the convict-clergyman editor of the Hobart *Guardian* wrote a long leader about California. He admired all Yankees' "characteristic tact for business and go-ahead-ism." The goldfields, he told his readers, would soon be connected with the United States by a railroad across the American continent. This would give Australians seven or eight weeks' shorter communications with Europe.[17]

With Tasmanian interest increasing, the *Osprey* left Hobart for California on February 13, to be followed four days later by the *Martha and Elizabeth*, still loaded with cargo that Edward Gilbert had been unable to sell. These first three vessels carried no passengers. As in Sydney, most Hobart newspapers discouraged emigration. One paper said that a man named Sam Brannan, a Mormon, had already claimed all the gold-bearing land and was charging a percentage for the ore mined. California, it was prophesied, would become "the greatest concourse of scoundrels that ever met in one place: deserters from the American and Mexican armies, runaway sailors, escaped convicts, and ruffians who for years had been perpetrating atrocities among the islands."[18]

Such accounts seem to have put an idea into the head of a convict who had been assigned the job of caretaker aboard the Bishop's yacht which lay at anchor by the Coal Yard Wharf in Hobart. This trim, cutter-rigged craft of about 12-ton burden was being fitted for a cruise around Tasmania. During the night of February 20, the caretaker, with three other "assigned convicts" who came aboard after dark, weighed anchor and floated down the Derwent unseen by the water police or the guard-boat crew anchored forty yards away. Next morning at half-past ten the yacht was missed. A signal to stop her was semiphored to Port Arthur, but with favorable westerly winds she had rounded Cape Raoul and was now safely on her way to California.

In later years, people believed that the yacht reached the coast of South America, changed her rigging, and cruised north to San Francisco. Australians in California claimed to recognize the craft's lines when she arrived. However, men's minds and memories play odd tricks, and the Bishop's yacht had a very different fate. Adverse winds or faulty navigation crashed her on the Great Barrier Reef, where two of the four men died, either by drowning or in a fight with their companions. The other two were picked up by a cruising bark and eventually returned on a vessel bound for Sydney. Both slipped ashore after entering the Heads. One was recaptured, but no trace of the other was ever found.[19] If he eventually reached California, it must have been under an assumed name.

After the disappearance of the Bishop's yacht, almost two months elapsed before another Hobart vessel cast off for California. People in town settled down to their everyday occupations, apparently immune to the gold fever until John Morgan, editor of the Hobart *Britannia*, decided, for some reason best known to him, to revive interest in the gold rush. On March 27 he devoted two and a half columns of his paper to a reprint of those parts of Dana's *Two Years Before the Mast* which described the California its author had observed thirteen years earlier.

Morgan may have lacked news. He was an odd character who had traveled to the United States, Canada, and the West Indies; perhaps he brought Dana's volume back with him. An impractical "man of principle," he had lost a government position because of his debts. In addition to editing the *Britannia*, he enjoyed writing poetry and delivered lectures on the sins of others. To amuse readers he spiced his paper with absurd ribaldry and sometimes with vulgar abuse. He hated American slavery, admired abolitionists, and boasted that he had helped several hundred Negroes escape from Charleston, South Carolina, to the British fleet.[20]

Some other Hobart newspapers followed editor Morgan's lead by printing months' old extracts from the *New York Herald* concerning the goldfields. Finally, when English journals arrived, the editors showed real interest, for whatever Britain did was scripture in Hobart. All local papers began copying long accounts from the London *Times*, explaining that the gold discovery would cause inflation. Everybody would suffer from a "general rise in prices which some ingenious philosophers think so necessary an element of prosperity."[21]

One editor thought that a gold rush might provide a social safety valve for blowing out undesirable citizens. Another editor, writing for the *Colonial Times*, urged ambitious people to go. He said that in California, by working hard, a man could succeed, while in "a colony like this . . . labor is unpredictable, and business of almost every description is in a depressed state; and with no cheering prospect of better times."[22] This editor even dared quote a London writer's description of how to make a "miner's cradle," but he also pointed out that in California an Indian willow basket had proved sufficient for collecting the golden treasure. An enterprising merchant, with more salesman's imagination than brains, offered butcher knives suitable for cutting California soil preparatory to washing for gold.

In May, with the people becoming really interested, many Australian newspapers published, for the first time, President Polk's message of December, 1848, officially announcing the gold discovery. Then column after column was filled with letters from Americans in California, all copied from eastern United States papers. This information was, of course, more than six months old, but the letters told of two men digging gold worth $17,000 in two days; of one man taking the equivalent of $30,000 from a ravine in three days; and a clergyman, unused to work, making $50.00 in five hours. Another letter, dated October 8, 1848, reported that a ragged man on the dock in San Francisco with no crown in his hat, a greasy buckskin shirt on his back, an old shoe on one foot and a moccasin on the other refused to work as a stevedore because he had two quarts of gold dust in a bag in his hand. The letter also stated that clerks earned the magnificent sum of $1,500 a year, that waiters in hotels made $1,250 to $1,500, and that common laborers were paid $10.00 a day. Furthermore, United States Army officers in California could no longer afford servants.[23] A captain receiving $60.00 a month sometimes had to pay his cook $75.00 and his steward $100.00. The editor of the *Britannia* admitted that the California news "has made quite a stir in our little commercial tea-pot."[24]

The accounts of such an abundance of money in the gold-fields stimulated trade in Hobart. Several papers printed United States customs regulations. Six freighters were laid on. The stagnant flour and provision market came to life. Ship chandlers settled overdue accounts and started new ones. Merchants took a tip from the London printers and packed "notions" of their own to sell in California. Tailors and grocers advertised cloth-ing, beef, and wines for the voyage under such captions as "EMIGRANTS TO CALIFORNIA" and "EXPECTATIONS REALIZED."[25]

Most of the newspapers, even as they printed shipowners' ad-vertisements for freight and passengers, warned readers to stay at home: the colony needed them. The *Courier*, in a long leader, told prospective emigrants that in California they would be-come aliens, "strangers to their mother's children; they will lose the paternal care of Earl Grey and the wisdom of our Colonial Secretary; they will forfeit the honour of electing their first Legislative Assembly; in short, they will become burly Republicans—*tarnation* proud—impudent—prone to *guess* and speculate—and should war break out, they may, by the chances of war, reappear on these coasts in the character of Paul Jones, and be hanged as traitors!"

The article went on to say that large purchases of drugs and arms for California indicated that health and security would be endangered there. "Nor is the medley of all tribes a very pleasant prospect. . . . There are red and yellow Americans, slaves and slaveholders, and Sandwich Islanders; and to crown all, the quintessence of Australian knavery—the debris of our penal masses sublimated by a savage life in the islands and among whalers."

The editor of the *Courier* also pointed out that "educational and religious institutions" would be lacking in California. Economic opportunities might not be so rosy as pictured, and prospective emigrants should await reports from travelers who had been there.[26]

Late in May more English newspapers arrived in Hobart. These familiar and authoritative sheets drove the last doubts about the California goldfields from Tasmanians' minds. They reported that eighteen ships were outfitting in Liverpool for California, that Englishmen had organized companies of adventurers for the expeditions. Some papers prophesied that America was bound to be hurt by losing its middle and lower classes, thus depriving the country of labor and forcing it to purchase more British goods. This, in turn, might cut English taxes and liquidate the national debt.[27]

So much for London's latest reaction as reported in Australian papers. Hobart editors also quoted from American newspapers. The *New York Herald* had pronounced the discovery of gold the greatest event of the century, one that would change the economy of the world. The *Boston Herald* reported the arrival of a whaler which brought $7,500,000 in gold. The happy seamen told tales about the precious metal being piled up in San Francisco streets for lack of storage room. Nails and bolts, one old salt said, were being made of gold. Ships were sheathed with it in lieu of copper. Gold nails were used on the railroad from San Francisco to the diggings. Buffalo were killed with golden bullets, and golden gridirons were common in kitchens.[28]

Of course there was neither railroad nor buffalo near the California diggings, but how was an Australian to know that?

Tasmanian editors copied column after column of similar statements from British and American papers. Readers learned that the fare from New York to San Francisco was $250 by sea— a trip of four to six months—or $500 across the Isthmus of Panama, a journey taking half the time. (The latter fare was $350 to $400, excluding the canoe trip up the Chagres, mule transportation over the divide, and hotel accommodations en route.) These figures were important, because they disclosed that Americans must pay twice as much to get to California as Hobart shipowners were asking and three or four times the price charged from Sydney.

Along with the California news from New York and London came a new commodity to be sold in the colonies. British publishers were sending bales of printed verses about the gold rush, some set to music. Australian bards immediately began writing their own ditties. Guests at Mrs. Mills's "First Rate" Devonshire House in Hobart played and sang "The Age of Gold," "Put Money in Thy Purse," and "The Good Times Come at Last." Another, "The Race to California," was advertised as "a comic song written to a golden measure."[29]

The first sign of this burgeoning interest in California did not seem to worry His Excellency, Sir William Denison. At this stage of the gold rush he showed no fear of losing his colony's population, nor even his Irish prisoners. After all, by the end of May only four vessels, all freighters, with a total of only nineteen passengers had sailed for California. Two more ships cleared on June 6 with twenty-six on board. This minor exodus was hardly large enough to deplete Tasmania's population. Fifty-three more passengers booked on the *Vansittart*, the *William Melville*, and the *Munford*. Many of them were merchants, one a Mr. A. M'Pherson. An A. W. MacPherson would appear later among members of the San Francisco Committee of Vigilance. These three vessels were loading lumber, potatoes and portable houses, commodities that should be salable in a new country.[30]

On June 16 another vessel became available. The *Agenoria*,

an emigrant ship, arrived from England bringing 246 "assisted passengers," persons whose passage had been paid in order to populate the colony. Her agents immediately began scrubbing 'tween decks and advertising for California gold seekers. Several others offered space on their vessels, and John Thomas Waterhouse was still trying to fill his *John Bull*, but passengers seemed to be afraid of the little tub. Apparently desperate now, he distributed a new set of placards announcing "CHEAP PASSAGE! CHEAP PASSAGE!!" His reduced rate finally persuaded thirty-three emigrants to book accommodations. With holds loaded to the hatches and decks piled with excess freight, the *John Bull* hoisted anchor on June 27. Next day the little overloaded brigantine returned; she had almost wrecked before clearing the estuary and needed repairs.[31]

While the *John Bull* was still in the harbor Edward Gilbert, whose *Martha and Elizabeth* was now far on her way, sent furious letters to at least three local newspapers and paid to have them published. He belittled the *John Bull's* size by eleven tons, pointed to the danger of embarking on her, and urged the authorities to protect the safety of all passengers.[32] The feud between Gilbert and Waterhouse had reached a climax, but Gilbert's letter did not appear in the papers until after the *John Bull* had set out to sea once more. Obviously too late to hurt Waterhouse financially, the letter's publication did not even slow down bookings on other California-bound vessels. The gold rush from Tasmania had really begun now. Many vessels in addition to the *Agenoria*, the *William Melville*, and the *Munford* were filling their berths with emigrants. A large number of people regretted that hard times had prevented them from accumulating enough to pay the fare. An even larger number were scheming how best to raise the passage money.

4

Australia's New England
Starts for the Diggings

Now it's blow, blow, blow,
For Californi-o
For there's plenty of gold,
So I've been told,
On the banks of the Sacramen-to.

Other Australian cities felt even less excitement than Hobart concerning the first news about the gold rush, but it should be remembered that the first reports in the eastern United States also failed to interest people there. In fact, three months elapsed before a real agitation developed in America.[1] It is therefore not surprising that Adelaide and Melbourne, both on the south side of the Australian continent, showed little enthusiasm until the rushes from Sydney and Hobart were well under way. Of the two southern cities, Adelaide was the farthest west, and was the most conservative city in Australia. Settled as an idealistic economic experiment, Adelaide had never permitted the importation of convicts, and prided itself on being the capital of a province with many cultural interests.[2]

News of the discovery came to Adelaide first from England, a fact that emphasizes the vast distances between Australia's settlements. Shortly thereafter, a ship from Hobart brought packets of Sydney and Sandwich Island newspapers confirming the earlier accounts.[3] A few merchants considered sending goods to San Francisco, and the editor of the *South Australian Register*, true to the cultural interest of his readers, suggested that a cargo vessel going to California might take along a man of science with "experience and integrity" who could report on the geology of the new country. Such particulars, the editor said, would be exceedingly interesting to Australians, as some gold in virgin purity had already been found in their own country.[4] This statement was, of course, made before the editor heard about the alleged discovery in the Pyrenees near Melbourne, so he obviously referred to the rather common, although not generally accepted, belief that a goldfield of commercial importance might develop in Australia.

Finally, on March 3, fifty-four days after Sydney's *Plymouth* had set sail, the *Sophia Margaret* left Adelaide carrying twenty-nine passengers to California. With this the agitation subsided, but in May, ships' agents advertised that the brigantine *Joseph Albino*, from Launceston, and the 200-ton brig *Jack*, from Cape Town, would stop for gold seekers. The announcement renewed interest in California and prompted owners of the 163-ton ship *Mazeppa*, which had served sixteen years in the opium trade, to outfit her for California.[5] She sailed on June 8, manned by a Malay crew. Sixteen passengers were packed between decks in a space sixteen feet square by four feet ten inches high—unbelievably cramped quarters for 127 days at sea. Moreover, rats and cockroaches infested the hull. Five cabin passengers escaped some of these horrors.[6]

Thus by early June, two vessels had outfitted in Adelaide for California and two others had agreed to stop there for passengers. Six ships had left Hobart and thirteen, Sydney. Melbourne had as yet sent no vessel. The town was southeast of Adelaide a distance of more than four hundred miles as the kookaburra flies, or some five to eighteen days by sail, depending on the wind. Situated on the north shore of turbulent Bass Strait, the town, like so many others in Australia, stood at the upper end of a wide bay some fifty miles from the open sea. Although Melbourne was located in New South Wales, its inhabitants felt closer to Tasmania than to Sydney, which was about five hundred miles to the north across rough mountains. At the time of the gold rush Melbourne had fewer than five thousand inhabitants, most of them living in two-room shingle-roofed cottages, with open hearths in brick-floored kitchens.[7] From this town many roads radiated out across the hills to gigantic sheep stations. Coastal vessels operating between Sydney, Launceston, and Hobart often stopped at Melbourne, so the gold discovery was soon known there. Local promoters, like those in other seaboard towns, saw a chance to make money transporting gold seekers and determined to make the most of it. One man with more brains than money called a mass meeting of all would-be Argonauts, and asked them to pay him £10 each on his promise to charter a vessel and take them to California.[8]

This scheme failed for lack of subscribers, but in the weeks that followed, as passing vessels delivered newspapers and letters describing the excitement in other colonies, the *Melbourne Daily News* printed a two-column account of conditions in California and the miraculous discoveries there. It was reported, too, that a small vessel, the *Petrol*, had sailed for San Francisco from Geelong, with 14 men and £150 worth of firearms.[9] Geelong was a hamlet forty miles down Port Phillip Bay, in a cove west of Queenscliff Head, where wool was loaded on oceangoing craft. If the wild colonial boys in that harbor under the stormy headlands dared sail a 69-ton schooner to California, Melbourne's adventurers must be outclassed. To meet this challenge, the 480-ton bark *William Watson* was laid on. She sailed on June 27, 1849, the largest vessel to join the rush from Australia up to that time, and she carried 161 passengers. None of the California-bound vessels preceding her had booked that many. Eighty-two days later she arrived in San Francisco with 157 on board.[10] The editor of the *Melbourne Morning Herald* expressed the hope that she carried arms to ward off pirates on her return trip with gold.[11]

Another vessel, the *Union*, followed the *William Watson* on July 15 with 40 passengers and arrived on October 4. Thus, by the middle of July a total of thirty vessels had left the colonies for California, and a dismaying number of gold seekers had gone with them. Robert Towns in Sydney, waiting for his big *Inchinnan* to arrive and pick up the cargo John MacNamara had left, complained constantly. To him the excitement was uncalled for, and as every incoming vessel brought fantastic rumors, Captain Towns noted with his usual caution that no ship had come directly from California, except the questionable American *Sabine*. Sensible people, he wrote in his journal, should await the return of the *Despatch*, now long overdue. She would bring that dependable financier, F. Montefiore, whose report on shipping prospects as well as emigration could be relied upon, but instead of doing this, Towns complained, everybody had gone mad, "completely bit by the yellow fever."[12] Half of Australia's New England, he wrote, seemed to be on the move.

The growing excitement attracted enterprising businessmen in all Australian ports. Ships bringing immigrants from England began advertising for California passengers before unloading. In Sydney, stock was sold in a corporation that planned to buy or charter vessels and pay investors dividends from the gold discovered. One group of speculators chartered the dilapidated 93-ton *John and Charlotte*, then advertised for adventurers willing to pay £60 for transportation to and from California with found for seven months. Applicants must furnish references and were told they would be expected to formulate a code of regulations before sailing—a sort of Mayflower compact. The vessel was to carry whaleboats for transportation from San Francisco to the diggings, and all adventurers were to share equally in the gold acquired, whether they went to the diggings or remained to guard the ship. This expedition failed to materialize, however, because the old brigantine required months of work to make her seaworthy, and the candidates for the voyage were refunded their money.[13]

The exodus to California, which started so suddenly, reminded some observers of the Irish migration to America during the potato famine.[14] Employers grumbled about "sarvents" quitting without the required "notice." Merchants urged the publication of the names of all emigrants, complaining that many were dodging their debts—complaints that would become more insistent in the months ahead. Even more important to the colony as a whole was the repeated assertion that hundreds of so-called pauper immigrants, who had had their way paid from England to Australia, were embarking for California without refunding their passage money or working a day in the colony.[15]

The gold-rush enthusiasm grew when newspapers stated that two vessels at Auckland, New Zealand, were laid on for California, and that nine gold-rush ships had sailed from Valparaiso, four from Callao, three from Guayaquil, and five from other South American ports.[16]

Letters and clippings from American journals were reprinted in Australian papers under such headings as "IMPORTANT NEWS FROM CALIFORNIA."[17] Accounts of lynchings and general lawlessness were verified. Indeed, they came from the best of authorities: Thomas Jones, commander in chief of the United States naval forces in the Pacific, blamed the disorders on runaway sailors, deserters from the army, and disbanded Mexican War volunteers.[18] There was no reference yet to Australian criminals.

A more discouraging pronouncement came from another American. General Persifor F. Smith, new commander of the army's Pacific Division, had not yet arrived at his new post, but while waiting for transportation at Panama he stated officially that foreigners would not be allowed to trespass on United States soil. This caused some concern among Australians who planned to emigrate, or whose friends were already at sea. In Hobart, John Thomas Waterhouse saw a new chance to make a fast quid. Under the heading, "BAD NEWS! BAD NEWS!!" he offered to accept subscriptions from relatives of the unfortunates who had gone, promising to bring them back and thus save them "from great misery and even *death*."[19]

This scheme provoked another protest from Edward Gilbert, who wrote to the newspaper again, exposing Waterhouse's duplicity. Gilbert called attention to the man's promise of superior accommodations for emigrants and his failure to furnish them, also his glowing accounts of opportunities in California followed by his appeal to the emigrants' relatives to bring them back, even before they had had time to land in San Francisco. "He is the son of a minister," Gilbert wrote, "disgracing the memory of his father."[20]

The local quarrel may have caused guffaws in coffee houses. But more serious people worried not only about General Smith's order against trespassing foreigners but also about a report that heavy tariffs were being levied on California imports. The local newspapers, however, reassured their readers on both these counts. The United States consul, according to the *Hobart Courier*, reported that no port of entry had been established in California and that revenues would therefore be waived.[21] As for General Smith's proposal to keep foreigners away from the goldfields, the *Colonial Times* said that the United States would have to send an army to enforce such a rule and that, if she did, the soldiers would desert and begin digging when they arrived.[22]

Baffled by these uncertainties, newsmen met every incoming ship to inquire for letters from emigrants which might have been posted at Pacific ports on the route north. Such letters made headline news for the papers, but they could not be depended on. As an example, the *Star of China* had left Sydney on June 28. One writer reported that his craft had spoken her and learned that forty passengers had died. A letter from another ship that spoke her later reported no calamity.[23] Which account were people to believe?

Stories of death on shipboard haunted the minds of many Australians. The British government had recently sent to the colony, passage free, four hundred "poor but virtuous" women. The trip consumed half a year. During the second month out of London someone noticed a shark alongside. Sailors baited a hook for him, but the monster showed no interest—a bad omen. The creature must be waiting for better food—a human, of course.

Every morning when passengers climbed up to the vessel's waist, they stood on boxes and rope coils to peer over the bulwarks and ask one another, "Where is he?"

"Look! Look! There he be." Trembling hands pointed to the ominous torpedo-like shape that swam without apparent effort beside the hull, never leaving it for long. When the grisly monster disappeared on the starboard side, passengers on the port bulwark spied the sinister form dimly outlined in the water below them.

On the third day after sighting the shark, a female passenger was reported ill with fever. The ship's doctor prescribed calomel, but it did not help her. Next morning two more young women complained of fever and remained in their berths. The ship had reached tropical waters now, and the heat below decks became stifling. The ill women were given pallets under an awning on the foredeck, good for them but harrowing for the other passengers. Their delirious cries, "The shark! The shark!!" could be heard throughout the ship.

That evening the stricken women were left at the fore companionway, where a breeze might comfort them. During the night one of the crazed girls rose from her bed and leaped overboard. A sailor standing guard on the quarterdeck heard the splash and saw her white figure drift past in the inky water. He shouted "Man overboard," and ran along the gunwale tying a rope to his belt. Passing the floundering figure, he leaped into the sea and clutched her floating gown. The watch came running and pulled on the rope, but the sailor felt the girl being jerked from his grasp and he was hauled aboard clutching only a piece of wet cloth. The shark had dragged his victim down into the depths.

There was no more sleep on the ship that night, and in the morning more women were down with fever—so many in fact that a canvas wall had to be constructed to form a hospital. The stench 'tween decks became worse than that of a dissecting room. The ship's doctor claimed that he had never witnessed anything so horrible. Before climbing down to his patients, he braced himself with a stiff "nor'wester," then practiced all his arts to stop the fever. He applied blisters and ordered the women's heads shaved. They protested, wailing that they would rather die than lose woman's crowning glory. Besides, as corpses without hair, they would look ghastly.

Burial services were performed daily. The ship would be hove-to, trembling under flapping canvas. The bodies, sewed in their bedding, lay on a ship's grating as the captain read the Episcopal burial service. Then the grating was tilted, and the bodies slipped into the sea with a final splash which invariably caused mourners to shudder visibly. Sick and dying Church of Scotland patients moaned that an Episcopal burial condemned them to everlasting perdition, to all the horrors of hellfire. Passengers who survived and landed in Australia could never forget that nightmare cruise.[24]

Quite a different story was brought by another vessel. She had spoken the *Martha and Elizabeth* at the Sandwich Islands, learned that she had sold her cargo there for a whopping 200 percent profit and then cleared for China to get more freight. Her only trouble was caused by the desertion of two crewmen who were in a hurry to get to California.[25]

Certainly, this news confirmed the genuineness of the gold rush, and, to stop a general exodus, John Fairfax, that bushy-haired John Bull in Sydney, tried a new argument in his *Herald*. He reminded prospective emigrants that by sailing now, in July, they would arrive at the beginning of the American winter, when hundreds of miners were congregating in the wet tent cities looking for employment. Fairfax dismissed General Persifor Smith's proclamation as an order leveled chiefly at the hordes of desperadoes who were flocking to San Francisco from the ports of South America. He admitted that lynch law might be used to discipline these undesirables, but he did not intimate that it would be applied to Australians.[26]

In August John Fairfax tried another device to discourage emigration. He had received a copy of the *London Economist* which declared the gold discovery a delusion. Although this contradicted Fairfax's previous admission, he reprinted it. According to the *Economist*, American journals had published forged letters of success, thus increasing the rush and causing a glut in the market for goods. "Lynch law is supplying the place of other modes of administering justice," the English editor said, "and scenes of outrage and blood are more certain realities than large lumps of gold to be had for the picking up."[27]

Many newspapers in other Australian colonies rejected the stories of violence, but some confirmed them. Both points of view were backed by letters received from California. Readers could take their choice, but it was certain that lawlessness and violence were considered by many to be the American way, the democratic-republican way. Three columns in the Hobart *Advertiser*[28] were devoted to a reprint of the Astor Place riots in New York, led by a fanatic British-hater named Edward Z.

C. Judson, another of those lawless Americans. The aspersion that violence was characteristic of a democracy seemed less fitting when another despatch told about a Canadian mob of so-called conservatives burning down Parliament House in Montreal. However, a patriotic editor could ignore that.

The newspapers down under did print reviews and abstracts of six books about California, three by Americans, three by Britishers. The American volumes, by Edwin Bryant, T. J. Farnham, and Lieutenant Charles Wilkes, described California before the discovery of gold. The English books were more recent and pertinent. A brief *Digger's Hand-Book* sold for five shillings. In *The Gold-Seeker's Manual*, David T. Ansted described the technique of gold washing as practiced around the world, calling especial attention to the success achieved in Brazil by flushing gravel down a plank grooved to catch the precious metal.[29] The third English book, Dr. J. Tyrwhitt Brooks's *Four Months among the Gold Fields*, was a money-making hoax written under an assumed name by a professional writer who had never seen California. Claiming to be a returned gold seeker, he wrote what conservative stay-at-homes wanted to be told. He described his troubles with Indians, the prevalence of illness at the mines, and the slim chances of finding gold. This imaginary account deceived the London *Times*, the *Athenaeum*, and the astute *Quarterly Review*. The *Sydney Morning Herald* quite naturally accepted the opinions of these journals, praised Brooks's book highly, and admonished prospective emigrants to heed its warning.[30]

Brooks's book may have deterred some Australians, but many still seemed eager to emigrate. In Hobart three new vessels were laid on: the *Eagle*, the *Raven*, and the bark *Cacique*. The latter had come from Malacca, via Singapore and Adelaide, in May, bringing a black tiger. However, the *Cacique* did not go to California and was returned to the local Adelaide run instead.[31] Before any of them cleared, the 219-ton bark *William Melville* floated away on July 3, loaded with 30 passengers, 100 portable houses, and an assortment of store goods including kangaroo blankets. She arrived in San Francisco on September 29, 1849.[32]

Building portable houses for California started a new enterprise in Australia, as did the construction of machines for extracting gold from sand. In Sydney a Pitt Street storekeeper, Arthur Gravely, offered to supply gold washers made of iron which could be taken apart so the pieces might be carried on the backs of mules.[33] A news note called attention to a Yankee invention, "California Gold Grease." According to the article, a prospector had only to grease himself with it and roll down a California hill and loose gold would adhere to the grease. Mining was as simple as that! The "Gold Grease" story appeared eight months later in a California paper.[34]

As the summer of 1849 advanced, the demand for passage to California increased. In July the teak-built clipper *Hero*, 204 tons, advertised in Adelaide for California passengers. In Sydney the brigs *Margaret* and *Spec* were laid on. The latter offered cabin, intermediate, and steerage accommodations with "separate cabins for ladies." Her owners claimed she was the only vessel on the line having fixed berths fore and aft. It was also announced that the brig *Susan*, expected from New Zealand, would be laid on for California.[35]

Reports about all these ships outfitting for the gold rush were slow to reach the stockmen in Australia's outback, but when they did, talk turned instantly to action. The graziers were frontiersmen in the American sense of the word. For years they had been pushing their flocks and herds over the next divide, hunting free grass and defying hostile aborigines. Many had already acquired title of a sort to vast areas of grazing land. Some lived in manorial fashion, drinking imported claret with their meals and reading the *London Illustrated News*—eight or ten months after publication. These were the romantic-minded Englishmen who inherited the characteristics of their merchant-adventurer forefathers, the shopkeeping warriors who had made fortunes in the West Indian sugar islands, in the East India and Hudson's Bay companies, in South Africa, and in the North American colonies. Only eight years ago James Brooke had become sultan of Sarawak, the same year China ceded Hong Kong to English merchants. It would be a mistake, however, to consider all Australian graziers merchant princes. Some of the rich ones could neither read nor write and were so stingy they sat at night in the dark to save burning a candle, but along with this extreme thrift they possessed stamina and courage, knew livestock, and possessed a faculty for bargain and trade.[36]

Among the graziers, too, were many adventurers who hoped to become rich by speculation, making small down payments on large mobs of mortgaged sheep. These fellows found themselves in straitened circumstances after the bottom fell out of the wool market in 1842. Some of them quit and went to Sydney. Others tried to save themselves by deeper speculations in cheap livestock. Sheep sold for as little as two shillings and sixpence and even a shilling a head. Some flocks with scab fetched only sixpence each. Since 1845 the price had begun to improve, but by 1849 a drought made it necessary to boil 743,000 sheep and 45,000 cattle for fat and glue—a terrible squandering of meat at a time when people in Ireland were starving to death.[37]

Australian graziers with adventurous spirits and moderate means saw a great opportunity in California. Several who joined the gold rush wrote about their experiences, but none more graphically than Thomas Archer.[38] Born in Glasgow in 1823, he came to Australia at the age of fourteen with his parents and grew to manhood on a sheep station at Wallerawang, on the Bathurst plains, 125 miles northwest of Sydney. Here he and his brothers learned about a new country of rolling hills called Darling Downs, where lush grass beckoned any stockman unafraid of the boomerang-throwing aborigines up there. Tom Archer and his brothers decided to take the chance. They oiled their guns and with 5,000 sheep, undulating like a white carpet over the green hills before them, the Archers drove north for 350 miles where they established Durundur and Cooyar stations east of the Dividing Range. From here, young Tom explored central Queensland and staked out a third station on the remote headwaters of Burnett River. California was no wilder, no farther away from his home in point of time, than these rugged highlands. He liked life in the wilderness and learned with joy that many young men were congregating in Sydney for the trip to San Francisco.

Tom decided to join the gold rush. He saddled his horse and

with Jacky Small and Davy, two Durundur blacks who had deserted their wild brothers for the dependable food to be had on a sheep station, joined three other young stockmen and their black servants. Together they rode southeast across the hills, lush now after June's winter rains. The black servants followed the horsemen as faithfully as hunting dogs but also with true hounds' uncontrollable appetites. The pyramid form of a bunya bunya pine invariably attracted them. Seeking edible cones, they ran toward it—a comical sight always. The white soles of their flat bare feet twinkled like cotton pads on licorice-stick legs. Being trailers, they eventually followed the tracks of their masters' horses through the bush and overtook them.

Occasionally the travelers had the good fortune to arrive at a station just before sundown. They could always rely on the owner's hospitality. Workers who made a practice of subsisting themselves during periods of unemployment by traveling past stock stations were called "sundowners." Such fellows would be known as "chuckline riders" in the American West a generation later, when ranching became established there.

On an earlier trip Archer had stopped at Clifton Station near the fountainhead of the Darling River, a stream 1,700 miles long and somewhat like the Missouri. This was the seat of Sir Francis Forbes, late chief justice in Sydney. Sir Francis was one of the aristocratic graziers. Travelers could expect to be treated here according to their class, owners at one table, white servants at another, and blackfellows outdoors. In such establishments the master, often educated in England, might come in from his stockyards smeared to the elbow with tar from marking sheep, but he would dress for dinner and serve the right wines with the right meat. At the end of the meal, the tablecloth was removed and all ladies present withdrew. The men, sitting around the uncovered board, drank a last brandy or two and told stories— all as English as could be.

Now in the summer of 1849, Tom Archer learned that Sir Francis' son, Francis, Jr., had already left for California.[39] The youth was more interested in learning how to mine gold than in acquiring it in America. Riding his father's downs he had become convinced that the precious metal existed in Australia,

had printed a pamphlet to prove it,[40] and hoped to come back
with the know-how for unearthing it. Tom Archer would probably meet him in California, and the two young men should
have much in common.

Settlements became more numerous as the riders approached
Brisbane. Occasional inns stood beside the cart tracks which led
to civilization, but they were notoriously bad. Some of these
inns were mere shanties of eucalyptus bark where cheap grog
was sold to itinerant sheepshearers, or to an occasional shepherd
who dared pay for a drink with one of his master's ewes. When
beds were available they usually crawled with fleas. Archer and
his white companions preferred to roll themselves in their
possum-skin rugs under the steady tropical stars where good
grass nourished their hobbled horses. Beside them the lanky
blackfellows kept warm by digging a shelter from the evening
breeze and curling around hot coals. The temperature rarely
dropped below 60 degrees, and the cones of "cubby pines"
would glow comfortably until some bellbird's musical gong announced the coming dawn.

Reaching the coast at Brisbane, Tom Archer and his black
servants boarded a coastal schooner for Sydney.[41] The city was
always a recreational spot for graziers after months in the outback. Archer found the streets that led down to Circular Wharf
pulsing with life. At one end of Macquarie Place, John Mac-
Namara had erected a rubber-topped tent. He offered for sale
to California-bound travelers others just like it, complete with
poles. Farther uptown vegetable carts lined the "futpaaths"
with costermongers holding up fruit and shouting, "Twofa-
haypenny! Twofa-haypenny!" Ringing bells announced the approach of a wagon selling milk by the dipperful. Barristers in
powdered wigs, and chimney sweeps as black as their English
counterparts, walked the streets—all a bit confusing to a bushman who found himself unconsciously grouping passers-by in
fours, the way a man does when counting sheep as they stream
out through a seven-foot gate.

At the shipping agency Tom learned that his brother, John
Archer, master of the *Harriet Nathan,* had already left Hobart

for California. The *Elizabeth Archer*, a 338-ton bark, stood in Sydney Harbor ready to follow her. Tom booked passage for himself and his two blackfellows, purchased some goods he believed salable in California, and moved his scant personal luggage into the cabin. Then, his sailing arrangements complete, he set out to have a good time until the ship's gun warned all passengers to come aboard. The town was full of gold seekers awaiting their vessels' departure. They soon met one another, loafed and drank together.[42]

"Here's how!"

"The sun is over the yardarm" (signifying a head tipped back to look).

"One more hair of the dog that bit you can do no harm!"

In the homes of friends they sang around the pianoforte, repeating the words of gold-rush songs imported from England. They also composed a song of their own which appealed to young adventurers, especially those who had found the sheep business disappointing in recent years.

> Hurrah, hurrah, we're off, my boys,
>   Off to the golden shore,
> Where want of cash, or want of "tick"
>   Shall trouble us no more.
>
> Then fill your glasses to the brim,
>   Let them our raptures speak;
> For see! our topsail's sheeted home,
>   Our anchor is a-peak.
>   Our anchor is a-peak, etc.
>
> Buf if, in following our bright schemes,
>   We happen to be "sold,"
> And each man digs his early grave,
>   Instead of digging gold,
> Our bones will rest as well as in
>   A gully or blind creek;
> Regret in vain, the die is cast,
>   Our anchor is a-peak.
>   Our anchor is a-peak, etc., etc.[43]

On July 17, 1849, the *Elizabeth Archer* cleared and drifted into the bay. She carried seven cabin passengers and well over a hundred steerage. (The records vary from 124 to 150.* In any event, she landed in San Francisco with a total of 140.) Midwinter had now settled over Australia. Cold rains peppered Sydney Harbor and deluged the ship's decks. Captain Cobb refused to sail in such foul weather. His cabin passengers huddled in the "cuddy" and became acquainted with one another. There were two graziers, a Mr. T. W. Bowden who, like Archer, brought along goods he hoped to sell in San Francisco,[44] and a Mr. Ned Hawkins with two black and two Chinese servants. A Mr. Edward Hammond Hargraves and a Mr. Simpson Davison shared a cabin. The former was destined to loom large in the history of the world's gold discoveries, the latter to complain about his own lack of recognition. Both men were ex-graziers. Hargraves had been an unsuccessful one, a fact that really hurt his more competent cabin mate when Hargraves achieved fame, knighthood, and a luncheon with Queen Victoria.

For three days the rain slanted down from a gray sky, shellacking the decks, screening from view the nearby city. Each of the cabin passengers had ample time to tell the story of his life. Tom Archer, regardless of his exploring experiences, was the "baby" of the group, aged only twenty-three. Davison was twenty-nine, and Hargraves, "daddy" of them all, was thirty-three, so old his hair was thinning on top although it curled luxuriously over his ears. He had a square, pleasing face topped with a high, intellectual forehead. In addition to his age and giant height, he outweighed all the others by tipping the beam at 15 stone (210 pounds), some say 18 stone (252 pounds).[45]

Hargraves had been born in Gosport, near Portsmouth, England, on October 7, 1816, the son of a lieutenant in the Sussex militia, and baby Edward was on the march with his parents when he was six weeks old. At the age of fourteen he was placed in service as cabin boy for Captain John Arthur Lister, com-

---

* Edward Hammond Hargraves, *Australia & Its Goldfields* (London, 1855), p. 74, states that 150 passengers sailed on the *Elizabeth Archer*. Charles Bateson, *Gold Fleet for California: Forty-Niners from Australia and New Zealand* (Sydney, 1963), p. 156, says there were 124 passengers. The *Alta California* (Oct. 11, 1849) notes that 140 landed in San Francisco.

mander of the merchant bark *Wave of Fortune*. Mrs. Lister and her two-and-a-half-year-old son were also aboard.

For more than two years Hargraves cruised the Oriental seas. Anchoring at Sydney, he quit the ship to work for a short time on a livestock station. He was growing fast, shooting up like a stalk of bamboo, and dreaming of adventure. He joined the crew of a French schooner hunting tortoiseshell in Torres Strait. All but seven of the crew died of typhus fever in Batavia. Hargraves, weak and wan, managed to get passage back to England and by 1834 returned to Australia. Aged eighteen now, six feet five inches tall, and gaining weight constantly, he brought a letter to Captain Thomas Hector, who operated a station near Bathurst. Hargraves' employment there was short. Within a year he married Clara Mackie, a merchant's daughter, and with her dowry established himself as a small squatter on Manning River, north of Sydney.

This venture failed, and for thirteen years Hargraves worked sporadically at Illawarra and East Gosford on Brisbane Water, where he and his wife finally operated the Queen's Inn. During those years he acquired four or five children and seventy bullocks. A near-failure at business, Hargraves possessed the buoyancy of some fat people and continually made big plans. Always he was sure his next venture would be a great success, my word, yes, a great success! Thus, when he heard the enticing reports brought by the *Spencer* and the *Sabine*, he sold his cattle for the bargain price of £1 each, left his wife to run the inn, and used his meager funds to purchase a cabin-class ticket on the *Elizabeth Archer*.[46]

Hargraves' roommate, Simpson Davison, related a very different life history as rain pelted their vessel anchored in the bay. He was born in Burlington, on the coast of Yorkshire, England, the son of a well-to-do banker. As a small boy, Simpson enjoyed hunting shells and fossils on the nearby seashore. This interest in natural history, especially geology, boded well for a gold seeker. In his father's bank he rose rapidly, but he disliked confinement and pined for adventure somewhere in Her Majesty's far-flung dominions. Several trips to the Continent on bank business, or on vacation, served only to whet his appetite for distant climes. In 1844, at the age of twenty-four, he determined to strike out for himself. His father gave him £1,000 and his blessing.

Simpson considered going to Jamaica, Canada, or Hong Kong but finally settled on Australia. He came to the new country with several letters of introduction and soon found himself in the outback inspecting cattle and sheep with a banker's concern for values. In the next five years he rode thousands of miles of open range from Darling Downs, west of where Archer's family lived, to the Murrambidgee where Canberra would be established as the Australian capital. In this vast area Davison owned and operated several stations, buying and selling as opportunities presented themselves. Always to the east of him as he rode he could see the long, flat-topped wall of the Blue Mountains which separate Sydney from the western grazing plains. The wall appeared black in some lights, bluer than the sky in others. Sometimes it glowed with lavender, purple, mauve, but always as Davison rode along he noticed the geology of nearby downs as well as the distant splendor, and he remembered the rock formations cut by the prairie streams.[47]

In this Never-Never Land, as Australians called it, Davison faced the stockman's usual financial problems, buying great herds on credit, selling often on "book count" when cattle were scattered too widely to be mustered. Droughts sometimes decimated his herds. He suffered from the depredations of savage aborigines, who had a provoking way of spearing livestock or a lone herdsman found asleep in a hut. Irate shepherds got revenge by dosing "dampers" (baking-powder biscuits) with the arsenic used to poison dingoes, then leaving them for black-fellows to eat.[48] Davison, with other squatters, had occasionally hunted aborigines as he did big game, but this troubled his conscience for he realized that they were humans—Her Majesty's subjects, like himself.

Explaining all this in detail as the rain beat on the portholes and ran in little rivulets down the heavy glass, Davison went on to say that last spring, after finishing his second shearing at Good Good, he rode to Sydney to arrange for shipping his wool, which was being drayed to town by oxen. As he approached the city, he noticed banners on coaches proclaiming them to be bound for California. Public houses along the way called themselves "California Hotels." At the edge of town he turned his horse into Pitt Street, which cut like a theater aisle down the slope to Circular Wharf. The houses on both sides stood regular as stairsteps, one above the other, the upper windows of each peeping over the roof of its neighbor below. On the skyline behind them St. James's spire watched over the city. Shutters had been removed from all the stores, and Davison noticed so-called California drapers' shops exhibiting shovels, picks, and buckets. Dismounting at the mew, he heard exciting accounts of the goldfields which had been brought by the *Spencer* and the *Sabine*. To learn more, he purchased a *Morning Herald* and read John Fairfax's conclusion that "if only one-half of the extraordinary reports ... are to be taken as truth ... the effects on the civilized world ... will be most extraordinary."[49]

The hard-riding banker's son could not withstand participating in such an adventure. He determined to join the rush, but being 200 miles from his station he could not do so at once. First he arranged for shipping his wool, then rode west across the mountains to his run where he leased his sheep to one man and his station store to another. Finally, after three months of preparation, he jogged back to Sydney in time to sail on the *Elizabeth Archer*. Always watching for a chance to make a shilling, he invested £300 in rum, biscuits, and kegs of beef to sell in California, as his companions who could afford it had already done.[50]

Davison talked endlessly about his own affairs. Hargraves and the others would have to listen for the next two and a half months to his long descriptions of livestock deals, his recounting what he had paid, what he had received, the discounts for cripples, and the complicated loans and margins necessary in frontier negotiations. He explained how a £1,000 deal failed because he would not throw in six brock-faced yearlings; how he had accepted another man's price but insisted that 33 1/3 percent of the mob fetch a lower figure. Babbling on and on, as persistently as the rain sluicing the portholes, he was a competent chap withal, and his knowledge would be important in California.

One day a rowboat from shore splashed out through the downpour with a package of the latest newspapers. A shocking headline stopped Davison's endless narrative: "PORT PHILIP A GOLD FIELD!" Under this caption the cabin passengers read details about the discovery of gold near Melbourne and decided that this was another hoax to check emigration, as the reported gold strike down there last February had been. In any event, they had paid their passage, had been assigned their cabins, and the *Elizabeth Archer* had cleared the port authorities and was waiting only for the weather to moderate.

Regret in vain, the die is cast,
Our anchor is a-peak.

5

Cruise of the Elizabeth Archer

When you start for San Francisco,
They treat you like a dog.
The victuals you're compelled to eat,
Ain't fit to feed a hog.

The storm cleared on July 20, 1849, and Captain Charles Cobb ordered up the *Elizabeth Archer's* anchor. Off at last, the bark slipped down Jackson Bay and out between the Heads. No one on board seemed to realize that the calm weather was the center, or eye, of a cyclone, but that night after all passengers had crawled into their bunks the storm broke. Tom Archer later said that he thought the bark had been knocked on her beam-ends. Seabags, chests, and stools slammed against the cabin's wall, then crashed against his berth. He was almost thrown out of bed. God help heavy Hargraves in such a storm!

Next morning the ship sailed on an even keel, and the passengers who ventured out found the decks a heap of water-soaked wreckage. Those traveling steerage were still sealed in the hull, the black boys in the depth "cooreeing" and "kinda-barring," no doubt. Overhead, sails hung in rags, but sailors already perched along the glistening spars stretching new canvas.

With fair winds the *Elizabeth Archer* sailed almost due east. On the eighth day she skirted the north coast of New Zealand.[1] Slim, white flying fish leaped from the milky wave at the bark's prow, flitting away "like a flight of silver fruit knives," one traveler later recalled. The next landfall, nearly 4,000 miles beyond, was Pitcairn Island—considerably farther than the distance across the United States. In 1789 the mutineer Fletcher Christian, after setting Captain Bligh afloat in an open boat, had fled with the *Bounty* to this far-off island, hoping never to be found. Australians knew the story well, for Bligh had been appointed governor of New South Wales after his rescue.

Pitcairn Island, from the sea, appeared to have a precipitous coast, but Captain Cobb's chart showed a good landing place. The white line along the foot of distant bluffs must be breakers on that beach. However, Captain Cobb feared to sail close to a lee shore lest his vessel, helpless without wind, drift aground. He told his cabin passengers that if they wanted to land and buy fresh vegetables for a change in diet, he would lower a small boat for them. This seemed a strange concession considering that their found was part of their passage costs, but perhaps the gold-rush chantey was right: "The victuals you're compelled to eat ain't fit to feed a hog."

However that may be, five of the passengers—Archer, Hawkins, Hargraves, Davison, and one other—decided to go ashore. The mate barked an order; the anchor plunged into the sea; a small boat swung out on davits and was lowered. The men climbed down a Jacob's ladder into her and took their places on the thwarts, each with an eight-foot sea oar. Hargraves, although an ex-sailor, displayed his clumsiness with his first few strokes, caught a "crab," and upset himself into the bottom. As a reward for awkwardness he was assigned a position in the "after-sheets," where he did no work and his weight helped elevate the prow.

The helmsmen soon spied a whaleboat coming to meet them. It brought a pilot who leaped into the *Archer's* boat and took the tiller. This man used great skill as they approached the beach under the bluffs. He restrained the oarsmen until he saw a big wave behind the boat, then shouted for them to pull with a will. The breaker soon overtook them and shot the boat high on the beach. A dozen natives grasped the gunwales to prevent her from washing back with the tide.

The passengers scrambled out on the wet sand, Hargraves heavily, of course. Women and children clustered around them. All spoke English, for these were mixed-blood descendants of the mutineers. The entire population numbered 152. They were devoutly religious, and the chief man among them introduced himself as a resident missionary. He happened to be an ex-before-the-mast sailor from God only knows what passing craft, and his first concern, he said, was for his flock. Could the gentlemen spare them a few bottles of rum "solely for medicinal purposes?"[2]

The gentlemen could, whereupon the good missionary proceeded to get drunk while the visitors were assigned lodgings with various families. Davison established quarters at the hut of one Isaac Christian, who said he was the great-grandson of the notorious Fletcher Christian.[3]

The passengers seemed to be in no great rush to reach California and remained on shore three days purchasing plantains, yams, coconuts, bananas, oranges, limes, and breadfruit—all preventives of the dread shipboard scurvy. The produce filled the landing craft. Banker Davison estimated the bill, settled the account, and shoved off, leaving Archer and Hawkins to follow in a native boat. As soon as Davison was gone with the supplies, the missionary told Archer and Hawkins that $10.00 was still due on the account. Davison could no longer be consulted, and the missionary controlled the only transportation for following him back to the ship. Although the request savored of blackmail, the two men paid the sum and were happy to be off toward the *Elizabeth Archer* in the Pitcairn Islanders' whaleboat. When Archer and Hawkins arrived at the bark's side and climbed over the bulwarks, they reinventoried the greengroceries and found that Davison had paid the bill in full. As they suspected, the missionary had cheated them.[4]

Captain Cobb ordered up the anchor. Sailors scampered to their stations and chanted lustily as they trudged around the capstan head, pawls clicking against the ratchet, each man stamping to the tune as he stepped over the straining anchor chain. At last the great hook rose dripping from the water. The anchor was apeak! Everyone, even those in steerage, cheered, the blackfellows "kindabarring" on their own account, of course. A moment later the sails unfurled, caught the wind with a jerk, and heeled the decks to leeward. Passengers jostled one another as the bark floundered away with a rush of white water.

The rest of the trip north was uneventful. Cabin passengers

watched the constellations every night, each man aspiring to be first to sight the North Star, which would tell them they had crossed the equator. One day, when a school of porpoises played alongside, an adventurous man, hoping to harpoon some fresh, hot-blooded meat, climbed down on the martingale beneath the bowsprit. While he waited for his target, the bark buried her nose in a swell, completely immersing him. Anxious watchers thought the bow remained under water an agonizingly long time, but when it came up the unfortunate harpooner still clung, dripping, to his perch. He had, however, lost his harpoon and his appetite for porpoise; he also lost no time in scampering aloft before being ducked in the next oncoming wave.

Finally, seventy-nine days out from Sydney, the great pillars of sea-girdled rocks known as the Farallons were spied over the port rail.* Charts showed the Golden Gate to be thirty miles east of them. As the sun set, passengers watched irregular white streaks above the eastern horizon. Were they clouds, or snow on the California mountains? Tom Archer climbed to the cross-trees of the Australian bark's mizzenmast, hoping for a better view. Heavy Hargraves remained on deck. The aspect from aloft proved nothing, but as darkness settled over the ocean, a full moon rose, and Archer enjoyed watching a school of whales playing around the vessel[5]—probably killers. Gray whales passed here in large numbers going north in March and April, south in November and December, but this was early October.

Next morning, when the travelers came on deck they saw distant mountains plainly, but no snow. They must have seen clouds last night. The wind had died and the *Elizabeth Archer* floated, hour after hour, becalmed. Around her on the circle of blue ocean lay other becalmed vessels—at least a dozen of them, all headed for California. One stood on the glassy waters within a mile. Captain Cobb studied her through his telescope and said the name on her stern was *Mount Vernon*. As he watched, a flag broke from her mizzen. The Stars and Stripes!

---

* Thomas Archer, *Recollections of a Rambling Life* (Yokohama, 1897), p. 183, says the passage consumed eighty days. The *Alta California* (Oct. 11, 1849), reporting the vessel's arrival, states that the voyage took eighty-one days. Did some one forget the international dateline?

A few minutes later, a whaleboat pulled away from the American ship and came toward the *Elizabeth Archer*. Sun glinted on the wet sweeps as the craft darted forward. When it swung alongside, ladders were lowered and four Americans, dressed like farmers in "billy-cock hats," climbed aboard.

The Britishers were somewhat taken aback by the strangers' "republican fashion" of shaking hands with everybody and talking to them without inquiring their stations. The Yankees also spoke with an odd accent, spiced with amusing expressions such as: "Do tell," "Waal, waal," "I reckon," and "I guess." Sydney papers had warned them that Americans talked this way, but here the strange creatures were actually doing so, and not in fun either.

Archer and some of the others who felt nimble enough to climb up and down Jacob's ladders decided to visit the American vessel. As they approached it, they noticed how tall a ship stands when seen from a small boat. Climbing on board, they marveled at the Yankees' industry. The *Mount Vernon* was a cooperative venture bound for the goldfields, and in the half-year cruise from Mattapoisett, Massachusetts, these fellows had kept busy making small boats and constructing kegs and barrels to sell. The Australians, when they returned to their own vessel, remarked that it seemed quiet and that their own men seemed slothful.

Next morning, as the sun peeped over the rough edge of California's Coast Range, a fresh breeze from the east ruffled the ocean. The Australians hurried out on deck to watch sails being trimmed on their own and on other becalmed vessels surrounding them. In no time all "hauled" into the eastern wind, racing for the Golden Gate. Foam creamed from prows, and hulls listed until their copper bottoms showed. The *Mount Vernon* dipped her colors to the *Elizabeth Archer*, and Captain Cobb replied in kind.

The Yankee craft pulled steadily ahead. English sailors admired these American-built vessels,[6] but their speed hurt the pride of the greatest maritime people of the century. As the coast came closer, the passengers watched for the Golden Gate. Soon they spied it, a narrow opening like a strait, with more blue water visible beyond the headlands. They were surprised, as others before them had been, to discover that San Francisco Bay was an inland sea.

The *Elizabeth Archer* passed through the channel on October 6, 1849, one of eleven vessels arriving that day.[7] Tom Archer climbed to the foretruck, and, as the bark rounded Clark Point and Telegraph Hill, he beheld the famed city of tents and tatters. In front of the settlement stood hundreds of vessels. The *Elizabeth Archer* glided toward them. Tom noticed that the anchored craft flew a bewildering number of flags. He recognized the colors of more than twenty nations—England, France, Spain, Portugal, Italy, Belgium, Holland, Sweden, Chile, Peru, Russia, Mexico, Ecuador, Norway, Hawaii, Tahiti, and a halfdozen fantastic banners of the German city-states. Many of the ships appeared deserted—crews gone to the goldfields. Surely so many people from so many climes had never before been thrown together in a land without law or order.

Captain Cobb dropped anchor in this city of deserted ships. Almost immediately a dozen small boats bumped the *Elizabeth Archer's* side. Watermen looked up from the thwarts, eagerly calling for "fares" to shore and offering to sign up steerage passengers for labor at $10.00 a day.[8]

San Francisco had changed completely since Catton came on the *Eleanor Lancaster* last April. A city had risen in six months, and was still growing. To the west, shanties, tents, and some houses dotted the rugged slopes almost to the top of Telegraph Hill. To the east, huts encroached on the cemetery in Happy Valley[9]—a name revealing the literary intelligence of a wandering population that was familiar, remotely perhaps, with Samuel Johnson's Rasselas of the Happy Valley. Ships stood, side by side, along the bay shore for a mile. In July, six vessels had brought 889 immigrants in a single day. In September, more than 3,000 arrived in one week, and the last steamer from Panama brought 400 more. On the day the *Elizabeth Archer* arrived, and on the day following, a total of 699 people came ashore.[10]

In the mob of excited, yelling immigrants, the cabin passengers from the *Elizabeth Archer* were rowed to Central Wharf, a new pier projecting for almost eight hundred feet across the tidal flats. Along the pilings stood ships already stuck fast in mud. They were being operated as stores, and the plank walkway to shore between them was lined with booths offering coffee, cakes, and sweetmeats. Jewish "slop-sellers" displayed their goods on wires—shirts and drawers waving in the breeze. Gamblers behind folding tables, or with trays suspended from their necks, tempted new arrivals to try their luck. The thimble game seemed to be a favorite.

The *Elizabeth Archer's* passengers walked through this hubbub to land. They saw, along Montgomery Street which paralleled the shore, more costers peddling fruit, fish, and goodies. They noticed that half a dozen other piers were being constructed into the bay, but immigrants arrived faster than landings could be built.[11] Trudging up the street, ankle-deep in dust, they detoured around piles of goods and baggage which lay apparently unguarded while awaiting storage space. Many sacks had split, letting flour and rice stream out, to be ground under the solid wheels of passing oxcarts. The Australian graziers noted that the bullocks were yoked by their horns, instead of across their necks as in Australia.[12] All the drivers seemed to be dark-skinned Mexicans, called "greasers" by the Americans.[13] Indeed, these democratic republicans were very undemocratic in their contempt for "furriners." Perhaps Britishers would have trouble here among them.

One block from the waterfront the strangers came to Portsmouth Square, a plaza on a hillside, where people might look down on Kearny Street, along its lower edge, as upon a stage with a backdrop of newly built hotel facades. The Australians saw the flamboyant front of the three-story El Dorado Hotel with its canvas roof, also the two-story Parker House. Jumbo letters on other buildings proclaimed them to be the United States House and the California Restaurant. On the steps leading to doorways, itinerant peddlers offered oranges and peanuts for sale.[14]

Up on the Clay Street corner of the sloping plaza stood the post office. Mail from the East Coast was supposed to come monthly by steamboat via Panama, but was already one month overdue.[15] Across the plaza from the post office, on the Washington Street corner, the Australians saw an old adobe customhouse. In the open space below it an American flag hung limply from a tall pole. Obviously, American influence, too, was limp here.

An odd assemblage of men crowded the plaza: Americans, Kanakas, Peruvians in brown ponchos, almond-eyed Chinese with long pigtails swinging across their blue blouses, soft slippers on their feet. Dark-skinned Malays carried wicked-looking creeses. The varicolored throng gabbled a dozen languages.[16] In the motley multitude, Archer recognized a familiar face, an old friend named Swanson from Hobart Town. The chap had arrived a fortnight earlier on the *Harriet Nathan*, commanded by Tom Archer's brother.[17] Swanson had read about the new Australian gold discovery. Was there anything to it?

The newcomers admitted they thought it a hoax. Swanson seemed pleased, for he was making money here. He and another Tasmanian had formed the mercantile firm of Swanson & Taylor. As soon as the *Munford* came in from Hobart, they planned to team up with her captain and buy one of the deserted vessels in the harbor, then bring in their own supplies.[18] With a storeship of their own they would be independent of San Francisco's erratic market. At present, when a cargo arrived, goods were auctioned in the plaza and sometimes sold for a song; yet, a week later the same goods might fetch an exorbitant figure. For instance, molasses had been worth $4.00 a gallon until a shipload of it reduced the price to 65 cents. In June, merchants had not been able to give away their surplus flour. Now it was worth $40.00 a barrel. Sugar that had sold for 3 cents a pound now brought half a dollar. Milk, fruit, and vegetables were all high-priced luxuries. Fresh butter was practically unknown.[19] The price of labor was almost as spotty. Indentured Chinese were auctioned like other goods in the plaza, and the captain of a ship from Australia offered the "sarvices" of three women for five months. They had been unable to "settle their passage," and the highest bidder gave only $15.00 for each one.[20]

The fluctuating figures dismayed those passengers on the *Elizabeth Archer* who had imported parcels of goods to sell.

They learned that some speculators ahead of them had made good profits, although some had not. One man from Sydney, who brought the materials of an old shed, had sold it for £120, receiving £5 a day for nailing it together.[21] Tasmanian boards, onions, and potatoes were selling well. So were bottled ale and porter,[22] but spirits and wine were fetching less than cost. Australian tradesmen told one another to remember one thing: Americans were a temperate people. "If you see a man in the streets drunk and abusive take it for granted that he is an Englishman."[23] But gambling, as the Americans practiced it, was really exciting. A Mexican game called monte was faster than Australian "two-up." French faro had become popular. Low-grade gamblers were called "tin-horns," for the tin cups in which they shook dice. Already the Parker House boasted four billiard tables, and grandiose columns of silver dollars and gold bars stood on twelve other green-topped gambling tables, each tempting the venturesome to try his luck.[24] One "establishment" attracted patrons with a band of Ethiopian serenaders. Another flaunted a female violinist. The exciting roll of drums invited the inquisitive into others. The air inside most gambling halls smelled of the heavy fragrance of Chinese punk, kept burning for customers who wanted to light their cigars.[25] All the larger public houses stationed armed guards to watch constantly for fire—the greatest fear in this rich, flimsily built city.

Swanson talked enthusiastically about the town which was growing miraculously around them. From a village of 1,500 it had grown to 5,000 last spring and now numbered 15,000.[26] Although still a city of many tents, six hundred houses stood where only twelve had been six months earlier.[27] Several of them were built of brick, that precious ballast brought by the *William Hill* from Australia.[28] Every day twenty to thirty new buildings appeared, and the canvas roofs of old ones were being replaced with boards and tar paper. A block of new shops, three and four stories high, was already open for trade. A theater was being built.[29] A new customhouse, down at the corner of California and Montgomery streets, was almost completed. Four stories tall, this brick building had front balconies on each floor, with outside stairways leading to them.[30]

Lodgings were still hard to find. The big iron ship *Antelope*, from Liverpool, was being used as a rooming house in the harbor.[31] Many Australians had congregated in an area known as Sydney Valley or Sydney Town, which sprawled from the slope of Telegraph Hill to the lower end of Pacific and Broadway near Clark Point.[32] Being close to the crescent of the harbor, Sydneyites could watch all vessels coming and going. A few other Australians found lodgings across town in Happy Valley, where they were unhappily packed together eight and nine to a tent, and, true to the "nation of shopkeepers," almost every one of them seemed to have goods, lodgings, or drinks for sale. The road through Happy Valley (later Market Street) led up a dry hollow to the old Spanish mission, three miles away. Meandering through sandy hills, people said that voices of riders coming down the draw could sometimes be heard before the sound of their horses' hoofs.[33]

In all the confusion of rapid growth and daily arrival of hundreds of immigrants speaking different languages, crime seemed relatively rare. Yet, there was no satisfactorily established constitutional government. The United States had acquired this country from Mexico in the recent war, but Congress had failed to arrange for its administration.[34] In midsummer of 1849 a semipolitical organization of New Yorkers engaged in a short, active, and disreputable career, which was difficult for Swanson to explain to his countrymen. Claiming to be democratic representatives of the common man, this group of so-called Hounds modeled their society after Tammany Hall, ignoring the fact that that organization of "common men," like so many successful "liberal groups," became dominated by wealthy political adventurers. The Hounds, after parading in grotesque costumes, openly robbed foreigners, pilfered from the stores of some Americans, and in August raided the Latin-American suburb called Little Chile, tearing down tents and beating the occupants. This incensed the better element in San Francisco, who called a mass meeting in Portsmouth Square to take the law into their own hands and organize a constabulary. Sam Brannan was a principal speaker. Some Hounds were arrested, tried, and confined in an old brig, probably the *Euphemia*,

which served as a prison ship soon after she arrived in the bay*
—a utilitarian climax for the old lumber-carrying brig. More
than nine months earlier she had carried, as far as Hawaii, the
first news of the gold rush to reach Australia.

The complacency with which Americans took the law into
their own hands instead of leaving it to General Persifor Smith
and the military was enough to confound the colonial British,
but some of them, as we shall see, quickly adapted themselves
to the new environment. Having dealt successfully with the
Hounds, San Franciscans were beginning to look upon the natural slope of Portsmouth Square as their tribunal. Down at Monterey a convention was formulating a constitution to govern the
state, but a bad precedent had been established up here and
later, when officers, even though legally elected, failed to suit
this ebullient populace, trouble might follow. Britishers were
used to political tumult and bickering, but they felt the need
of a monarch to maintain the state.

Swanson had met most of the arriving Australians. He recognized his countrymen by their cabbage-tree hats and moleskin
trousers. A close observer could even tell the colony they came
from by the color of their bedding. Possum-skin rugs from Tasmania were darker than those from the mainland.[35] A goodly
number of the Australians arrived without money and immediately sought jobs to earn transportation to the diggings, more
than a hundred miles away. Many remained permanently in
town. As editor Fairfax had warned, the seething throng of
strangers offered tempting opportunities for crooks, absconders,
and vagabonds from all settlements in the South Pacific.

Were these bad characters beginning to engender prejudice
against all foreigners? Tom Archer must have wondered! So far
the worst rascals had been the New York Hounds. One Australian had been arrested for robbery but was acquitted.[36] Some
people complained that a prejudice against British subjects was

* *Alta California,* July 19, 1849; Felix Paul Wierzbicki, *What I Saw in Cali-
fornia* (Launceston, 1850), p. 159; Frank Soulé, John H. Gihon, and James
Nisbet, *The Annals of San Francisco* (New York, 1855), p. 556 ff. According to
Soulé, Gihon, and Nisbet (p. 233), the *Euphemia* was sold in August, 1849. The
vessel's owner, William Heath Davis, states (*Seventy-five Years in California*
[San Francisco, 1929], p. 306) that he sold the craft in 1850.

growing. Others said the British and the Americans were much alike and both looked on the Latins as foreigners.[37] Swanson did not know which opinion was right. Archer, Hargraves, and their friends would have to find out for themselves.

Returning to the ship, the Australians found Captain Cobb in a desperate situation. His entire crew had deserted for the mines. The distraught master could unload none of his cargo. He could not even give his cabin passengers the goods they had brought along for speculation. And worst of all, a threatening storm might pile all the anchored vessels into a jackstraw heap.

6

Off to the Mother Lode

"Cockbill all yardarms." What did that mean?

Some port authority in San Francisco sent the order, but Captain Cobb could not comply without a crew. Indeed, he was in an ugly mess. When his passengers returned to the ship after their shore visit, they learned about his predicament and the threatening storm. They understood at once that in case of a blow the anchored vessels standing so close together were sure to tangle yardarms and tear one another's rigging to tatters. To prevent this, every yard must be lashed in a vertical position like the bill of a crowing cock. That was what the order meant, but Captain Cobb had no men to carry it out.

The passengers admired Captain Cobb. They also worried about the unloading of their own cargo, so they decided to do it themselves. Master and servant, white, yellow, and black, along with some steerage passengers, set to work in the brisk October weather. The storm failed to materialize but the job lasted for days. While the men worked they discussed future plans. All agreed that, as had already been said in Australia, General Smith's order prohibiting foreigners from mining "proved perfectly inoperative,"[1] but they were uncertain about the most suitable place to begin prospecting for gold. Three inland towns should be good for trade, and two of them were close enough to the diggings for a tradesman to prospect in his spare time.

Benicia seemed to have the best future, and might even become the capital of the state, but it had no nearby diggings. Sacramento was close to a good mining area, but the first of the 20,000 to 30,000 overland gold seekers' wagons had been trundling in there since late July.[2] Such a horde had surely staked all the best claims already. A third town, Sonora, stood in the heart of the southern Mother Lode and seemed to offer the best opportunities for both mining and commerce. That area could be reached by way of Stockton, or Tuleburg as it was called, on the San Joaquin River. The Australians decided to go there first.

Hargraves, a promoter always, suggested that several of them form a company, pool their resources, and prorate expenses. Seven men agreed to this proposition and Davison, possessing both banking experience and the most money, became company treasurer. Hargraves, having a commanding presence, became president. They engaged passage to Stockton on a local schooner. Thomas Archer, Hawkins, and a few of their shipboard companions decided to remain in San Francisco, retail their goods, and join the others later.

Before he left, Davison exchanged most of his goods for gold dust at a 50 percent profit, but he found no buyer for a half-ton of sea biscuits and two casks of pickled beef. An import duty of 40 percent on alcoholic beverages caused him to ship his two puncheons of rum back to Sydney along with 30 ounces of gold dust to be credited to his account there. He loaded the "hard-bread" and casks of beef on the schooner, hoping to sell them at Stockton or in some mining town beyond.

With this cargo the company set sail on October 27, 1849, joining a long procession of sailboats, scows, launches, whaleboats, and some raftlike canoes made of tules by the Indians. They traversed the blue bays, turned into the channel, passed Benicia, meandered through Suisun Bay's maze of inlets and islands, then up the tule-lined San Joaquin River. On November 1 they came to a high bank where twenty-five sizable vessels stood, moored end to end. This was the landing for Stockton. Although more than a hundred miles inland by water—sixty as the crow flies—tides rose and fell here four feet daily.

The Australians climbed the steep bank and found Stockton to be a line of 200 tents, one house, and at least a dozen dwellings under construction. Men everywhere worked on the run— the most active people Davison and Hargraves had ever seen. Stevedores, carrying heavy burdens, trotted from the moored vessels up swaying gangplanks. Draymen shouted to their teams. Drovers' whips popped like pistol shots.[3] Stockton, as yet, had no jail, and law without punishment was hard to enforce. During the past summer two Negro criminals had been tied to a tree and publicly flogged, with the alcalde and the sheriff present. This was unsatisfactory justice, certainly very different from the way Queen Victoria administered authority in Australia's outback.

Davison found no market for his supplies in crowded Stockton. The next town, Sonora, was seventy miles away, in mountains not yet visible across a plain that stretched eastward to the horizon. From here on, everything would have to be hauled in wagons. The weather was still fine, but people said the rains might start any day now.

"You better be in camp, pardner, before they come!"

No time could be lost, so Hargraves and Davison inquired about hiring a teamster. They were told that a Hoosier was in town with some work cattle. The Australians went to see him and learned that a Hoosier was not a Red Indian, but a citizen of the state of Indiana. They also learned that quaint American tavernkeepers who catered to businessmen furnished a bundle of fagots on each table[4] and a spittoon beside it. Men liked to whittle during negotiations, and a chew of tobacco gave them time for consideration before committing themselves. The "Aussies" learned, too, that Americans called work bullocks "steers," their drivers "bullwhackers," and referred to camp equipment as "plunder." Davison finally reached an agreement on a fair price for transporting the camp outfit and his half-ton of hardtack. His heavy kegs of pickled beef had to be left behind.

By early afternoon the Hoosier's wagon was loaded, and the travelers walked out of town beside the lurching vehicle. This resembled the life they all knew so well in Australia's outback. The day was sultry. A dark-brown road stretched ahead of them across an endless plain of yellow, sun-cured wild oats.[5] It disappeared in shimmering heat waves, and a covered wagon far ahead seemed to float, wheelless, on a glistening quicksilver sea. The mirage dissolved the trunks of distant trees, leaving them suspended in the hot sky. Smoke from invisible tule fires clouded the air.

That night the Australians camped by a creek near Dancing Bill's public house. They stretched a canvas from the wagon to the ground and fixed their pallets underneath, as they would have done in their own New England. Sitting around the supper fire after dark they heard, for the first time, the wild staccato howl of coyotes, and noticed that California in late November felt much colder than Australia.

Before morning, the first of the winter rains pelted against their canvas and dripped from the underseams. At daylight the men built a little fire for tea and munched biscuits around it. The rising sun cleared the sky and glistened on the wet plain. The travelers packed quickly and set off along the road which tapered to a threadlike line at the horizon—all much flatter than Australia's Bathurst plains. The brown earth in the wheel ruts had turned black in the rain and stuck to the wayfarers' boots. They plodded only seven miles before the sky clouded and another downpour threatened. This time they camped by the roadside, barely stretching their canvas before the storm hit them.

All afternoon and all night the rain sluiced down. By morning the road was impassable for their heavily loaded wagon, and water still poured from the leaden clouds. Throughout the day the men remained in camp. Davison worried lest the water damage his precious half-ton of hardtack. The Hoosier, watching the dreary sky, finally remarked in his slow drawl, "I guess the rainy season has set in."[6]

At the end of the second day a covered wagon, heading east, trundled in out of the storm and halted. The travelers were New Yorkers who had hired a Buckeye in Stockton to haul them to the diggings. A Buckeye, the Australians learned, was a citizen of Ohio, a state joining the Hoosier's Indiana. The two parties decided to go on together next day, rain or shine. If one wagon stuck in the mud, there would be sufficient men and bullocks to pull it out.

In the morning they set off, slipping, sliding, splashing, and "doubling" teams at every mudhole. By dark they had covered so short a distance that the Hoosier said this would never do; too much time was being wasted hooking and unhooking. Tomorrow he would add his team to the Buckeye's, and together they could pull the New Yorkers to the foothills, where wood and water were plentiful. Then both teams would come back and haul in the Australians. This seemed to be a reasonable solution, but instead of coming back in two days, the Hoosier left the Australians in camp for eleven. They had a rough time. On the first morning, fog obscured everything, making the sun look like a silver moon. The campers had no firewood and dared not go out of sight of the wagon to seek some, lest they become lost in the ashy atmosphere. Unhappy because they could not make tea, they waited until midmorning when the air cleared. Then they saw with dismay a great swamp ahead of them—or was it a mirage? The nearest tree seemed to be at least two miles beyond it.

Davison and Hargraves, president and treasurer of the company, shouldered axe and gun, and started toward the tree for firewood. They came back with armloads and reported game to be plentiful. They had seen quail, hare, ducks, and geese. Being inured to bush life the graziers lived well, made their camp comfortable, and baked "damper" in the coals, although they had no bullock's tail to dust off the ashes, Australian style.[7] The bushmen pronounced the cooking coals from California oak inferior to those from the cones of "cubby pine."

Almost every day, travelers came down the road from the mines, passing the Australians' camp. Davison opened his boxes of "hardbread" and sold the biscuits profitably. Among the travelers he recognized some steerage passengers from the *Elizabeth Archer*. These men were already discouraged, disgusted, bankrupt, and anxious to return to Australia. They were full of tales about the miners' illegal enforcement of order. The punishment for petty crime at the diggings, they said, was flogging or banishment from camp. Up at Hang Town last January a Chilean and two Frenchmen had been flogged, then hanged by a drunken mob after a mock trial in which the foreigners were allowed no interpreter. A thief, for his first offense, usually lost one ear; for the second, his other ear was cut off. He might also be branded with a T on the cheek. If caught a third time, the penalty was hanging. Australians with long hair were accused of hiding marks of punishment.[8] This posed a threat to Hargraves, who liked to cover his ears with curls.

At last, Hoosier and Buckeye returned with the double yoke of oxen. The Australians upbraided them for the delay and were told in no uncertain terms to "jump in the swamp." The Americans had come to unload the "furriners' plunder," take the Hoosier's wagon and go, leaving the Australians stranded.

Hargraves, a big and determined-looking man, protested. He pointed out that his party exceeded the Americans eight to two. The property in that wagon belonged to his company, and the Americans had better not touch it. In this predicament Hoosier and Buckeye agreed to haul the Australians and their "plunder" across to the foothills and leave them where they could find sufficient wood to encamp until spring.

This concession failed to satisfy the Australians, but, as the proffered move was in the right direction, they permitted the Americans to haul the wagon eastward. That night they all camped among scattered oaks on rolling hills below the mountains. Next morning the Americans began to unload the graziers' "plunder."

"Hold on!" Hargraves warned. "Don't touch our goods."[9]

The Hoosier turned angrily, said he would go to a nearby camp and come back with a sufficient number of Americans to whip the British. Hoosiers and Buckeyes had a traditional dislike for Englishmen which stemmed from the War of 1812 when, according to tradition, Britain had sent Indians to scalp Midwestern settlers. American politicians had never let the voters forget that alleged wrong.

The two Americans trudged away with their cattle to get help, and the Australians, their goods still on the Hoosier's wagon, prepared to defend themselves. At least the fight would be in the open, not like the vicious ambushes laid by blackfellows on Darling Downs. But, instead of returning with sufficient help to take the wagon, the Americans came back with one cowboy who dismounted on unsteady, sugar-tong legs, listened attentively to the Australians' account of their predicament, then thoughtfully pushed his sombrero back on his head and "allowed as how" the Americans were wrong. As far as he was concerned, they could go to hell.

The Australians had obviously won the argument, but they were unprepared for the next turn of events. The Hoosier said that his steers lacked the strength to pull the loaded wagon up the hills ahead; more oxen would be necessary. Treasurer Davison offered to pay the Buckeye $60.00 to help with his bullocks as far as the diggings. This was agreed to and the wagon, with its double line of oxen, plodded up the oak-studded slope, an open, parklike country yellow with rain-beaten wild oats. Here and there in open spaces among the trees the Australians saw odd clusters of black lava slabs resembling their native black-fellows in council.

On the crest of the divide the travelers paused to rest the animals. Before them lay the famous Mother Lode country—a vast jumble of round, tree-stippled knobs and tangled gorges sprawling endlessly into misty distances to the north and east. Eager to reach their destination, the drivers spoke to their oxen and the wagon lurched ahead into the jumbled wilderness. On downgrades the wheels had to be rough-locked to make them skid like runners. Eight miles of such driving put the company at the bottom of a wide gorge—Knights Ferry, on the Stanislaus River. Both banks were lined with Indians spearing salmon that skittered up the rapids. A few white men were working on a ferryboat to be used when the water rose next spring. Treasurer Davison purchased some fish from the Red Men, and at tea that night the Australians declared the meat less pink and delicate than the Scottish variety.

For the next three days the Argonauts proceeded along the rough Table Mountain road. Their oxen strained up steep pitches, bumping the wagon over quartz outcrops and creek-bottom boulders. Leaves of bay trees in the gulches smelled as fragrant as eucalypti when crushed between a traveler's palms. Finally, the Australians reached Wood's Creek,* a likely spot

---

* Simpson Davison, *The Discovery and Geognosy of Gold Deposits in Australia* (London, 1860), p. 33. Note that Hargraves mistakenly calls the stream Hood Creek.

five miles from Sonora. A month's time had been required to travel the seventy miles from Stockton. Below them in the shallow gorge they heard the clink of metal shovels and the swish of water running out of cradles. Looking down through the tops of poplars whose leaves were yellow now with autumnal color, the Australians saw red-clad figures working in the white sand. "Redcoats" meant British law, authority, discipline. Trudging closer, the graziers realized that they had made a mistake. The red coats were miners' red shirts, and, whether red flannel stood for discipline and authority in California, the Australians would soon find out. They unloaded the wagon, paid the bullwhackers, and picking up axes and shovels began to construct a winter camp. They worked fast, hoping to finish in time for some gold panning before winter came.

Back in San Francisco, after the Hargraves party left, Thomas Archer, together with his friend Hawkins, planned to open a shop and sell his goods at the best possible profit, then follow Hargraves and Davison to the diggings. In Sydney, Archer had purchased dollars. With this specie in a bag, he joined a queue of importers on the upper side of the plaza waiting before the old customhouse to pay duty on their goods.

His turn came finally. Half a dozen men examined his invoices and cleared the goods. Archer had it hauled to Happy Valley just inside Rincon Point. Here, with the help of his blacks, he pitched a tent and opened shop. The lower end of the street was lined with booths of a dozen other merchants, and competition was keen. To help finance his venture, Archer left the blacks, along with Hawkins and his two Chinese, to keep store while he worked as deputy sheriff to make extra money. Men with sufficient education for such a job were difficult to find, and there certainly seemed to be no prejudice against him as a foreigner. One of his first duties was to serve a paper on an Australian sea captain who had dodged the service by taking refuge on a British man-of-war anchored in San Francisco Bay. Not to be thwarted, Tom obtained an authorization from the captain of a United States flagship and served his man. Tom Archer was making a good start in the new country.

The Archer tent-store stood close to the Happy Valley grave-yard. On one of the wooden crosses Tom recognized a familiar name: FRANCIS FORBES, son of the owner of Clifton Station, the lad who had come to California to learn about gold in its natural state so that he might discover it back on Darling Downs. Two other Australians had died since Archer's landing. They had come on that gigantic and heavily loaded *William Watson* which lost four passengers on the trip from Melbourne. Another Australian, the former shipping master in Sydney, was also buried in Happy Valley.[10]

Indeed, illness seemed to be distressingly common. The chief complaints were diarrhea, colds with rheumatism, fever, and ague. Archer heard that physicians of all nations were permitted to practice without a license. Some of them kept private hospitals where the charges were "an ounce" a day, with ten days' payment in advance. The fee for a house call was also an ounce. Poor men who succumbed were tumbled into rough coffins in the suits they died in.

On October 28, the rains, which hit the Hargraves party east of Stockton a few days later, began in San Francisco.[11] The storm swept in across the bay, shrouded Telegraph Hill, and beat a tattoo on tent roofs and new board sidings. In no time, dusty streets turned into quagmires of mud so sticky it could pull the boot off a pedestrian. In front of buildings empty boxes served as sidewalks. To prevent wagons from bogging down, Montgomery Street was corduroyed with the branches of trees. William Tecumseh Sherman, who lived in California that winter, reported the street to be so bad that a saddle horse might get its legs tangled in the mired branches,[12] fall, and thrash around until drowning.

Many tent-stores were flooded, and Archer admired his fellow merchants' good nature. They were, of course, all young men. Some stood behind their counters in water to their knees, swapping jokes. One chap told about seeing a new hat in the muddy street. He laid planks out to it and claimed that he found a man's head under the beaver. The submerged fellow said he was all right because he was mounted on a stout mule.[13]

This joke would grow on the American frontier in the years to come, until the man under the hat could say that he was all right because he stood on a load of hay.

Three days after the beginning of the rainy season, a memorable incident occurred: Mail arrived from "the states" on a steamship from Panama. A watchman on Golden Gate sighted the vessel and signaled across the sand dunes to Telegraph Hill, where a flag notified all townsmen. Immediately, a queue formed at the post office and soon extended for several blocks. After the steamboat docked and the mail sacks were delivered, the queue moved slowly; office-window deliveries took time, because postage must be paid by the receiver. Many people held their places all night. Some sold theirs for $10.00 to $25.00. Hawkers peddled pies, cakes, and coffee along the line.[14]

Tom Archer had many things to learn in this strange community, and perhaps the strangest was sending soiled clothes to Hawaii to be laundered.[15] He retailed his goods at a reasonable profit, then joined three former shipmates on an expedition to meet Davison and Hargraves at the diggings. The party consisted of ten men: four masters and six servants, two of the latter Chinese and four, blackfellows. The masters chartered a barge, loaded it with goods to sell in Stockton, and steered the floundering craft north across San Francisco Bay. All went well until they passed Benicia. Night overtook them in the dreary wastes of tule swamp in Suisun Bay, at the junction of the Sacramento and San Joaquin rivers. To await the dawn they anchored in deep water, where there was no danger of an ebbing tide stranding their precious cargo in the mud. This was a great mistake because the tide was coming in instead of going out, and the rising water pulled the barge's anchored bow down close to the surface. A sudden gust of wind blew water over the gunwales. The old craft began to fill. She tipped forward, her heavy cargo tumbled into the bow, and her hull dived to the channel's bottom.[16]

Archer and one companion, named Mackenzie, wallowed and swam through tules to the quaking shore. They called and waited for their comrades, but heard no sound in that wilder-

ness of reeds except the beating of countless wings as hundreds
of wild geese flew close overhead. In the morning the two white
men found the bodies of Hawkins and Hicks floating in the
water, but there was no trace of the six servants. Archer and
Mackenzie returned to San Francisco, proceeded to Stockton
overland, and continued to the Stanislaus River by the road
Hargraves' party had followed. In the Sonora country, where
their friends had settled, they made camp.

Here Archer's two thin-faced blackfellows, Jacky Small and
Davy, joined their master. Their story was simple. On the day
after the wreck, they returned to the submerged barge and
waited endlessly. Ships passed them, but the blackfellows talked
English incomprehensible to Americans. At last a party of Australians, floating down the river, understood the Durundurs'
lingo and took them back to San Francisco. There the Australians learned Archer's whereabouts and shipped his servants
to him.[17] The fate of the other blacks and the Chinese is unknown.

The Britishers found American miners to be cordial fellows.
No introductions or "letters" seemed necessary. Without any
formalities, a man would stop work to show the newcomers
how to twirl gravel and water in a pan, sloshing the small stones
and dirt over the sloping sides until only "black sand" remained
in the groove at the bottom of the dish. Old-timers explained
that gold settled in this black sand. Tiny particles, called
"colors," could be seen sparkling in it. The number of colors in
a pan determined the richness of the strike. When a miner located "pay dirt," he laid aside his pan and employed a cradle,
which extracted much larger quantities of gold with less work.
Of course this required cooperation, with one man at the cradle,
two or three others pouring in water and shoveling in dirt. However, a cradle cost £12 and, with everything being exorbitantly
expensive, the Australians hesitated to pay that much.

Banker Davison solved the financial dilemma. Noticing that
each man averaged 7 shillings a day with his pan, he got a pledge
of this amount from every member of his party and lent the company sufficient money to buy a cradle. With this they set to

work and, in the days that followed, learned how to "rock a cradle"—not so simple a performance as it seemed. They also learned the California word "gulch."[18]

When freezing weather stopped their work, they had made more than their expenses. Many diggers were "fixin' to go to San Francisco" for the winter, although Sonora now had a population of 5,000. Hargraves and Davison decided to relax in their camp until spring, a rest that proved not so restful as they had hoped. The streams froze and they often broke the ice to dip water for cooking. Sometimes at night they got up and beat snow from the tent, lest it fall down.[19]

Archer and his blackfellows trudged off into the wintry hills prospecting the High Sierra, bent more on adventure than on accumulating wealth. The aborigines had never seen snow before, and it set them to "cooreeing." They danced with joy when they found digger-pine cones—so like the pineapple cones of their beloved bunya bunya trees, but they wailed ruefully when they found none of the prized meat inside. One day black Davy spied the tracks of a grizzly bear. Neither he nor Archer had ever seen a monster that left such a gigantic spoor.

"You see that fellow track?" Davy asked. "Bel me know that fellow."

Archer understood this to mean that Davy knew enough to stay away from "that fellow," and when night overtook them they lighted a big fire hoping it would frighten away the beast. Later, Archer and the blacks learned that grizzlies, although dangerous antagonists, do not hunt humans.[20]

Back at the diggings once more, Archer remarked that his aboriginal servants learned California manners quickly. He pronounced them more aggressive and self-sufficient, more proud and arrogant than the miserable Red Indians who slunk into Sonora begging refuse. The blacks, of course, were Durundur warriors who, with spears and boomerangs, had made a good fight for Darling Downs. Archer, who had read James Fenimore Cooper, expected Red Indians to be like *The Last of the Mohicans*. Only one thing about them impressed him—their bows and arrows. He had seen no such ugly weapons among aboriginal Australians. Even a spent arrow had a deadly way of darting around boulders and piercing any flesh in its path.

Jacky Small and Davy displayed markedly different characteristics. Jacky "turned republican," as Archer called it, got drunk, and threatened camp with a revolver. Davy, when drunk, became homesick, shed tears, and sat in his tent looking out at the snow as he sang a "corroboree."[21]

During these idle days, both Hargraves and Davison—according to their recollections—noticed that the gold country in California resembled Australia, and this convinced both of them that gold must exist down under. Which man was first to reach this conclusion is controversial, but it became very important to them for it meant fame and fortune for one, disappointment for the other. Davison was always certain that Hargraves got the idea from him,* for he, Davison, knew intimately the back country of New South Wales, whereas Hargraves had not seen it for seventeen years. As a matter of fact, the idea really amounted to little. Everybody knew that shepherds in Australia had frequently found small quantities of gold in the outback. Young Forbes had left Darling Downs ahead of Archer to note how gold was washed in California, so that he could repeat the process on his father's station.[22] Moreover, the Mother Lode country really bore little resemblance to the Australian gold country; even flat-topped Table Mountain southwest of Sonora could hardly be compared with the majestic Blue Mountains in New South Wales.

Undoubtedly Hargraves, and Davison too, heard miners tell how the appearance of the creek below Sutter's mill, where the first gold was discovered, reminded many men of other similar creeks they knew, and how the length of the Mother Lode had thus been developed. It was commonly said that a man named Charles Weber, looking at the site of the first discovery, was re-

---

* George F. Parsons, *The Life and Adventures of James W. Marshall, the Discoverer of Gold in California* (Sacramento, 1870), p. xiii, reports that Marshall in 1857 claimed to have met Hargraves at Coloma in 1849, and convinced him that he could find gold in Australia. Hargraves, however, was not in Coloma in 1849.

minded of the Stanislaus River down here, fifty miles south, and came to open the Sonora field. Another man who saw the original site was reminded of a stream he knew seventy-five miles north of the Feather River. He went there, discovered gold, and established another field. Still a third man came, looked, was reminded of the Mount Shasta area he knew far to the north, and opened up that region. Therefore, if Hargraves and Davison were reminded of country they knew in Australia, they were following a pattern. It should be noted too that Hargraves, when he wrote about his experiences, said erroneously that the James W. Marshall who discovered gold in California was an engineer from New South Wales[23]—a misstatement that caused several Australians who were descended from another Marshall to claim the honor.

By midwinter of 1849–50, the bottoms of all the streams around Sonora had been turned upside down in a search for alluvial gold, and shafts had been driven for forty to fifty feet into quartz veins on the hillsides. This skillful tunneling had been done by Latin Americans, who were experienced miners and for whom the town of Sonora had been named. Indeed, Sonora was an old mining community—almost two years old—and California's generally adopted Miners' Code was said to have been originated on nearby Wood's Creek.[24]

The winter weather, with intermittent rain and snow, tempted idle American diggers into mischief. Pursuing their rights, as they called it, they organized kangaroo courts to "jump" the Latin Americans' claims and persecute them by levying a tax on local miners. The near civil war that followed prompted the first California legislature, then in session at San Jose, to pass a law imposing a tax on foreign miners, directed against Spanish-speaking diggers, not English colonials. Indeed, Archer, Hargraves, and Davison pronounced their relations with the Americans as cordial as could be. They were accepted as Englishmen, which they were, but a change was coming. Englishmen from Australia were soon to be considered convicts and treated accordingly.[25]

Gold Rush Crescendo:
A Good Outlet for Expirees

Then come along, come along,
You that wants to go.
Here's "the best accommodations"
And "the passage very low."

More than six months passed before people in the colonies could learn about the experiences of Hargraves, Davison, Archer, or any other Australians who had sailed to San Francisco. Nonetheless, interest in California was growing, and two events soon precipitated a real rush. As has been said, Sydney's newspapers did their utmost to discourage emigration. At first they had urged people to wait for more news, "wait until a vessel arrives straight from the gold fields." Then, after arrival of the American *Sabine* in March, the press changed its plea: "Wait until one of our own vessels comes back."

Some people may have taken the new appeal seriously, but not all. Towns's *Inchinnan* came in from New Zealand, and he started refitting her. The owner of a little brigantine, the *Chearful*, began advertising for passengers on July 18, 1849 (the day after the *Elizabeth Archer* left). This little craft, according to the owner, was of light draft, could run up the Sacramento River, and thus save passengers the expense of an overland journey after arrival in San Francisco.[1]

Both the *Chearful* and the *Inchinnan* promised to be first away, but both failed to sell all available space. Perhaps the newspapers had checked a rush. Then, on August 4, a momentous event occurred: Lookouts reported a vessel approaching the Heads. Seamen recognized the schooner rigging of the *Des-*

patch; at last a Sydney ship was returning from California, though already one month overdue.[2] The news was semaphored to town, and excitement swept over Sydney like a thunder-shower. Men and boys ran down Pitt and George streets to Circular Wharf. Shopmen on Hunter, Macquarie, and King streets put up shutters in front of their stores and joined the throng. In the cold mid-August weather drinking saloons near the docks soon filled with noisy, rum-drinking customers. Outside, other people waited, stamping their feet and swinging their arms as they watched for every signal from the castellated walls of Admiralty House across the cove. Among the crowd, Punch and Judy showmen set up their booths. Jugglers tossed their balls and solicited coppers.

At the upper end of Circular Wharf, Robert Towns paced to and fro beside the wet pyramids of cargo on his dock—cargo he was loading aboard the *Inchinnan* hoping to get it on the San Francisco market ahead of MacNamara's shipment. Towns ached with influenza. Moreover, his wife and daughters were also suffering from the malady and he longed to be with them near the glowing coal grate in his house—but business was business, and he could not rest. The incoming *Despatch* might bring reports that would change his shipping plans. He ordered the loading of his *Inchinnan* stopped pending the news. Owners of the *Chearful* did likewise.

Finally the *Despatch*, gliding slowly under the harbor steamboat's tow, rounded Bennelong Point. The schooner nosed toward the quay as rolling swells from her stern splashed on the wharf's pilings. Before she docked, passengers climbed down her side and jumped into small boats. Among them were F. Montefiore and J. C. Catton. Towns immediately buttonholed the latter to discuss trade opportunities.

The *Despatch* had experienced a rough trip. On arriving at San Francisco, she found seventy vessels anchored there—all without crews, some of them still not unloaded.[3] Her own crew promptly deserted for the mines. Merchants came out and purchased her cargo, but the captain found himself unable to employ sailors to bring back his ship. Finally he hired two youths, both "full to the bung," too drunk to know where they were going. With them he navigated the vessel out through the Golden Gate. Beyond the Farallons, hardly out of sight of the mainland, the *Despatch* tacked into a head wind so strong that she raced along with the lee gunwale cutting the water. Her bowsprit pierced oncoming waves, going through them, wetting the jib halfway up. The schooner's masts groaned under the strain. Captain Plant pleaded with his few passengers to help shorten sail, but they refused. All feared to risk their lives in the roaring gale on a pitching deck that sloped into hissing water. After seven blustery days the *Despatch* raised Diamond Head and sailed safely into Honolulu, where the captain employed regular seamen—able-bodied if not white—to bring the vessel back to Sydney.[4]

Now, at last, Australians talked with fellow countrymen straight from the diggings. Moreover, they could see with their own eyes 2,865 ounces of gold actually on board. In addition, dozens of letters came from friends who had gone to California and stayed. The news was copied at once and sent skimming out across the ocean to other Australian colonies. People learned that San Francisco had two- and three-story houses, respectable hotels, and an abundance of drinking places. The stories about lawlessness were denied. Life and property on the hilly streets were pronounced as safe as anywhere in the world. The population had an average proportion of women (a statement contradicted later when single women joined the rush). Earlier hearsay stories about the high price of everything were confirmed and enlarged upon. Skilled laborers were reported to be getting $15.00 to $20.00 a day. A porter received $5.00 for carrying a bag. A man and dray could make $100.00 a day. There was, as yet, no bank—a great opportunity for the Montefiores. Specie had to be stored in the adobe customhouse.[5]

Beyond San Francisco, other settlements such as Stockton, Sacramento, and Marysville seemed to be growing equally fast. A letter from one Australian told about watching a town of canvas and boards grow in one day. "I have seen men laying a house foundation as I went to breakfast," the writer said. "At tea time

I saw the edifice complete and filled with goods. Before bedtime
the owner had, no doubt, sold enough to pay for his store-room
twice over."

As people read these exciting tales, another great event came
to pass. On August 18 the *William Hill* arrived straight from
California, having left there on May 23. E. S. Hill had been
unable to sell his paint, glass, rum, and tobacco, but he was enthusiastic about the California market. He reported horses to
be in great demand and offered investors an opportunity to buy
suitable animals at Valparaiso, Chile, where he would pick them
up for delivery in San Francisco—a much shorter haul than
from Sydney, he said.[6]

With the news brought by these vessels, the rush from Australia really began. Editors printed extracts from letters telling
about great opportunities in California. So much material came
to their desks that they printed only parts of it, but in editorials
they stressed the chances of failure, the bad climate, the fact
that high wages had been paid several months earlier, before so
many people had arrived. Now there might be unemployment.[7]

Such discouraging words had little effect. The *Chearful's*
owners sold more berths than they had on their brigantine and
set carpenters to work improvising additional ones. Three other
vessels offered passage. People flocked to Robert Towns's counting room with their savings and purchased the last steerage
space on his *Inchinnan*.[8] To take advantage of the demand, he
chartered two more craft, the *Chasley* and the *Duke of Roxburgh*. Thus seven vessels were laid on for California, and the
exodus became big business.

Towns played his old game of sending some goods on his own
account, although he saw to it that his transportation costs were
paid by cargo he carried for others. Three bits of information
brought by the travelers impressed him: San Francisco lacked
building materials, firewood, and draft horses. Think of a dray-
man making $100 a day! Towns noticed that speculators were
buying horses for California. Splendid! He hoped to profit by
shipping them. He became enthusiastic when a man named
Palmer, who represented himself as an outback horse raiser, offered to fill a vessel with good draft stock. The *Chasley*, Towns

said, could be refitted for such a cargo, and he set men to work
at once.

Down on the wharf the August weather became beastly cold.
Towns, still suffering with the grippe, sniffled miserably and his
bones ached, but he kept stevedores loading the *Chasley's* hold
with 30,000 bricks, 120 tons of coal, and a quantity of lime.
Above this ballast he constructed stalls for horses. He under-
stood how to build them, having been successful in shipping
Walers to British cavalrymen in Calcutta, Madras, and Hong
Kong.

Then, just when Towns was up to his aching ears in projects,
a new excitement hit Sydney Town. A British ship, the *Randolph*, entered Jackson Bay, her decks black with convicts. Such
transportation to New South Wales had been abolished, but the
law was being evaded by calling these immigrants "ticket-of-
leave men." Here was a supply of servants sufficient to offset the
emigration to California. Employers welcomed them, but they
did not reckon with the cabbage-tree-hat boys who wanted to
keep labor scarce, force wages up, and get advantageous social
legislation. In no time, all streets leading to Circular Wharf became packed with a protesting throng. Leaders harangued their
fellows:

"New South Wales is no longer a penal colony."

"Get that ship out of here, and fast!"

"Let shippers try to import criminals and there will be a
Boston Tea Party in Sydney Harbor"—and fat sharks.[9]

The mob knew its American history!

A similar importation had been tried down at Melbourne in
June, accompanied by a similar protest. The Sydney shipment
of convicts was consigned to Smith, Campbell & Company, who
dared not disembark them. But Towns's grazier customers
needed these convict-laborers for their stations. Consequently,
ill as he was, Towns arranged to land the best hands after dark
at W. C. Wentworth's manor. Other employers engaged in similar negotiations, and next day Towns could tell his diary that the
entire cargo had been "snatched off before a cat could lick her
tail."[10]

As a matter of record, all but fifty-nine of the convicts landed, and the *Randolph* took these undesirables to Moreton Bay.[11] Empty of prisoners, she hurried back to Sydney where Smith, Campbell & Company laid her on for California. They advertised her as a new ship, pointed to her patent ventilators—the latest improvement installed now even on convict ships—her competent surgeon, her limitation on the number of passengers which conformed to parliamentary regulations, and the novelty of her special cabins for families and single women. (This appeal to single women to venture into the pioneer world of men was reiterated during the months ahead.) The owners also announced that Captain Dale was prepared to make arrangements with passengers who wished to remain on board for *three weeks* after arrival "without any other charge than the cost of Victualling."[12] A fine inducement, indeed!

Newspapers printed new advertisements. Tailors offered to make clothes suitable for California. One man wanted to sell an omnibus to carry passengers from San Francisco to the diggings and then bring back the gold. He assured prospective purchasers that it would provide excellent sleeping quarters for six men. Joiners, following the example of those in Hobart, proposed to construct portable houses. Mrs. M. Brignell offered to sell her home to be taken to California. Another householder offered two two-room cottages and one with two stories and six rooms suitable for a lodging house, pub, or store in San Francisco. William Beaumont, on Castlereagh Street, advertised a new design for portable houses that would pack well and thus cut shipping costs in half. Towns wrote in his journal: "The whole affair (to use a hackneyed phrase), beggars description—a perfect phenomenon . . . *wonderful* and at the same time *true*."[13]

The *Despatch* and the *William Hill* had both been in Sydney a fortnight before any vessel could be made ready to put off for the "promised land," but the owners of four, in addition to Towns's three, were pushing shipwrights and stevedores in order to be first away. The extra amenities which her agents offered on the convict ship *Randolph* forced the owners of other vessels to improve their accommodations. MacNamara began overhauling the big, 460-ton ship *Maria*, knocking out bulkheads and extending storage space. He renewed his campaign, deprecating Towns's vessels and praising his own. He told prospective passengers that the *Maria* had lofty 'tween decks and Gilbert's patent ventilators equal to any on the *Randolph*; no expense was being spared. *"The whole of the berths"* he promised, *"will be enclosed* and erected on the same plan as emigrant ships from England, thereby affording passengers the comfort and privacy, the absence of which has been so justly complained of in other vessels, especially when there are females. The system of *packing* human beings *six in a berth like a slave ship,* will be avoided in this vessel and sufficient space will be given for passengers' luggage."[14]

Towns replied to tirades of this kind by saying that his vessels were all fitted according to the rules passed in London for the *Randolph*.[15] MacNamara changed the subject, said his *Maria* would supply more bounteous food than any vessel leaving Sydney. To this Towns replied that he would give his passengers a written list of provisions to be issued them. MacNamara beat this concession by promising to furnish intermediate and steerage passengers with plates, spoons, and tin pots—articles that travelers in these classes usually brought on board themselves.[16] This was a step further than Towns seemed willing to go, but in spite of MacNamara's largess the berths on his *Maria* remained unfilled while Towns booked all available space on his *Inchinnan* and advertised that his *Duke of Roxburgh* would follow her in fourteen days.

While the two big shippers quarreled, the 186-ton *Margaret* sailed with eighty-seven passengers on August 27. The little brigantine *Chearful* prepared to clear; her holds were full and her deck was piled high with cargo to sell in California. However, the port authorities refused to let her go, maintaining that the little overloaded vessel was sure to encounter tragedy in rough water. Cranes began to swing cargo back onto the wharf. A check of the passenger list showed more people on board than allowed by the law providing that only three could be carried for every five tons of capacity. Eighteen ticket holders were ordered ashore, but the troubles of the *Chearful*'s owners were not yet ended. A mortgage holder wanted his money before letting the vessel clear for so unpredictable a destination as San

Francisco. With this debt paid, the *Chearful* finally slipped away on September 25 carrying eighty-six passengers, still eight more than permitted by law. She was required to take food for sixty days—a ridiculously small amount for so long a voyage. Her galley was empty before she reached Tahiti, so the hard-pressed owner-captain remortgaged his brigantine there to purchase provisions. (She arrived in San Francisco on February 20, 1850, after 148 days. Of all other vessels leaving Sydney in 1849, only the *Lindsays* took so long.) [17]

Eager emigrants who had paid for passage on the *Inchinnan* complained about Towns's slowness in getting them to sea. A new worry now perplexed that cautious man. Suppose the market in California was glutted—especially with English goods! Already in the first nine months of 1849, a total of 509 vessels had anchored at San Francisco. During the two weeks from August 30 to September 13, forty-one had arrived. Many more would come before year's end. Such a surplus of goods might ruin Towns's speculations. On the other hand, he might profit greatly by it. He decided to send J. H. Catton, accompanied this time by his wife, with written authority to sign drafts on him for the purchase, at half price, of any goods that might be salable in Sydney or in the South Seas. Catton was also to serve as San Francisco agent for all of Towns's shipments and to investigate the demand for portable houses which was prompting so many people in Sydney and also in Hobart to ship sheds, shacks, and shanties. If the market really seemed permanent, Towns could build portable houses on his dock and hoist them aboard ship, thus producing them more cheaply than others could—or so he thought.

Finally, the *Inchinnan* stood ready to cast off ahead of Mac-Namara's big *Maria*. God be praised! But at the last moment an unexpected event stopped the *Inchinnan*. The sheriff served Captain Pearce with a writ for payment of a personal debt. The suit automatically detained the vessel and might permit rivals to beat her to San Francisco. "A shabby trick," Towns wrote in his diary, especially since he, Towns, had lent money to the party who brought the suit.

Towns was not a man to assume other people's—even his captain's—obligations, but the ship must sail. Just what was done to have the suit dropped is uncertain, but on September 12, 1849, Towns wrote his correspondent in Calcutta with apparent relief that, after much worry, "the thing is over"[18] and the *Inchinnan* was gone. The big bark carried 219 emigrants and left many who would have to follow on his *Duke of Roxburgh*.

Towns now began booking gold seekers not only on the *Duke* but even on the *Chasley*, a vessel designed primarily for transporting horses, but he made room on her for twenty-five passengers. MacNamara continued to publicize the advantages of his *Maria*, which was still being fitted. Then that man Palmer who was to supply Towns with horses failed to deliver, said all the beasts had died. Towns investigated, and learned that the scamp never owned a hoof. In this predicament Towns sought genuine horse owners and tried desperately to interest them in shipping. When they complained about being asked to pay £30 to transport a £20 horse, he admitted that the stallage seemed high but assured them that, if landed safely, the animal would fetch five times the investment.[19]

These negotiations postponed Towns's sailing date. The *People's Advocate* and the *Herald* took advantage of the delay and did everything possible to discourage his passengers. The former cried out for more social legislation, denounced emigrants for deserting their families, and called them cowards for lacking the courage to remain and fight for their civil rights at home.

John Fairfax admitted that a "perfect mania" had developed, that well-to-do people were joining laborers in the exodus, and he complained that the sale of residences, especially in the suburbs, had dragged down house values at least 30 percent in the past two months. He pointed out that America's high protective tariff would usurp any shipping profits, and that by leaving now—in September—emigrants would arrive in the middle of California's worst winter weather.[20] Better wait a few months!

In spite of these warnings, many letters from friends in the goldfields, written at the height of last summer's boom, continued to fire the imagination of Australians. The lack of passage money did more than all the newspapers could do to hold back the population. Neither emigrants nor shippers were perturbed by the unfortunate experiences of others. Newspapers printed accounts of cargoes that failed to pay their freight, of shipmasters who were fined for providing passengers with insufficient food.[21] Nobody seemed much concerned, unless it was Robert Towns. Not only were his booked passengers threatening to go on other vessels, but the *Chasley's* charter called for a demurrage of £8 per day if still at dock after October 1.[22]

Towns was pondering this business predicament when the whole town of Sydney was aroused at dawn on September 26 by newsboys shouting excitedly. During the night the American *Sabine*, which had left Sydney on April 4, slipped into port— another vessel that had made the round trip to California. In San Francisco her crew had deserted. The captain and mate purchased the brig for a song and, leaving on August 23, navigated the 175-ton craft to Honolulu. Here they engaged a crew of Sandwich Islanders and proceeded to Sydney in ballast, but loaded to the gunwales with fabulous tales equaling those brought by the *Despatch* and the *William Hill*. To prove their yarns they displayed £10,000 worth of gold dust straight from the diggings.

Newspapers hoping to hold back emigration realized now that they were playing a losing game. The seamen assured Australians that the rush had in no way abated. There was no glut in the labor market. Why should there be? Every man at the diggings averaged an ounce a day. True, such foreigners as the Latin Americans had been driven out, but they went quietly because they had already made all they wanted. It was said they took $15,000,000 with them. The people of Sydney also learned that some Australians were making a bad name for all colonials. This annoyed the editor of the *People's Advocate*. Too many of his subscribers' relatives had been steerage passengers to California. He admitted that some of them were crooks but "most of the migrants are honest people"—quite a change from his earlier statement that all who went were cowards afraid to fight for their rights at home.[23]

The *Sabine* brought reports from many Australian vessels whose fate was unknown since they sailed away. She saw both the *Spencer* and the *Lady Leigh* in San Francisco, in Honolulu the *Joseph Albino* from Adelaide and the *Bandicoot* from Hobart Town.[24] No report had been received of the *Sophia Margaret* since she left Adelaide in March, nor of the *Mazeppa* which followed her in June with those sixteen steerage passengers packed 'tween decks in a space sixteen feet square.

The *Sabine* delivered a letter from a passenger on the *Joseph Albino* which was widely published. It gave the following account of the sea voyage. The brigantine had left Adelaide on July 14, reaching New Zealand on the 28th. For a week the vessel refitted in the dreary, rockbound Bay of Islands, then sailed to Pitcairn ten days behind the *Elizabeth Archer*; but instead of landing, the brigantine turned north. On the equator she was delayed by calms. The moon was full, and passengers lay for hours on the idly rocking deck. At night "many gentlemen and some ladies" slept there, being careful to cover their faces lest lunar rays make them lunatics![25] Occasional showers relieved the daytime heat. Sailors stretched canvas to catch the precious rain and refill the water casks which had been under guard as the supply diminished. Passengers set out tubs and basins, filled canteens, and washed clothes in the soft, frothy rainwater. Drying lines on deck fluttered with laundry. Between washdays, passengers growled—as always—until the trade winds gave them something to talk about. In the days that followed, their water supply became low again and the captain steered west to the Sandwich Islands which they found full of vessels en route both to and from California. Here the much-published letter was mailed.

The *Sabine* also brought copies of the Honolulu *Polynesian*, which printed a letter dated June, 1849. Signed "Panama," it was reprinted in the colonies. The writer described California as follows:

Here's San Francisco—the oddest little square mile of sand hills and scrub oaks, tent houses and tabernacle stores, Yankees, Chinese, Dutch, Africans, French, and Kanakas the sun ever strove to look upon through the flying banks of Nova Zembla fog, driven by polar hurricanes—in fact, a meteorological paradox—soft and summer-like in winter, raw and winter-like in summer. . . . Walk around the public square, Portsmouth-square they call it; see those cloth houses, half timber, half canvass [*sic*]; those mushroom tenements of wood, shut up at night, while billiard and card tables and all the appliances of gambling [are] in full blast, and with a group motley as mosaic— of all colours, coats, and classes—gloating over piles of silver and gold, like crows over carrion.[26]

Such letters at the height of the rush tantalized, without discouraging, the eager passengers who had paid for transportation on the *Chasley* and were now being held at dock, while Towns tried to decide between waiting for more horses or paying demurrage. As the exasperated Argonauts fretted, the brig *Deborah* skimmed into port on October 2. She had left San Francisco on July 20, more than a month earlier than the *Sabine*. Unlike the American brig, she brought passengers who could tell about their experiences in California, instead of ship's officers seeking business for a return trip. Her crew, like the *Sabine's*, had deserted in San Francisco, except for one seaman with a bad foot who was now first mate. The captain fortunately enlisted a few Kanakas at $100 each for the trip to Honolulu, and there he employed a regular crew for Sydney. Like earlier captains, he brought a hundredweight of precious gold dust for all to see.

The passengers who climbed down the side told conflicting stories. Disappointed gold seekers repeated the accounts of California lawlessness, of murders and robberies. Others told of marvelous opportunities. Israel Solomon said he had come back to get his family and any friends who wanted to become rich. What was more, he intended to charter the brand-new *William and Mary* for them and any other passengers who cared to go along. He even offered to accept fares in four installments.

The glowing accounts from the *Deborah* coming so close after those from the *Sabine* increased the excitement. A dog-eat-dog competition soon developed. On October 3, one day after the *Deborah* docked, MacNamara turned away applicants for passage on his *Maria*, promising that he would fit out another vessel "in the same manner." C. S. Deacon, a businessman with no shipping experience except one round-trip excursion to California, chartered the big, 586-ton British ship *Victoria* and began booking gold seekers by the hundred. Agents for the small *Lady Howden* cut rates to £25, £15, and £10 according to the class of accommodation selected.[27] Towns complained that too many people were going into the transportation business. There would be no profit for any of them. He believed in competition, but not when everybody competed!

With these and other vessels equipping to take passengers at cut rates, Towns could hold his *Chasley* no longer. He purchased some heavy harness and carts, which he unwheeled and stowed aboard. Next he waived his required advance payment for shipping horses, accepted some COD, and finally decided to send his pet dock horse, Duke. The big animal was quiet, would carry a lady, hoops and all, without fright. An unusually powerful beast, Duke had once moved a ton-and-a-half load alone on the wharf. Towns loved the animal, but always business was business, and he told the head groom to sell Duke into good hands. Towns also sent "a very fine pointer dog." Whether or not he thought the bird dog would be helpful for hunting gold or chasing the rats that had swum ashore from the hundreds of deserted vessels and were swarming in San Francisco storehouses, Towns did not say. Finally, he added some cases of bottled beer in the last available space. "These things cost little and sell well," he wrote in his journal.[28]

On October 7, the *Chasley* cast off with twenty-four passengers, forty-two horses, and her bricks, as well as lime, coal, and beer. In the vessel's mail pouch Towns sent a letter that would have displeased her captain, Charles P. Aldrich, had he known its contents. Addressed to supercargo Catton, who had gone on the *Inchinnan*, and to Stanley, Jenner & Company, should anything happen to Catton, the recipient was warned to beware of Captain Aldrich, to advance him no money for unloading without ample security. Towns had spied on Aldrich while preparing for the voyage and found the fellow was "not frugal."[29] Towns also told Catton again to watch for surplus British goods which might be bought for the value of the packing cases "or thereabouts." Towns said he wanted canvas, rope, blue dungaree, calico, blankets, and a few gaudy prints for the sandalwood trade.

With the *Inchinnan* and the *Chasley* on their way to California, Robert Towns had only one ship left for the gold rush. The *Duke of Roxburgh*'s charter had cost him £1,500, half to be paid before sailing, the other half on arrival in San Francisco. As usual, Towns operated on shares, promising Captain George P. Collard half the profits. Steerage passengers alone would more than pay for the charter. Freight and cabin fares would be clear gain.

Carpenters were still busy reconverting the *Duke*, and dozens of would-be emigrants came to Towns seeking jobs. Even more annoying were scores of letters from friends of friends back in England who had placed ne'er-do-well sons on outback stations —"jackeroos," such tenderfeet were called. Now these frustrated young fellows appealed to relatives to better their "situations." Towns, never more busy in his life, chartering ship after ship, loading cargoes, booking passengers, replied to all requests that he had no jobs because business was so bad that he had been forced to curtail operations.

Of all the applicants, Towns seemed most suspicious of seamen who wanted to sign for the cruise, promising to come back with the vessel. He warned his first mate to watch out for such fellows. "Like all others," he said, "the moment the anchor is gone so are *they*." The only compensation for the rush, he confided in his diary, was ridding the country of "a multitude of idle people." Certainly California was "a good outlet for expirees."[30]

Towns understated the facts. Many of his so-called expirees were really escapees, like Sam Whittaker on MacNamara's *Louisa* who was destined to be one of the worst gold coast criminals. At least two women, Mary Ann Hogan and Harriet Langmeade, were neither expirees nor escapees from any "past" of record, but both would be notorious molls in San Francisco's gold rush. Two genuine escapees failed to escape. Private Peacock, deserting from the 99th Regiment in Hobart, and a female "pass holder" were arrested after they boarded a California-bound bark in Launceston. Harriet Langmeade was on that vessel, but whether she participated in the couple's conspiracy cannot be determined. The guilty pair had traveled together 120 miles across Tasmania along the partly finished Royal Mail coach road. Among laborers and camp followers they were not recognized or overtaken, but police intercepted letters they wrote to conniving passengers on the *David Malcolm*; thus California was spared two potential troublemakers.[31]

Robert Towns vowed constantly that he would not cut passenger fares, but, with others doing so, he made some exceptions on the *Duke* as he had for horses on the *Chasley*. To sail with a cubic foot of vacant space seemed heresy. He agreed therefore to give Mr. and Mrs. Newton passage to San Francisco for £20 in hand paid, and a pledge for the balance in the form of a gold lever watch to be held by the captain until redeemed in California.

These negotiations and the *Duke*'s repairs seemed to take an unusually long time, and MacNamara's *Maria*, equipped with Gilbert's patent ventilators, sailed ahead of the *Duke*. Although smaller than the *Duke*, the *Maria* carried twenty-eight more passengers than Towns had booked.[32]

Three days later, on October 15, the *Duke of Roxburgh* set sail. Her master, George P. Collard, carried a long list of instructions from Towns in addition to Mr. Newton's gold lever watch. Like Towns's earlier captains, Collard was to keep his eyes open for bargains and buy surplus British goods in California if available at one-tenth their worth, but he must guard against accepting gold dust unless sure of its genuineness.

In all, twelve ships carrying at least 471 persons on board left Sydney during October for California, 363 of these passengers leaving within four days. Only twenty-four vessels had gone since January 8, and the passenger lists totaled 1,448. Thus more than 32 percent of the emigrants recorded thus far left in October, 1849—as soon as they could get away after the *Sabine* and the *Deborah* had confirmed the reports of the *Despatch* and the *William Hill* concerning the true richness of the California discoveries.

Among this multitude of gold seekers, one of Australia's brilliant financial geniuses sailed on his own yacht. Benjamin Boyd had begun blowing an Australian bubble before he left Scotland in 1842. The British Isles were booming, and investors seemed eager to support his plan to develop the colonies, to establish the Royal Bank of Australia, and to purchase ships, sheep, and sureties. By 1844 he was reckoned to be one of the largest squatters down under with more than 2,000,000 acres of land, three steamers, three sailing ships, and nine whalers— all owned by the slimmest margins. Finally a lawsuit over a ship- wreck bankrupted him, and the bubble burst. Benjamin Boyd saved his 84-ton yacht *Wanderer*, and in her set off on October 26, 1849, to make another fortune in California.

Although the crescendo of Sydney's gold rush reached its 1849 peak in October, more than 750 emigrants embarked in Novem- ber and December. The demand for berths was so insistent that Captain George Barmore, whose *Sabine* was booked full, char- tered another vessel, the 134-ton *Bee*, which, like the *Chearful*, was small enough to pass San Francisco and anchor on the Sacra- mento River near the diggings. He offered a special freight rate and promised passengers that they might have "a comfortable home on board as long as they like."[33] Hustling off the *Bee* on December 5, Barmore followed her next day on the *Sabine*. The *Bee* reached San Francisco on April 10, 1850, with twenty-six of the twenty-nine passengers she had booked, but the *Sabine* wrecked off Upolu, the future home of Robert Louis Stevenson. Although a total loss, all passengers on board were saved.[34]

In addition to the 1,840 emigrants who had left New South Wales for the goldfields by the end of 1849, at least another thousand were reported to be waiting for transportation. News- paper editors admitted now that California could not be so bad as they had represented. Too many people were coming back for their families. If the rush continued, however, the colony would be ruined. The Sydney Council was urged to do some- thing about that.[35]

8

Keep Women Out
of California!

*Then pause, ye heedless voyagers, and shun
the golden snare;
Oh, listen to the warning voice that cries
beware! beware!*[1]

The last two months of 1849 showed a slight decrease in the number of emigrants to California from Australia—probably owing to the increasing difficulty in obtaining passage money—but no noticeable slackening of the rush. Shipowners continued their blandishments and also their cutthroat competition, while the press did everything it could to discourage emigration. Then an entirely new element complicated the problem—women. As Australia already had two men for every woman, it was doubly important to keep them at home, but the Argonauts' letters hinted that any girl who was white would find little competition in California. "There are but few females in San Francisco," one gold seeker wrote, "but the number of Indian squaws at the mines, who appear to be most filthy and disgusting beings, [are] as bad if not worse than the black gins in this country."[2]

Another writer described the scarcity of women in more jocose terms: "Dancing is the principal amusement here; but it is pretty much on the stag order, as we are short of pettycoats—except the squaws, which indeed wear no pettycoats, but only a light wrapper. They are of an affeckshynut disposition, but all-fired yaller."[3]

To counteract the possible effect of such accounts on some unmarried women in Australia, the newspapers kept harping on the danger to health in California. A letter from a man who had gone to San Francisco on the *Eleanor Lancaster* was widely published. This unhappy fellow wrote:

"From the number of people that arrive here from the Australian colonies an indifferent person might suppose that you are all a nation of madmen. Surely, the good people of Sydney must know before this that gold is not picked up in the streets, or do they rush down here without making inquiry as to what becomes of those who have preceded them? After a residence here of seven months I am led, from my observation, to believe, that if any 100 Australians who may leave the colonies in health were correctly accounted for at the end of the year, it would be found that about twenty have died, thirty have been so injured in their constitutions that their recovery is hopeless, twenty will have disappeared altogether and cannot be accounted for, ten will be about as well off as when they left Sydney, and ten may have made money—and if anything, I think this rather too favorable a view of the case. [What about the 10 percent not mentioned by this statistician?]

"Now, the much-vaunted climate of California I fancy is nearly all humbug; and now that winter is set in, I find it more changeable than the worst part of England in the worst season of the year—add to this the fact, that the people are badly clad, badly fed, and badly housed, and you need not wonder at the mortality."

Certainly, these tidings should have made all but the hardiest females pause and consider.

Another letter stated that "enormities of every imaginable kind are committed, and in all probability will increase as the season advances." Large numbers of people were reported to be leaving California, some with money but most of them as poor as when they came. "Upon the whole," this writer concluded, "I am of opinion, that California will be a curse to the whole world for some time to come; for of the vast numbers that come here from all parts, but few that return will leave without being more or less brutalized by their sojourn."[4]

Let thoughtful women ponder this!

None seemed perturbed, however. The rush in Sydney continued unabated. Vessels lined Circular Wharf, bow to stern. In the bay, others waited for places. Robert Towns, with no more ships available, towed in an old discarded wreck of a bark, the *Avon*, which he had saved for spare parts. He put carpenters to work making her seaworthy, or at least floatable—if not suitable for ladies. To his dismay prospective gold seekers failed to apply for passage on her, while at least two vessels, advertised by his rivals and still anchored out in the bay, were booked to capacity. Towns complained that one of them, the *Seringapatam*, was an old craft built in Bombay fifty years earlier and as leaky as his *Avon*. He told his journal that he knew who was prejudicing passengers against his boat but, a cautious man always, he omitted writing any names.

Never one to be stopped, however, Towns's next move typified the indomitable versatility that made him rich. He ballasted the old hulk with coal, brick, and lime. Commissioning Captain Alfred Silver to take command, he supplied him with kegs of nails, also empty packing cases for potatoes, and ordered him to sail to New Zealand, where both lumber and labor were less dear and cheap potatoes might be purchased for California. If no passengers were available over there, the captain was to take the *Avon* "sandalwooding" and recoup expenses thereby. If, however, gold seekers in New Zealand sought passage, Silver was to remodel the old hull into a transport. The sail room, Towns said, might be filled with extra berths. Moreover, the lumber used in refitting could be torn out in San Francisco and sold there to advantage. After that was done the bark, herself, should be offered separately. He estimated that she must fetch £2,000 if he was to break even. "I expect more," he said, "but she looks old, although good for another twenty years."

Towns also told Captain Silver to enlist a crew of Maoris in Auckland. They would be less apt to desert in California, but he must keep faith with them and be sure they got home if the bark sold.

With these instructions Captain Silver sailed away on the *Avon*, while Towns noted in his journal that he hoped she would make the voyage without leaking too much. Having fixed the *Avon*'s value at £2,000, Towns thought better of it and wrote Catton in San Francisco to cut the price to £1,500. Later, when he learned that the *Avon* got a bumper cargo out of Auckland, he wrote Catton again to cut the price still further, but instead of being elated by the continued good news, cautious Towns appeared disturbed. The "rush" which he had considered a good outlet for "expirees" worried him now. He feared that the excitement "will unhinge the minds of our Labouring Classes much to the prejudice of the Colony. A great deal of our useful labour is leaving us, much better people & more than we are receiving in exchange."[5]

Towns's own mind became a bit unhinged as he watched 353 men and women stream up the side of the docked *Victoria*, and recalled that his Avon had departed empty. He also knew that 200 passengers* were waiting to board the *Seringapatam* as soon as there was loading space along the dock. His own *Duke of Roxburgh* had carried only 165. Moreover, Deacon, that inexperienced charterer of the *Victoria*, set aside freight he had agreed to take at a cheap figure and began loading goods for shippers who paid him a premium. Towns did not intend to stand for much of that kind of competition and predicted in his diary: "Deacon will find himself in a fix."[6]

On November 1, 1849, a wharf steamboat nosed the *Victoria* away from the dock. Passengers had been tucked in her every nook and cranny. Cargo stood in perilous piles on deck. The big bark hoped to clear customs the next day, and her dockside berth was filled immediately by the waiting *Seringapatam*, commanded by Captain F. Lovett. Port authorities refused to let the *Victoria* depart, however, until she unloaded the cargo on her decks.

Towns was right—Deacon was "in a fix." The *Victoria* had lost her place at the wharf, and lowering cargo into lighters while she lay at anchor out in the bay consumed valuable time. To make matters worse, dissatisfied passengers on board sent letters ashore complaining that the food was terrible, that they were packed like Negroes in a slave ship on the Guinea coast, and that the terms of the Passenger Act should be enforced to

---

* These numbers are from the *Sydney Morning Herald*, April 2, 1850. Charles Bateson, who bases his figures on port records, says (*Gold Fleet for California: Forty-Niners from Australia and New Zealand* [Sydney, 1963], p. 157) that the *Victoria* carried 272 passengers and that 158 embarked on the *Seringapatam*. The *Alta California* (Feb. 19, 1850) states that 231 landed from the *Victoria*, and (March 19, 1850) that 160 landed from the *Seringapatam*.

assure adequate hospital facilities on board. Even more deplorable was the discovery that an unqualified man had been installed as "ship's doctor," an appointment evading the intent of the law which required vessels with more than fifty passengers to carry a licensed physician.[7]

These complaints may have pleased Robert Towns, but whether or not they helped the emigrants on board is uncertain. For almost two weeks their ship floated under the scorching sun while they remained virtual prisoners in sight of their old homes. At last, on November 14, they sailed. Eleven of the passengers would receive considerable notoriety in the Vigilance Committee disturbances a year after their arrival in California, some as criminals, some not. It should be noted, however, that all cannot be identified except by the similarity of names, but of one there is no question. Thomas Berdue, who was leaving his wife in Sydney, would be a principal in one of the most famous of the vigilance trials.

The *Victoria*'s supplies began to run low by Christmastime, while the ship's passengers sweltered on the equator. They were put on half rations until they reached Honolulu a month later. When they arrived in San Francisco, the captain turned a mutinous crew over to the American frigate stationed there.[8] But more shocking news was yet to come. The passengers filed down the gangplank, trudged into town, and read in the *Pacific Daily News* that their vessel had brought 200 abandoned women. Of course, that many women did not arrive on board the *Victoria*, and those who did happened to be married. Although the *News* contradicted its story next day, the damage had been done. Australians realized more than ever that their fellow countrymen—good or evil—were acquiring a bad reputation in California.

The quarrels between passengers and captain on the *Victoria* were duplicated on the *Seringapatam*. Arriving in San Francisco, these unhappy travelers sued Captain Lovett and obtained a judgment against him. When he proved to be insolvent, his ship and papers were confiscated.

Both incidents pleased the Sydney editors. They publicized these events as examples of the disagreeable uncertainties that emigrants must expect. Furthermore, John Fairfax warned his readers, the day for profitable shipping had passed. He said that an average of four vessels were entering San Francisco Harbor every twenty-four hours, more than half of them from the eastern United States. Australians could, therefore, no longer be first at this market.[9]

No one in Sydney understood this better than Robert Towns, but he could not resist the California gamble. Thus, when the bankruptcy of Benjamin Boyd put the steam-propelled *Seahorse* on the bargain counter, Towns bought the battered old cattle boat, ripped out her boiler and engine, shipped them to England, and remade the hull into a sailing craft for California.[10]

Every spare stick that would float was now on the way to the gold coast, and Sydney businessmen advertised a bimonthly sailing of packets to San Francisco as well as a regular steamer to Hawaii.[11] Neither materialized, but it was probably no coincidence that a third report of two gold discoveries at home appeared at this time in the Australian papers. One of these alleged strikes was in the Torrens range of South Australia and the other near Bathurst, in New South Wales, a town west of the Blue Mountains 132 miles by road from Sydney. The latter discovery was on the estate of W. H. Suttor of Brucedale, Bathurst, who did not want his sheep run ruined by prospectors' holes. A convict bullock driver had made this strike but refused to tell its location, saying that he had "already served one lagging, and felt no inclination to run the risk of a second." Editor Fairfax doubted that the precious metal had really been found. He had heard too many similar stories for too long, but down in Hobart the *Town Guardian* reported that a gold rush had started from California to Australia, that the first gold seekers had already arrived, and that large numbers might be expected in Sydney by the end of the year.[12]

People in Sydney, especially the women, knew better. The only gold seekers "rushing" to New South Wales were men coming for their wives, and insufficient vessels had been equipped to take them all back. To meet the demand, owners of small craft schemed constantly to raise sufficient money to outfit their vessels for the trade. Captain Sullivan offered to sell a half interest in his schooner *Vixen*, equip her as a transport, and sail to the gold coast. The little Sydney-built *Phantom*, only 34 feet 6 inches long and 11 feet 6 inches wide with a single mast, set sail on November 10 and arrived in San Francisco 100 days later—the smallest vessel to make the trip.[13] C. S. Deacon, regardless of the adverse reports from his *Victoria*, laid on another ship, advertised first-class accommodations on her, and accused his competitors of all the transgressions his faultfinding customers had heaped on him. "Passengers," he said in a printed announcement, "will not be *stowed away in bulk*, nor will they be *half starved* on the voyage, as has been the case with *some* vessels which have left Sydney (more like slave ships than otherwise). Passengers are, therefore, cautioned not to be gammoned by the *blarney* of a certain advertiser. The conditions of the above will be *guaranteed* to every person engaged and also a *certain space* allotted to each passenger for sleeping, in addition to their space for luggage."[14]

The excitement over opportunities in California received a boost in December when letters arrived from travelers on the *Sophia Margaret*, which had not been sighted since she left Adelaide in March. She arrived in California after a tempestuous voyage of 107 days. Her cook was now employed in a restaurant in Sacramento at the princely salary of $200 a month, and a young man passenger named Byron now earned $150 as a hotel dining-room waiter in San Francisco. Obviously, fortunes in California were not made exclusively with pick and pan.

An even bigger boost for California came from an Adelaide plasterer named King, who came back on the *Sabine* as far as Sydney, where he got passage on a small coaster for home. His stories of the gold coast set Adelaide on fire. Many citizens knew King, or knew of him; he was one of their own kind. His reports seemed more genuine than newspaper stories. King said that when he first landed in San Francisco he worked as a lumper unloading cargo and earned £19 in one week, paid him in hard cash. After he hurt one of his hands at this job, he went to work as a plasterer, earning only £12 a week but getting board and lodging. Having saved £80 in six weeks, he decided to return to Adelaide for his wife. California was a great country for women!

If King could get rich, why not the next fellow!

King told strange tales of prices in California. He said a two-pound loaf of bread cost a shilling, while the flour in it was as cheap as in Adelaide. Cattle were brought in by the Spaniards, he said, a hundred at a time, and after being driven to a "krael" were slaughtered by the knife, the beef selling at sixpence per pound. The principal hotel in San Francisco, he reported, cost £100,000, though it was no larger than the Waterhouse Hotel in Adelaide, and not so tall. In houses of entertainment where spirits were sold, an interesting American custom prevailed. The customer put a shilling on the bar and poured his own drink. The Yankees, according to King, had brought with them their proverbial "go-ahead" activity and did not like to see an idle man. As for the security of life and property, women need have no fear; life was as safe in San Francisco as in Adelaide, and people were getting rich there. He saw merchants who had come with little money sporting around town in light two-wheeled carriages drawn by flashy teams driven by highly paid, liveried coachmen. Hundreds of people who had nothing, a year earlier, were now worth $10,000 to $275,000.[15]

Before the receipt of these fantastic stories, a scant hundred emigrants had left Adelaide on the *Sophia Margaret*, the *Mazeppa*, and the *Joseph Albino*. Now the newspapers announced that from 200 to 500 people wanted to sail as soon as possible. The Bunce brothers offered to take passengers steerage for £20 each. Another shipper, John Newman, immediately undercut them, offering to arrange such passage for £15 plus his commission. South Australians always prided themselves on their cultural superiority, and the editor of the Adelaide *Register* noted that the higher-priced accommodations were in greatest demand, an indication that the emigrants were neither destitute nor improvident.[16] Adelaide's renewed activity started too late in 1849 for the equipping of more vessels that year, but seven left for California during the early months of 1850, carrying more than six times as many gold seekers as had gone the preceding year.

Back in Sydney the December rush continued, with people hurrying off to the gold coast in anything floatable. On the 17th, the bark *Gloucester* left her wharf to make room for another vessel and dropped down the harbor, anchoring between Pinchgut Island and Bradley's Head. She planned to clear customs there the next day and sail on the 19th. Her passenger list contained 115 names, many of which would appear in the San Francisco Committee of Vigilance troubles.

One man on board, William M'Andrew, must have watched with relief as the distance increased between ship and shore. He was escaping woman trouble in Sydney, and the bay seemed comfortingly wide at the anchorage eight miles from the Heads, but not wide enough. The December weather, as usual, turned suffocatingly hot, especially on the tarred deck of a becalmed sailing vessel, and the temptation to swim in the cool water was great. However, a shark had bitten a bather at the beach below the nearby promontory known as Mrs. Macquarie's Chair. The fellow bled to death almost instantly. Passengers on the *Gloucester* could see the grinning V-shaped mouths and wicked dorsal fins of man-eaters cruising around the vessel. Garbage thrown overboard seemed to attract them.

William M'Andrew found to his dismay that not only sharks were watching for him. A small boat came out from shore with an officer and a warrant for William's arrest. The complaint was signed by Mrs. M'Andrew, who accused him of deserting her. Taken back to the Sydney jail, he was ordered to supply her with either a home or passage with him to California. Many other guilty persons were no doubt more successful in getting away.

A Sydney merchant complained that three-quarters of the passengers on all vessels leaving for California were swindlers with bad reputations, or men who ran up last-minute bills before leaving. Many, he was sure, sailed under assumed names. He suggested that every emigrant be compelled to have a certificate from a Sydney householder or a county minister, and that these certificates be approved by the police and posted three days before each vessel cleared.[17]

The *Gloucester's* troubles did not end with her final clearance. When only a hundred miles on her way she began to leak. Her pumps proved defective, so she sailed back to Sydney for re-calking. Just before New Year's Day she resumed her voyage.

While the *Gloucester* was at sea the schooner *Sea Gull* sailed with twenty-one passengers and arrived in San Francisco with nineteen. Curiously enough, the passenger list included "two aboriginals of New South Wales"[18]—a forgotten people in gold-rush annals. Perhaps these blackfellows' fate would be somewhat similar to that which lay in store for Jacky Small and Davy.

The *Gloucester* had hardly disappeared across the horizon on her second trial before a new ship was advertised for California. The *Johannes Sarkies*, built as a frigate, had been re-equipped to take women. Her owners promised good food and quarters, also "an ample supply of medical comforts for the voyage."[19] The rush was continuing, but she cleared port after year's end, so she cannot rightfully be considered a forty-niner. Another vessel that barely missed the distinction of going in 1849 was Solomon's *William and Mary*, which sailed with 263 passengers in February, 1850.[20] As she passed through the Heads she met the incoming brig *Spec* loaded with disappointed gold seekers, many of whom had gone on the *Inchinnan* and lost heart soon after landing. Some of them, having spent all their money, were working for their passage on the homeward voyage. These unhappy people crowded along the bulwarks and shouted to the outgoing emigrants: "Come back—you will repent it if you go on."[21]

In the United States the summer before, overland forty-niners who gave up as they crossed the high Rockies had said the same when they turned their covered wagons eastward. In Australia, however, the example might have more influence. Certainly both newspapers in Sydney hoped for discouraging reports, and these were numerous in the many letters the *Spec* brought straight from California. Among them was one from the *Herald's* special correspondent, Thomas Hinigan, who had gone on the *Maria*. Writing just after landing, he said that a fire had consumed the heart of San Francisco, that the cost of living was exorbitant, and work scarce, with unemployed diggers crowding in from the creeks. Gamblers, he reported, sat behind their tables with six-guns in their belts and piles of money in front of them.

This was the picture of conditions the editors wanted, but even as Hinigan maligned California, his enthusiasm for the new country's activity showed plainly enough. New buildings, he said, were going up everywhere. Men were busy, working furiously, carpenters shingling roofs while others nailed down the sides, hammers pounding, saws squealing.[22]

Hinigan's letter may have disappointed John Fairfax but, being a conscientious newsman, he printed it. His rival, the editor of the *People's Advocate*, supplied more adequately the horrendous conditions in California which both desired. In an editorial he stated:

By letters and passengers arrived here by the *Spec* from San Francisco, we learn that the setting in of the winter rains had, as anticipated, taken thousands of the new arrivals by surprise; and the consternation occasioned by finding themselves without a roof or shelter from the piercing cold are [*sic*] perfectly indescribable. Those who had been longer there had suffered equally, and the shattered constitutions, which their weakly and sickly forms presented, almost prevented recognition by old acquaintances. The fever and ague, diarrhoea and dysentery, had made dreadful havoc in the neighbourhood of the city; and the awful pictures of the tent-town or encamping ground at Happy Valley are horrifying in the extreme. To multitudes it had proven "the valley of the shadow of death"; and some of our informants, who went there by the *Inchinnan*, could with much difficulty find enough of unoccupied ground on which to pitch a tent, the cleared surface presenting the appearance of numerous graves, and forceably impressing on their downcast spirits that they had been thrown by their own voluntary exile into a Golgotha, instead of the fanciful Paradise which their imaginations had pictured to them on deserting their homes in New South Wales. Men with hearts full of sorrow and repentance, with tears in their eyes, implored some of the passengers by the *Spec* to warn their relatives of the fate that must await them if they ventured going to California; and requested that their distresses might be made as public as possible [which the *People's Advocate* was doing admirably] in order

to deter others from risking their lives in adventures to that part of
the world.

So much were the people who came from Sydney changed in their
appearance, scarcely one in twenty could be recognized. . . . Labourers were at the port offering their services at very reduced rates; and
one of our informants saw dozens of doctors, lawyers, and others of
learned professions, so miserable that they were glad to work as
carpenters' labourers, and were staggering under shoulder loads of
planking at the numerous erections in the city; while several of them,
the doctor of the *Star of China* among others, were employed as
watermen on the harbour, and thankful of that means of procuring
a living. Many hundred others, whose names cannot be remembered,
were walking about the streets and the dreadful "Happy Valley"
more like spectral skeletons than men of flesh and blood. When the
Inchinnan arrived, the first sight that met the passengers on landing
were [*sic*] the dead bodies of men lying at the water's edge in a
state of decomposition, unclaimed and unnoticed; and in the streets
of San Francisco a man was lying dead, exposed to the view of every
passerby. The tents presented fearful scenes. In corners, and boxed
up betwixt packages of luggage, which served to shield the emaci-
ated bodies of ague patients, were seen unfortunate victims of that
disease wrapt up in blankets, their teeth chattering, their limbs
shivering, and their countenances distorted by disease. Despair had
silenced their calls for assistance, which could not be rendered them,
and resignation to the approach of death only permitted them to
solicit as a dying favour that thoughtless emigration from New South
Wales should be discouraged by a detail of their individual mis-
fortunes. [And the editor of the *People's Advocate* was doing just
that, but let him continue.]

The lodging-houses were in a dreadful state, one hundred and fifty
sleepers were thronged into one apartment, and there lay mingled
the healthy and the diseased, men of all nations and tongues, the
once exalted among the most debased, the filthy and the clean in one
indiscriminate mass. Returned miners, enfeebled by fever, were seen,
careless of their dreadful fate, with not the slightest regard to personal cleanliness, and their inability to help themselves, and the
want of others to assist them; in many instances they were covered
by crawling lice, and shockingly disgusting. . . .

The editor concluded his leader by saying that many Australians, after being in port only thirty days, became so disgusted
they waited daily for a vessel to bring them home. They all expressed outraged fury at the Australian shipowners who had
duped them with false representations concerning California.[23]

This emotional tirade elicited immediate replies from travelers who had just returned. Editor Fairfax printed a letter denouncing his rival's report as being nothing but the notional outbursts of emigrants too shiftless to work. As for the dead bodies on San Francisco beaches, this writer said, the only dead things there were dead fish. To be sure, some people had died of exposure in California, but the exposure was usually a consequence of excessive drinking and all the victims had received a proper burial. The *Advocate*'s adverse propaganda, this writer said pointedly, was much too exaggerated to stop emigration.[24]

As the year 1849 closed, the most noteworthy items in the Australian papers continued to be those about the emigration of women. The *People's Advocate* unearthed the fact that a Mrs. Farnsworth in America was enlisting for California a cargo of poor and marriageable girls "who have no prospect but the needle at home."[25] Undoubtedly, the editor meant Mrs. Eliza W. Farnham, who was known for her social work among destitute women and her husband's books on California. Diggers were reported to be toasting "the lady who so warmly exerted herself to bring a few spare-ribs to this market."[26] Certainly, Australian lassies could hold their own with such competition, and a later Australian paper reported the *Daily Pacific News* as saying more women were coming from Australia than from Yankeeland.

A threat of more serious competition came from South America. A Hobart paper reported that a merchant in St. Jago (Santiago), Chile, was advertising for "200 young, white, poor and virtuous girls to be taken to California and there honorably married to the thousands of North Americans and other strangers who have made their fortunes at the mines."[27]

Ambitious women in Australia received encouragement in a letter from California which was published in Tasmania. The writer said that San Francisco contained barely 50 women. Among them was a Mrs. Ellis who formerly kept a public house in Hobart Town, and she was now worth £170,000. In Sydney, *Bell's Messenger* repeated this fiction of only 50 women in San Francisco and added that 20 of them were Americans. What an opportunity for Australian beauties! "The arrival of a ship load of female emigrants," the *Colonial Times* said, "would be a cause of public rejoicing, and all the single ones would receive offers before they landed."[28]

At best these figures must have related to immigrant women and not to Spanish and American Californians already in San Francisco. Even so, the numbers did not correspond to other statistics published in Australia which showed that 161 women arrived in San Francisco prior to April 11, and that all but 8 of them were Latin Americans. The 8 included 3 from Australia and 5 from New York. In the month of August, 86 women were reported to have arrived, only 6 of them married. Half of these were North Americans. Certainly, this indicated a very small female population in California, but the report noted that the overland emigration of forty-niners numbering 8,000 (an underestimate) had not yet arrived, and 17,000 to 20,000 were known to be coming by ship. The percentage of women in these contingents was unknown, but certainly plenty of sunbonnets accompanied the covered wagons.[29]

Other statistics released in Australia disclosed the presence in California of 1,421 women and 38,467 men[30]—figures that certainly should have been doubled for California by the end of 1849. Since this preponderance of men was bound to attract hardy women seeking mates, John Fairfax presented an argument that he hoped might hold the better ones in Australia. Such a discrepancy between the sexes, he said, would keep away virtuous females. Apparently backing his statement, a booklet appeared in Sydney which also discouraged female emigration. The author, Charles H. Chambers of Pyrmont, a suburb of Sydney, was a playwright and writer who had made a special tour of the gold coast. In *A General View of the State of California* he assured readers that the region was healthful and "neither licentious, drunken, dissolute nor disorderly," but few get-rich-quick fortunes would be made there. Then, to discourage the immigration of women, he said: "I have just heard that hosts of adventurous females were expected before winter, and that a project was entertained to send a cargo of Chilean ladies. The rape of the Sabines was never so wholesale"—a reference, no doubt, to the Santiagoans reported earlier in the newspapers. In spite of this, the prospects of finding a husband in California seemed rather good. According to San Francisco port records, 102 Australian women arrived between July 1 and December 31, 1849. In Sydney during January, 1850, the *John Munn*, one of the largest vessels to make the trip that year, advertised special accommodations "set aside for single females." By January 1, 1851, port authorities in San Francisco had checked in 869 more women from Australia.[31]

The total emigration of both men and women from Sydney in 1849 amounted to 1,840 passengers, carried in forty-four vessels. Seventeen ships left Hobart and Launceston with at least 500 travelers on board. The only vessels to leave Melbourne, the *William Watson* and the *Union*, carried some 200 emigrants. From Adelaide 105 were reported to have sailed in three vessels.* Thus Australia furnished only approximately 8.5 percent of the gold rushers who came to California by sea in 1849. Australian newspapers admitted that the percentage of former criminals among them was large, although statistics kept for the last three months of 1849 and the first three of 1850 show only 12.5 percent of the emigrants from Sydney to have been emancipists. One-third of the total were free emigrants, who had been brought to New South Wales at government expense. The records from Tasmania tell quite a different story. Apparently more than 21 percent of the gold rushers from Launceston and Hobart were ex-convicts.[32] Hence, although Sydneyites—called derisively Sydney Ducks—earned the bad name, the percentage of bad characters was much larger among the Derwent Ducks. But, as shall be told, two of the three Australians lynched by the Committee of Vigilance came from Sydney.

* L. G. Churchward, "Australia and America" (unpublished M.A. thesis, University of Melbourne, 1941), p. 67; Charles Bateson, *Gold Fleet for California: Forty-Niners from Australia and New Zealand* (Sydney, 1963), pp. 104, 160. Only three vessels with a total of ninety-two passengers left Adelaide for a direct passage to California in 1849. A fourth, carrying twenty-nine, stopped en route at Hobart hoping to pick up more gold seekers.

Three Musketeers in California's Outback, 1850

In the spring of 1850, Davison, Hargraves, and Archer, having failed to make a fortune panning gold in Wood's Creek, decided to separate and try other areas. During the winter Banker Davison had watched the Sonora merchants receive fabulous prices, and he determined to try his hand once more at trade. For some weeks rumors had come to the southern mines about new discoveries up north, discoveries much richer than anything yet unearthed in the Sonora area.

Local businessmen scoffed at such tales. They pointed to a fresh strike at Columbia, only ten miles from the Australians' camp, displayed a lump of gold weighing twenty-three pounds, and said all sensible people would remain. Davison did not listen. He had scratched the Sonora hills all winter, wanted to see the northern diggings and make money selling goods on the way. He packed his few belongings, walked to Stockton, and found the village very different from the one he had left last fall. A fire at Christmastime had wiped out the line of tents and shacks along the riverfront. A new theater, a bowling alley, and a billiard room now offered entertainment. A weekly paper printed the news. At the landing a ship and an oceangoing schooner were unloading all manner of goods—boots, clothing, wine, pickled oysters, hardware, carpenters' tools, blankbooks, gold scales, crockery, and cases of revolvers.[1] Certainly, goods were being landed here more cheaply than Davison could hope to do.

Davidson boarded the steamboat which now made regular

trips through more than a hundred miles of tule-lined open water to San Francisco Bay. The Golden Gate city had also changed mightily during the winter of 1849–50. Indeed, California had changed. The future state already possessed close to 100,000 inhabitants, and foreigners no longer predominated. One-half to two-thirds of the people were Americans now, and all but 20,000 of them had come within the past year. San Francisco alone boasted a population of 30,000. Last fall the shore had been lined with ships for a mile. Now vessels lay along it for more than twice that distance. At least thirty of these craft operated as storeships, among them the *Lindsays* and the *Eleanor Lancaster*, back from Benicia, both competing for trade here as they had for speed at sea. A hundred or so other vessels lay in the bay, and the thud of pile drivers told where new piers were creeping out toward them; one pier was already a third of a mile long. Some ships, clinging to old pier sides had already become stuck in the mud. There was talk of filling the shallow water between piers with dirt so stores could be built on the new land. Last winter's muddy streets, where a horse might drown, were now planked and dry.[2]

On December 24, 1849, the heart of San Francisco had been devastated by a fire which broke out in Dennison's Exchange. Flames licked up from the painted cotton ceiling to the tar-paper roof and crackled across one side of Portsmouth Square, consuming the big hotels and many business offices. Some Australians suffered, among them the Launceston firm of M'Kinzie, Thompson & Company.[3]

Fires caused confusion which robbers welcomed. A second blaze in January, although quickly extinguished, caused people to suspect that criminals from Sydney had set it. Moreover, that anti-English sentiment in the eastern United States was coming west with Irish immigrants, and Australians noticed that Democratic newspapers, seeking the Irish vote, blustered against John Bull.[4]

The fires had actually benefited San Francisco. New buildings rose almost before the ashes cooled. Old gambling tents and shanties were now replaced by brick houses and handsome shops. Davison read that a brick theater had just been completed, and that the Olympic Circus had engaged a company of comedians from the Victoria Theater in Sydney. Shipping agents, real estate brokers, dealers in gold dust, and law firms now occupied new and comfortable offices. The Montefiores of Sydney had established a permanent commercial business house.[5]

Indeed, San Francisco had changed so completely that Davison could recognize nothing except Telegraph Hill and Happy Valley with the sandy road leading up to the old mission. Sydney Valley was well established now, and already had a bad reputation. On the steep hillside shabby little dens, tents, and hovels, patched with canvas, carpet, boards, and linen, dispensed drinks behind the usual Old World ale-house names: the Magpie, the Bobby Burns, the Boar's Head, the Bird in Hand, the Jolly Waterman, and Tam O'Shanter. In the doorways villainous-looking vagabonds watched the street furtively. Their features were concealed by slouch felts or tattered cabbage-tree hats, and they had a way of sliding out of sight when looked at steadily. Australians like Davison, who were used to convicts, noticed that some of these hangdog fellows walked with the peculiar swinging gait a man learns during years in leg-irons.

Davison watched this scum from Australia with disinterested but understanding eyes. Poverty and crime had been at the tail end of all civilized societies he had ever known, whether in England or in the Orient. But here in California he saw something new. Many of the poorest Australians who had landed a few months earlier with insufficient money to go on to the diggings had worked honestly as carpenters, painters, or waiters. Some had saved their money, speculated, and already were rich men. An Australian cabdriver on the corner, where Kearny Street entered the plaza, was demonstrating a new way to acquire wealth. He wore the correct English coachman's uniform, tall black hat, with rosette on one side, and a coat of many capes. He held a whip in hand, correctly on his knee, and could be depended on to perform with the aristocratic training of a Royal Horse Guardsman. He charged $10.00 an hour if engaged for three hours, $15.00 if engaged for two, and $20.00 for one hour or less. The fellow was becoming wealthy; newly rich Americans liked to copy British ostentation, even as they scorned it.

Some poor but honest Australians had failed miserably. Broken and discouraged, they were going home. Others scoffed at the tales of woe, said thousands in the colonies would give their ears to come when they learned about the true state of affairs.[6] Davison, having money to invest, made careful purchases of goods he hoped to sell at the northern mines. He found shipping costs exorbitant and, rather than pay them, he purchased a small schooner. While loading her he met Hargraves, who had followed him to San Francisco. The poor fellow was as restless as Davison and he also wanted to try his luck in a new country. He had wagered the last of his few bullocks back in Australia for this trip to California, but so far his gamble had failed. Perhaps Fortune might smile on him in the northern diggings. Genial, clumsy Hargraves had been a sailor in his teens. Davison, who could use the big fellow's skill in navigating the schooner, offered him one-third of the profits if he joined the expedition.[7]

Before they cast off, Davison and Hargraves rested in the home of a colonial friend. Both wrote letters to Australia, stating that gold could be discovered in the colonies. The date, March 5, 1850, is important, because these letters were the next step in the controversy over who first noticed the resemblance of California's goldfields to Australia's outback. At the time, neither letter caused any commotion down under. Davison's, written to a sheep farmer, was shown to a few friends, then destroyed. Hargraves sent his letter to a Sydney businessman. It was filed and temporarily forgotten, but later published, to Hargraves' advantage. Read today, it truly reveals the writer's salesmanship, his expansive nature, his belief that he alone could find Australian gold. The letter said, in part: "I am very forceably impressed that I have been in a gold region in New South Wales, within 300 miles of Sydney; and unless you knew how to find it you might live a century in the region and know nothing of its existence."[8]

The letters from Davison and Hargraves, each of whom hoped to be first to lead a gold rush in Australia, were sent to New

South Wales on the same vessel. But it should be noted that Davison claimed later that he had written a duplicate letter to the same man "a few weeks" earlier and was therefore the first man to record the resemblance of the California goldfields to Australia's. If written, this letter must have been sent from Wood's Creek, which is improbable. Davison always procrastinated, and it seems much more likely that he waited until Hargraves came to San Francisco before writing any letter. Unquestionably, he was a more able man than Hargraves, more studious and careful, but he usually let details divert him from his main objective. Hargraves, on the other hand, was a born promoter, an expansive disseminator of ideas, always eager to talk big and use his head to save his hands.

A third man who would claim the distinction of recognizing the similarity between the California and Australian goldfields now appeared. E. W. Rudder had just arrived from Sydney with his two sons, Julius and Augustus. Rudder was an English-born man of substance, forty-nine years old—elderly for California. The son of a brass foundryman, he had been a partner of Harriet Martineau's brother and was active in the English reform movement of the early 1830's. Going to Australia in 1834, he selected a good piece of land, imported fine stock, and started a school. Rudder's purpose in coming to California was not to dig for gold but to sell gold-washing cradles. He had improvised a metal contrivance similar to those used at Freiberg in Saxony for amalgamation processes. Constructed in sections to be carried on the backs of mules, one of his cradles had been sent to mines in the Andes and another, properly crated, was following him to California. He expected it on the next vessel. To meet current expenses, he had brought a few bales of workingmen's moleskin breeches—salable surely![9]

Rudder had known Hargraves slightly in New South Wales.[10] He showed him and Davison the gold-washing machine's plan. The two studied it carefully and convinced Rudder that it was much too complicated for California mining. Other clumsy and unworkable washers had already been brought to the goldfields, at least one from Australia. Several came around the Horn, and one American hauled a 1,200-pound cradle overland from Missouri, but when he found how easily washers were made at the diggings, he kept his foolishness a secret.[11]

As for the workingmen's trousers, other shipments had sold poorly. Nobody seemed able to compete with a young Bavarian from New York named Levi Strauss, who was making pants out of canvas from the sails of deserted ships in the harbor—just the thing for rough work at the diggings. Rudder, deciding to forget his washing machine as well as his bales of breeches, asked Davison and Hargraves if he might accompany them on the schooner up the Sacramento River.[12] They welcomed him and enlisted a few extra hands to man the sweeps for the 180 tortuous miles of waterways to Sacramento. For this ten-day trip, men were often willing to work for nothing in return for free transportation toward the mines. The schooner's sails and Hargraves' skill put the cargo across San Francisco Bay and through the strait past Benicia. At the upper end of Suisun Bay, where mosquitoes were almost unbearable, a warship stopped the Australians and examined their cargo. Already many smugglers in small boats had learned how to take goods from vessels in San Francisco, slip through the tules, and thus deliver imports, duty free, at the outfitting towns.

Cleared by the man-of-war, the Australians' schooner proceeded up the Sacramento River. The stream was two or three hundred yards wide, and in places where the water seeped around marshy islands it was difficult to recognize the main channel. However, many boatmen waited for the flood tide to help them upstream, and Hargraves was able to follow them along the course. Also, there were several woodyards on the banks where inquiries could be made. At one point the travelers spied an Indian village of tule huts.[13] Hargraves, Davison, and Rudder noticed, as Archer had, that these California Red Men seemed degraded, confused, and inferior to the proud, naked blackfellows down under.

Sacramento stood at the junction of the Sacramento and American rivers. As the Australians approached the town, they noticed a long line of ships cabled to tree trunks and exposed roots along the bank. On the riverbank above they could see big signboards advertising goods for sale. A man in brilliant and grotesque costume—evidently employed by some company —greeted strangers before they landed. He extolled the wonders of the town, named the best shops to visit for bargains, and told them the date of the next auction sale. Evidently there was a surplus of goods in Sacramento, and Davison would have to investigate the market before unloading his goods.

The Australians jumped ashore and strolled into the city. A little over a year ago there had been only four houses here. Now the tents and houses of 10,000 inhabitants sprawled under the shade of a square mile of great, gnarled oaks and sycamores. Along the main street parallel to the river, ships' galleys and deck cabins, evidently lifted from river craft, served as places of business. At one end of the red dirt thoroughfare a gigantic, umbrella-shaped live oak shaded a horse market. The venerable tree's branches had an odd way of bending to the ground and growing prostrate on it, thus furnishing long log seats in the shade. Farther up the street, behind grandiose false fronts, stood shops, restaurants, a newspaper office, and a daguerreotype gallery. Signs printed in large letters on flimsy facades and swinging shingles announced business locations of lawyers, exchange brokers, overland stage agents, contractors, and realtors.

In January a flood had covered this entire area. Only Sutter's old fort, with its twelve mounted cannon a mile and a half back from the rivers, had remained above water. An epidemic of sickness followed, and the timber and adobe fort had been converted into a hospital. It was half demolished now, and gamblers and shopkeepers had appropriated the remaining rooms. Sutter, despoiled of his property, was trying to collect something from the hundreds of acres of his land being overrun by gold seekers and squatting speculators. The majority of the people, being landless, considered it equitable and just to divide his property.

After the flood receded, Sacramento scraped off the red mud and began rebuilding. Only the high-water marks on tree trunks reminded citizens of the disaster. Some of the new buildings were brick, among them the town's second theater. Colonial troupers from down under played here as they did in San Francisco. Mistress Ray "of the Royal Theatre of New Zealand" had enjoyed only limited success. Perhaps her cockney accent had been a detriment. Among the stores a barnlike structure, operated by Sam Brannan a year ago, appeared to be the largest. Goods overflowed the shelves, and were piled in pyramids on the floor. From the low, wide ceiling hung buckets, lanterns, log chains, horse collars, and hobbles. On the counters scales stood ready to weigh customers' gold dust. Beside each one lay a magnet for removing particles of iron.[14]

As night fell a fog obscured everything. Davison and his companions saw rats by hundreds venture from underneath houses. Lights from saloons shone wanly through red curtains. The sound of music, stamping feet, and laughter lured men from the ghostly shadows. Few gold seekers could resist "Oh, Susanna, Don't You Cry for Me" or "Carry Me Back to Old Virginny." Inside one drinking tent, garish pictures reminded forty-niners of their overland trip. With a good deal of imagination the men might recognize Independence Rock, Sweetwater Valley, and Fort Laramie.[15]

The Australians had seen none of these historic landmarks, and Davison, as he looked at the well-supplied stores and loaded wagons in the streets, decided that Sacramento would be no place for his trade. Come morning he must go upriver and try to sell his goods at Marysville, the next outfitting town, about one hundred miles north by water, although only fifty overland. As soon as the goods were disposed of profitably, he and his associates would go into the mountains and try their luck at the northern mines.

On the broad, sluggish Sacramento River, Hargraves could still use sails. Although the schooner moved upstream, the current was hardly perceptible, flowing down scarcely three to four inches per mile. Only where an overhanging sycamore branch stroked the surface, causing a little V-shaped riffle, could an observer be sure which way the river ran.

At night the Australians tied up their craft. Climbing the mast, they looked across the endless plain. No mountains were in sight, east or west, but they knew that the gold-bearing sierra must stand behind the eastern haze. As they sailed on next morning they followed other vessels going upstream and waved to craft floating down. At last they came to the Feather River. Hargraves steered the little schooner up that channel, for he knew that Marysville lay at the junction of the Feather and Yuba rivers. The town had been named for Mary Murphy, a survivor of the tragic Donner party who married one of the hamlet's founders.

Navigation was more difficult on the Feather River for there was less water and the stream soon became even smaller above the mouth of Bear River. Twenty miles farther the Australians saw on both banks ahead of them, tents, cabins, adobe and portable houses. A line of vessels was unloading cargo. Marysville at last!

The men jumped ashore and climbed the east bank. From the top, looking up a shack-lined road, they could see hazy foothills. Ox- and mule-drawn freight wagons plodded toward them. Ragged miners trudged into town with exciting tales as well as leather pokes of glistening gold. Marysville, like Sacramento, was an anthill of activity.

People said the snow had not yet melted from the mountains. Prospectors back yonder were grubbing in the wet earth under soggy drifts and discovering unbelievable wealth. New cities would grow out there!

Marysville's alcalde, Stephen Johnson Field, was a thirty-four-year-old Connecticut lawyer who had come to town this past January with only $20.00 in his pocket. He invested this sum the day he arrived, in $16,250 worth of town lots, all bought on credit. Three days later he was elected to his exalted office, winning by nine votes. His election was contested on the ground that three days' residence was insufficient for such high office. But, as his opponent had resided in town only six days, the contest failed.[16] In 1863 Abraham Lincoln would appoint Field to the Supreme Court of the United States. Things like that did not happen in Australia!

Davison auctioned his goods wholesale and decided to go back to San Francisco for another load. He would wait until the snow melted before inspecting the distant northern mines. Hargraves and Rudder also participated in this second mercantile venture. All three of them had certainly discussed the similarity

of California's goldfields to the outback in Australia, although
Rudder had as yet seen no California diggings. If each of the
men planned being first back to Australia, as they all claimed
later,[17] they forgot their haste in the prospect of making money
now. The trip downstream was a merry one. Their vessel
skimmed along past cottonwood trees, sycamores, and willow
thickets. The weather turned sultry, but the moist air near the
water's surface fanned their faces, and every evening they could
count on a refreshing tule fog.

In less than half the time required for the upriver passage,
the three men reached San Francisco. Davison and Hargraves
purchased a new supply of goods, and Rudder wrote a letter of
historical importance, at least to himself. Dated May 4, 1850,
it explained how Australians might discover gold in their own
country, and was published in the *Sydney Morning Herald* on
July 22. Thus the third epistle in the Australian gold-rush story
was sent from California. Each letter was intended to stop the
Australian exodus and start a gold rush down under,[18] but all
were ignored. The three dedicated letter writers—like the three
musketeers, loyal to their queen, to her dominions, and out-
wardly to one another—each planned secretly to be the principal
who would lead an Australian gold rush. To start a rush down
under always seemed more important to them than finding gold
there for themselves.

When the Australians left San Francisco on their second upriver trip, Rudder's sons went along to help man the sweeps.
Reaching Marysville once more, the party learned that the gold
discoveries, since the snow had melted, exceeded everyone's
expectations. The size of the town had doubled; it was now the
third-largest settlement in California, but unfortunately happened to be overstocked with supplies. Davison's second speculation had failed. And that was not all! The Australians, with
this boatload of goods on their hands, could not walk away and
visit the diggings.

In this predicament, big Hargraves, who disliked physical
exercise, came to the rescue. Let Davison and Rudder go to the
mines and try their luck. He would remain, sell the goods and
the schooner.[19] Davison accepted this proposition. With Rudder

and his two sons, he set off up the Yuba for the diggings. They found the old river bottom completely turned over by gold seekers ahead of them. Pebbles and smooth boulders lay in the sun, dry and white. In many places the channel had been diverted in order to wash away the banks. Nothing remained now but a dazzling flat of gray gravel and white sand half a mile wide. Even the side gulches were being worked by hundreds of men, their spades clicking in the gravel, the air everywhere heavy with the smell of sweat.

All the gold in this sand must have been washed down by nature from the mountains above, so the Australians plodded upstream amid the sloshing cradles. Before realizing it, they entered the foothills. The first perceptible difference in the landscape was timber on hills skirting the wide, gravelly stream bed. Thirty-five miles above Marysville, south of the stream, they came to a hamlet called Rough and Ready, for President Zachary Taylor. He had died on July 9, but no one here learned about it until months later. At the present time the diggers were incensed over a miners' tax and threatened to secede from California rather than pay it. Thus the Australians had a second lesson, like their earlier one in Sonora, about the danger of levying a miners' tax—a form of taxation which would be the cause of a revolution when gold was discovered in their own country.

Five miles beyond Rough and Ready, Davison and Rudder came to Grass Valley, a green park in the gloomy pines. Here in the timber where gulches cut through the hills, great gold discoveries had been made. One strike on a nearby hill was called Ophir—a name to be famous in Australia. Everywhere men were working, thick as bees, leaving no room for newcomers. The Australians could only follow other travelers trudging along a wagon road up hill and down, through the pines. It ended at Camptonville, but a rich gold country lay beyond along the North Yuba near a place called Downieville. Reports said that a single lump had been found there weighing 25 pounds,[20] bigger than the one discovered at Columbia last year! One site was called Tin Cup because a digger could wash a cupful of gold daily from its soil. All supplies used by miners up yonder in that land of treasures must be carried on the backs of animals or men.

Davison and the Rudders set off into this new wilderness. On the trail, pine needles cushioned the ground under their feet. In the silence there was something ominous in the eerie cry of Clark's nutcrackers, curious birds which followed travelers, flying above the pine tops. The tinkle of bells on an approaching packtrain came as a relief. Shortly thereafter, the bobbing packs appeared among the red-boled trees, the lead mule with ears pricked forward, those following with ears turned back. The muleteers waved cheerily and were soon out of sight.

Four miles beyond Camptonville, a chasm 1,000 feet deep opened before the travelers. The trail zigzagged down among rocks and trees. Saddle girths must be tightened for the descent. A stumble here would send a rider hurtling through rocks and brush to the jagged granite boulders in the bottom far below. The climb up the northern slope was equally precarious. Animals scrambled on the steep grades, kicking rocks into the precipice.

On reaching the top, the trail plunged down again into the canyon of the North Yuba, an icy, sparkling stream different from anything the Australians had seen in the southern mines. For the next ten miles they followed this stream along a narrow slot between steep mountain walls. Gloomy forests of bull pine prevented grass from growing on the slopes, and there was no feed for horses. Small wonder that all supplies back here cost double the price asked in Camptonville.

At a fork in the canyon the Australians came to Downieville. Already it contained 5,000 people—as many as in the Sonora they had left. Also, like the southern diggings, every gulch and sandbar was already appropriated. Beds of sand and gravel which had been worked over were selling for $500 to $1,000 per claim.[21] On every trail troupes of baffled prospectors kicked at boulders, struck picks into exposed banks, examined loose rocks and tossed them aside. All talked hopefully about rich strikes in some other area, and how a "fella" might be first to strike it rich somewhere else.

Davison and the Rudders found themselves as baffled as any

of the latecomers. Soon they were startled by one of those events characteristic of goldfields. A rumor spread along the creeks that the biggest discovery yet known had been made 120 miles back on the Stanislaus River, where they had wintered. All four of them joined this rush, trudging overland across the rugged foothills, following the southbound lines of men. At night they all crowded into mountain taverns or shivered around open fires. With other bearded prospectors they argued about the route for tomorrow, complained about the heat, the cold, the bad water, and told how much worse, or better, conditions had been on the last rush.

Over at Marysville in his store Hargraves heard about the new strike. He closed shop and boarded a river steamboat, one of those clumsy craft with the boiler on deck and passengers crowded fore and aft. Below Sacramento the vessel entered the desolate labyrinth of tules where the Sacramento and San Joaquin rivers join. Skilled pilots knew the right channels in the bulrushes and steered the vessel south to Stockton. From here Hargraves could ride the stage back over the route he had taken last autumn when first going to the diggings. On Wood's Creek, at the site where he had camped during the winter, he met Davison and Rudder. The ground where they had built their cabin and pitched their tent was now a sand heap. Already it had rendered a fortune for its present claimants.[22]

As the Australians tarried, laughing at their ill luck and wondering what next to do, they saw, above the silver-gray leaves of a manzanita thicket, a familiar figure approaching with two blackfellows. He had the odd Australian habit of plucking and smelling the crushed leaves of every tree he passed.

"Must be from the colonies," it is easy to imagine Hargraves as saying. "See 'im sample the fragrance of every gum! A better habit, eh what, than the Ammerican custom of sluicing tobacco juice along the futpaath."

Tom Archer and his aborigines had found even less gold than the other Australians, but they had enjoyed fine sport hunting game. They had been amused, come spring, to notice that the snowshoe rabbits turned from white to brown except for the soles of their big feet which remained white and flashed comically when they ran—just like an aborigine's. The black-fellows had experienced bad luck with the first rattlesnake they heard. The warning buzz sounded to them exactly like the chirp of an Australian cricket, an insect they considered a crisp and luscious tidbit. Creeping up to pounce on the creature, they spied the writhing serpent. Unlike the snakes they knew, rattlers coiled to fight instead of slithering away. The only serpent in Australia, Archer said, which remained when man approached was the deaf adder, which, people believed, was unable to hear.* It, like a rattlesnake, he said, moved slowly, and both were an easy prey for an aborigine's spear.

With thousands now congregated in the Sonora region, miners passed more resolutions against foreigners. This time the Australians heard that Sydneyites and Chinese were included, along with Chileans, as undesirable citizens who must be expelled. With this prejudice growing noticeably down here, and with opportunities for gold strikes better back at Downieville, the Australians decided to retrace their steps from the North Yuba and renew prospecting there. Thus they left before angry miners took four Mexicans from the authorities and almost lynched them. Obviously, the Californians were beginning to feel no compunction against ignoring a local government that failed to serve their conception of justice—a practice that would soon cost some Australians dear.[23]

The prospect of the long trip back perplexed Hargraves, for he was broke. The expensive steamboat ride down from Marysville had consumed all his money. Davison solved Hargraves' problem by employing him to prospect on shares, being careful to explain later that in America employer and employee did not have the status of superior and inferior recognized in a British community.[24]

---

* Thomas Archer, *Recollections of a Rambling Life* (Yokohama, 1897), p. 245, undoubtedly meant the "death adder," described in Raymond L. Ditmars, *Reptiles of the World* (New York, 1936), p. 216. "Deaf adder," however, seems to have been an accepted Australian name, for it is used by Mrs. Charles Clacy in *A Lady's Visit to the Gold Diggings of Australia in 1852-53* (London, 1853), p. 250, and by R. G. Jameson in *Australia and Her Gold Regions* (New York, 1852), p. 45. Nevertheless, Alan Moorehead, *Cooper's Creek* . . . (New York, 1963), p. 136, refers to "death adders."

On the return hike over roads familiar to Davison and Rudder
but new to Hargraves, they all continued to discuss the possibility of finding gold in Australia. Each still planned, should
they fail here, to return and start that rush. In July they separated, Rudder and his sons going to the pine-clad canyons
around Downieville, Hargraves and Davison to the Slate Range,
an area northeast of the North Yuba (not to be confused with
the Slate Range near the Mojave Desert). Archer rode on to
the Mount Shasta country for more prospecting and high adventure fighting Indians during the coming winter of 1850–51.[25]

As autumn approached with a tingle of iced seltzer in the
mountain air, the oaks in northern California, unlike the evergreen live oaks around Sonora, changed to russet and tobacco
brown. Red and gold leaves on cottonwoods and quaking aspens
came spinning down and rustled underfoot—so different from
the colonies where trees never shed their leaves seasonally.
Davison had found no more gold than he had last year. Hargraves' bad luck had also continued. The big gamble on which
he had staked so much was, like the business ventures he had
tried all his life, a complete failure.

The two men decided against spending another winter in the
mountains. When cold weather locked these northern ranges,
warm weather would be creeping over Australia's lush Blue
Mountains. The time had come, they were sure, to go back and
find the Australian gold about which they had talked and
dreamed and schemed. Both were still working together more
like partners than master and servant, but it was obvious that
each, deep in his mind, hoped to be first to make the Australian
discovery. Now they would go quickly, without disclosing their
plans to Rudder, who was mining with his sons thirty miles
away.

On the day of Hargraves' and Davison's departure from the
Yuba diggings, according to Davison's later recollections, they
told their plans to American friends. Men in heavy boots and
flannel shirts assembled to bid them farewell. One miner shouted
jocosely: "There's no gold in the country you're going to, and
if there is that darned queen of yours wouldn't let you dig it."

Davison recalled that Hargraves struck a theatrical pose,

took off his hat, and replied: "There's as much gold in the country I'm going to as there is in California, and Her Gracious Majesty the Queen, God bless her, will appoint me one of her Gold Commissioners." Turning to his employer, Davison, he added, "Then I shall get my friend Davison here a like appointment."[26]

Perhaps Hargraves spoke in such a dramatic manner, perhaps not. This is the way jealous Davison remembered the incident, but memories are tricky. In any event, the two Australians did leave for Australia, although the date of their departure is controversial. Rudder, meanwhile, seeing frost tinge trees along the watercourses, felt the haunting excitement that comes with a change of seasons. He sent his two sons to the Slate Range to tell Hargraves and Davison that the three of them were ready to return to Australia. Should they all go together?

The boys came back on October 1 with disturbing news. Hargraves and Davison were packing to go. Although they said they would meet Rudder in San Francisco, these men were plainly hoping to get away ahead of him.* This information infuriated Rudder. His rivals must not reach Australia ahead of him! He determined to be there first.

Settling his affairs as quickly as possible, Rudder started on October 3 with his sons but, to his dismay, one obstacle after another blocked his way. Travel was slow in the late autumn. The rivers were low for navigation, and regular steamboat service had been discontinued at Marysville.† It was necessary to go by stage downriver for twenty miles to Nicholas, which had been built at the new head of navigation. Travelers changed

---

* Simpson Davison, *The Discovery and Geognosy of Gold Deposits in Australia* (London, 1860), p. 49. Note that Enoch William Rudder, *Incidents Connected with the Discovery of Gold* (Sydney, 1861), p. 36, states that Hargraves and Davison had already gone. In his unpublished manuscript notes, however, Rudder says that they were packing to go. The reason for this change seems obvious. If Hargraves and Davison were merely packing, this did not prove that they were planning to return to Australia ahead of Rudder, but if they had gone without telling him, Rudder was justified in trying to arrive there ahead of them.

† An unclaimed letter for "Mr. Ruder" was advertised in the *Marysville* [California] *Herald*, September 10, 1850. If this referred to E. W. Rudder, he may have picked it up on his way down river.

boats again at Sacramento where a new fast steamboat, big enough to accommodate a hundred passengers, made night trips to San Francisco. Carrying searchlights, she could thread her way through the tortuous tule channels after dark, and thus was able to paddle across the open bays in the early morning ahead of the usual wind.[27]

San Francisco had changed marvelously, even since last summer, and the problem of finding Hargraves and Davison perplexed Rudder. Central Wharf, where the steamboat docked, was almost a mile long now. Other piers parallel to it had become thoroughfares, with cross piers making cross streets. High tides lapped under many pierside business houses. Vessels that had stuck in the mud were now two and three town blocks from the open bay, and shops had been built between hulls. During the summer two bad fires had swept away hundreds of wooden houses, as well as the docks and buildings on them. When the tide receded, long lines of piles with charred heads stood in the shallow water. Rudder was told that some of the worst sufferers had been Australians with property. Catton had lost not only all his goods but all his records as well. People blamed the fire on arsonists planning robbery. Sydney Valley men had been arrested although not convicted. An ugly rumor accused the courts of corruption, and threatened lynching of future offenders.[28] No one who knew Hargraves or Davison had seen them recently; all doubted that they were in town.

New brick buildings stood on the burned-over areas, but Hargraves and Davison were not in the crowds attracted to the cafes by music—bands, drums, and chanteuses accompanied by pianists. Nor were they to be found in the novel establishment that catered to diverse tastes by serving liquor over a bar on one side of the room, while on the other side a lady in a black silk dress dispensed tea, coffee, and chocolate.

Obviously, Rudder had won a lap over his rivals in the race to Australia, and he learned to his delight that a fine bark, the *Rosetta Joseph*, was scheduled to sail for Sydney on October 11. Rudder bought passage on her for himself and his two sons. A shipping agent informed him that the grandiose cradle he had shipped to San Francisco was awaiting him on the dock. Rudder did not take time to uncrate it. Instead, he arranged for its shipment back to Australia[29] and, on the appointed day, he sailed out through the Golden Gate. Of the three hopeful musketeers, he would certainly be first to start a gold rush in Australia!

Rudder was well on his way when Hargraves and Davison arrived in San Francisco. No Australian ship was immediately available, so Hargraves embarked for Hawaii.* Surely he could pick up some fast vessel there for Sydney and still beat Rudder. Davison wanted to accompany Hargraves, but was obliged to wait for a shipment of trade goods which might arrive any day; always Davison let immediate details divert him from the main project. Haunting the wharves now for bargains, he made money buying and selling imports, accumulating capital to help him promote a gold discovery back home. Finally, his deals completed, he prepared, with his usual exacting care, to sail. But the delay ruined him. The great San Francisco fire of May, 1851—the fifth in sixteen months—destroyed his goods stored in three warehouses and also the records of his bank balance at Wells & Company. Months were required for the careful man to straighten out his affairs. With this accomplished, Wells & Company suspended payments. Another delay! Davison finally reached Sydney on the *Orpheus* in September, 1852.[30] By that time an Australian gold rush was well established, and Hargraves had become a famous man.

Davison's continued bad luck put him out of the race. Rudder, in spite of his early start, fared no better. On December 1, 1850, the *Rosetta Joseph* crashed on Elizabeth Reef at the lower end of the Great Barrier Reef, that barely submerged coral plateau stretching for 1,500 miles just out of sight of Australia's east coast. Rudder and his two sons, after ten days in an open boat, landed at Moreton Bay.[31] When they reached Sydney, Hargraves was there ahead of them, but he had failed as yet to

* The records fail to disclose when Hargraves left California. He arrived in Sydney on the *Emma*, but, as a search has failed to reveal such a vessel leaving San Francisco, it is assumed that he boarded her in Honolulu, or possibly Tahiti. Since he arrived in Sydney five weeks after Rudder should have, had he not been wrecked, it seems safe to say that Hargraves left San Francisco after Rudder did.

start a gold rush. The monumental honor of that achievement still lay in tempting splendor before the rivals. Of the two, Rudder had more money and more influential friends. Robert Towns could have told the two aspirants: "In trade there are no friendships. Let the best man win!"

10

Hargraves Returns to a Different Australia

Edward Hargraves, racing across the high seas to Australia, knew nothing about the Rudders' mishap. He arrived in Sydney on January 7, 1851. On the ship with him came at least $100,000 worth of gold, but Hargraves owned little of it and debts incurred by his family during his absence absorbed the little he possessed. However, with the optimism characteristic of many corpulent people, he felt sure of future success and persuaded a friend to write Governor FitzRoy's secretary, Deas Thompson, one letter on January 23 and another on February 3 stating that he, Hargraves, could find gold in Australia.[1] To these letters he received no reply. Inconsequential eccentrics often wrote the Colonial Office about gold, and men of consequence had admitted for years that moderate quantities might exist in Australia's outback. As early as 1823 a convict had claimed to have discovered gold near Bathurst. The authorities, suspecting that he had stolen a watch and beaten it into a lump, rewarded him with 150 lashes. The presence of gold had also been noted by Count Paul E. de Strzelecki in 1839, by the Rev. W. B. Clarke in 1841, and by W. J. Smith in 1846. Surveyors had reported gold as recently as 1848.[2]

News of all discoveries had been suppressed for fear of "agitating the public mind." Certainly, Hargraves had nothing acceptable to offer the administration. If Australia became a goldfield, criminals might consider it a blessing, not a punishment, to be sent here. FitzRoy's predecessor, Governor George Gipps, had frankly told Mr. Clarke to put away his sample "or we shall

all have our throats cut." A stable government needed no gold discovery, and, thanks to California, the depression of 1848 had passed.[3] The coming year of 1851 promised continued prosperity.

Everywhere Hargraves went he learned that the excitement over the far-off gold rush had increased tremendously during his absence, especially among the working classes. Conversations turned continually to California, not to the possibility of discovering gold at home. Servants, people said, answered the bell dreamily, lost in thoughts of the goldfields. Clerks—"clarks" they were called—responded to the commonest questions with bewildered stares, for their minds, too, had wandered overseas. The new four-horse coach built in Sydney for the run to Parramatta was named "California." A chart of San Francisco Bay, copied from a map by William Tecumseh Sherman, was published locally. Men who had returned from San Francisco advertised their services on future trips as supercargoes. The Union Bank of Australia planned establishing a branch in San Francisco to take advantage of the 10 and 20 percent monthly interest paid there. The seaport towns had become so America-minded that even the Royal Circus in Hobart, which performed while ships were loading, added a new equestrian act entitled "The Red Man of the Far West." Everyone looked forward to good times, cooperation with the American cousins, and cordial hands across the sea.[4]

The letter E. W. Rudder wrote from San Francisco saying gold could be found in Australia had been published in the *Sydney Morning Herald* on July 22, 1850, but caused no stir whatever. Instead, poets waxed lyrical about California and found publishers for their verses. A pamphlet, printed in Adelaide, described not only how to avoid dysentery on the gold coast but how to build a rocker there.[5] Edward Hargraves had certainly arrived at an inopportune time to reverse the trend.

In the pubs along George Street and on the wharves dozens of returned gold seekers told anyone who would listen to them amazing stories about the opportunities in California. All said they had come home only to take their families back on the first outbound vessel. One man had left Hobart in July, 1849, as a steerage passenger on the *William Melville* and returned in February, 1850, to fetch his wife. He said he had gone straight to the diggings after landing in San Francisco and had made enough while the bark was in port to come back on her cabin class.[6]

"Where've you been, mate," many people must have asked Hargraves, "that you don't know what transpired down here in 1850?"

Not only had California become a haven for ambitious young Australians, but older men who had accumulated property in the colonies counted on the gold coast as a permanent outlet for products that had previously clogged the home market. Tasmanian flour, which had been unsalable in 1848, was now worth £11 a barrel in Hobart and £40 in San Francisco. And that was not all. California's population was growing and would soon reach half a million—enough to consume all of Tasmania's "corn-stuff" and warrant planting more. Australian flour had already proved superior to the Chilean product, and it could always be delivered in San Francisco much more cheaply than the Yankees could bring their flour from the eastern states. In fact, Tasmania hoped to become the breadbasket for California, and as such would attract ambitious farmers to her own shores.

Other goods readily salable in California were pickles, dried fruit, fresh apples, garden seeds, potatoes, onions, and carrots. Possum-fur rugs and kangaroo knapsacks and panniers for mules were also in demand, as were tents, tarpaulins, and camping equipment. Australian mechanics were doing well making carts, small wagons, window sashes, and doors. Even Australian typesetters were prospering, for shippers had learned that it paid to arrive in San Francisco with handbills describing their goods and thus save the exorbitant California printing charges.[7]

The shipment of lumber and prefabricated houses was no longer profitable. Both wood and iron houses were supplied now from the eastern United States. Australian eucalyptus was also out of favor. Hard and heavy, American carpenters found it difficult to work. Nails bent when driven into it. Recent shipments had been unsalable and were either kept for ballast or thrown overboard. The beach at San Francisco was reported to be strewn with discarded Australian lumber.[8] So what! Plenty of the colonists' other products were in demand, and fortunes were being made shipping them.

In addition, look at the profits from transporting emigrants! To provide passage to California, vessels had been taken from the India, China, and Singapore runs—even from the lucrative opium trade, as the old *Mazeppa* had been last year. In fact, one-third of all the Australian ships were now operating to California. Yankees had entered the colonial trade, too, with fast clipper ships of slim build carrying a cloud of sail, including skysails and moonrakers. Such ocean greyhounds hurt the Tasmanian shipwrights' pride, and editors urged exporters to offer a challenge cup to any local ship architect who could beat the foreign rivals.[9]

"My word, cobber, a really fast Australian vessel would be more welcome now than the discovery of gold down here!"

In May, 1850, it had been reported that seventy-five vessels had already left Australia that year carrying some 3,500 emigrants to California, not counting stowaways and others working for their passage.[10] This was 31 percent more than had left in the entire year of 1849, and by the end of 1850, just before Hargraves returned to Sydney, reports showed that 5,000 had left New South Wales alone. In Tasmania the shrinkage in population was so severe that Governor Denison ordered printing of the census withheld, until large shipments of paupers and convicts, including many women from Ireland, would enable him to show a favorable balance.

Responsible citizens worried because the best people were leaving for California and Britain was filling the vacuum with undesirables. In Hobart a mass meeting called attention to the danger and protested further importations of convicts (which did stop in 1853).[11]

The tempting profits to be made in the California trade, as well as the opportunities for young men up there, made it difficult for Hargraves to finance a prospecting adventure in Australia. Too much easy money could be made by other means, although some of them were questionable. The demand for transportation to California prompted a number of people to attempt evading the port authorities and sail without sufficient supplies, or without a physician on board, or to book more passengers than allowed for their vessel's tonnage. A few shipowners may have succeeded, others certainly failed. A little 15-ton ketch cleared the Sydney water police for a small port along the coast, but was stopped when the authorities learned she had booked passengers for California. A more ambitious swindle was attempted up at Moreton Bay where, away from emigration officers, a big vessel capable of carrying 180 to 200 gold seekers was equipped. The secret leaked out, however, and she never sailed.[12]

The rush to leave Australia seemed to have engendered a new carelessness, a new lack of the reserve so characteristic of the British. Even the discipline of their world-renowned maritime inspection relaxed. Certainly, the increased clamor for passage resulted in more ill-equipped ships slipping to sea than had done so in 1849—and coming to grief. The *Rosalind* left Sydney on October 16, 1850, with only sufficient supplies to reach Tahiti. When three hundred miles from land, she began leaking badly. The captain brought her back, but experts could not find the cause so her owners finally decided to unload and examine her copper bottom. The cargo and passengers were transferred to the big, 413-ton *Louisa Baille*, a J. B. Metcalf schooner, already overladen.

With this extra load the *Louisa Baille* floundered out to sea on November 11, and after passing the Heads labored fearfully in a "sow-sow-easter." The strain opened some planks, and water started to fill the hull at the rate of 13, and finally 20 inches an hour. Crewmen soon became exhausted at the pumps. When the schooner was only 200 miles out from Sydney, Captain H. H. Green gave up and wallowed back to port, arriving on November 21. The passengers made a second transfer and finally set off on December 6 aboard the *York*.[13]

Such mishaps and delays occurred much too often and people showed interest, even concern, about them, but nobody seemed to care about financing Hargraves to prospect for gold in Australia. Perhaps the most noteworthy of the vessels that failed to reach California during the 1850 rush was the *Widgeon*, out of

Hobart. Like the others, this 260-ton brig was overloaded with timber, horses, salt beef, and in addition she even carried extra casks of the famous Hobart water. Much of this cargo was stowed on deck, leaving scarcely room to pass fore and aft. The *Widgeon* had advertised A1 accommodations in cabin and intermediate classes.[14] Families were quartered below deck, where it would be smoother in rough weather. Single men occupied a cabin on deck.

As with all outgoing vessels, the *Widgeon's* passengers realized the dangers ahead. They floated on an even keel down the long Derwent estuary, watching the pleasant green landscape sloping westward to the foot of snowcapped Mount Wellington. There was no finer vista in all the colonies, and the travelers sang "Isle of beauty, fare thee well" as the cool sea breeze fanned their faces. Long lines of black, angular cormorants and trim flights of wildfowl—the Derwent ducks—skimmed past the vessel. At sunset the *Widgeon* rounded the basaltic point of Cape Raoul, with its screaming gulls, and entered the sea under heavy, lowering clouds. Before she was out of sight of land a gale hit the heavily loaded brig: her timbers groaned, water splashed across her deck. The bow plunged forward recklessly. Seamen high on the rocking masts shortened sail in the inky storm.

At midnight an antarctic hurricane swept overhead. All off-duty hands in the fo'c'sle were called to reef topsails. Sleepy, grumbling, many still sobering up from their shore spree, they climbed up the ratlines, with the wind tugging their trouser legs. Cold rain pelted their faces. Ropes slapped the wet masts threateningly. On wide-swinging yardarms a man hung dangerously over the boiling sea one moment and the next he circled high up into the dripping clouds.

Soon breakers began to roll across the *Widgeon's* deck, sloshing over and swirling around kegs and boxes, snapping lashings, piling cargo up against one bulwark, then tumbling it to the other side. The captain, clinging to the shrouds above the water, shouted commands through a trumpet. The second mate brought him word that the hull was taking water. No hands were available to man the pumps. The captain told him to rouse the passengers in the deck cabin. Set them to work.

These gentlemen refused to get up. Warm in their berths while water splashed against their cabin walls, they maintained that they had paid for A1 accommodations. A ship should be sailed by those hired for the job.

At dawn the mate knocked on the cabin door once more. With a trembling voice he explained that water was filling the hold rapidly, that the ship might sink if the gentlemen refused to help. This had the desired effect. The passengers dressed hurriedly and soon two pumps, with two men at each, drew water gurgling from the hold.

The cook's galley was already flooded. His fires were out, and no food could be served except sea biscuit and water. All hatches had been battened down, leaving the families 'tween decks in darkness with no ventilation, but better for them surely than having waves come crashing down the companionway. To lighten the hull, loose cargo was cut from the decks and rolled overboard. Horses were led onto gratings and one side was hoisted until the animals slipped into the churning sea.

All day long the gale continued. Nobody noticed that the gaskets that reefed the topsail were slipping until the canvas whipped furiously overhead, jerking the mainmast, wracking the whole vessel. Finally the topsail broke loose and flew away like an open umbrella. Only one sail, the jib, remained to hold the lumbering vessel to her course.

On the second day the crippled vessel's jibboom snapped, taking the last sail with it, and the *Widgeon* tossed helplessly in the sea. As she rolled from beam-end to beam-end, remnants of tangled rigging clung to the hull like seaweed to a wharf. The naked mainmast whipped back and forth threatening to capsize her.

"Chop down the mainmast," shouted the distraught captain.

Footing was uncertain on the wet, rocking deck, but Australian axmen knew their business and chips began to fly. In no time the great stick splintered and crashed into the water, but the butt end swung inboard, slid along the lee rail, tearing loose deck gear, crushing the longboat, and sweeping off the last of the deck stowage before plunging into the sea.

The ship was now free of this gigantic battering ram, but a

near accident lay in store for a passenger named Johnson Dean. A wave crashed over the *Widgeon's* bulwarks, snatched him from the pump handle, and tumbled him toward the lee rail. Two sailors caught his clothes and saved Dean from being washed overboard. A close call!

The vessel now became a mere bit of flotsam. Lacking the heavy mainmast, her bow nosed low in the water and lifted her rudder to the surface, thus making it impossible to steer. On the third day the storm abated, and on the fourth the sky cleared. To lighten the bow and thus trim ship, the forehatch was opened. Heavy cargo was lifted out and dropped overboard. Hatches to the hold, which housed the steerage passengers, were also lifted and miserable men, women, and children climbed up blinking into the brilliant light. Dean went down to inspect their dungeon and said "a pigsty would have been a parlour in comparison."

The crippled vessel, with a sail rigged on a jury mast, limped up the Australian coast, turned through the Sydney Heads, and floundered to a repair dock.[15] Dean, still eager to reach California, sought accommodations on another ship but found all vessels in the harbor filled with passengers. Not a place available for even one man! He learned that coalers were being loaded at Newcastle up the coast; black diamonds had become a profitable export. Although shiploads of coal were reaching San Francisco from the nearby Columbia River and the convict mines down at Port Arthur in Tasmania, both areas were failing to supply the demand.

Dean boarded one of the two steamboats which made the seventy-five-mile run to Newcastle in twelve hours. He found the coast town to be a ragged village at the foot of a steep hill. Orange-colored sand filled the streets. Shabby shops and miners' cottages seemed to emerge through it. In the harbor stood the largest fleet of square-rigged vessels ever seen at this port. Among them eight American vessels and five British hulls were waiting their turn to load.[16] The first in line was taking on twice as much coal as her registered tonnage allowed, but the captain was determined to make money. Dean welcomed the opportunity to join her twelve passengers for California.

Overladen, this craft wallowed away from shore. Speed was

important. To get the best price, the captain realized that he must beat all other coalers to San Francisco. He bent every sail: above topsails he set royals and skysails so far aloft, the seamen seemed to be clinging to threads as fine as spider webs. Not satisfied, the captain ordered booms lashed to the square sail yards and rigged them with studding sails. Dean admired the captain's ingenuity. In steady trade winds the heavy old hull surged ahead, sunshine in the spray from her bow making a rainbow.

One day tall towers of cloud loomed in the sky—sign of a tropical storm. The ocean became breathlessly still, the surface so glassy it reflected the clouds—another bad sign. Sails hung limp, but the captain refused to shorten them. No time must be lost trimming sails in this race!

Dean, writing about his experiences, recalled that the gale, when it came, tore the sea to tatters, ripping the wave crests into sheets of foam, knocking the old hull over 45 degrees, and "making things lively for a while." But she weathered the storm.

Days later, in the doldrums, passengers and crew prayed for wind, even a gale, as the empty sails flapped occasionally against a sun-scorched spar. To relieve the monotony, men swam in the lazily folding waves. Someone on deck spied a box floating in the sea. What could that be? The seamen speculated about its contents. Was it a pirate's treasure or cargo from a wreck? Finally a boat was lowered. On the surface of the water oarsmen could not see over the long, barreled swells that rose and fell as though breathing. Up in the shrouds sailors signaled the box's location until the boatmen located the treasure—a box twenty inches square with Chinese characters on the lid. A rope was tossed around it, and the oarsmen towed the find back to the idling vessel.

The box was hoisted on deck—a real sensation in the monotonous days on shipboard. What fabulous riches from the Orient might it contain? A man came running with an ax from the ship's rack. But the investigation was interrupted by a call to dinner. Few events on a voyage are so important as meals, and a ship's cook gets cranky when diners are late. The men scampered to the galley but continued to speculate about the box as they stowed their victuals.

After dinner all hands off duty clumped back on deck. The

box was opened. Inside they found Chinese clothing, an unlined tunic, damp, moldy, smelling of seawater. Below it lay some "drawers," a sailor's term for trousers. Next, the curious men discovered dominoes, a saucer painted with odd artistic designs, chopsticks, and a few "cash" (copper coins with square holes). Deep in the box they resurrected a human foot, evidently a Chinaman's.

Here, indeed, was material for days of speculation as the vessel loitered across the equator, with restless passengers watching hour after hour the blue ocean, mackerel-purple at noon, glittering every morning and evening with golden stars of reflected sunshine. One day a lump appeared on the thin straight line of horizon. The captain looked through his telescope and pronounced it a sail. An American whaler inched toward the Australian coaler. The two vessels exchanged names, lowered boats for visits, and traded Sydney fruit bags for Yankee "hardbread." It was good to see new faces after tiresome months at sea, but not so good to find the ship biscuits full of white grubs. Perhaps the apples, too, had rotten cores.

Finally, the northern trade winds sent the coaler lunging northward on long tacks, and in due time the coast of California rose from the blue waters. Dean climbed the rigging for a better view, watched with wonder as the mountains loomed higher and higher before the vessel. He saw the Golden Gate, and remembered later that the blue waters turned green as the ship sailed between the mountain walls. Rounding Clark Point, the vessel came to the city of ships—more than five hundred deserted vessels with bare masts, swinging gently on the channel tides. A launch carried passengers to Central Wharf, where small steamboats from the inland waters waited to take travelers up the Sacramento and San Joaquin rivers—pronounced "San Warkeen," Dean noted in his journal.

One of San Francisco's periodic fires had just burned a city block, but it interrupted the gambling only temporarily. Like most Australians, Dean was impressed by California's games of chance. He gaped at the stacks of golden eagles, Spanish doubloons, Mexican dollars, sometimes a nugget on top—all in the open, "not sly dens, but public as an auction-room." One member of Dean's party who thought himself clever at cards lost all he had, including "some nice possum rugs and a fur coat" brought for the northern winter ahead.[17]

The sight of gold made the Australians eager to leave for the mines. They were bushmen, accustomed to wilderness camping, and the prospect of a new outback with strange wild animals intrigued them. On June 22, a 500-pound grizzly had been lassoed and killed near the old Spanish mission. Later, an Englishman who had struck it rich purchased three grizzly cubs and took them home by the Panama route. The roly-poly beasts walked over the tropical divide with him and made the canoe trip down the Chagres River. On the transatlantic passage they romped on deck. It cost their master $800 to get them to London, but he paid this, besides his own fare, and still had $25,000 left in dust.[18]

Finally Dean and his shipboard companions set off. They found the California desert somewhat similar to Australia's. Barrel cactus took the place of spinifex tussocks, creosote bush of mulga thickets. Turtledoves, the white in their tails visible when they flew, resembled Australia's gregarious Twelve Apostles. Sagebrush, the Australians learned, made a very hot but short-lived fire. When the travelers entered California's foothills, the woodlands seemed strange. Being used to evergreen bush, they looked in wonder at the naked branches of living trees etched against the sky. Squirrels and woodpeckers were also new to them, as were light American wagons with spoked wheels. No wonder Americans had been able to come overland for 2,000 miles. The drivers of these vehicles all seemed much alike. Their first question when they met the Australians on the road invariably was, "I say, captain (or colonel), what part of the States are you from?"

When Australians replied in their peculiar accent, Midwestern Americans who had come overland "guessed" them to be from New York or Dublin.[19] When told the strangers were from Australia, the Americans "reckoned" them to be convicts. All colonials were being labeled with that unsavory designation, but this did not stop the immigration.

Dean and his friends, going toward the goldfields, may have

met Hargraves coming out. With so many people joining the miners' ranks, many Australians believed that Hargraves quit too soon. Why leave the Land of Promise! Perhaps the one person in Sydney Hargraves could find who lacked enthusiasm for California was Robert Towns, down on Circular Wharf. Even as he reaped good profits, that tight-fisted conservative wrote in his journal that he hoped only to get back the money he had ventured on speculations. His disgust with the California trade had increased in June, 1850, when the *William Hill* arrived with no accounting from Catton. He did learn that of the forty-two horses he had shipped on the *Chasley*, twenty-four had died, but he admitted that the survivors fetched splendid prices. Australian horses were selling in California for from $875 to $1,220 each. However, both the *Chasley* and the *Avon* had been gone more than seven months, and Towns had received no hard money from Catton—only drafts for expenses. No profit in that! If he ever got those two vessels back, Towns vowed he would put them both at whaling or "sandalwooding."[20]

Even as Towns fumed he decided to buy an old American whaler offered him at a bargain and put her in the California trade, thus throwing more good money after what he continually stated in his journal was bad. He also decided to discharge supercargo Catton, and sent a power of attorney authorizing J. L. Montefiore, of Hart & Company, to take all the goods in Catton's charge. A. H. Hart was a prominent Sydney Jew who could surely be trusted.

The document was hardly out of Towns's hands when he read in the *Herald* that Catton had been burned out in the San Francisco fire on May 4.[21] So that explained, although it did not excuse, the lack of a report! Then, to increase Towns's embarrassment, his own *Eleanor Lancaster* sailed through the Heads. Having served profitably as a storeship at Benicia and at San Francisco, Captain Lodge now brought her back for more goods. He delivered gold dust sent by Catton to Towns, together with a splendid accounting which, that skinflint admitted, was "not so much to be complained of."

Of course there were a few things a cautious merchant like Towns might still "complain of" in the California trade. Captain

Silver had failed to sell his *Avon*, saying that she leaked too much to attract buyers. Leaked, indeed! Towns blamed that on Silver—probably drunk instead of attending to business! Also, something about the sale of his big horse Duke displeased him. The details are obscure, but Towns wrote Catton a letter of censure. "Shame, Mr. Catton," he said, "is much too mild a term for it." Obviously, the animal had not died and may well have been the "powerful London dray horse, a very giant in harness," which Bayard Taylor saw in San Francisco pulling a load through mud which stalled other draft animals.

Towns, complaining constantly, hurried to reload the *Eleanor Lancaster* with goods and passengers—the biggest booking of the month, he noted. On board he was sending a new man to take the *Avon* from Captain Silver and either sell or take her sandalwooding. Invested capital must not stand idle. In a letter he restored Catton's authority and warned him that the new captain was careless with money. Every shilling must be watched. As for worthless Silver, advance him no more currency. If obliged to give him passage back to Sydney do so, but make him pay for his wife should she accompany him.[22]

Towns had reason to be in a hurry to get the *Eleanor Lancaster* out to sea, for he realized that every country in the world was competing with him. Crazy as it seemed in 1849 to ship horses to California, good draft stock had proved so highly profitable that many shipowners were converting their decks to stalls. The gigantic, 700-ton female prison ship, the *Earl Grey*, advertised for horses before she arrived in Hobart. Once in port she started building stalls while disposing of her cargo of "first-rate servants." Another shipment of female convicts in July on the *Baretto Junior* was offered for quick bids to vacate the ship. Over in Adelaide, where the importation of convicts was prohibited, two extra vessels became available when an English emigrant aid society sent shipments of "unemployed needle-women who have been unable to get employment in service." In order to dispose of them as rapidly as possible, it was announced that they were something special and had been kept 'tween decks under lock and key by a matron.[23]

In this year of 1850, with profits booming and the colonies

becoming more and more dependent on California for prosperity, Hargraves' chance of finding an investor for his wild-
goose chase in Australia's outback seemed slim indeed. However,
a new and ugly relationship with California was developing.
Australians learned that of sixteen men arrested in San Francisco
by the end of 1849, twelve were from Sydney. Of seventy sus-
pects arrested after the December fire, forty-eight were Sydney
men. It was claimed, rather feebly, that the $50.00 miner's
license fee which foreigners had to pay prevented poor Australians from digging and caused them to rove the country and
live by crime. Being city people and much traveled, many
Australians, unlike Dean's luckless companion, could outsmart
rural Americans at the gaming tables. One Hobart correspondent
wrote home that the professionals in San Francisco's gambling
hells were "French crooks, London sharpers, and the coarse
rogues from Sydney." [24]

Australians who were both honest and successful admitted
that the worst people in San Francisco came from the colonies,
and they blamed their own countrymen for permitting such
characters to emigrate. It is notable that some of the upper-
class Australians, including Thomas Hinigan, J. H. Levien, and
A. W. MacPherson, either helped, or were members of, the
committees that met incoming vessels and prohibited some of
their own countrymen from landing.

The political development of California impressed Australians who had been struggling for half a century to increase
their population and get a constitution of their own. Some said
openly that California's example struck a deathblow to Old
England's pretext that the colonies were not yet ready for self-
government. Said another: "Australians will not fail to recognize
in the California constitution a model after which their own
might be moulded. . . . The result of this recognition may
lead, even during the existence of the present generation, to
the establishment of independent Australian republics."[25]

Here was an early premonition of the coming revolution
which would be blamed on Californians. A third writer com-
mented:

Schooner Similar to the *Despatch*
Courtesy San Francisco Maritime Museum

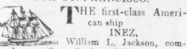

Newspaper Announcements of
Ship Sailings, 1849

The *Joseph Conrad*, a Ship the Size of the Brig *Spencer*
Courtesy San Francisco Maritime Museum

Fast Sailing Ship the Size of the *Sabine*
Courtesy San Francisco Maritime Museum

Giant Tasmanian Eucalyptus
Courtesy Captain Harry O'May

VOL. 37.]   [PUBLISHE

Return Passage

BAD NEWS—BAD NEWS.

CALIFORNIA.

THE Golden Statements, in reference to this place, are declared to be *FALSE*: and (independent of the place being inundated with goods) gold has become scarce, and obtained with great difficulty.

If any of the friends of those who have gone will give the Undersigned security for their passage-money, they may have a return passage, which may be the means of saving many of the unfortunates from great misery, and even *death*.

Application to be made within seven days from the present date —Apply to

JOHN THOMAS WATERHOUSE.

Packet Office, New Wharf,
August 3, 1849.

N. B.—Any but American citizens found digging or trespassing, will be fined and imprisoned ; and any gold found upon them, will be forfeited to the State. Suitable rewards will, " most probably," be off red for their apprehension, and any American citizen be rewarded for apprehending the same.   1893

CALIFORNIA.

FOR SAN FRANCISCO,

Touching at the Sandwich Islands if necessary,

THE fine fast-sailing Barque *DUCHESS OF CLARENCE* HARRY GILBERT COLE, Commander. The above vessel, of 500 tons burthen, is admirably adapted for passengers, for the accommodation of whom, she will be fitted up right-fore-and-aft. Having the greater part of her cargo already on board, she will meet with quick dispatch. For freight or passage, early application is necessary to

LOWES & MACMICHAEL,
Exchange ;
or,
F. A. DOWNING,
Davey street.

Hobart Town, June 28, 1849.

"Bad News—Bad News"
From Hobart *Colonial Times and Tasmanian,*
August 14, 1849

Gold Seekers Climbing up Ship's Rigging

Montgomery Street, San Francisco, 1849
From Frank Marryat, *Mountains and Molehills* (London, 1855)

The Bar in a Gambling Saloon, San Francisco
From Frank Marryat, *Mountains and Molehills* (London, 1855)

Deck Scene on a Gold-Rush Vessel, 1849
From *Century Magazine* (August, 1891)

Vessels Stuck in the Mud Converted into Stores and Hotels
From Frank Marryat, *Mountains and Molehills* (London, 1855)

Montgomery Street, San Francisco, 1850

From a Contemporary Print

Deserted Ships, San Francisco Harbor, 1850
Courtesy San Francisco Maritime Museum

Nugget Sent by Hargraves to Deas Thomson in 1851
Courtesy David S. Macmillan, University of Sydney

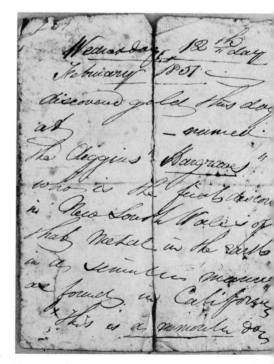

Hargraves' Announcement of His Discovery of G
in Australia, February 12, 1851

Sixth Great Fire in San Francisco, June 22, 1851

Courtesy Bancroft Library, Berkeley, California

Lynching of James Stuart at Foot of Market Street, San Francisco, July 11, 1851

Courtesy Bancroft Library, Berkeley, California

Hanging of Whittaker and McKenzie by the San Francisco Committee of Vigilance

From *Illustrated London News,* November 15, 1851

American Gold Diggers in Australia Reading
the *New York Herald*
Courtesy Argosy Gallery, New York

The Fight at the Eureka Stockade
Courtesy Mitchell Library, Sydney

An Australian colonist cannot see without some envy the rapid
establishment of self-government in a late desert. Had California
been subject to the British rule, beside a thousand vexations and de-
moralizing schemes to give the aristocracy a virtual monopoly of the
gold, it would have been impossible to obtain a constitution for
twenty years to come. We should have heard that the population
was too mixed—that some were aliens and others democratic. They
would have expended years in useless expectation, and many pounds
in parchment, fairly written, and graciously received, but not read.
But the Americans, accustomed to action, not whining and petition-
ing, have elected their governors, and accepted their constitution,
without a moment's obstruction; and have offered a practical lesson
to these colonies which has produced a profound impression. The
great republic, of which they are now a part, has displayed a mag-
nanimity in reference to the golden treasures, which demonstrates
how widely sound economical and political principles have been
spread among them. . . . We cannot but feel mortified to contrast
the spirit of that young nation with the still jealous restraints which
fetter the enterprise of our own colonies; and the unwise reservations
under the name of Crown rights, which remind us in the most painful
form that we are subject to an office essentially dull and despotic.[26]

One thing seemed certain: The California gold rush either
was going to revolutionize Australia, or the working people
would emigrate to the New World. Edward Hargraves may
have felt vaguely that what he hoped to do would stop the
emigration and bring about the revolution, but he was much
too practical a man to use such arguments in his efforts to raise
money. However, he finally succeeded with his financing. William Northwood, a Sydney alderman for the urban government,
advanced him £105 as a grubstake, an American custom by
which the prospector reimbursed his benefactor with half of
any gold he found.[27] For an extended exploration beyond the
Blue Mountains £105 was not much, but Hargraves started the
first week in February, 1851. He had worked on a station belonging to Captain Thomas Hector in the Bathurst region
eighteen years ago. Perhaps some of his old acquaintances
would still be there and he could live with them. Certainly
Australian stockmen, like ranchers everywhere, were notable
for their hospitality.

Hargraves Crosses the Divide

On February 5, 1851, Edward Hargraves rode along the toll road from Sydney to Bathurst. Forty miles ahead of him stood the Blue Mountain wall he must cross. Since he weighed well over two hundred pounds he needed a big horse, and its purchase had reduced his available cash. The sturdy animal plodded along a red clay road which meandered through rolling farm country. The Homebush racecourse on the Wentworth estate was out this way, as were such popular drinking places as the Crispin Arms and the Elephant & Castle. Sailors came here often to relax as far as possible from the sea. At noon, having passed fifteen mileposts and as many pothouses, Hargraves reached Parramatta.

The town in many ways was finer than Sydney—certainly an odd jumping-off place for a gold rush. The official residence of the colony's governors was located here until two years ago when Governor-General Charles FitzRoy's wife was killed in a carriage accident while driving around the park. After that tragedy, the Governor established quarters in Sydney. In addition to Government House, Parramatta had a hospital, a military barracks, an orphan school, and an institution for derelict trollops called the "female factory." Women were paraded here periodically for men to select wives from among them. On one occasion, when the inmates' hair was ordered cut, a riot ensued.[1]

The headmaster of the King's School at Parramatta, the Rev. William Branwhite Clarke, M.A., Cambridge, had discovered gold in 1844 across yonder Blue Mountains, but Hargraves said later that he knew nothing about it. Mr. Clarke had published the details of his discovery in last September's *Quarterly Review*, prophesying that the vast numbers of Australians going to California for gold might soon be returning.[2] However, it seems that no one except a few intellectuals read the *Review*, and they apparently had little influence on mass opinion. Hargraves probably was telling the truth when he said he never saw the article. With plans of his own, he plodded quietly out of Parramatta on his big horse.

The next town on his route was Penrith, nineteen miles beyond and only three miles from the base of the Blue Mountains. Penrith had a courthouse, a lockup, a livery stable, an inn or two, and a government-operated paddock where pastoralists fed and rested livestock before driving over the mountains. Hargraves stayed here all night.

In the morning he continued his journey. The rising sun shone on the black barrier ahead and he saw deep canyons—as they were called in California—which had been invisible to him yesterday. He had heard many times that the early pioneers tried and failed to cross this divide by riding up the bottoms of these defiles. Invariably, they found themselves in box canyons, or cul-de-sacs, and reported that crossing the Blue Mountains was impossible. Finally, in 1813, a new approach was tried by Gregory Blaxland, Lieutenant William Lawson, and twenty-year-old W. C. Wentworth, the now wealthy, political power in the colony. With four convict-servants, four pack-horses and five dogs, these men, instead of traversing the bottom of a canyon, climbed up the steep mountain's face until they emerged on its flat summit—a route that much of the road in 1851 followed.[3] Here the Blaxland party found themselves in a forest with no noticeable landmarks. Great slabs of rock lay horizontally under the trees, and passage was slow, but the explorers worked their way westward. Time and again they came to precipices 2,000 feet deep, with skeins of fog rising from the chasms' amethystine depths. Believing, correctly, that these gorges led back to the Pacific seaboard and need not be crossed, the explorers edged ever westward on the broken plateau's summit, following a mazelike watershed until they came at last to a mound from which they looked over the

escarpment and saw below them a vast plain stretching westward to the horizon. Here was pasturage enough for untold
generations of sheep and cattle, as yet unborn.

The present road, which Hargraves planned to travel in his
search for gold in this stockman's paradise, had been finished
in 1815. Mobs of sheep had crept along it, caterpillarlike, almost
before the convict-laborers had laid down their picks and
shovels. Blaxland, Lawson, and Wentworth were rewarded for
their discoveries with pastoral principalities. Other capitalists
followed them. During the ensuing forty years these early
graziers entrenched their holdings, and men of lesser means
also crossed. When Hargraves first visited that country eighteen
years ago, the economy seemed firmly established, the open
land all gone. Stockmen knew every foot of it, but the ever
optimistic Hargraves was sure he would discover gold and
change all that.

A mile west of Penrith, with the mountain wall towering
above him now, Hargraves forded the Nepean. A prolonged
drought had made the river so low that the rope ferry was no
longer necessary. His horse climbed the far bank, followed the
road through a border of droopy-limbed she-oaks and on past
the government farm for juvenile offenders. The Emu Plains
beyond had acquired a bad name from the severity of the farm's
discipline. Two miles past the buildings, the stage road started
its 2,000-foot climb to the mountain's summit. Hargraves knew
this rocky country to be notorious for bushrangers—"road
agents" to a Californian. Squatters on the western side made it
a practice to pay employees with orders on Sydney banks
instead of specie and thus save their "sarvants" from being
robbed while crossing for a spree in town. Moreover, many
herdsmen got drunk and "orders," if written on thin paper, were
often lost before cashing, thereby saving money for employers.
Travelers made it a practice to ride through this dangerous
area without arms; guns or pistols would mark them as tempting
victims for robbers. Hargraves could see, as his big horse plodded up the grade, that this country afforded perfect hideouts
for highwaymen. Soft clay had eroded from the horizontal
strata, creating caves everywhere as well as breastworks for

surprise attacks. A man unfamiliar with the nooks and crannies in these rocks would be almost helpless, and only a heavy guard could take quantities of gold through this country.

On the lower slopes Hargraves saw familiar eucalypti, with long streamers of bark waving gently from their smooth, naked, lemon-colored trunks. In the morning sunlight they glowed as though illuminated from within. Above them, in the black slide-rock, stood groves of somber stringybarks. At higher altitudes he noticed white gum trees; against the black sandstone rim-rocks, their branches and twigs etched delicate white veins. Finally horse and rider reached the summit. Turning in his saddle, Hargraves could look back eastward across a panorama of checkered farms to Penrith, Parramatta, and a pale-blue cushion of smoke where Sydney must be. Beyond it the ocean rose steeply into the sky like a flat-topped wall—an odd optical illusion.

The records do not tell where Hargraves stopped for his second night, but mail-stage stations had been erected every ten or fifteen miles across the Blue Mountains and he probably unsaddled at one of them. He noted later that innkeepers along the way complained because the low price of wool prevented pastoralists from patronizing their hostelries on trips to Sydney. Perhaps wool values were responsible, but more discriminating travelers had other reasons to shun the miserable accommodations offered. One observer, who knew frontier inns in both California and Australia, excused the primitiveness down under by saying that Americans, not being home lovers, patronized inns more than did Australians, thus prompting California bonifaces to make theirs more attractive.[4]

On the third day, Hargraves came to the western escarpment of the mountains. The plains below were gray now under February's late summer sun. He could see a threadlike road leading to Bathurst, twenty-five miles away. Hargraves knew that somewhere to the south and west across the great gray plain lay the station of the famous William Lawson, who had died last year. The brand "WL" on cattle or horses and the name "Lawson" in a human pedigree indicated the best breeding in Australia.

The Lawson station was a settlement in itself. The owner's residence, a veritable ancestral manor, was modestly called, in true Australian fashion, "a cottage," but hospitality here was known to be regal. Thirty-five guests might sit down to a dinner served on handsome china and silver. The host would offer a profusion of hock, claret, and champagne. Dainties and savories were imported from Europe; all had been brought on a four- or five-month ocean voyage, then hauled by oxen for two weeks across the mountains. Ladies wearing imported satin slippers and crinolines attended levees here and danced on the brick-floored veranda with bronzed swains from distant stock camps. These young men dressed for the occasion in white linen, their sunburned wrists showing beneath straw-colored gloves. All very democratic in theory, yes, but pastoralists were looking forward to the day when they might be established as landholding nobility, like Englishmen at "home." Already their wives and daughters sniffed at Bathurst women as being "tainted with trade." Certainly, a landlord in Australia must outrank a money changer, and the grandees of these grasslands would not welcome gold prospectors trespassing on their precious runs.

The low price of wool and the drought had hurt many graziers, and even bankrupted some; others, like Archer and Hargraves, had quit. Wentworth and men of his status could afford to stay in business until prices improved. The drought, of course, was not expected to last forever.

Hargraves followed the road down the escarpment to the plains—a rolling country, not so flat as it appeared from above, but certainly unlike the gold country of California. The thoroughfare stretched monotonously ahead. The sun stung his eyes and lips. His big horse had a rough, jarring gait. In the dusty roadside, bearded lizards and blue-tongues watched him pass. Now and again a flock of parrots, feeding on the ground, exploded into the sunshine like a dazzling fountain of gems.

Summer days are long in February down under, and the sun was still high in the sky when Hargraves rode into Bathurst. The town was almost thirty-six years old and had been laid out with the precision of imperial planning, so different from the haphazard construction of California mining towns. Although the population was less than 2,000, ample stores supplied stock-men's wants, a newspaper kept them informed, and the stage-coach and bullock trains of freight brought business activity. The Church of Scotland (Presbyterian) had completed a new brick edifice since Hargraves' previous visit. The pubs, two at every corner, seemed the same as they had always been, and the convict stockade was still guarded by tidy redcoats.[5]

Hargraves met many people in Bathurst who for years had heard rumors of gold in the surrounding country, but none of them took these tales seriously. There was a vagabond named MacGregor, who went to Sydney periodically with lumps of the precious metal he traded for drink. Some blokes thought him another of those imposters who pounded stolen jewelry into a resemblance of ore. At present he was in Sydney serving a jail term for debt.[6]

Undoubtedly, the most reliable person for Hargraves to inter-view about gold in these hills was Thomas Icely, a man of means who belonged to the New South Wales Legislative Council. His station, "Coombing," pastured 25,000 sheep, 3,000 cattle, and 300 horses. Forty-five miles of rail fences enclosed his paddocks. His Arabian stud was as fine as any in Australia.[7] Like other big pastoralists, he lived in what he liked to call "a cottage" which was English except for a broad veranda covered with fra-grant honeysuckle imported from "home." An English garden supplied his "people" with cutting flowers and European vege-tables. An orchard furnished fruit. Icely was already mining copper successfully on his estate and had found samples of gold there. Hargraves resolved to see him at once. Obviously Har-graves did not remember a definite location where he had seen gold, nor had he told the whole truth in last summer's letter from California stating that he remembered a gold-rich area in New South Wales and "unless you knew how to find it you might live a century in the region and know nothing of its existence."

Hargraves rode out of Bathurst early the next day intent on meeting Icely. He said later that he carried a letter of introduc-tion to him. A touch of approaching autumn chilled the Febru-ary air until the sun peeped over the distant Blue Mountains and scorched the dry, grassy slopes. Somewhere along the road

Hargraves made a wrong turn: never much of a bushman, he became lost on King's Plain, about twenty miles from Bathurst. Here, perspiring and confused, he met a carriage drawn by high-tailed Arabian horses. Thomas Icely held the reins. The great man was driving to Sydney, furiously angry with one of his fellow councilmen and eager to talk. The Rev. John Dunmore Lang, he said, had done it again. That old trickster never knew how to keep his mouth shut, although the bloke did accomplish things. He had dared call Governor-General FitzRoy a "he-goat"—with some justification, perhaps, since FitzRoy's wife had been killed in that accident.

Icely might have forgiven this statement, but now the cleric had published derogatory details about the personal lives of every colleague who had voted against him at a recent council meeting. Icely, having also lost his wife, was an easy mark, but he determined to sue the tactless clergyman for defamation of character—much better, surely, than a Californian reply by bowie knife.[8]

In spite of being angry with Mr. Lang, Icely restrained his tongue long enough to tell Hargraves that the son of a Mrs. Lister, who kept Guyong Inn above the Cornish Settlement (later named Byng), had found some gold and probably knew the source of more. Icely pointed out the track leading to the hostelry and drove away.

Hargraves followed the wheel ruts Icely had pointed to, again lost his way, and that night "laid out"—a California term for "bushing it" or camping campless, without food or bedding. Dozing beneath the unblinking southern stars, he must have pondered the familiar name "Lister." Was Mrs. Lister kin to Captain John Arthur Lister, the merchant seaman to whom he had been apprenticed at the age of fourteen? If so, her son John, the tot Hargraves had tended on the *Wave of Fortune*, must be in his twenties now and the baby daughter, Susan, a young lady.

In the morning Hargraves rode on to Guyong Inn. He found it to be a shabby little place on a tributary of Lewis Ponds Creek, twenty-one miles from Bathurst. At this time of year the creek was dry except for a few disconnected pools. Hargraves dismounted and watered his horse at a well between the house and barn. Mrs. Lister failed to recognize him at first, and her son John, a full-grown cornstalk now, did not recall the fourteen-year-old boy who had grown to the middle-aged giant standing there beside his horse. However, both mother and son received their guest with Australian cordiality.

Mrs. Lister had changed as much as Hargraves. Life in the outback had been hard after her captain-husband had retired and later died one night from a fall out of his gig on the way home from Bathurst. With seven children, five more since Hargraves had first known her, she had done her best with this little hostelry. Like most pioneer women, she had not tried to adapt herself to the new environment. To her the golden acacia (she called it wattle), the brilliant, feathery bottlebrush, and the amber honeypot were all weeds. Yet she cherished, as she would have done "at home," a scraggly little garden of English irises, the tips of whose sword-shaped leaves browned dismally under the scorching Australian sun.

Hargraves' life, since they had met last, had been as precarious as Mrs. Lister's, but he was sure the hard times were ended. Indeed, yes, for he was going to discover gold and make them all wealthy. John Lister replied that he had already found gold but never enough to buy a beer. He led the way into the inn and pointed to the brick fireplace where guests warmed themselves when evenings became chilly in July. On the mantel stood some chunks of white quartz: unmistakable gold was embedded in them. John said he had picked up the rocks on Lewis Ponds Creek, below the Cornish Settlement.[9]

Hargraves' California experience stood him in good stead now. He knew that constant erosion through the ages washed gold out of the quartz, and that this gold accumulated in sand downstream, where miners could pan it profitably. He remembered the lower end of Lewis Ponds Creek. It was quite different from the dry pools up here and should be good for panning. Years ago, when he was working for Captain Hector, some dray bullocks had strayed. Hargraves said that, with an aboriginal tracker, he had found them chewing their cuds on Lewis Ponds Creek. He and the "abo" had stopped that night at the 640-acre homestead of a Cornishman known as Parson William Tom.

Young John Lister's weather-beaten face brightened. He told Hargraves that Parson Tom lived only three and a half miles down the "crick." The parson, a deeply religious man, was a local preacher who told his congregation many times how he had come from England as a free emigrant in 1823, with a wife and three children: John, aged three; James, one and a half; and William, junior, a babe in arms. On the Indian Ocean a storm stripped the vessel of her rigging, while Parson Tom and family, sealed in the darkness of the hold, prayed as they had never prayed before. After this harrowing passage the Toms prospered in New South Wales and added five sons and three daughters to their original three children. To house them all the parson had just completed a dignified Georgian mansion named "Springfield" on a knoll overlooking the treetops along Lewis Ponds Creek.[10]

Twenty-three-year-old Johnnie Lister and middle-aged Hargraves decided to pan the sands on lower Lewis Ponds Creek. But Hargraves, tired and hungry after his night's bivouac, first rested two days at Mrs. Lister's inn. Then, on February 12, the two men shuffled down the dusty road through the Cornish Settlement. They rode past stately "Springfield" and, at the estate's lower boundary, entered an open forest.

Australian trees made peculiar shade. Their narrow leaves, hanging on edge, created a strange light which artists have found difficult to reproduce. On the ground, flocks of sulphur-crested cockatoos fed in the grass. But always, when riders approached, a sentinel on some lofty perch sounded an alarm and the whole flock roared into the air, like a column of white smoke.

As the men rode downstream they noticed that the country became more hilly, with water holes (locally called "water howls") closer together. At Radigan's Gully, ten miles from the inn, they stopped to rest the weak, grass-fed horses and make tea. Waiting for the billy to boil, Johnnie Lister could tell Hargraves that they were now only about five miles from the end of Lewis Ponds Creek.[11] Farther downstream the country became rougher and the "crick" often flowed between precipitous bluffs, sometimes 50 or more feet high. To pan gold down there a man might have trouble getting to the water. The country opened out again at Yorkie's Corner, where Lewis Ponds Creek joined Summer Hill Creek. The Corner was named for a Yorkshire shepherd who had built a sheepfold there. The combined streams flowed on for ten or fifteen miles to the Macquarie River.

After tea, with the unforgettable tang of burning gum leaves, Hargraves walked down to the sluggish stream. The soggy banks of weeds and rushes were ideal for duckbilled platypuses, and there was ample water at last for panning. Hargraves scooped up some mud and sand in his pan and swirled it, as he had learned to do in California. Sloshing the roily water and light gravel over the side, he saw tiny, glistening colors in the heavy black sand that remained. Of five pans, he said later, he found colors in all but one. A color is, of course, only a speck of gold, and from all his panning here Hargraves failed to net twopence' worth. Moreover, this is all the gold of record Hargraves ever discovered in Australia, but he was jubilant.

"This," he shouted to Lister, "is a memorable day in the history of New South Wales. I shall be a baronet, you shall be knighted, and my old horse will be stuffed, put in a glass-case, and sent to the British Museum"[12]—a revealing statement from Hargraves' autobiography. And let us believe that a kookaburra, Australia's laughing jackass, had been attracted by the smoke and, from the limb of a coolibah tree, uttered his idiotic giggles.

In any event, the two men plodded back to the inn that night. Hargraves, apparently realizing he had made no great discovery, persuaded twenty-nine-year-old James Tom, son of the parson, to guide him and Lister on a 150-mile circle down to the junction of the Macquarie and Turon rivers, crossing the cattle run belonging to a Dr. Kerr. James Tom had learned to know that lower country while working as a stockman. The three men carried their supplies on a packhorse. Since their animals were weak at summer's end, they traveled slowly. Water being scarce in the creeks, the men panned only a few sandbars and found scarcely any colors. Riding on to the mouth of Summer Hill Creek they decided to go no farther, and plodded up the rock-strewn stream bed to Yorkie's Corner, and thence home by the familiar Lewis Ponds Creek.

The expedition returned to "Springfield" after a fortnight's absence, bringing no gold.[13] Having failed miserably, most men would have quit—but not Hargraves. He could even delude himself by saying in all seriousness that he must hurry back to Sydney lest "some miner from California should make a similar discovery."[14] The only miners from California who might make such a discovery were Rudder and Davison, both of whom he believed to be far behind him now.

Before leaving for Sydney, Hargraves showed Johnnie Lister and William Tom, James's younger brother, how to make a California cradle, explaining that it was more efficient than a pan. The young men promised to experiment with it in his absence. Johnnie Lister then rode as far as the Blue Mountain escarpment with Hargraves, who did not care to take a chance on getting lost again.

A storm was brewing and east of the divide rain drenched Hargraves, but he went doggedly on, reaching Sydney on March 23. In spite of his grandiloquent boast to Johnnie Lister on the banks of Lewis Ponds Creek about the "memorable day in the history of New South Wales," he brought no gold and his grubstake from Alderman Northwood was exhausted. Being an ever-optimistic man he decided to call on the colonial secretary, Deas Thomson, and sat for three hours in a wet coat waiting for an appointment. Admitted finally to the Secretary's presence, Hargraves failed to convince him that a great goldfield lay across the Blue Mountains. Cold and wet, Hargraves left the office with no encouragement.

To climax Hargraves' accumulating ill luck, he heard startling news. His old rival, Rudder, was in town! Already a letter of Rudder's, describing how to pan gold, had been published in the Sydney *Herald*. Moreover, Rudder was scheduled to deliver a lecture on the subject at the School of Arts on March 25.[15] Was it possible that Rudder, with his extensive friendships among wealthy people, might be planning some new way to start the gold rush about which both of them had dreamed and schemed? Rudder might even succeed where Hargraves had failed.

Edward Hargraves could only await developments. He returned to the inn his wife was keeping at East Gosford, Brisbane

Water. Here he learned more bad news. Conditions in the colony had deteriorated during his trip west of the mountains. The business boom due to the new California market had burst: merchants everywhere complained about a new depression, and the hotel business had collapsed. Trade was hurt further by the separation of Melbourne and its surrounding territory from New South Wales. The people of the new colony, to be called Victoria, were determined to build their own economy and let Sydney go to the dingoes. More than a thousand persons had already left for California since Hargraves had returned in January. Vessels continued to bring back gold seekers "with money in both pockets,"[16] but these men came only to get their families and go away again.

Newspapers urged them to invest their funds in Australia, but in the same sheets Hargraves read that capitalists were being bankrupted by lack of labor, and that promoters were at work on a new and desperate plan to encourage immigration from England. The next item in the press dismayed him: his old rival, Rudder, was one of the promoters.

Hargraves determined to investigate Rudder's new activity; he might find possibilities for himself. Boarding the steamboat for Sydney, Hargraves planned to hear Rudder's lecture on how to pan gold and, if possible, learn his rival's scheme. Hargraves still hoped to achieve his own ambition. In Sydney, he learned plenty. Rudder, it seemed, along with well-to-do Thomas S. Mort, was deep in plans to offset the California exodus. Mort, the son of an English master weaver, had emigrated to Australia in 1838 as an employee of a mercantile firm. Within five years he became an independent wool auctioneer, and now, aged thirty-five, he headed the chief wool-selling agency in Australia, had acquired mining and shipbuilding interests, held 38,000 acres of land, and was working on plans for a railroad. The elaborate iron cradle that Rudder had shipped to San Francisco and later sent back to Sydney was now on display in Mort's yard.[17]

The lecture Rudder delivered was poorly attended. No one seemed interested in finding Australian gold. Perhaps everybody was too busy making arrangements to go to San Francisco.

Rudder told the few who came to hear him that a third of all who went to California would die within a year.[18] He repeated, to empty seats, all the other clichés that had been voiced to hold laborers in Australia but had failed to do so.

The disappointed propertied class, the employers, tried another procedure. They called for a mass meeting on the Domain —Sydney's great common—to discuss California and the labor problem. The meeting was well attended. Cabbage-tree-hat boys by the hundred trudged up Hunter and King streets from George Street. They stood thick as penguins in front of the speaker's stand and sprawled on the massive, exposed roots of Moreton Bay fig trees. "Swells" came up the hill from fashionable Woolloomooloo in gigs and phaetons. Pastoralists rode in from their estates astride thoroughbreds. Mr. Mort came from his counting room on a sleek pony. Sydney's first city clerk, C. H. Chambers, brought a list of proposed resolutions. He had published a pamphlet concerning the horrors of California, based on details furnished by Rudder.

Speaker after speaker offered plans to counteract the exodus to California by importing labor from England. All were shouted down. The cabbage-tree-hat boys opposed having their wages reduced by competing with cheap English labor.[19] The meeting broke up with employers wondering what could be done to save Australia.

A few days after the meeting, probably on April 2, Hargraves told Rudder about his futile expedition across the mountains and his frustrating meeting with Deas Thomson, but instead of depicting these occurrences in their truly drab colors, he described them as glowing achievements. Then, encouraged by his own enthusiasm, he decided to go with his story over the head of the Colonial Secretary and appeal to the Governor-General himself.

He found Sir Charles to be a plump, well-fed, handsome John Bull, with pleasing smile, curly hair, and side-whiskers. The Governor-General's manners were gracious, his bows punctilious and low. He owed his position to high connections, being the first cousin to two dukes and brother-in-law of a third. An assignment to India would have suited him better than to this

colony, but, with the *noblesse oblige* typical of British aristocrats, he came to New South Wales and was now pronounced
the best judge of claret in Sydney. An accomplished whip, he
brought a pack of hounds from the Duke of Beaufort's kennels.
Sir Charles always made a fine appearance—and a poor speech.
All his sympathies were with the property holders. Convicts
were called his and Earl Grey's "pets." He was wont to defer
his actions until tomorrow and thus, with a gracious smile,
waved Hargraves over to the rooms of the Colonial Secretary
who, as a matter of fact, was the real executive.[20]

Ushered once more into Deas Thomson's office, Hargraves
repeated his story of a gold discovery and requested a reward
of £500. The Colonial Secretary seemed unimpressed by the
stale account, especially since Hargraves had brought no gold
to verify his discovery. But inasmuch as the California rush was
disturbing Australia's economy, Deas Thomson, as diplomat-
ically gracious as his superior, told Hargraves to present his
facts in a letter to the colonial government and it would receive
proper consideration.

Whipped again? Not Hargraves! He went immediately to see
Rudder with a new proposition: Why not help your wealthy
friends and stop the emigration to California by writing a letter
for publication in the Sydney *Herald*, saying that gold has already been discovered in New South Wales? Rudder agreed to
this proposal and prepared the letter, while Hargraves journeyed
back to his wife at East Gosford, where he wrote and sent the
letter Deas Thomson had requested from him.*

Rudder's letter, stating that the discovery had been made by
a gentleman recently returned from California, was printed in
the *Herald* on April 4, 1851—the same day that Hargraves' letter
reached Deas Thomson's desk. This coincidence may have
prompted the Colonial Secretary to consult the Governor-

---

* Simpson Davison, *The Discovery and Geognosy of Gold Deposits in Australia* (London, 1860), p. 460; Enoch William Rudder, *Incidents Connected
with the Discovery of Gold in New South Wales, in the Year 1851* (Sydney,
1861), p. 17; Edward Hammond Hargraves, *Australia & Its Goldfields* (London,
1855), p. 119. Hargraves says that this interview took place on April 3 and
that he wrote the letter to Deas Thomson on the next day. However, his letter
is dated April 3 and Rudder's is dated April 2.

General and suggest that Hargraves' request receive special consideration. Such little incidents can be important. On April 5 Sir Charles initialed a memorandum asking the Secretary to send Hargraves an encouraging reply,[21] but Deas Thomson was slow writing it, and the delay may have changed the history of Australia's gold rush. Had the colonial government asked for proof of Hargraves' discovery during the first week in April, he could have shown nothing. And to make a bad situation worse, while he was waiting for the reply from Deas Thomson, a discouraging letter came from William Tom, saying that he and his brothers had tried the cradle again without success; all their prospecting had failed.[*]

Certainly, the goldfield over there seemed unpromising, and it was lucky for Hargraves that the government seemed to have forgotten him. Finally, however, after holding Hargraves' letter eleven days, Deas Thomson replied on April 15. He said that the government could not agree to pay the £500 requested, but that, if there should be a valid discovery, a reward would undoubtedly be granted, the amount depending on the field's nature and value.[22]

Hargraves was really in an embarrassing position now. He must "put up or shut up," and the only thing he had to show was that letter from William Tom saying that he and his brothers had failed to find gold.

---

[*] Frank Clune, *Wild Colonial Boys* (Sydney, 1948), p. 150. A search has failed to reveal this letter, but there is evidence to show that the Toms tried without success.

Gold Discovery in Australia!

If ever any man was born under a lucky star, that man was Edward Hammond Hargraves. Thwarted so often during his life, the great opportunity he had been seeking came to him in that letter of April 15, 1851, from the Colonial Secretary. At last the authorities wanted to know the whereabouts of his goldfield. And Hargraves, of course, had neither a goldfield, nor anything else to show except his repeated efforts to find one— his repeated failures, that is. While the poor fellow was pondering what to do in this predicament, his bad luck changed. Another letter came to him from across the mountains. Over there a recent storm, the first of the winter rains of 1851, had filled the gullies and exposed many new rock surfaces. Lister and William Tom had gone prospecting again on April 7. (James Tom did not accompany them this time, for he was taking delivery of 300 cows on the Bogan River.) The two young men packed the cradle down to Yorkie's Corner and HOORAY! They washed out gold dust worth £13 and found one lump weighing two ounces.[1]

With this good news Hargraves hurried from East Gosford to Sydney, reported to Deas Thomson, and then, without waiting for the Colonial Secretary to act, showed the letter to editor John Fairfax and hurried on to Bathurst. The *Herald* announced on April 29, 1851: "GOLD DISCOVERY," but gave few details, and Hargraves was now far on his way. Arriving at "Springfield" he found Parson Tom as excited as the boys, and the parson was later credited with giving the name "Ophir" to Yorkie's Corner. According to the parson, "Hiram brought gold from Ophir. Yes, first book of Kings, Chapter 22, Verse 48."

Perhaps the parson was first to give this name to the area; perhaps not. The first recorded use of the new name was written by Hargraves, who knew the town of Ophir in California.[2]

The young men showed their samples to Hargraves and the next day Rudder turned up. He had read the papers, and wanted to take part in the discovery. He examined the gold, pronounced it genuine, and separated it from the black sand for Hargraves, who was always more the promoter than the skillful worker.[3]

Hargraves was now too excited to go back quietly with his gold to show Deas Thomson. Instead, he invited a few gentlemen to Arthur's Inn in Bathurst, where he proclaimed his discovery and organized nine men into a company to return to the diggings and work for him. The commissioner of crown lands, C. H. Green, heard about this proceeding with amazement. What right did these men have to trespass on private runs or the Queen's domain? He wrote to the Governor-General for instructions. However, Hargraves arrived in Sydney at the same time as Green's letter, and he showed the gold dust to Deas Thomson. The Colonial Secretary poured the glittering grains from one paper to another: they certainly looked genuine, but he was still skeptical. This sample could be from California![*] He agreed, nevertheless, to send geological surveyor Samuel Stutchbury to investigate the discovery. Stutchbury had come to the colony last winter to inspect the coal veins up at Newcastle, which had boomed extraordinarily with the California trade. If Stutchbury pronounced the discovery really substantial, Deas Thomson said, Hargraves would be rewarded suitably. He did not name the amount.

Hargraves hurried back to Bathurst, proclaiming the gold strike as he rode along. A dozen riders accompanied him, and more joined the cavalcade en route. With thirty-seven hopeful

---

[*] *Sydney Morning Herald*, May 15, 1851; F. Lancelott, *Australia As It Is* (London, 1852), I, 284; letter from Governor-General FitzRoy to Earl Grey, May 22, 1851, in W. R. Glasson, *Australia's First Goldfield* (Sydney, 1944), p. 12. The nugget at the University of Sydney (see illustration) was sent to Deas Thomson "some months afterward," according to Hargraves' own statement. See "Minutes of Hearing before Select Committee of Legislative Council" in 1852, printed in Simpson Davison, *The Discovery and Geognosy of Gold Deposits in Australia* (London, 1860), p. 462.

horsemen Hargraves arrived at Yorkie's Corner.[4] The Tom boys were working there, and prospectors trudged in hourly. Stutchbury came also and Hargraves, eager for the certificate from him verifying the discovery, watched the geological surveyor examine the sands for three agonizing hours. This man's report, Hargraves knew, would be the turning point in his life—success at last, or final failure. He was overjoyed when Stutchbury found undeniable indications of the precious metal and signed the certificate for Hargraves. The geologist also wrote a report for Governor-General FitzRoy stating that grain gold existed in the locality, but added with scientific caution that he was not prepared to estimate the quantity. (As a matter of record, £10,000 in gold was washed by the end of the week.)

In the meantime, Hargraves returned triumphantly to Sydney with Stutchbury's certificate of discovery to get his reward, but instead of being acclaimed on arrival he was greeted with disheartening news. Many people had begun to dispute his right to any reward and they wrote protests to the newspapers. Gold, they said, had been discovered long ago. They recounted previous instances, from the days of the convict who received 150 lashes for finding gold near Bathurst in 1823 to the shepherd MacGregor, now in Sydney jail, and they did not forget the geologists who had recently reported auriferous rock.

John Fairfax printed these letters in the *Herald*, admitted their truth, and deplored the prospect of a gold rush with its inherent lawlessness. He hoped Her Majesty would prevent a repetition of the California chaos. To do so, the number of police might have to be doubled, perhaps tripled, and that meant an increase in taxes which were already too high. Only the *People's Advocate* saw benefits in Hargraves' discovery. Its readers were neither property owners nor heavy taxpayers. The editor was sure this discovery must be genuine, and he crowed that it "will end convictism and squatterism."[5]

Soon fantastic tales came from Bathurst which no editor could ignore. Two hundred men were reported at the diggings. One "little shrimp of a fellow with a forked stick and old frying pan" had made £5 in one day. A "poor but honest Scot" fainted when he found a gold lump weighing 46 3/4 ounces.

Two other men came into Bathurst with sufficient "dust" to balance 35 sovereigns on the apothecary's scales. A third, elated over his discoveries, jumped on a table set for dinner, kicked off all the dishes, and set the astonished guests to drinking and rollicking.[6]

While Bathurst was in a state of ferment over these exciting developments, a few men hurried to Sydney with gold samples. When they showed their gold to John Fairfax he became almost enthusiastic. "Mr. Hargraves," his paper announced, "deserves the credit."[7] A second report from Stutchbury dated May 19 said 400 persons were washing along about a mile of creek, many getting an ounce or two a day with no other equipment than a tin dish. This convinced Governor-General FitzRoy, and on May 22 he announced that gold had been found in commercial quantities. He could not very well do anything else. Besides, the exodus to California must be stopped. Hargraves had discovered no appreciable amount of gold personally, but he had taught others how to pan and cradle, and he had shouted "gold" until a rush began. Government must recognize a fait accompli.[8]

Hargraves received an immediate reward of £500 and considerably more later. When offered a position under the chief gold commissioner, he refused any subordinate situation. Consequently, a new post entailing a handsome annuity was created for him. As "Crown Commissioner for Exploration of the Gold-Fields" he traveled in a covered cart with two horses and an extra saddle mount. Two servants in police uniform attended his wants and at night pitched a tent for him to sleep in. As soon as he received his first award he went at once to his grub-staker, Alderman Northwood, and gave him £250, but insisted on getting back the partnership papers. Thus he escaped from sharing subsequent payments. For this Hargraves was censured. The alderman, however, had more than doubled his money in a few months.[9]

Even before Governor-General FitzRoy made his announcement, the rush from Sydney was well under way. Two of the city aldermen were among the first to go. In front of the *Herald* office a crowd watched the bulletin board for the latest despatches. On George Street people who usually walked from shop to shop began to run; old folks with rheumatism had to skip. The overland stage company received applications from five times the number of passengers it could accommodate. Service was doubled, with stages rolling night and day to make the approximately 125-mile trip in twenty-four hours. Seats must be booked a fortnight in advance. Independent omnibus owners offered to take fares at £5 each and to load not more than ten in a vehicle. Drays carrying chests of tea, steam-pressed biscuits, "Virginia cradles," and gaily shouting passengers rumbled up the Parramatta road behind long strings of plodding bullocks. The highway was inadequate for so many vehicles. One observer counted 30 drays queued up in front of the first tollgate and 168 on the road beyond. A thousand people crossed at the Penrith ferry in a single day. An extra detachment of mounted police was sent.[10]

Down at Circular Wharf, MacNamara's big, square-rigged *Johnstone* was loading for California. Thirty emigrants on board forfeited their passage money and came ashore. The boatswain tried to break his contract to sail by having his wife apply to the water police to hold him on the pretext that he would desert the ship, and her too, as soon as he reached California. The police pronounced this a ruse to enable him to join the Bathurst rush and refused to intercede. MacNamara's sailors also rebelled, and he had to pay them £20 a month to man his ship. The *Johnstone* cleared on May 22 with only ninety-three passengers, about a third of her capacity.[11] She carried Governor-General FitzRoy's announcement. How California would react to a gold discovery down under remained to be seen.

In Sydney, laborers' pay rose from 17 or 20 shillings a week to 48 shillings. Clerks complained that their meager pittances could not support them since the price of groceries had risen 50 percent almost overnight. They must either get more pay or join the rush.

For the *People's Advocate* and its Chartist readers, the sun now shone. The editor gloried in the fact that no more money would be sent out of the colony to import "virtual bond servants." Instead, hundreds of settlers would come at their own expense. He repeated once more that the rule of the grazier had terminated, and that henceforth herders of sheep would be treated like men—not like dogs. No longer would they have to buy tea, tobacco, and "slops" at the station store paying a 300 percent write-up; no longer must servants be tried for delinquencies before a grazier's brother magistrate. With apparent delight the *Advocate* reported that Wentworth had gone over the mountains to herd his own sheep since his "servants" had abandoned them to the tender appetites of dingoes.[12]

Only one cloud disfigured the *Advocate's* rosy view of the rising sun. Suppose criminals from Van Diemen's Land were dumped on them! In that event, the editor said, the people of New South Wales must take a tip from the Californians and organize a brotherhood more powerful than either police or law —a vigilance committee, if you please—to protect themselves.

The *Advocate's* rival, the *Herald*, bombarded readers with contrary opinions. Fairfax saw nothing amusing in Wentworth's herding his own sheep. He bemoaned the fact that the failure of the woolgrowers would drag into bankruptcy Sydney's merchants, who made a practice of extending credit between shearings. He admitted that the colony's economy would change from agriculture to mining, but he urged the people, as persistently as he had during the California rush, to stay home. And he was as persistently disregarded. Jewelers displayed tempting trays of glittering gold behind large panes of glass. Merchants filled their stalls with picks and shovels, "California cradles," and goldwashing pans, red and blue "California shirts," and "California hats." Special prices were posted for convenient packages of tobacco, "magic-stoves" for gold seekers, rum, and Porter's Family Antibilious Pills "for diggers."[13]

G. C. Mundy, kin of the Governor-General, went out to the races at Homebush one day. On the Parramatta road he saw a typically English race crowd but among them were hordes of gold seekers wearing "California hats" and hauling camp outfits on carts. Another observer regretted that many members of the mob bore firearms. This, he said, might have been necessary in California, "but Englishmen respect constituted authority"—or was this whistling in the dark? One man carried all his belongings on a wheelbarrow, with his son harnessed in front and his wife walking behind, carrying a child on her back. Gold seekers turned and cheered as this odd family passed (and rumor said they returned before Christmas with £1,000 in gold). Another group accompanied the shepherd MacGregor. They had paid his debts, gotten him out of jail, and now hoped he would lead them to his gold vein (but he did not). One troop of Sydney exquisites rode along with "bright spurs, kid gloves, and opera ties, and smelling sweet in hair oil and eau de Cologne." A party of seventy men and six wagons marched with bagpipes skirling.

Several companies of women joined the rush. They hoped to make a living at the mines with their washtubs. Other women, with more questionable plans, were arrested before reaching Penrith and herded to police court. "They seem of all classes, some in tatters, some respectably dressed, but all bearing marks of dissipation," one observer remarked. "They were followed by a motley crowd of urchins and larrikins of both sexes." Another writer said that many of the gold seekers begged for bread while they trudged along. Hargraves wrote the *Herald* that of the 800 to 1,000 he saw on the road, not 10 percent had the necessary tools or equipment for prospecting. Villages and inns on the western slope, he said, could not cope with such an influx of destitute people.

By the last of May, Bathurst resembled an aboriginal village with ragged humpies and bark shelters erected by white gold seekers. Out at Yorkie's Corner, good-natured gold seekers congregated helplessly along the creeks, looking at one another and wondering what to do. Some tried clumsily to pan sand in washbasins, saucepans, and even their hats. Only a few had brought tents or sufficient supplies. The rainy season was approaching, and every shower dismayed these city folk.

Meanwhile, back along the road they had traveled, constables and officers with red stripes down their trousers combed the crowd for deserting sailors. Ships' officers offered handsome rewards for the tars' return, in spite of the fact that some captains would have to pay the seamen six months' overdue wages.[14]

On May 28, with the rush increasing daily, an American bark, the *Edgar*, sailed for San Francisco. Many of her 146 passengers were the wives and children of Australians who had already gone to California. They were the last of the 1,684 emigrants who went to California in the first five months of 1851. Henceforth the traffic, which had been mostly from Australia to California, would be in the opposite direction.

In June the winter rains began in earnest. Snow dusted the dark flat-tops of the Blue Mountains. Smoke from the camps hung ceilinglike over the wet valleys. Roads from Bathurst to the diggings became so soft that drays hauling supplies traveled in pairs to help each other in case of trouble. Twelve oxen on each dray hauled a two-ton load and at mudholes, when the drays sank to their axles, it became necessary to double up. So slow was this procedure that one campsite sometimes served for two days' travel.[15]

The Bishop of Sydney, returning from a visit to the diggings, reported 3,000 people at Ophir in mid-June. A week later 4,000 were there, and eventually 10,000 congregated at the junction. Strangely enough, some American Negroes were there cooking for the crowds. Native blacks straggled in from the hills with their gins and pickaninnies and received good pay for fetching firewood as well as bark for hut roofs. "Black fellow rich now," they said as they smoked cigars which many diggers could not afford. Riders gave the blackfellows their mounts to herd. "Three shillin and tix pences, mind it horse," was the regular price. Troops of near-naked aborigines from the far outback trudged in to look in wonder, display their skill throwing mulga boomerangs, stamp out their rhythmic corroborees, and beg gratuities.[16]

At night, after work, the diggers congregated around big fires singing the national anthem, "nigger" melodies, brigand and California muleteer songs. On Sunday, the Bishop reported with satisfaction, they usually attended religious services. True enough, but the congregation often turned around in their seats to watch a fight, and in some tents gamblers "pursued their soul-debasing occupation." However, "California lawlessness" was reported to be rare in camp, although highway robbery of gold trains crossing the mountains was a common occurrence. In short, a long background of strict discipline seemed to produce more incorrigible blackguards and fewer gray ones than in California. American revolvers were said to be used only for celebrating the Queen's birthday—a striking contrast, indeed, to the "lynch law, and brute force allegedly dominant at California."[17]

Regardless of whether these reports were true or false at the beginning, it is noteworthy that the Australians who returned from San Francisco strutted around in high-topped boots, "California hats," and other conspicuous garments. A Mr. Alexander, of Sydney, appeared in scarlet shirt, buckskin breeches, pistol, dirk, and cartridge pouch. It was explained that "he has been to California and is uniformly obliging and communicative, not withstanding his somewhat fierce aspect."[18]

To discourage workmen from quitting their "situations" and thereby disrupting the colony's economy, and to raise sufficient money for proper administration of the goldfields, a licensing system was inaugurated. Without a permit no man would be allowed to dig for gold. On June 3 police arrived at Ophir with licenses that cost 30 shillings a month. Some diggers paid the fee dutifully and continued their work. Others slipped away deeper into the outback, where they hoped to evade the police. Still others, discouraged by the persistent June rains, looked at the lowering sky, the dripping trees, and said, "I know a country that looks like this nearer home, and will get my gold there."[19] Hargraves had heard this statement many times in California before he voiced it himself.

Hundreds of unlucky prospectors who had found no fortunes and had no money for licenses plodded back across the mountains through mud and slushy snow. In Sydney they met some 800 gold-seeking immigrants from other colonies—Hobart, Melbourne, and Adelaide—who had come by boat. A surprising number of young women were among them,[20] but before they could be warned to turn back, amazing news came over the Blue Mountains. One of the fabulous discoveries of gold-rush history had just been made on Dr. Kerr's cattle run beyond Ophir—the desolate country where Hargraves with his pack outfit had found nothing.

13

Australians Learn about California Lynchings

"'E caan't soy, 'Split a sixpence,' 'e caan't." The stockman loafing in front of the Bathurst pub flipped a coin into the outstretched palm of a flat-faced, bearded blackfellow. The white man's companion laughed at this standard test of the aborigine's difficulty with English pronunciation. The black man grinned even as he shivered in his new government blanket, for July mornings were chilly and hoarfrost whitened the ground until sunup.[1]

When the first excitement over gold waned, and before news of the recent breathtaking discovery reached town, Bathurst reverted to its old, easygoing routines. A few thousand diggers still toiled down around Yorkie's Corner, but a third of them scarcely made enough to pay for their monthly licenses. Each day grumblers streamed back into Bathurst, telling tales of disappointment: Australia a goldfield, indeed!

These discouraging stories were hardly out of discontented mouths when a horseman pounded into town announcing the approach of a tandem of gray horses hauling a lump of gold weighing more than 10 stone (140 U.S. pounds). Figure that for one nugget!

Down on Dr. Kerr's run, a black shepherd named Jemmy Irving had stumbled across the treasure. While examining it he saw a neighboring herder approach. Jemmy tossed his blanket over the exposed gold. The two sat on it and talked for an hour. After his visitor left, Jemmy penned the sheep and hurried off to report the discovery to his master. The white man rode out to see the great yellow boulder and decided to send it to Bathurst for analysis. The town was more than fifty miles away, and three days elapsed before the precious cargo could be hauled there over the muddy roads. Almost half of the big lump was quartz but, even with this crushed out, the scales in Bathurst's Union Bank of Australia registered some eighty pounds of pure gold—a tidy sum. John Fairfax, when he learned about its magnitude, wrote: "It will startle England, Ireland, and Scotland. It will startle even California."[2]

A new rush began at once, emptying Bathurst of clerks and shopkeepers. Travelers crossing the mountains from Sydney found the town all but deserted.[3] This second wave of prospectors pushed farther into the outback, into the great, gray distances of spinifex flats, rocky hogbacks, and dry gulches. On the Turon, where Hargraves had failed so dismally during the dry season, the newcomers washed out alluvial gold in unbelievable quantities.

Since May, John Fairfax had been deploring the damage that gold discoveries might do to Australia. Now he submitted to the inevitable. Like it or not, Australia was to start a new life, and his *Herald* had better move with the changing times, influence events as much as possible, and attract the best people as immigrants. "Our fellow-subjects at home," he declared, "would mark the superiority of our Eldorado over all others, in point of civilization, industry, social order, and all that Englishmen deem essential to the calm engagements of domestic life."[4]

The contrast between the way the Crown might regulate a gold rush and the way lawless republicans had failed to do so was becoming increasingly plain. Conditions in America seemed to have gone from bad to worse, and were now almost out of hand. Fairfax noted that in Sacramento the mob had had the effrontery to *demand* of the courts—*demand* mind you, not *beg* of them—more prompt prosecutions of murderers. The mob had even proved its viciousness by taking an Englishman named Frederick T. Rowse from the constituted authorities in Sacramento, trying him in a lynch court, and hanging him. Perhaps he was guilty, but why take him from the legal courts?

A later issue of the Sydney *Herald* reported a worse defiance of the law by an infuriated mob. Two men had slugged and robbed a prominent merchant in San Francisco named C. J. Jansen. John Fairfax did not know the blackguards' nationality and printed the story merely as an example of life in California. Before the law had time to act, he reported, placards were posted calling on all citizens to ignore the constituted courts and meet in the plaza to decide on a new method of freeing the city of robbers and murderers. This, of course, was revolution![5]

Several weeks elapsed before Australian readers learned who was accused of the robbery and what the mob's leaders intended to do about it. In the meantime, other reports announced the lynching of two more men, James Baxter of Maine and Charles Simmons of Massachusetts, caught as they were driving stolen horses across a ford in the mountains beyond Sacramento. The horse thieves spoke with an accent that made their captors suspect them of being Australians under assumed names. Both were summarily hanged, even as one of them cried, "For God's sake let us live a little longer."[6]

Reports of the grim fate of these men whose nationality was uncertain worried some Australian families who had not heard recently from husbands, sons, or brothers. Was the California mob, which had acted so violently against Latin Americans now turning against British subjects? A mob, it seemed, must always smother its own frustrations by attacking some minority group.

The next ship, which arrived in Sydney two weeks later, brought more details about the Jansen assault in San Francisco, details unpleasant for an Australian to hear. Jansen, newspaper readers were told, owned the principal emporium on Montgomery Street. He was robbed at midday on February 23. (After dark on February 19 would have been more correct, but no matter.) Two men, according to the report, entered Jansen's doorway. The big, gloomy storeroom was lighted only by a candle. The men said they wanted to purchase blankets. The shorter of the two remained at the entrance, his cloaked figure and peaked hat silhouetted in the oblong aperture. As Jansen turned to his shelves to lift down the blankets, he heard the man at the door say, "Now." A moment later Jansen was struck on the head by a slungshot and fell unconscious to the floor. When he revived, his head ached and his till had been robbed of $2,000. He staggered to the door and shouted for help. Neighbors came running. Some said they had seen English Jim, an alleged murderer who had escaped jail in Sacramento, and another man hurrying toward Central Wharf. However, a search among the storeships proved futile.

So far the dispatches from San Francisco had failed to implicate any men from the colonies, but later reports, reprinted by Fairfax, stated that, in the days following the crime, several characters were brought to Jansen's bedside for identification. The stricken man pointed out two: both were Australians. One claimed to be William Windred and the other, Thomas Berdue. (Fairfax printed their given names differently, but again no matter.) The *Herald's* editor said further that two such individuals of good family from nearby Windsor, New South Wales, had joined the rush in 1849. Their wives followed them a year later, and everyone supposed that their husbands had prospered by industry, not crime. To make their case even worse, the man who claimed to be Berdue had been identified as none other than that much-sought criminal, English Jim. Popular indignation against both Windred and Berdue was reported to be so strong that they might be lynched.[7]

More details of the story came to Australia later—more examples of American disrespect for law. At first the accused men were confined in the basement of San Francisco's new City Hall, a four-story structure with galleries surrounding all but the top floor. Jansen was a popular man, and angry mobs assembled outside the building on February 22 and again on February 23. Handbills demanding quick justice circulated in the crowd, and from the gallery Sam Brannan—that man who had a hand in everything—harangued the multitude, urging them not to lynch the men now but to appoint a committee to work with the authorities in prosecuting the case. As Brannan was suspected of distributing the handbills, his conciliatory speech seemed a sly step to assure an ultimate hanging.

On the top floor of the same building the mayor, big, handsome John Geary, pleaded in his best auctioneer's voice for the mob to go home. Let the law take its course. During this debate shouted from housetop and gallery, the prisoners heard both arguments and also the angry hoots of men intent on killing them. Jail guards, fearing the worst, hid the captives under their own cots and draped blankets to the floor.

Brannan's inflammatory speech seemed to be winning the argument. The mob was becoming more demanding, when a third voice boomed from the gallery. William Coleman, an educated merchant and shipping agent, who had been voted by his school class to be its handsomest member, spoke with youthful assurance and ear-catching persuasion. He suggested that instead of hanging the men at once, the mob should form a court and give them a fair trial.[8]

This plea for immediate action pacified the multitude, but not John Fairfax, reporting it in Sydney: Picture the travesty, an impromptu judge, jury, and attorneys, not one of them wearing the powdered wig of his profession, being selected from the mob when legal courts had been established! Some might call this democracy, but to John Fairfax it was revolution, no doubt about that! Who would want to live in godless California! Such conditions must not develop in Australia now that gold had been discovered there. A later dispatch reported that the mob court, being thus extemporaneously organized, proceeded to hold the trial in a hotel room, with dissatisfied members of the rabble shattering windows, shouting vengeance, and even pushing against the improvised jury-box rail until it gave way. Yet in spite of the turmoil, the jury failed to agree, and the accused were remanded to the lawful courts. These Americans were odd people indeed!

Then a strange thing happened. The two Australians, Windred and Berdue, when tried in the legal court, attempted to clear themselves with alibis, but they selected witnesses who hurt their case. One witness was a Captain Robert Patterson, former master of a cattle boat which operated between Launceston and Hobart Town. He kept a public house on Pacific Wharf and was acquainted with so many underworld Australians that people distrusted him. Later, when the San Francisco

Committee of Vigilance was formed, he tried to join but was not accepted, because it was feared that he might warn criminals before they were arrested. After this rebuff, Patterson opened a booking office for the return of Australians exiled by the committee.

Another alibi witness was George Cooper Turner, a sporting gentleman who owed Robert Towns money, had evaded the debt, and slipped away on a ship out of Newcastle, north of Sydney, taking some race horses with him. In California he won considerable money from the racing fraternity. However, one of the track stewards happened to be the ubiquitous Sam Brannan, so George Cooper Turner was too well known to be popular in the community.

The defendants' alibis, sworn to by Patterson and Turner, were contradicted by two other Sydneyites. The man and wife who kept the San Francisco lodging house where the accused men boarded maintained that the defendants came to their rooms at the very time they were said to have been elsewhere. Moreover, these witnesses alleged that both had also dressed in dark clothes as Jansen testified. The jury pronounced both men guilty. Berdue, called English Jim, who allegedly struck the blow, was sentenced to fourteen years in jail; his accomplice, Windred, to ten.[9] John Fairfax considered the procedure fair, the sentence just, the example of good men going bad during a gold rush worthy of notice. How wrong he was on all three counts soon became manifest.

Neither man served his term. Berdue was wanted at Marysville, California, for the murder of Charles Moore, so he was transported by boat to be tried up there. Windred escaped from the station house in San Francisco before being shipped to the makeshift penitentiary. The manner of his release hurt the already bad reputation of other Australians. A Hobart convict, T. Belcher Kay, had been elected San Francisco's port warden. He was an illiterate fellow who ran "a gymnasium of self-defense" and lurked around houses of ill-fame. He offered the girls a cut for putting "knockout drops" into the drinks of gold-rich patrons who accompanied them upstairs. No one suspected T. Belcher Kay of being involved in the Jansen robbery, but he deemed it wise to help Windred escape before the fellow talked too much. As port warden, Kay knew the corrupt police and, according to reports, smuggled a key to Windred. When the prisoner came out, Kay drove him to a hiding place in the home of an English physician on Mission Road. Windred's wife, disguised in men's clothes, visited his retreat. Together they were smuggled onto an Australia-bound vessel and left the country secretly.[10]

Meanwhile, a curious and unbelievable incident marked the trial of Berdue in Marysville. On the stand, he maintained again that he was not English Jim, the murderer. However, witnesses who claimed to know Jim testified under oath that Berdue was that notorious fellow. Jim, they swore, had this man's curly hair, the same bald spot on top, and telltale India-ink stains on his hands. Moreover, Jim had a stiff middle finger on his right hand, a scar on his right cheek, and an unmistakable cockney accent. The prisoner in the dock had the corresponding bald spot, a slightly deformed middle finger on his left hand, the India-ink stains, and the unmistakable accent. A full beard covered a possible scar, and when the accused was shaved this incriminating mark appeared. The only difference in the alleged similarity between the two men was the deformed finger, which happened to be on the prisoner's left instead of his right hand. The jury considered this a possible error of memory and adjudged Berdue guilty of the murder committed by English Jim. The date for Berdue's hanging had not been set when dispatches describing the two cases were carried by outgoing ships to Australia.

John Fairfax, as has been said, considered the trials of both men as legal as any they might have received in New South Wales—no mob courts. Besides, much more important and disturbing events were occurring in Australia under his very nose. Down in Melbourne, the people who had seceded from New South Wales to set up a separate colony named Victoria were now coming back to join the rush to the Turon River. Such a loss of the new colony's much-needed population embarrassed the mayor of Melbourne, and he called a meeting in the Mechanics Institute to devise some inducement to hold the citizens. A fake gold discovery had been tried in 1849 and had failed, but times were changing. In April of this year, 1851, a German geologist had really found gold in Melbourne's Pyrenees, although not in commercial quantities. However, this discovery seemed as propitious as Hargraves' original strike and other minor finds that had been reported. Consequently, the meeting voted a reward of 200 guineas to anyone who located a paying vein within 200 miles of Melbourne.

John Fairfax noted this reward in his paper and dismissed the distant California convictions, saying that the fate of Berdue and Windred was another example of what might be expected for even "very respectably connected" people who emigrated to a degrading environment like that of California.[11] God forbid that the Turon would create a similar situation!

John Fairfax once again spoke before he knew all the facts. William Windred might be "very respectably connected" around Windsor, but a Joseph Windred had a bad name there, having been convicted of "bailing up" and robbing his aunt. Some Windsor people, when they read about the Jansen robbery, believed William and Joseph to be the same man. The Windred who left San Francisco secretly and arrived in Windsor during July boasted that he had set the San Francisco fire of May 4, 1851—a questionable assertion. Although he did sail two days after the fire, he seems to have been hiding on shipboard during the preceding week, and he would hardly have risked being captured by going ashore to set the blaze.[12]

In Windsor, the Chief Constable read American newspapers and noted that a large reward was being offered for Windred's arrest. As Joseph and William seemed to be the same person, the Constable wrote the Inspector General of police in Sydney on July 24, 1851, that he knew the wanted man and could arrest him. This communication was immediately forwarded to Governor John McDougal in California for further action. The Governor wrote the American consul in Sydney concerning a requisition,[13] but, before he had time to receive the consul's reply, several events completely changed the Australian situation.

First, the offer of a reward for a gold discovery near Melbourne produced tremendous results. A woodchopper named James Esmonds had come back from California on the same vessel with Hargraves. The two may, or may not, have met on shipboard. Both lacked cash when they arrived in Sydney and Esmonds also lacked Hargraves' salesmanship. He worked his way south to Melbourne, arriving there by sail three months later, and got a job as a tree chopper in the Buninyongs. Here he learned about the reward. Being familiar with California prospecting, he found gold within a week and panned $5.00 worth in ten minutes at a likely spot ninety miles from Melbourne. He said, as had Hargraves, Davison, and Rudder before him, that he was impressed with the resemblance of the country to California. He was probably more impressed with the fact that several people had already discovered samples of gold in the country but did not know how to mine it.[14]

This discovery on June 28 marked the beginning of a new era in Melbourne. Four days later, on July 1, 1851, the town became the capital of the new colony of Victoria, under Lieutenant Governor Charles Joseph La Trobe—or just "Joe," as the diggers would call him in contempt after trouble began. He was a scholar, a theorist, much traveled, and easygoing. Well acquainted with the wealthy squatters and their aristocratic ways, it remained to be seen whether he could cope with the revolution that gold was bound to bring to Australia. John Fairfax already realized that he and the *Herald* would have to adjust or perish. Could Joseph La Trobe do as much?

The next ship from California brought more dismaying news, another reminder of what gold could do to a new country. Sam Brannan and other leaders of the San Francisco mob that had tried Windred and Berdue had organized into what they seemed proud to call the Committee of Vigilance. Members even quoted the Irish rebel, John Philpot Curran, who allegedly declared: "Eternal vigilance is the price of liberty." Liberty to lynch, John Fairfax thought. The committee's first act, on June 10, had been to string up an Australian named John Jenkins. Described as a waterman from Sydney, he was actually an ex-convict from Tasmania.[15] Little more was known about him, but people in

Sydney were duly outraged. The American consul wrote Governor McDougal that he believed an application to extradite Windred for trial in California, where lynching was condoned, would be futile. If, however, the Secretary of State requested the suspect for trial by the United States, Windred might be surrendered.[16]

The Sydney newspapers printed lurid accounts of Jenkins' lynching. According to stories received in the colonies, he had rowed a boat out beside Central Wharf at nine o'clock one night, floated under the dark floor of a shipping office and sawed out enough boards to enter the building, and let down the safe into his boat.* Someone watched him row away toward a deserted vessel in the harbor. Several boatmen followed him to investigate. When Jenkins saw them, he heaved the safe overboard and shortly thereafter was captured. The safe was hauled up from the shallow water, and Jenkins was taken, not to the police as he should have been, but to the Brannan Building, which the Committee of Vigilance used as headquarters.[17]

Jenkins was formally tried by this unofficial organization of citizens on the same evening he was apprehended. They found him to be a low, brutal fellow of herculean frame, with loud mouth and coarse red hair and beard, who formerly operated a disreputable groggery named Uncle Sam in San Francisco's Sydney Valley. He had rented this brothel to a Mr. and Mrs. Connolly from Launceston. The woman was known as a talkative and stupid shrew, who could neither read nor write and made a cross in lieu of signing her name. She was prone to blurt positive incriminating gossip and, in the same conversation, deny it with equal barefaced assurance. Five days after leasing the Uncle Sam her husband died, presumably of apoplexy. Neighbors who did not like the woman maintained that she had poisoned him in order to live, undisturbed, with Jenkins.

---

* *Bell's Life in Sydney*, Aug. 30, 1851; Hobart *Colonial Times*, Sept. 9, 1851; *Hobart Town Guardian*, Sept. 10, 1851; *Hobart Daily Courier*, Sept. 10, 27, 1851; *Sydney Morning Herald*, Sept. 12, 1851. The account of Jenkins' lowering the safe through the floor is apocryphal. He probably walked out of the door, carrying it in a sack.

Of this murder she was later exonerated, but the ugly stories and Jenkins' relations with her damaged the reputations of both.[18]

Another of Jenkins' close associates was a short, stout man with small features, who had served four years in irons at Port Arthur, then, like many convicts, became a turnkey in Hobart Town before emigrating to California.[19]

Jenkins' disreputable associates, his obvious connection with the Sydney Valley underworld, and his unquestioned guilt as a safe robber convinced the Committee of Vigilance that he should be hanged in the plaza as an example to other wrong-doers.[20] The legal courts, they believed, had become so corrupt that he would be freed if tried there.

During this illegal trial inside the Brannan Building, a police-man on the street suspected something irregular to be tran-spiring. He noticed that a password was required of all persons at the door, and, edging closer, through an open window heard Jenkins exclaim, "Shoot me like a man. Don't hang me like a dog."

After that, the window was slammed shut. The policeman heard no more, but word spread over town that the man had been convicted and would be lynched. The Rev. Dr. Flavel S. Mines, rector of Trinity Church, was called to console the doomed man. Dr. Mines found the prisoner sullen, revengeful, and unrepentant. With indecent language, probably the only words Jenkins knew, he told the minister that he preferred a cigar and a drink of brandy to divine consolation.[21]

That night, June 10, 1851, with a full moon shining down on the city, the bell on the Monumental Fire Company station began to toll. People thought another fire had started. A crowd of 2,000 assembled—many more than the police could control. At about one in the morning Sam Brannan addressed the multi-tude from a sandbank, saying that Jenkins had been duly tried and condemned to be hanged.

"Do the people approve?" he shouted.[22]

An almost unanimous roar affirmed the sentence.

Shortly before two o'clock in the morning the door of the Brannan Building opened and the prisoner appeared, surrounded by an irregular column of men who marched three and four abreast toward the plaza. The moonlight glistened on the prisoner's handcuffs. Here and there a policeman tried to take the doomed man from his captors, at times snatching hold of his clothes, but pistol-wielding men in the crowd held back the officers. Someone climbing the abandoned customhouse flagpole shouted, "Hang him here."

"No! no! That's too good for him."

"Hang him on the adobe!" another voice shouted.[23]

David C. Broderick, a leader of the Democratic party and president of the California Senate in its second session, just adjourned, tried to mollify the mob and stop the execution, but was shouted down. A crowd with a rope, at the northwest corner of the plaza, elbowed their way through the throng and tossed a hangman's loop around Jenkins' neck. The rope had already been passed over a projecting beam on the old adobe customhouse. Frenzied men struggled with one another for holds on the rope and tugged exultantly. Jenkins was jerked down, dragged along the ground, then pulled up in the air until his head hit the beam. For a few minutes he struggled violently, twitching the rope like a big fish on a line. Men spelled each other holding him. Finally he hung limply and someone who seemed to be in charge tied the free end of the rope to the veranda railing on the customhouse. Police attempted to cut the rope but were held back. The crowd stood silent now, apparently awestruck by what they had done. Above them in the moonlight Jenkins seemed to nod and grin.[24]

Twelve days later the fire of June 22 swept across the city. Many people believed Sydney toughs had set it to revenge the lynching of Jenkins. Right or wrong, one thing was certain: prejudice against all Australians had reached fever pitch. In the heat of this bigotry, Berdue wrote a pathetic letter to a friend saying that the unfavorable attitude toward Sydney men had prevented the jury from giving him a fair trial, that he was to be hanged for the crimes of the real English Jim. This was followed four days later by an announcement that startled the entire city. The real English Jim, alias James Stuart, had been arrested and, in a long confession, admitted that he and a man named Samuel Whittaker had committed the Jansen robbery. So both Windred and Berdue were completely innocent![25]

The capture of English Jim so near the time to be set for Berdue's hanging is one of the fortunate coincidences in criminal history. Moreover, it was pure chance. The Committee of Vigilance in San Francisco happened to arrest a man for burglary while Berdue was awaiting his execution up in Marysville. The newly arrested fellow gave his name as Stevens, and the evidence against him seemed dubious. The committee was on the point of releasing him when somebody noticed a discrepancy in his story. The prisoner said he had walked in from Sonora without changing clothes, yet he was wearing a fresh shirt. This discrepancy saved Berdue's life because the committee decided to hold Stevens for further questioning, and his guard noticed something peculiarly familiar about the man. His nose was aquiline, his swivel eyes sharp as a fox's. His curly brown hair hung below his collar, and he wore his beard trimmed as in pictures of Christ. Stevens also had a defiant way of raising his head and looking around when questioned, and he walked with a measured step as though pacing a distance— a cell perhaps? The guard noticed India-ink stains on his hands. The middle finger on his right hand seemed slightly deformed. In addition, there was a scar on his right cheek, and he spoke with a cockney accent.[26]

The guard believed that this man might be the real English Jim and reported his suspicions to the committee. They cross-examined the man, confronted him with incriminating evidence, and even promised, with a signed contract, to release him for a legal trial if he would incriminate his accomplices.[27] Inasmuch as organized criminals felt reasonably safe in the San Franciso courts, which were supported by their votes, this offer broke the man's resolution. He admitted that he was James Stuart, alias Stevens or English Jim, that he was thirty-one years old, and that, at the age of sixteen, he had been convicted of forgery in England and was transported to Australia for life. In Sydney he had been assigned to a master but ran away from him for adventure in the South Pacific islands. After some ten years of vagabondage, he happened to be on the coast of South

America when he learned about the California gold rush and joined it.* Arriving in San Francisco in November, 1849—a month after Hargraves, Archer, and Rudder had landed—Stuart began supporting himself in the frenzied crowds by stealing. He found willing confederates among other ex-convicts from the colonies, and he named twenty-six, including Sam Whittaker who, he stated, had helped him rob Jansen. This confession, as has been said, exonerated both Windred and Berdue. The former had already escaped. A messenger hurried off to stay the execution of Berdue.[28] Jansen, who had mistaken Berdue's identity and thus caused him to be convicted, contributed to a collection taken for the abused fellow's relief. A free man once more, Berdue was last seen in the fall of 1851 dealing three-card monte on Central Wharf.[29] That vicious Whittaker must be found and punished at any cost!

* Mary Floyd Williams (ed.), *Papers of the San Francisco Committee of Vigilance of 1851* (Berkeley, 1919), p. 225. In an earlier confession (*ibid.*, pp. 137-139), Stuart claimed that he came from England to Canada as a boy with his parents, grew up there, and, when the gold rush started, went to California via Panama.

14

The Greatest Goldfield
of Them All

Fairfax gave the Stuart confession full coverage in the Sydney *Herald*, but he seemed more interested in explaining that California's placers had been exhausted and that gold-bearing quartz was now being crushed by expensive machines while dredges, big as houseboats, were operating in the streams. Such equipment might soon be necessary on the Turon and the Bathurst plains. Fairfax's lack of bitterness toward the Californians' brutal handling of his fellow countrymen may have been partly due to the reports he had received from Thomas Hinigan, who wrote that the ex-convicts from the colonies were the worst kind of scoundrels, that more were coming constantly —some so recently out of jail that their hair had not had time to grow on their heads. To protect life and property in San Francisco, the Committee of Vigilance was a necessity, and several well-to-do Australians belonged to the organization.

Thomas Hinigan's enthusiasm for California had become boundless. He wrote Fairfax that San Francisco was destined to be one of the great cities of the world. He did not say that he had applied for American citizenship and accepted a position on the *Alta California*. Before permanently quitting the *Herald*, however, Hinigan wrote Fairfax that Benjamin Boyd had failed to strike it rich in the mines and planned to return to Sydney by way of China, a plan that never materialized. Boyd left San Francisco on his yacht in June, 1851, landed at the Solomon Islands on October 15, went ashore with a native for some shooting, and was never seen again.

Hinigan reported also that several Australians with their families planned to live permanently in California. Most diverting of all was his statement that some females who were remembered as loose characters in Sydney had married respectable men, had reformed, and would, no doubt, mother the social leaders of San Francisco's next generation. Fairfax printed this with apparent amusement. He even seemed to understand how men of substance might feel justified in protecting their property by extralegal, Committee of Vigilance means, although he did not condone it. He was disturbed only by fears of what might happen in Australia's goldfields.[1]

None of this tolerance appeared in the columns of the *Empire*, a new Chartist paper appealing to the same readers as the older *People's Advocate*. The new journal's editor felt little concern for protecting property and showed great scorn for American lawlessness. "The blood thirsty mob," he wrote, "cannot fling calumnies against Australia when guilty of such acts [as lynching Jenkins]. . . . When the infuriated citizens of San Francisco strangled the thief whom they had caught in their streets, they hanged that liberty which they seemed to think they could preserve. . . ."[2]

Melbourne newspapers also deplored California's outrages, but more important events were occurring in their own outback. Another gold strike had been made in the Buninyongs on August 8, 1851. On August 24, two wandering prospectors scraped up two and a half pounds of gold worth $600 on a sheep run called "Ballarat"—the richest alluvial goldfield ever known. That green and leafy paradise soon became a hive of workers. Ballarat alone produced 300 million dollars worth of gold, more than all California had by 1853, and almost one-third of California's total production by 1870. Seventy-five miles to the north, Bendigo produced an even larger amount of wealth. The camp was named for a local shepherd who considered himself a great man with his fists, so great he was nicknamed "Bendigo" after the famous English boxer. During this same year discoveries at Mount Alexander, later called Castelmain, set men to ripping open that heavily timbered country. Forests disappeared, leaving only brown dust to cover diggers' tents.[3] These strikes were all miles apart, and the ranges separating them promised to contain some of the richest goldfields on earth.

Such marvels were sure to start a rush from Europe, from the eastern United States, and even from California. Already streams of ox-drawn drays were trundling southward through the Australian Alps below the Bathurst region. From the city of Adelaide gold seekers came on foot, on horseback, and in carts. Others braved the rough waters of Bass Strait to make a faster trip by sail. A total of 94,664 people disembarked in Melbourne in 1852, an average of more than 1,800 a week. This was a larger number than had come to San Francisco in the first year of the California rush. So eager were emigrants to reach Melbourne that two vessels refused to wait for pilots to guide them and were wrecked attempting to navigate the thirty-five miles of inland water above Geelong. The coming of the winter rains failed to check an ever-increasing throng of gold seekers on all roads to the diggings. Every few miles along the way inns, coffee tents, and sly-grog hovels offered refreshments. At night travelers bivouacked around fires of stringybark logs which were so steeped in natural oil that they burned when green. Crown Commissioner Hargraves, with his liveried servants, came from New South Wales to show prospectors how to pan.[4]

Lieutenant Governor La Trobe, deep in problems of separating the new colonial government of Victoria from New South Wales, and already reluctant to forego his personal investigations in the field of botany, found himself caught in an emergency which demanded versatility, practical executive experience, and boundless energy. Australia's economy presumably depended on wool. The shearing season had arrived, but the shearers had thrown down their blades to prospect for gold; the Geelong stevedores, who customarily loaded the wool bales into ships' holds, had also quit their jobs. Then, to add to the perplexing situation, the hated Californians suddenly became much in demand for their knowledge of prospecting and mining gold, even though the newspapers continued to incite people against them.[5] Lieutenant Governor La Trobe, like John Fairfax in Sydney, feared that his new colony might "parallel California in crime and disorder" unless strictly regulated. On August 15, he followed the precedent set by Governor-General FitzRoy and asserted the Crown's right to all gold in Victoria, thus inaugurating a licensing system similar to that used in New South Wales. This move met wtih protests, as it had in the Bathurst region, but most of the first diggers accepted it.[6]

Passengers on the next vessel to arrive from California had not heard about the Australian gold discoveries, but they brought word of Jim Stuart's fate. The Committee of Vigilance had found an excuse acceptable to it for not honoring the pledge to deliver him to the state authorities. Certainly he had implicated a sufficient number of his confederates to fulfill his contract,[7] but he was kept a prisoner, and on July 11, 1851, citizens of San Francisco heard the foreboding clang of the bell on the Monumental Fire Company's engine house—an accepted signal, since the hanging of Jenkins, for assembling the crowd. Curious citizens gathered before the closed doors of the Vigilance Committee's headquarters. A man stepped out to face them and shouted that James Stuart had been sentenced to be hanged this day. Did the crowd approve?

A bellow of affirmations greeted this announcement, with only a few shouts of "No!"

The man stepped back in the doorway, and shortly thereafter the prisoner was led out, neatly dressed in dark jacket, white shirt, brown pantaloons, and patent-leather boots. Some four hundred men surrounded him. They all marched down Battery Street and out to the end of Market Street Wharf. Here the rope from a derrick was tossed over his head. He asked that he not be blindfolded, and a few minutes later he swung above the spectators who respectfully uncovered their heads. In the harbor flags broke out on ships and cannon fired. The dying man's body twitched. His hat blew off. The long hair on his head blew across his forehead.

Twenty-five minutes later the body was lowered, and the coroner stepped up to take charge. He pronounced the man not yet dead and tried vainly to revive him as the mob melted away.

All this was horrible for Australian readers, and the same

vessel that brought these details also announced the lynching of a Spanish woman. Readers were not told that this had occurred at Downieville, 200 miles from San Francisco—almost twice as far as Bathurst is from Sydney.[8] Instead, readers assumed that lynching women, as well as men, had become common practice in San Francisco. What would be done to the twenty-six criminals implicated by Stuart's confession, especially to Sam Whittaker, English Jim's confederate in the Jansen robbery?

Accounts of California lawlessness continued to come to Australia by every ship, but the news of the discovery of gold down under was slow in reaching San Francisco. The first report arrived there on a British bark from Hobart, the *Black Squall*, which arrived on August 5 after an eighty-four-day run. The information she brought was indefinite and caused little concern, but two days later MacNamara's *Johnstone* from Sydney via Honolulu confirmed the report, adding exciting details. A rush to Australia began. Only nine days later, when the *Edgar* arrived in San Francisco with the wives and families of Australian gold seekers then in California, two vessels, the *Dorset* and the *Walter Claxton*, had already sailed for Australia, and two more were loading equipment for the voyage. Captain Patterson was advertising berths on a third, the *Mary Catherine*.

The editor of the *Alta California* greeted this exodus without comment except to say that many good people had come from the colonies and he hoped only the bad ones would go back. He concluded the article by adding that the Pacific Ocean was evidently destined to be the great area of democracy in the future—a prophecy Australians had expressed more than a year earlier.[9]

The rush of ships from California to the Australian goldfields had come too late to offer a mode of escape for the criminals exposed by the Stuart confession. They scattered immediately, despite efforts of the Committee of Vigilance to apprehend the worst of them. Two, however, were caught and lynched on August 24. One was British, the other Australian, although the difference is difficult to distinguish. Robert McKenzie, a big, roughly clad laborer, could neither read nor write. Now twenty-six years old, he had left Liverpool with his parents when thirteen, and had lived in New Orleans until news of the gold rush lured him across the Isthmus of Panama in 1849. Like so many others, he failed to find the precious metal, and supported himself first as a sailor along the coast, then as a volunteer soldier fighting Indians in northern California as Thomas Archer had done. After that episode, although not an Australian, he joined the Sydney Ducks and became a notorious criminal.

The man hanged with him was the much-sought Samuel Whittaker, a very different character. Shorter physically, only 5 feet 6 inches tall, he made a good appearance and had evidently associated with people of some means. When he learned that his partner, Stuart, had implicated him in the Jansen robbery, he fled from town as so many of the other criminals had done. The committee determined to find him, if possible. They learned that he had lived in Sydney Valley with a Mrs. Mary Ann Hogan, English-born, who was taken to the colonies when a baby. She married there and, before coming to California in 1849,* helped her husband, Michael, run a public house at one of the stagecoach stops on the road out of Sydney. On arrival in San Francisco, the couple established another pub, and, to help finance it, Mr. Hogan went to the mines. Mrs. Hogan could neither read nor write, but she could add accounts and make change well enough to run the business. During her husband's absence she began living with dapper Sam Whittaker. They were seen together drinking in taverns and driving to the races. The Stuart gang had planned their robberies in the Hogan barroom. When Michael Hogan returned, Whittaker left, but it was believed that Mrs. Hogan kept in touch with him. The committee therefore arrested and interviewed her but gained no helpful information. In Australia the papers, learning only part of the facts, complained that this lawless mob had apprehended an apparently "highly respectable lady, and kept her carriage."[10]

---

* *Alta California*, Aug. 25, 1851. The ship that brought Mrs. Hogan is difficult to identify. Two couples named Hogan are listed as passengers in 1849. The first came on the *Inchinnan* with two daughters; the second came on the *William Hill's* second voyage with a son. Neither couple resembles the notorious Hogans in the text.

The Committee of Vigilance, thwarted by Mrs. Hogan's testimony, suspected that Whittaker might be hiding in the southern mines. A vigilance committee had been formed on Wood's Creek the year after Hargraves and Rudder left. Its members were notified to watch for Whittaker. Then this most wanted man appeared from the least expected place, a little seaside village 250 miles down the coast. Sheriff Valentine W. Hearne, of Santa Barbara, read Stuart's confession in the newspapers, recognized Whittaker as a visitor in his town, arrested him on August 8, and brought him in irons on board the *Ohio* to San Francisco. But before the sheriff could deliver Whittaker to the authorities, members of the Committee of Vigilance boarded the vessel at Central Wharf and took the prisoner to new headquarters they had leased for $400 a month on Battery Street between California and Pine.[11] This building stood on land that had been covered by water until dump cars on a little railway filled the area between wharves. Whittaker was held a prisoner here for a week while he was interviewed, cross-examined, and faced with incriminating witnesses. Certainly he was unprepared for one of them.

Harriet Langmeade from Launceston, who had arrived in San Francisco on the *David Malcolm* in December of 1849, reenters the story here. The committee, having failed to learn much from Mrs. Hogan, hoped to get more information from Harriet. Before Whittaker was arrested in Santa Barbara, the committee's secret police had followed Harriet's uncertain trail through Sacramento, Stockton, and Sonora. Finally apprehended by one of these illegal officers, she was brought before the committee on the day after Whittaker had been taken from the vessel on Central Wharf.

Harriet Langmeade, alias Langley, alias Gardner, testified that she had been born in Middlesex, near London. When twenty-six years old, in 1838, she went to Van Diemen's Land with her sister and married there. In 1849 she and her husband came to California. On arrival he asked her to support them both by becoming a prostitute. This, she said, she had refused to do, whereupon he left for the mines and she began living with another man, supporting him by washing clothes, dressmaking, and occasional prostitution—remarkable versatility for a woman who was now at least thirty-nine.

In some manner not plain in the testimony, she had been insulted by T. Belcher Kay, the onetime port warden who acted as go-between for strumpets. To redress this insult, Harriet's male companion of the moment attacked Kay with a knife and "cut open" his head. Belcher Kay's partner, Sam Whittaker, had tried to avenge the injury by shooting her. The bullet knocked down a lamp but did no further damage.

During the unsavory testimony revealing these facts, Whittaker was held in an adjoining room. At the interrogation's conclusion, he was brought in and Harriet identified him as the man who shot at her. This, along with incriminating statements from others, broke Whittaker's silence. He signed a long confession and was sentenced by the committee to be hanged on Wednesday, August 20, 1851, from the yardarm of a ship anchored in full view of Telegraph Hill and the rascals in Sydney Valley.

Whittaker had influential friends in the legitimate government, which was supported by votes from the underworld. On the evening preceding his execution he offered his captors $100,000 in cash and bonds, guaranteed by men of unquestionable financial standing, if they would either banish him from California or remand him to the established courts for trial. This bribe was peremptorily refused, and the executioners were ordered to continue their preparations for hanging him and his fellow prisoner, McKenzie. The pair were allowed razors to shave themselves. Whittaker already wore a fine shirt. McKenzie was given a clean one to be hanged in. The new spring handcuffs on his wrists were substituted for an older model, so that the better ones might be saved for future arrests.[12]

On this same evening, Governor McDougal, in Benicia, learned about the proposed lynching. He was faced with a predicament: members of the Committee of Vigilance were his friends, and as a lame-duck governor he might seek employment from some of them as soon as his term expired. Often an opportunist, in this instance he showed real character and acted quickly. With little to expect from the electorate and much from members of the committee, he decided that lawless vigilantism must be defied. Ultimate good did not justify illegal acts. The elected government, corrupt or not, must be upheld!

A steamboat was scheduled to leave that night for San Francisco, and Governor McDougal boarded her. Arriving in town at three o'clock next morning, he appeared at the Vigilance Committee's headquarters with the mayor, the sheriff, a deputy sheriff, and a writ of habeas corpus. Risking their lives, the brave little party walked boldly in the front door, upstairs to the room where McKenzie and Whittaker were being held, and marched out with them. The rescue was made so quickly and with such assurance that the dumbfounded guard offered practically no resistance.

The prisoners were taken to the city jail to be held there for legal trial. The vigilance guards, when they came to their senses, tolled the engine-house bell—the usual announcement of an execution. This aroused the city. People scampered through the dark streets and alleys to see the spectacle, only to find the headquarters building closed and apparently empty. No one appeared to explain the bell's false summons. Indeed, there was nothing to explain, except that the legal authorities had taken the prisoners. One man in the mob, a reputed humorist, seeing a ready-made audience, tried to entertain it with a mockingly bombastic speech. Lynchings had obviously become an exciting spectacle, but when no one was hanged before dawn the crowd melted away.

The Committee of Vigilance determined to retrieve the prisoners and show the authorities who ruled the city. They decided to do so on the next Sunday, when the prisoners would be released from their cells to attend divine services in the jail hall. The vigilantes' plan was simple: they divided twenty-nine selected members into three groups, each of which could approach the jail from a different direction without causing comment. Next, a lookout was to be placed on the top of Telegraph Hill, where he could spy into the jail compound. When he saw the prisoners returning to their cells from the service he was to signal, and the three parties would storm the jail from different directions, thus dividing the defenders. A closed carriage behind two fine white horses was to stand innocently at the main gate, ready to carry away the prisoners.

The plan succeeded. Both the front and back doors of the jail were forced open. At pistol point the rescued convicts were led out and ordered into the vehicle. The driver lashed his horses and they galloped away. The thunder of hoofs on the DuPont Street wooden pavement, and the ominous tolling of the Monumental Fire Company's bell disturbed that quiet Sabbath. Crossing Washington and Clay streets just above Portsmouth Square, the carriage roared down Sacramento to Battery, where the crowd came running. Fifteen thousand people were said to have been massed between California and Pine watching the vigilance headquarters. One group carried a gigantic, blue satin flag, 9 by 7 feet, which had been presented to the committee by ladies of Mr. Mines's Trinity Church.[13]

Shops occupied the lower floor of the two-story frame headquarters. Above them, on the second floor, two large doors were situated under projecting beams for hoisting freight. Soon these doors swung open. On the thresholds stood two men in shirt sleeves, with their arms trussed. Whittaker, jaunty always, seemed composed. His boots were polished, his fine shirt open at the neck. Giant McKenzie wore the coarse shirt and gray pants of a workman. One reporter who watched said that no one who saw the big man's face as he looked at the crowd would ever forget his expression.

Ropes from pulley blocks on the overhead beams were adjusted around the men's necks. A few minutes later the two figures swung out over the street and were pulled up to the beams to struggle, chests heaving spasmodically. Then both hung quietly. If any police were present in the multitude they did nothing to stop the execution. A few of the hangmen at the open doors waved to friends in the crowd below. Hangings were losing their gravity and becoming more of an exhibition than a solemn duty.

Forty minutes later the bodies were lowered. By this time many of the spectators had wandered home. Those who remained heard that heavy McKenzie was pronounced dead, and his body was surrendered to the coroner. Life still persisted in the lighter body of Whittaker, so he was elevated for another twenty minutes.[14]

The details of this gruesome execution in violation of the law appeared in Australian newspapers, which also printed an account of a revealing San Francisco lawsuit. The plaintiff was a Sydney man named Peter Metcalf, a carpenter by trade, who had gone from Manchester, England, to Australia in 1841 and to California on MacNamara's *Maria* in 1849. In San Francisco he kept a public house and did some draying on the side while his wife and daughter took in washing. Now, in 1851, he brought suit for $20,000 damages against Felix Argenti, a banker and commission merchant who was one of the richest men in San Francisco. Argenti, as a member of the Committee of Vigilance, had surrounded Metcalf's residence with an armed guard one night. Demanding entrance, he routed the family out of bed and with a woman—the prosecution called her a common prostitute—they ransacked Metcalf's closets, trunks, and boxes, hunting for stolen goods.

Argenti defended his action by saying that he had employed Metcalf during the excitement of the last fire to haul away four loads of his furniture and goods. Metcalf had returned only three loads, and many of his lady's belongings were missing. While searching Metcalf's house Argenti found several trunks filled with fine merchandise for which Metcalf had no valid explanation. However, Argenti's mistress failed to identify anything belonging to her.

For a Vigilance Committee to sanction the arbitrary searching of a private citizen's residence demonstrated the abuse to be expected from such organizations. The court rightly found for the plaintiff, although only to the modest extent of $201 and costs, reduced later to six cents[15]—the kind of legalistic pruning which makes some people feel that lynching is justified.

During the trial for this outrage, Metcalf's counsel excoriated the Committee of Vigilance, claiming that it had done more to corrupt the civil government in San Francisco than all the rascals put together. Perhaps the original committeemen, he said, had meant well, but hell was paved with good intentions. Nor could the murders of Jenkins and Stuart be excused because the mob sanctioned them. He reminded the jury that in Jerusalem the mob had shouted for the execution of Jesus and the release of Barabbas, the robber. "For all we know," the prosecution charged, "Brannan may be a corruption of Barabbas."

Australian newspapers devoted column after column to this attorney's speech. The fact that the Committee of Vigilance "censored"—perhaps threatened—the law firm for accepting Metcalf's case was pounced on by Australian writers. Was there no right of trial by jury in liberty-loving America, no British justice entitling the accused to a legal defense?[16]

The same ship that brought the accounts of Whittaker's hanging and the Metcalf *vs.* Argenti case also brought the first Californians who had heard about the gold discoveries in Australia. It was an inauspicious time for them to arrive because the *Empire,* new organ of the working classes, had just told its readers that many well-to-do Australians who had left Sydney "untainted with any tendency toward democracy have been members of the Vigilants." Some of these unpardonable people were now coming back, bringing with them those despicable Californians, and the editor pontificated: "Let no door be opened to receive the blood-stained wretches."[17]

John Fairfax's more aristocratic readers must have felt equally shocked when they learned that T. B. MacManus—one of the four Irish rebels of '48, sentenced to be hanged, drawn, and quartered—had eluded his jailors on Van Diemen's Land and arrived safely in San Francisco on June 5, 1851. Instead of lynching him, the mob welcomed the traitor with a lavish public dinner and presented an engraved silver pitcher to the sea captain who helped the Irishman escape.[18]

Certainly all classes seemed to agree that Australians must conduct their gold rush very differently from the way Americans were doing.

The Irish Patriots Escape

The escape of MacManus in the summer of 1851 set a pattern for the remaining six patriots who had been convicted of treason and exiled to Tasmania. Four of them, sentenced in 1848 to be hanged, drawn, and quartered, were men of means. Being "gentlemen" they were not transported like 'tween-deck criminals on a convict ship. Instead, they sailed from the British Isles aboard naval vessels and were treated as befitted their class. Assigned a cabin to themselves under the poop deck, they received good food and wine and had an ample supply of books, pens, and paper. MacManus, a successful merchant in Liverpool before joining the revolution, brought along a backgammon board which helped while away many hours at sea. The prisoners also amused one another by reading aloud in Greek or Latin, by dancing Irish and Scottish reels.

Outside their cabin door a marine stood on duty. He allowed them to exercise on the deck above, provided that never more than two went together. After nine o'clock at night they were locked in their cabin until morning. At the end of the journey, sailing up the Derwent, they admired snowcapped Mount Wellington, the green hills below it, and the fragrance of flowering orchards, for October was springtime in Tasmania.

On their arrival in Hobart the naval captain delivered to Governor Denison written instructions to offer the prisoners tickets-of-leave, giving them liberty to live as they pleased, each in a separate district of Tasmania, provided they would sign paroles not to escape. The parolees must also promise not to confer with one another.

All accepted this liberal offer except the oldest of the seven. William Smith O'Brien was nearing fifty. A stately man with bushy, aggressive steel-gray hair and side-whiskers, he stood erect, his black silk stock tied tight and high on an erect, unbending neck. He belonged to a distinguished non-Catholic Irish family, had sat in the House of Commons, and had been a leader in the Young Ireland revolution of 1848. To sign a parole, he said, or to recognize the British Crown in any way, was unthinkable for one with his principles and beliefs. This moralistic quirk in his character, this insistence that he was always right, revealed itself in the contents of his portmanteau when seized before his arrest. It contained a carefully kept scrapbook of cuttings from the press, some of them very small, but all commending him.[1]

Governor Denison, having no alternative but to keep the inflexible man in confinement, assigned him to a two-roomed cottage on Maria Island off the precipitous east coast of Tasmania. The quarters, with a small garden, were as good as, but no better than, a field officer in the army might expect. A servant prepared O'Brien's dinners, and the Irishman's only complaint was that Denison neglected to supply him with his usual brand of cigars.[2]

This was in the late summer of 1849, when people in Hobart had become convinced that California gold was no hoax and the rush had commenced. O'Brien's friends saw their chance and they planned to smuggle him onto one of the vessels passing the island. They paid Captain William Ellis of the cutter Victoria—not to be confused with the ship by that name— £220 to pick O'Brien up on the vessel's way to California, promising an equal amount on O'Brien's delivery there. This was, indeed, an attractive fare for a captain who had been sentenced to the colonies for piracy. Thus, at an appointed time, along the storm-tossed bluffs, the Victoria hove to and lowered a small boat manned by three oarsmen. O'Brien waded out through the seaweed to climb aboard. To his dismay, guards suddenly appeared and carried him back to the cottage—kicking like a petulant child, his critics said.[3]

It was believed that Captain Ellis, after accepting the money, had revealed the plot to Governor Denison. However that may be, the Governor moved O'Brien to the dreaded jail at Port Arthur, where he could be kept securely. But instead of lodging him with other convicts, in the stone barracks, the Irish gentleman was assigned to a cottage formerly occupied by the hospital superintendent. Surrounded by hundreds of Britain's worst criminals, he was not in personal contact with them, but his windows overlooked the yard where prisoners were flogged on the triangle.

In these quarters O'Brien received a petition from 900 of his Irish sympathizers begging him to sign the parole. He did so in November, 1850, when the gold rush to California was at its height, and received permission to move to New Norfolk, twenty-one miles above Hobart. In this village he rented rooms at Elwin's Hotel on the left bank of the Derwent, across a wooden bridge from town, amid garden flowers, orchards, and hop fields. Strawberries and raspberries were already in season, dripping from the vines. Cherry-tree limbs bent with the weight of ruddy fruit. Roads and footpaths meandered among sweetbrier hedges. Here was a country resembling the best of his own Ireland, but Smith O'Brien professed to hate every green leaf of the new land, to love only his native sod. Although his sole restrictions were that he must be in his lodgings by ten o'clock at night and not meet with the Irish rebels, this was asking too much of a free spirit. He broke his parole almost weekly to meet secretly with the other "martyrs."[4]

Governor Denison learned about this infraction and punished the incorrigible O'Brien by sentencing him to hard labor in a convict camp above Port Arthur—serious punishment for a fifty-year-old statesman who had never done a day's work in his life. Colonial Irishmen cried out against the indignity and assembled in mass meetings of protest. Some demanded Governor Denison's recall. Others asked that all who had taken part in the Young Ireland revolution of 1848 be pardoned. Among the speakers, the ever-vociferous Dr. Lang's voice was heard. Whether criticizing his colleagues' morals or thundering for constructive civic reforms, he always attracted listeners. These protests may or may not have impressed Governor Denison. At any rate, he returned O'Brien to New Norfolk with a ticket-of-leave.[5]

The experiences of the other six convicted Irish traitors were more exciting. As has been said, the first to make a successful escape was Terrence Bellew MacManus. He accepted parole on landing at Hobart, when O'Brien rejected it, and was sent to New Norfolk. Here by the still waters of the Derwent he fished from the grassy banks and on hunt days joined the local gentry for a stirrup cup at "The Bush" as he might have done in Ireland. But he, too, was unhappy and, like O'Brien, violated the provisions of his parole to meet secretly with Irish confreres. For doing this he was sentenced, as O'Brien had been, to hard labor, though at a different encampment. His "hard labor" consisted of splitting shingles. Both men may have derived some consolation from hearing sympathizers play Irish tunes as police escorted them through Hobart but, although spared the humiliation of wearing the canary yellow of desperate convicts, they did have to don gray prison uniforms, each with a number on the back.

After two months MacManus was released, again on a ticket-of-leave, but he had not reformed. Learning that another of the seven convicted rebels, Thomas Francis Meagher, planned to marry a Tasmanian lass on February 22, 1851, up at Ross on the stage road north to Launceston, he decided to attend the nuptials. To disguise himself he plastered down his naturally curly hair, shaved off his sideburns, and posed as a sick man. In this counterfeit role he booked a seat on the four-horse stagecoach.[6]

The police learned about his plans and went to the wedding, but they made the mistake of arresting a genuine "sick man" who loyally refused to identify himself until after MacManus departed. However, the police followed the real MacManus and arrested him in Launceston. Pleading true illness now, MacManus was allowed to remain in his lodgings. Left alone by the constables, who were obviously lenient with Irishmen, he slipped out and boarded a vessel casting off for California.

The escape embarrassed Governor Denison, for it reflected on the efficiency of his administration. He worried about being unable to hold the remaining six rebels in his charge and wrote Earl Grey on March 22, 1851, stating that both people and police felt so much sympathy for Irish rebels that it would be difficult to keep them unless he was given authority to use more stringent methods.[7]

MacManus arrived in San Francisco on June 5, 1851. A committee including handsome Mayor Geary, scheming Senator Broderick, and wealthy Sam Brannan as well as others arranged a demonstration of welcome. In the plaza, speeches and cheers eulogized the Young Ireland revolution and the seven condemned rebels. The *Alta California* printed an editorial on the prospect of Australian independence from Great Britain. At a grand banquet in Happy Valley, MacManus sat among city officials, state political figures, and officers of the United States Army.

The newly appointed British consul, George Aikens, reported these proceedings to Governor Denison, saying that he could not learn the name of the vessel that brought the rebel. (MacManus probably came on the *President,* which docked at Monterey, California.) The consul also sent information about an American brig that was preparing to change her name to *White Squall,* go to Sydney under the English flag, and aid other Irish rebels to escape.[8]

Since MacManus was feted in San Francisco just before the lynching of Jenkins, it is obvious that Californians did not frown on escaped convicts—provided the crime was political. It should be noted, too, that many of those who attended the welcoming dinners and rallies were Southern Democrats evidently courting the Irish vote in a struggle against the pro-Northern wing of their party.

Ironically, a Tasmanian in San Francisco named Thomas Burns took advantage of the enthusiasm for Irish patriots by christening his rooming house the "MacManus Welcome." It was a disreputable dive offering lodgers fifty beds in a long loft, and a few single rooms with padlocks. The worst of the

Sydney Ducks congregated here, and on July 2 the Committee of Vigilance escorted Burns and two other undesirables to the harbor, where they were put aboard a vessel bound for Launceston.[9]

An even more ironic act was perpetrated by MacManus himself. Within the year Captain Ellis, commanding a new craft, the *Callao*, sailed into San Francisco. MacManus and six of his Irish friends, claiming—incorrectly—to be delegates of the Vigilance Committee, boarded his ship, kidnaped him, rowed ashore, and threatened to hang him unless he returned the £220 he had received in part payment for agreeing to bring O'Brien to California, although none of them had personally advanced the money.[10]

The second of the seven Irish rebels who succeeded in escaping to America was Thomas Francis Meagher, eldest son of a wealthy member of Parliament. On his arrival as a prisoner in Van Diemen's Land, Governor Denison kept him on shipboard until after dark. Then with a parole duly signed, the Governor shipped him up the Launceston turnpike to Campbelltown, a village with one main street, four hotels, a shop or two, a jail and stocks. Being at liberty inside the district to which he was assigned, Meagher moved seven miles down the road to Ross, a hamlet more to his liking. Here he boarded with a congenial family, hunted and fished with newly made friends, and attended jolly drinking parties at which he recited his poems, caricatured stuffy officials, and, with youthful self-appreciation, delighted in calling himself "O'Meagher." He married a local lass, as has been noted, and established a "fairy cottage" on Lake Sorell fifteen miles west of town. With sailboat, saddle horses, a gigantic Irish wolfhound given him by MacManus, books, servants, and sherry at his disposal, he entertained his friends.

Punishment indeed for treason!

The lake was seven miles long and three of the districts to which Meagher's fellow traitors were limited touched its shores. Thus the Irishmen could evade the terms of their paroles and meet, dine, sing, and sail together on the lake's sparkling waters. His fellow rebel, John Mitchel, described seeing Meagher at the tiller of his boat, healthily bronzed. Beside him on a crimson cushion sat the "fair and graceful" Mrs. Meagher.

The exiles organized horseback excursions to gallop beneath the tall, fragrant eucalypti where brilliant parrots flashed across the forest aisles. "The ladies ride like demons," poetic Mitchel wrote, "and thundering home in the moonlight, they send the opossums scampering to the tops of the trees." But always Meagher, like O'Brien and MacManus, dreamed of a free Ireland, the excitement of revolt, the exhilaration of enthusiastic crowds. Constantly all of them talked and planned escape. So, in 1852—only a few weeks before his wife expected a baby —Meagher broke his parole in an ingenious, if questionable, manner. On January 3 he wrote the police that he would end his parole as of noon next day, adding that, should they consider it their duty to apprehend him prior to that time, he would regard himself as fully absolved from "the restraint which my word of honor to the Government at present inflicts."[11]

After the letter was sent, Meagher's friends remained with him, "partaking of some refreshment," and engaged in merry conversation while strolling through the bush surrounding the cottage and along the shore of the lake. At five in the afternoon a servant reported that two constables awaited Meagher at the house. Meagher immediately mounted his horse and, riding within musket range of the police, shouted: "I am O'Meagher. Catch me if you can." Reining his horse away, he and his party galloped into the open woods.[12]

A fugitive could escape easily at this time. The whole world had learned that Australia's goldfields exceeded California's, and the rush to Victoria had become chaotic with countless strangers scurrying hither and yon. In this babel of eager fortune hunters Meagher was smuggled to Waterhouse Island in Bass Strait. There he boarded a vessel bound for Pernambuco, where he transshipped to New York, arriving on May 26, 1852. In America, patriots received him with rejoicing, and his escape also pleased many Tasmanian editors who, as has been seen, sympathized with the Irish. However, some of his fellow parolees deplored the tricky method he had used to break his word of honor. To erase this blot from his record, Meagher presented his own case to a "tribunal of American officers" who, he reported, declared that all the conditions of his parole had been honorably observed.

Meagher's baby son died in Tasmania on June 8, less than two weeks after his father had arrived in New York. The bereaved mother sailed for Ireland, where she lived with her father-in-law's family—visiting her husband once in New York —until she died on May 9, 1854, aged twenty-two.[13] Meagher became an American citizen and married an American girl in 1856; as the Civil War loomed, he organized a company of New York zouaves. In Washington, D.C., just before the Battle of Bull Run, he was reported to be strutting along Pennsylvania Avenue in a uniform covered with gold lace. Riding out to battle on a good horse, he was obviously drunk, and vociferously eager to kill "damned rebs." Within a year be became a brigadier general, fighting valiantly under a great green banner embroidered with a gold harp; beside it waved the Stars and Stripes. Meagher's Irish Brigade became famous for the fury of its charges and infamous for its delinquency. Once, in his cups, Meagher challenged his surgeon to a duel, which was settled amicably when both sobered. President Andrew Johnson appointed Meagher secretary as well as acting governor of Montana Territory. Out there, on July 1, 1867, he mysteriously fell off a steamboat at Fort Benton and drowned, aged forty-three. Some said he was drunk, but as he was unpopular in the West this may have been gossip. Later it was reported that a man who died in 1913 confessed on his deathbed that he had murdered Meagher.[14]

In 1852, about the time Meagher escaped to America, people in Australia were saying that the vile practice of lynching had spread from San Francisco to other California towns. Two robbers, reputedly members of a Sydney gang, had been strung up at a camp near Stockton. Shortly thereafter another man, said to be from Sydney, was arrested for forgery in the town itself. Australian papers also reported that in Sacramento a Sydney man named Henry George, who had been indicted by a grand jury, was taken from jail prior to his trial and lynched. These continued reports increased the already strong prejudice against Americans, and the United States consul in Melbourne (first to be appointed in the growing city) warned incoming Californians to expect trouble down under.[15]

In the Australian mining areas threats of California lawlessness and American crookedness started almost at once. Tricky traders were accused of using faulty scales, of weighing "dust" in small quantities, in order to take advantage of the fractional ounces. Cardsharps played the same tricks as they did in California. One of the most flagrant was for the dealer to have a confederate among the players who, as the dealer glanced away, peeped under a face-down card so that all could see it and bet accordingly. Later, when the dealer finally turned up that card it had somehow changed, and all the cheaters were neatly cheated. Australians, like Californians, complained about these tricks—and some enjoyed them too.

In Australia, as in California, men caught stealing were flogged by the mob and otherwise manhandled. At Ballarat a suspected robber was held over a hot fire, but whether Americans incited such summary punishment is open to question. Certainly the British commissioner at Bendigo reported: "A number of American adventurers, who had come in from California diggings, were inciting the people to set up Judge Lynch." Lieutenant Governor La Trobe wrote to Earl Grey that the diggings had become a mixed multitude of returned Californians together with the most profligate people of the colonies, including expirees from Van Diemen's Land. Desperate crimes, he wrote, were being committed among the tents, huts, and workings. An American, Charlie Ferguson, reported that no one was safe outside his own tent after dark in Bendigo. Sandbagging and garroting were common, and the burial ground looked like a plowed field.[16]

These horrendous accounts of developing lawlessness were contradicted by twenty-two-year-old Lord Robert Cecil who, as Third Marquis of Salisbury, would be four times prime minister of Great Britain. His statements disclose how a politician's vision may be shaped by his prejudices. He was positive that he observed a great difference between the respect for law in the Australian and Californian goldfields. Of course, he had not visited the American diggings but he dared say that, instead of the murders, rapes, daily robberies, lynch law, and Committee of Vigilance in California, the Australian mines had "less crime than in a large English town." He stated further that he found "more order and civility than I have myself witnessed in my own native village of Hatfield"—an assertion differing widely from those of Lieutenant Governor La Trobe and others.

Lord Robert attributed the difference between Australia and California to the fact that the former was a monarchy ruled from above, the latter a democracy ruled from below. He based his opinion of the Australian diggings on a trip he made to Mount Alexander in a passenger coach with six companions, one of them a woman who "supplied the shrieking whenever the cart dipped sideways into a hole." With the jaundiced eyes of his class and generation, he described an American passenger on the coach as "a coarse, hideous, dirty looking man, without an attempt at ornament or neatness in his dress; yet he wore in his ears a pair of earrings about the size and shape of a wedding ring. He wore a pair of pistols in his belt, and the words, 'put a bullet through his brain' were constantly in his mouth." The future political peer did confide in his diary, however, that highway robbery was much more prevalent in Australia than the government liked to admit.[17]

Many people complained that the worst thing about the gold rush in Victoria was the proximity of Van Diemen's Land, just across Bass Strait, where British convicts were still being unloaded. Australians now protested as bitterly about criminals coming to their goldfields from the island colony as the Californians had about Sydneyites. The Victorians copied California's 1850 Importation of Criminals Act by passing their Convicts Prevention Act, which imposed a fine for captains of vessels that crossed Bass Strait with any passengers who lacked an absolutely free pardon.* Yet despite this new and stringent law, the third of the seven condemned Irish traitors made his escape from Tasmania.

Patrick O'Donohue's life in exile had been harder than his compatriots' because he was the only one of them who lacked independent means of support. A bookworm, he relished good literature, read the Greek and Latin classics, memorized the Sermon on the Mount and the Epistle of St. James. Governor Denison allowed him to remain in Hobart on parole, but supporting himself there proved difficult for O'Donohue. Trying futilely to practice law, he decided in desperation to publish a newspaper called the *Irish Exile*. Friends, knowing of his outspoken hatred of English rule, warned him against this venture, but, as might be expected, he printed seditious articles that earned him repeated sentences in the local jail. Soon he committed an even worse offense. Like the other rebels he violated his parole by visiting O'Brien and MacManus at New Norfolk. Like them, too, he was condemned to Port Arthur, but having no money, he was assigned to the common barracks, where his ribs were broken during a fight with another criminal. In this sorry plight, guards carried him to one of the penitentiary's iron pallets in the hospital ward. Here he was dressed in a blue flannel robe and the warden allowed him a book—a solace that may have saved his life.

After serving his term, O'Donohue returned to Hobart, still bound by his ticket-of-leave. He found the city greatly changed by the gold rush to Victoria. New discoveries on the Ovens River in 1852 added to the excitement. Many people were moving north to Launceston, Tasmania's jumping-off port for Melbourne, and opportunities for jobs up there seemed excellent. O'Donohue received permission to ride the stage to Launceston, where the police would check him in. But when the coach arrived, he was not on board. Neither the driver nor the redcoated postilion could say when he had escaped—perhaps at

---

* The California law was passed on April 11, 1850. Note that the gold discoveries in Victoria during June and July of 1851 which resulted in the rush from Van Diemen's Land seem to have prompted the Hobart *Colonial Times* to reprint the California statute on August 1, 1851.

one of the horse-changing stations, or perhaps he had jumped out while the coach rumbled along the highway. In any event, he must be hiding somewhere in one of the numerous villages, manors, or sheep stations along the 120-mile road, or in the woods brilliant now, in October, with the spring growth of sweet-scented acacia blossoms.

For six weeks O'Donohue's whereabouts were unknown. Then on December 22, 1852, he knocked at the door of Irish friends in the gold-crazed city of Melbourne. He was hungry and had endured harrowing experiences. The details cannot be verified, but he had reached Launceston by some means and stowed away on a passenger ship bound for Melbourne. After clearing port, the little vessel sailed for thirty miles down the Tamor River before entering Bass Strait, and police were apt to climb aboard anywhere. Next came a hundred miles of the roughest water in the world. Ship timbers groaned under the strain. So did seasick passengers. Loose cargo rocked and thumped while captain and crew prowled everywhere putting things in place. They all knew the penalty for permitting a passenger to cross in violation of the Convicts Prevention Act, but O'Donohue remained well hidden.[18]

At last Queenscliff Head emerged above the stormy waters. A little fort stood here and more police might inspect the craft, but if they did O'Donohue escaped detection. Another forty miles of calm water in Port Phillip must be crossed to reach Melbourne anchorage at Hobson's Bay, packed now with gold-rush ships. This year 2,657 vessels had anchored here as compared with only 712 last year.[19] Such a concourse of vessels taxed the watchful eyes of the police and made it easier for O'Donohue to land unobserved.

Two towns of tents and shanties had mushroomed on the shore, Williamstown on the west of the Yarra Yarra River, Sandridge on the east. A stone bridge spanned the stream's mouth between them. Both communities were ports of entry to Melbourne, and it is not known which of them O'Donohue used. From Sandridge north to Melbourne was only two miles. Bullock drays traveled that route, but in wet weather the beasts sometimes sank to their bellies in quaking mud. Most travelers

preferred to ride a little side-wheel steamer up the Yarra Yarra
—a circuitous ten-mile journey on a filthy meandering stream
rank with the stench of sheep manure. Sheds for washing wool
lined both banks, and bloody pelts hung on the fences.[20]

Melbourne, a village of 4,479 people in 1841, had expanded
suddenly to a town of 39,000—larger than San Francisco[21]—
and would reach a population of 139,916 by the end of the
decade. Flinders Street, where incoming travelers landed, had
been macadamized. It paralleled the river and was lined with
barges and piles of tarpaulin-draped freight. Elizabeth Street
ran north up the valley and in times of flood lay waist-deep in
stagnant water.[22] A jostling crowd of Italians, Swedes, Swiss,
and Dutchmen elbowed past lascars, Manila men, dusky
Malays, Chinese in pigtails, Californians in Jim Crow hats
(sometimes called "wide-awakes"), black aborigines in blankets, and a surprising number of American Negroes, probably
escaped slaves.[23] A fugitive could disappear in such a mob, but
even here an Irish political prisoner must use his wits. Many of
these immigrants hoped to evade the law against foreign diggers by claiming to be British subjects. Thus the Chinese said
they lived in Hong Kong. Negroes with unmistakable South
Carolina accents maintained that they "knew massa in Bar-
badoes." Even the Yankees "guessed" they came from Canada.[24]

In this human kaleidoscope, Patrick O'Donohue avoided questions and made his way to his friends' house. He found them,
like everyone else, excited over making money, but they welcomed and fed him, gave him a place to rest, and surreptitiously
bought him a passage on the *Earl of Lincoln*, bound for Callao,
Peru, paying the captain an extra pound for the accommodation. The captain, suspecting something crooked in the deal,
gave back the passage money but kept the bribe, and nobody
dared complain.

Another captain accepted a fare to Sydney for "the mysterious
passenger." Thence O'Donohue proceeded on the *Oberon* to
Tahiti, where he found an American bark, the *Otranto*, whose
captain agreed, for $1,000, to take him to San Francisco, far
from the clutches of British law. Within a year the restless
fellow turned up in Boston, where he was held to bail for chal-

lenging the chairman of a festival held in honor of Meagher, who had arrived ahead of him.[25] These Irish rebels always rebelled against one another. Any three of them were said to have four opinions, and John Mitchel even went so far as to say that, if Ireland ever got her independence, he and his followers would have to hang O'Brien.[26]

John Mitchel, trained in the law and the son of a Unitarian minister, was the last of the Irish martyrs to escape. Thirty-five years old, he stood 5 feet 10 inches tall, had dark hair and nearsighted eyes that could scarcely recognize people across a large room. He was a brilliant, opinionated man who resented discipline. At school he found his lessons so easy he neglected them, making poor grades, but he immersed himself in Scott, Shakespeare, and Carlyle. Much impressed by Gibbon's *Decline and Fall of the Roman Empire*, he determined to aid in the decline and fall of the British Empire by establishing a fiery newspaper named the *United Irishman*. A British court sentenced him to fourteen years' exile in Van Diemen's Land. Suffering from asthma,[27] Mitchel arrived in Hobart in such ill health that Governor Denison permitted him to live with John Martin, another convicted Irish rebel who was wealthy in his own right.[28] The two had been schoolmates in Ireland, where Martin had married Mitchel's sister.[29] In Van Diemen's Land both signed the usual parole and purchased a farm in the highlands two miles out of Bothwell—a village 46 miles from Hobart, with sixty or seventy buildings, a church, four public houses, and a library they admitted to be better than they would have found in a similar community in Ireland.[30]

The gold rush to Victoria had not begun when they moved to the farm. This was months before MacManus, Meagher, and O'Donohue escaped to America. At first Mitchel and Martin seemed reconciled to starting a new life together, and Mitchel sent to Ireland for his wife and five children. They arrived in June, 1851. In the cool, hilly pastures the sheep thrived and the clear bracing air restored Mitchel's health.[31] With Martin, he violated the spirit of his parole by riding twenty miles to Lake Sorell for the gay reunions with Meagher, mentioned previously. But Mitchel, like his Irish fellows, failed to find contentment, especially after MacManus and Meagher absconded. Mitchel became even more restless when a young Irishman named Patrick J. Smyth arrived from New York, ostensibly as roving correspondent for Horace Greeley's *Tribune*. A commanding figure with a mustache and chin whiskers, Smyth wore a cloak over his frock coat. Twenty-five years old, the son of a wealthy Dublin tanner, he had participated in the 1848 insurrection and had escaped to America before being arrested. Enjoying mystery and intrigue, he fancied being a secret agent for the Irish Directory in New York. His real mission in Australia was to liberate the convicted rebels.

Smyth's plan for Mitchel's escape was daring enough for any Irish adventurer, and the parolee accepted it at once. First Mitchel purchased the local magistrate's gray horse, the fastest animal in the district, paying the princely price of £80.[32] Then, with young Smyth, he rode from his farm to the police station. The two men tied their horses to the hitching posts, walked in and confronted the magistrate at his desk. Mitchel announced formally that he had come to cancel his parole. Saying this, he turned abruptly and both men, with hands on pistols in their pockets, strode past the astonished police and rode away. As soon as they were out of sight in the Tasmanian woods, they exchanged coats and horses, then separated.[33]

Smyth rode south toward Hobart, hoping to lay a false trail with the fast gray horse. Mitchel jogged north, planning to be picked up on the wild south shore of Bass Strait by one of MacNamara's vessels. Smyth had made arrangements with this Irish magnate whose ships passed without suspicion through the gold-rush traffic funneling into Melbourne.[34]

Midwinter had settled over the Tasmanian highlands as Mitchel rode north. Gusts of snow and sleet pelted his face and froze in crackling sheets on his trousers, but friendly shepherds gave him food and shelter. For almost a month he hid in the hills, lurking along Bass Strait, watching for a rescue ship but seeing only police patrol boats. Finally a message came from Smyth. The plan was abandoned! A better and safer scheme had been worked out for Mitchel to escape from Hobart at the other end of the island.

THE IRISH PATRIOTS ESCAPE

To go to Hobart, Mitchel disguised himself as a priest. In clerical coat, standing collar, and broad hat he boarded the southbound mail stage. Friendly passengers accosted him in Latin. Mitchel proved their equal in this discipline, but he became embarrassed when asked personal questions about the bishop who had lost his yacht to California-bound convicts.[35]

Smyth in the meantime had brought Mitchel's family—there were six children now—to Hobart, where he ensconced them in the one place a priest would not enter, the Freemason Hotel. Mitchel, in priest's garb, lodged elsewhere. Smyth engaged passage for the Mitchel family on MacNamara's regular passenger brig *Emma* for Sydney.[36] The *Emma*'s captain, like her owner, sympathized with Irish exiles, and it was arranged for Mitchel to board the *Emma* from a small boat down the Derwent after customs and police had cleared the vessel. Other passengers who saw the strange "Mr. Wright" climb up over the side in midstream believed that he had missed the ship in Hobart.

Mitchel had great fun on board arguing against himself and upholding the government,[37] but his wife had difficulty preventing the children from recognizing their father. As the coast of Tasmania slipped below the horizon, poetic Mitchel wrote in his journal: "The last of my island prison visible to me is a broken line of blue peaks over the Bay of Fires. Adieu, then, beauteous island, full of sorrow and gnashing teeth; island of fragrant forests, and bright rivers, and fair women; island of chains and scourges, and blind brutal rage and passion."[38]

In Sydney, Mitchel stayed secretly at MacNamara's house. To obtain passage was very easy, because gold seekers were coming to Australia from California now and ships had to make the return passage with empty berths, but Mitchel encountered an unexpected obstacle. To escape suspicion, his wife and children sailed on one vessel and in July he was snugly established in the cabin of another, hoping to overtake them in Honolulu. Instead of sailing, however, the crew of the ship he had boarded deserted for the Bathurst diggings, and police came down to search the vessel.[39]

Luckily MacNamara received warning and smuggled the

Irishman back to his residence on shore. Not until October 12, 1853, did Mitchel arrive in San Francisco, to be greeted as Mac-Manus had been with a banquet attended by the Governor.[40] But Mitchel was no gold seeker. Instead, he had become a professional rebel and, at the first opportunity, crossed with his family to New York, where he was welcomed by comrades playing the rollicking Irish tune "Garryowen." Though he always hated the idea of being a slave to any man, he believed in Negro slavery, advocated reopening the slave trade, and sided with the Confederacy during the Civil War. Two of his sons died fighting for the Stars and Bars. Ironically enough, both had become the "damned rebs" Meagher wanted so much to kill.

Of the seven convicted Irish martyrs, only three now remained in Australia. Elderly William Smith O'Brien refused to make a second attempt to escape. John Martin, aged thirty,[41] abided by his parole until pardoned. The last and youngest of them all, twenty-five-year-old Kevin Izod O'Doherty had been a medical student when convicted for publishing the *Irish Tribune*. On arrival in Hobart he signed the parole and found employment in St. Mary's Hospital, where he soon distinguished himself.[42] When unconditionally pardoned in 1856, as all the rebels who remained in Tasmania were, he returned to Dublin and finished his medical studies. After that he moved back to Australia, where he became a leading physician and a member of the colonial legislature. He returned to Ireland once more and was elected to the House of Commons, but after a single term he decided to make his home under the Southern Cross, where he achieved fame as one of the colony's most eminent citizens. He died there in 1905.[43]

16

Are Californians
Dangerous Revolutionists?

The year 1853 was notable in the Pacific. Thousands of vessels scudded hither and yon among palm-fringed islands. British ships sailed freely into Chinese ports after the Opium War, and many other nations were now acquiring concessions. Most important of all, Commodore Matthew C. Perry, with four men-of-war, headed for Yeddo Bay determined to part Japan's bamboo curtain and force that ancient civilization to trade with the commercial world. The Australian gold rush added more sails—and some steamboats—to the unprecedented activity. Ships came to Melbourne from all parts of the globe. Many from the United States rounded the Cape of Good Hope, thus avoiding stormy Cape Horn. Moreover, they made the trip in three to four months—less time than was previously needed for the voyage to San Francisco.

Only a small proportion of the people coming to Australia were Californians. But the Californians' bad reputation, lawlessness, revolutionary background, aggression against Mexico, and crusading determination to save the world for mobocracy, by force if need be, tainted all Americans, just as the few ex-convicts from Australia had tainted all immigrants in San Francisco from down under. Of the first 100,000 gold seekers to reach Victoria, only 9 percent came from the United States, and most of these were not American-born. Indeed, many were disappointed Australians returning home.[1] One Californian, Charles Ferguson, who sailed from San Francisco on the *Don Juan* in 1852, wrote that his fellow passengers included one

American with another man's wife, several Englishmen, and a pack of ex-convicts from Van Diemen's Land who were being sent back by the Committee of Vigilance—a tough lot, he said, who constantly swore to get revenge on Californians in general and San Franciscans in particular. Ferguson himself was a questionable character, not above making a sly dollar or participating in a revolution should the Americans down under decide to take over.

The *Don Juan* was a half-wreck salvaged from the deserted gold-rush fleet. She had lain out of water until her timbers shrank and leaked at every seam. Passengers had to pump constantly, until the planks tightened. When they complained that they had paid for passage, not for work, the captain told them peremptorily to take their choice—sink or swim, pump or go to hell before eight bells struck.

Close to the equator the *Don Juan* was becalmed, as were most sailing ships. Provisions became scarce. Men grumbled like beasts and bellowed for water. To break the monotony and cheer voyagers, the sailors trailed ropes overside for swimmers to cling to. Small boats were lowered and passengers rowed across the swells until the blue peter, run up on the mainmast, called all back on board. When rains came, everybody caught fresh water to drink, and also for washing clothes. Soon shirts and drawers flapped and billowed on lines from stem to stern.[2]

The ceremony when crossing the equator was new to Americans who had crossed only the Plains, but it was an old story to Australians. Days before passing the invisible line, preparations were made to initiate the Californians. These victims watched ruefully while sailors converted a spare sail into a pool on deck and rigged a barber chair in front of it. On the fatal day most novices hid under bunks or high in the rigging, but all were caught and dragged forward with shouts of glee. Then, as they waited, Father Neptune emerged from below the bowsprit, climbed up over the fo'c'sle and, trident in hand, hailed the captain, who invariably welcomed him on board. Next, the bearded figure jumped down on deck and inspected the captured initiates. One by one they were seated in the chair, to have their faces dobbed with tar and shaved off with a barrel hoop. Each in turn was finally tipped back into the water-filled sail, and then allowed to wallow out. An initiated traveler now, he delighted in hazing those behind him.

Like many other poorly equipped and overloaded vessels racing from California to Australia, the *Don Juan* stopped at Tahiti for fresh vegetables to stave off dreaded scurvy. Many of the passengers went ashore, were arrested, locked up for the night, and released in the morning to continue their voyage. Skimming along in the southern trade winds, the sails overhead bent like summer clouds, booms squealed against the masts. Men said, "Girls in Australia must be hauling on the tow rope."

Day after day the glare of high noon on the rumpled, white-capped sea was relieved by a black velvet night powdered with stars. At dawn one morning, Norfolk Island rose mistily against the pale sky. At this dread penal station for Australian incorrigibles, the *Don Juan* stopped to purchase more vegetables. This time those passengers who had criminal records preferred to stay on board. Ferguson landed and was escorted through the notorious dungeons by soldiers of the 99th Regiment who seemed to derive grim satisfaction from the cruelty of punishments here. They explained that bad offenders were put in a dark cell which filled slowly with water. A prisoner must pump almost constantly to keep from drowning—as bad as the first week on the *Don Juan*, yes siree![3]

California diggers who arrived in Melbourne during late April and early May of 1853 found a line of incoming vessels waiting to cross Port Phillip Bay and then Hobson's Bay above it. Each ship in turn hoisted a signal flag for a pilot, who sailed out from the little fort on Queenscliff Head and guided the craft through the great inland seas. Two days were usually consumed before reaching the Melbourne anchorage. Here on every side stood hundreds of vessels flying the flags of all nations— whalers, steamers, American clippers, emigrant ships, fine East Indiamen, all stalled for want of seamen. It was worse than San Francisco in 1849.

Customs and health officers in small boats met each ship as it arrived. They quarantined one vessel from Liverpool. On her voyage 101 passengers had died of "ship's fever," and no survivor was permitted to land until the malady subsided.

The other big hulls in port were surrounded by venders in small boats offering to sell notions, fresh meat, and pastry. Petty merchants looked up at the rows of faces along ships' rails and shouted the prices they would pay for pistols—the one commodity that seemed to have great value here. Passengers threw soiled bedding and smoke-blackened cooking utensils overboard, now that the long voyage was finally ended. No more daily rations issued at the cuddy to be cooked as best it could be by their own mess 'tween decks. Here and there a splash showed where a deserting sailor had jumped overboard. Boats always seemed ready to pick up the dripping fellows and smuggle them to shore.[4]

One Yankee gold seeker who landed with other American boys at Sandridge described rowing past a vessel loaded with Mrs. Caroline Chisholm's "invoice of young women" who waved handkerchiefs at them and received a hearty cheer. After months at sea, these lads were eager to laugh at anything. Bathing machines hauled by big horses into the surf off St. Kilda beach excited them, especially when a scantily clothed female popped out into the protecting water. The Sandridge–Melbourne road was macadamized now, and the boys marveled at the sight of twenty-yoke bullock teams, but even more laughable were the first horsemen they met. These strange fellows rode with their feet thrust through short stirrups and seemed to urge their mounts forward by "jumping in their saddles."

The New Englanders found Melbourne a dirty city and attributed its tolerance for grime to Britishers' familiarity with the bituminous smoke of old England. However, the boys pronounced the barmaids pretty and the 300-acre botanical gardens more beautiful than Boston Common. Most noticeable of all was the Australians' peculiar talk. Americans chuckled when a fellow referred to a bloody bad meal, a bloody nice woman, or a bloody good sermon.[5]

Of all the Yankees who came to Melbourne in 1853, the most

notable was George Francis Train, a brash twenty-four-year-old with great ability and greater conceit. He always wanted to be the center of every activity and never stuck to anything long. Later, in London, he would become a notorious champion of democracy, advocating cheap newspapers, penny postage, and street railways (the poor man's cab). Still later, in the United States, he would crusade for the democratic North against an aristocratic Confederacy. Always seeking notice, he attended Lincoln's second inaugural ball with his wife, whose hair was elaborately powdered with gold. He vociferously recommended tolerant reconstruction for the conquered South, involved himself in the Union Pacific financial scandal, became a candidate for president of the United States in 1872, and eventually died penniless.

If the Americans fomented a revolution to further democracy in Australia, George Francis Train might be expected to take part. However, the brash young man had not come to Melbourne for that purpose. Instead, he came as junior partner in the firm of Caldwell, Train & Company, with a shipload of goods, and a plan to establish an office as importer, commission agent, and underwriter. He was backed by a wealthy uncle in New England who happened to be a partner of Donald McKay, the builder of newly designed clipper ships that were amazing the world of sail. One hundred and twenty-five of these ocean greyhounds had been launched in the United States this year of 1853. Already they had reduced the speed of transportation between Britain and Australia to approximately 85 days. Within another year, one of the clippers would set the record at 63.[6]

These New England seagoing merchants had traded successfully in California and knew—or thought they knew—what was salable in a gold rush. Moreover, the British Navigation Acts had become more liberal in 1851, and Americans now sought the open markets. Only 3 Yankee vessels arrived in Melbourne in 1851, but this number increased to 13 in 1852 and to 134 in 1853. Australians seemed particularly anxious to buy American mechanical devices like sewing machines, stoves, canned vegetables, and India-rubber clothing.[7] Strangest of all imports were American portable houses, outselling those made in nearby Hobart. American lumber did well, being easier to work than the iron-textured Australian wood.

Train arrived in Melbourne just before the Queen's birthday, when a grand celebration was planned. He elbowed his way through the mob at the Flinders Street landing without realizing that some people feared a demonstration by lynch-hungry Californians. Exploring Elizabeth Street, he found the roadways inches deep in red dust which filled the air, thick as a London fog. An enterprising American on a water cart sprinkled the streets in front of the homes of residents willing to pay for the service— a custom practiced in San Francisco. In the sweltering sun many people drove past Train in two-wheeled dogcarts. He had imported "New York buggy-waggons" with curtains and tops which, he hoped, would sell here to advantage.

In the shopping district, he noticed a predominance of females. Bonnets and parasols outnumbered California wide-awake hats. Most of the men had evidently gone to the mines. He noticed, too, that ladies of the better classes wore simple attire. Here and there among them rustled the spouse of some digger from the creeks in gaudy colors, gaudier perfume, and jewels fit for an Oriental princess.

Over a shop window Train saw a sign reading: "GOLD! GOLD bought here! The highest prices given for gold." In another, a mound of yellow dust stood among scattered piles of sovereigns and bank notes. In a third window, there was a skull with a bullet hole in it; nearby lay a revolver and a pile of nuggets. This display was labeled: "BEWARE IN TIME."

Everybody was friendly, wanted to talk. All repeated stories of lavish squandering by the new-rich. One man was said to have shod his horse with gold. Another lighted his cigars with £5 notes. A third had set up champagne bottles like tenpins for his friends to strike down. Actors in the Queen's Theatre were sometimes pelted with nuggets.[8] This outdid California!

As in San Francisco, wages had reached astronomical heights. Carpenters and masons received £2 a day, and the price of staples had increased accordingly. One man complained that he used to pay a shilling for a meal and leave a penny for the waiter, but now the same meal cost him 12 shillings. People with fixed incomes had become virtual paupers, compelled to sacrifice their treasures to middlemen who, in turn, made big profits selling to the diggers such items as gold and silver watches, patent lever-clocks, rugs, ladies' dresses, and gentlemen's tailored coats.

Caldwell, Train & Company profited 200 percent on their shipment and ordered more goods from Boston. Three days after Train arrived in Melbourne he was nominated a member of the Chamber of Commerce and began urging Americans to join. He added handsomely to his income by earning big commissions for selling other shippers' goods. His champagne luncheons for customers became famous. He claimed a net profit of $95,000 the first year, and of this he spent $60,000 for the construction of the finest building in the city, a warehouse on Flinders Street, east of Elizabeth, to store material shipped from Boston. He also built a six-story warehouse at the Sandridge anchorage, erected docks there, and promoted a railroad connecting them with Melbourne. (An enabling act had been passed prior to his arrival.)[9]

Train also organized a fire company (an enterprise that had failed in 1852), sent to Boston for two engines, and became secretary of one of the brigades. He completely reorganized the Criterion Hotel on Collins Street, establishing a commercial exchange in one of its rooms where market prices and import notices were posted regularly. Merchants and commission men from all eastern American cities as well as from Great Britain congregated here. Train swaggered among them garbed in immaculate clothes and swinging an obviously expensive cane. He insisted that the proprietor serve iced drinks, the ice having been brought on Train's vessels from Massachusetts. In short order, the barroom installed gigantic mirrors on the walls and stately decanters on a marble counter. American barkeepers amazed the natives by nonchalantly tossing iridescent crystal from hand to hand, then mixing strange drinks by slinging the liquid ceilingward in a great rainbow without a splash.[10]

Perhaps Train's most lasting innovation was the importation of American vehicles. Concord coaches with their gay colors, light hickory wheel spokes, and thorough braces——those peculiar leather springs that allowed comfort with speed—differed greatly from the bulky Australian wagons. Freeman Cobb, a little lame man from Boston, brought two of these coaches with American drivers and in July, 1853, operated his first stage line from Sandridge to Melbourne. Train claimed that he loaned Cobb the money to begin this business. However that may be, by January, 1854, Cobb & Company coaches with American drivers were leaving the Criterion Hotel on regular schedule for the Bendigo diggings. Each vehicle accommodated fourteen passengers inside and on top.[11] Freeman Cobb soon sold out for a reported $250,000, returned to Massachusetts, and sat in the state senate during 1864 and 1865.* The name of his firm, "Cobb & Co.," remained famous for seventy years as Australia's great coaching chain.

Melbourne, when Train arrived, had two newspapers, one liberal and the other conservative. The *Argus* championed the diggers and attacked the Lieutenant Governor at every opportunity, demanding more democracy and the "unlocking" of grazing estates for conversion into farms. In 1849 the editor had trod on graziers' toes by trying to start a gold rush to their lands adjacent to Melbourne. The *Herald* had quashed that rush, but the feud between the papers persisted. One of the first things that Train must have noticed in the *Argus* when he arrived was a bold advertisement:

WANTED
A Lieutenant-Governor. Apply to the people of Victoria.
Wanted
A Colonial Secretary. Apply to the same.

Was the *Argus* suggesting that the people of Victoria take over Her Majesty's prerogative? Train might well believe that such a statement foreboded a revolution. The newspaper's editor, Edward Wilson, was always outspoken in his opposition to the big landholders. A brave man on paper, he was one of those

---

* The *Australian Encyclopaedia* (East Lansing, Mich., 1958), describes Freeman Cobb erroneously as a United States senator from Massachusetts. Records in the Massachusetts Archives list him as a state senator from the Cape District.

quiet, retiring individuals who displayed no spark of violence except in the editorials that crackled from his pen. Such writers may be dangerous, and how far editor Wilson would urge Australians to go remained to be seen. Certainly he felt no love for Americans and, in spite of his alleged hope for democracy in Australia, he distrusted Californians and warned his readers to beware of them as "ripe for anything, disorder and rapine, under the specious pretext of serving the sacred cause of liberty." He even complained that the better-class Englishmen were staying away from Australia because of their "knowledge of what happened in California."[12]

George Francis Train was not the only Yankee who made a quick fortune in Melbourne without seeking gold. Roe's American Circus reputedly made more than half a million dollars, but the Queen's Theatre staged performances more to Train's taste. True, the audiences belonged to middle- and lower-class immigrants—as rough a crowd as ever congregated in front of a stage (unless it was in Shakespeare's Globe!). The lights were dingy, savories and ale were peddled from the aisles, and "ladies" in the boxes and dress circle smoked "short tobacco-pipes."[13]

In spite of the Australians' alleged aversion to Californians, American minstrel shows and the New York Serenaders drew crowds. Among the most popular actors were Edwin Booth, Laura Keene, and Lola Montez—all considered American, regardless of their close British Isles connections. Train claimed that Booth and Laura Keene squandered all their earnings and he gave them passage on one of his vessels to San Francisco. Lola Montez, the idol of California miners, came in 1855 and triumphed mightily. A temperamental Irish girl of many marriages, she gained publicity by constant brawls. Back in Ballarat she threatened to horsewhip the editor of the *Times* whose wife, being "as good a man as she," snatched the whip from her.

In her cabin on a ship in Hobson's Bay, Lola prevented the sheriff from serving her by screaming, "Don't come in. I'm naked." Debonair Train once called on her in the theater greenroom and sat on a sofa while waiting for her to appear. Suddenly, he said later, the door flew open and a great ball of feathers approached him. The next moment he was enveloped in a cloud of sweet-scented lace skirts and petticoats. The bold little dancer had tossed her foot over his head.[14]

One of the favorite burlesques depicted forty-niners in hip boots, pistols, and wide-awakes, bragging, shouting, and bullying. The "Flash American Bar-Man" became a popular song. A familiar theatrical skit presented a gaudily dressed Californian as one of the players. He strode across the stage bragging about his wealth, his "democracy," and his lynch law. In the last act, amid haw-haws from the pit, this fellow always turned out to be an Irishman in disguise. Perhaps it was more than coincidence that Irishmen and Americans seemed somewhat similar, and if that growing threat of revolution materialized in Australia, these groups would get the blame.

Another choice play was *Uncle Tom's Cabin*. The book sold readily in Australia, as did a song, "The Slave Mother," inspired by it. Popular lecturers delivered graphic summaries of the story and drew from it arguments against dreaded democracy. Audiences were told that girls in the United States "with eyes as blue . . . and complexions as fair as any of Australia's fairest daughters . . . were bought and sold like beasts of burden or chattels in the marketplace." Thus the book was a "withering exposure of the infidelity of a nation to its own political creed" of liberty and equality.[15]

These plays, lectures, and entertainments were being presented regularly back in the diggings. Ballarat, the closest and most famous of the camps, was located only seventy-five miles from Melbourne. The road out there—or "track," as Australians called it—traversed the Keiler Plains and Bacchus Marsh, and crossed twice, on bridges, the now dry and sandy Werribee River. At last, Mount Buninyong peeped above the gum tree-tops. Travelers said the dark, rounded headland, reminding them of the Scottish Highlands, served as a landmark until the road dipped into Ballarat. Along the track stood tall lemon-scented gum trees, naked of bark, smooth-skinned, and wrinkled at limb joints like an old man at knee and elbow. Often emus could be seen striding through the theatrical landscape. At every campground a kookaburra might perch boldly on a nearby branch to utter humorless guffaws, and always in summer the air was fragrant with golden acacia blossoms which fell to the ground under each tree, making oval carpets soft as velvet. The stagecoach came by this route and so did wayfarers, trudging beside their own drays.[16]

An easier, but longer and more expensive, route from Melbourne to the diggings was by steamboat down to Geelong. From there a good horse could cover the 45 miles along a wool haulers' trace to Ballarat in six to eight hours. It is not known which way Train traveled, but he found the camp more advanced than he expected. The original discovery of gold had been made along a small creek on a sheep run. Every summer the creek dried to a series of pools too stagnant to support frogs, but diggers had muddled around the rims washing out fortunes. Then it was learned that spotty beds of gold lay deep underground. At first a miner was allowed a claim of only eight feet square on the surface, although this area was enlarged later. In this limited space he could dig down as far as possible. Train noted with amazement that one shaft was 170 feet deep.[17]

Thus the Ballarat diggings appeared to be heaps of upturned earth, and more dirt was popping up constantly in buckets from holes so close together a cart could hardly move between them. Some shafts tapped subterranean springs. Men worked for days in water to their waists, shoring the flow with bark or timbers, thus enabling them to dig down to the precious metal they hoped to find below.

Back some distance from the diggings the hills were mottled with bark huts, aboriginal humpies, and small A-tents. Above them floated the flags of all nations, the most prominent, according to some travelers, being the Stars and Stripes. Perhaps this was so, or perhaps the chroniclers were overly conscious of the nationality that, some feared, might foment the dreaded revolution.

Ballarat had 20,000 residents. Large tents sheltered the post office and most of the stores, which seemed to be well stocked. They carried everything from sugar candy to potted anchovies, from ankle jackboots to corsets. Lack of counters or shelves and an excess of eager customers with money to spend resulted in great confusion. Here a pair of herrings on a string dripped brine into a bag of sugar. There, on a packing case, a half-empty bottle of ale sat upon a bundle of tangled ribbons. Cheese, butter, bread, yellow soap, pork, saddles, frocks, baby linen, and tallow candles were all scattered about. Housewives pawed over everything, gossiping as they worked, "tongues going nineteen to the dozen."[18]

Two big shops in Ballarat were operated by Americans. As in Melbourne, many Yankees supported themselves by trade rather than manual labor. One operated a large hotel called the United States. Others plodded among the diggings peddling pies, Colt revolvers, and copies of the ever popular *Uncle Tom's Cabin*. One American, the same Charles Ferguson who had come on the *Don Juan*, operated a restaurant, sold liquor without a license, presented minstrel shows and theatrical performances in a tent. California names appeared everywhere: California Gulley, Yankee Hill, Happy Valley, Jim Crow (a popular minstrel song) Diggins, the Eureka Lead, and the Eureka Hotel. California was known as the Eureka state, but Train learned a word that he believed peculiar to Australia. People said that "nugget" was first used by diggers up at Ophir. Californians admitted that they had not heard it at home.[19]

Train also learned how gold could be shipped safely to the coast. In California the Wells Fargo Company was making big money guaranteeing gold shipments from mine to city bank. In Australia such private enterprise was replaced by a gold commissioner in every community who bought dust and nuggets, paying in coin or giving a negotiable receipt. This bullion was carted weekly to the government bank in Melbourne with an escort of eight splendidly mounted troopers. Dressed in blue, silver-trimmed uniforms and high silver-ornamented shakos, they were admired by bonneted females everywhere. The troopers carried pistols and blunderbusses for quick, short-range shots. At night they encamped in blockhouses along the trace. Thus the government protected itself adequately from bushrangers, but not from unscrupulous Yankees, who, according to gossip, diluted Australian "dust" with less fine California gold before selling to the commissioners.[20]

A dozen other encampments similar to Ballarat stood along the roads beyond, and all had the same crowd of English, Scotch, German, Irish, and Italian diggers swarming in the muck, shoveling, bailing, and cranking windlasses. All these men complained about a licensing system that required a man to buy a license before he had found enough gold to pay for it, and punished him for violation of the act by chaining him to a tree. (There were no jails in the bush.)

This licensing had caused protest meetings at Ophir and on the Turon. "Taxation without representation," miners called it, and when the system was adopted by Lieutenant Governor La Trobe in the much larger and more complex fields in Victoria, with fees doubled in amount, the diggers' indignation boiled over—the first genuine hint of revolution. After several local protest gatherings, a monster meeting was called at Mount Alexander on December 15, 1851. Diggers came from as far away as Bendigo, twenty miles to the north. The assembly was estimated at from 15,000 to 20,000. A majority determined to pay nothing. La Trobe, who was present, compromised with them, offering to reduce the fee but not give up the right to levy it. George III's Parliament had made a similar tea-tax concession.

The crowd agreed to the Lieutenant Governor's proposition and dispersed, but a noisy minority dissented; thus the issue was not dead.[21] In 1852 these diggers organized the Mutual Protective Association, passed resolutions to resist the license system and defend themselves with arms if necessary, quoting the revolutionary slogans American colonists had hurled at redcoats in Boston almost a century earlier. Twice during the summer, soldiers and a heavy contingent of police came to the diggings to restore order and collect license fees. Each time they were greeted with shouts, boos, sticks and stones. Here and there recalcitrant diggers were reported to be "murmuring that in California this state of things would soon be altered, and that in a summary way."[22] In August, a popular demonstration in Bendigo proclaimed under great banners: "TAXATION WITHOUT REPRESENTATION IS ROBBERY!"[23] Within a year this was followed by the Red Ribbon Movement, devoted to the abolition of licenses. (The movement's supporters wore a bit of red cloth or ribbon on their hats.) Revolts against the system were becoming general. Meetings and demonstrations of protest were reported in McIvor, in Goulburn Valley, and in Ballarat.[24] The slogans sounded American, but if Yankees were behind them they kept well hidden. Even that windy Californian, Charles Ferguson, seemed to be minding his own business, but deep waters often flow smoothly.

Lieutenant Governor La Trobe tried to restore peace, tried to raise necessary revenue without raising license fees, even let the state run badly in debt, but all to no purpose. The diggers had become obdurate. To them Charles Joseph La Trobe represented all their troubles, and whenever an inspector appeared they shouted, "Joe! Joe!!" in order that men without licenses might hide. Rumors said that rifle clubs—minutemen—were being formed at the diggings. Gold seekers everywhere joined the Melbourne *Argus* in clamoring for removal of both the Lieutenant Governor and his colonial secretary.

The threat of revolution seemed more ominous when men with little legislative experience came to George Francis Train to borrow George Bancroft's *History of the United States*, Benjamin Franklin's writings, the *Massachusetts State Papers*, and a copy of the Constitution. Train believed that the crisis had arrived. Either the government or the miners would have to surrender.[25]

Some people began to suspect Americans of starting the disturbances. Others maintained that Yankees were loud, flashily dressed show-offs, but more law-abiding than the immigrant Germans, and much more so than the Irish who cherished a traditional hatred of Britain.[26] People of English descent distrusted them all. The prejudices acquired against Californians reasserted themselves and became more virulent when distressing news came from Earl Grey in London.

Britain's colonial secretary had heard rumors that American immigrants planned a revolution in Australia and wrote letters of inquiry to Her Majesty's ministers in Washington and Philadelphia. Both replied that they were unable to discover a definite plot among gold-seeking emigrants, but that an independent Australia would be "highly acceptable to the great mass of the American people," and that "extreme vigilance should be maintained."[27] The minister in Washington intimated that Americans—especially Irish Americans—would be disposed to assist the escape of Irish political prisoners. This was timely advice indeed, since MacManus, Meagher, and O'Donohue had already slipped away.

The threat of revolution might be increasing at the Australian diggings, but in Melbourne Americans like George Francis Train showed little concern for the rights of men at the mines. As loyal citizens of another country they drank toasts to liberty and independence, but paid no visible attention to the knots of radicals who preached on Melbourne's street corners and muttered in the pubs.[28] Train himself had become so rich he indulged in an extensive vacation. A steamboat, the *New Orleans,* a paddle-wheeler with massive walking beam and tall light sail, had come from San Francisco and now served the colonial coastal trade. Train booked a passage on her for Sydney and splashed away on a pleasure trip up the eastern coast of Australia. As the *New Orleans* turned in between the Sydney Heads, she announced her arrival by firing a cannon.[29] This was a mistake, because the paddle-wheeler was unpopular in Sydney. She had brought ex-convicts from San Francisco—Sydney Ducks sent back by the Committee of Vigilance—and her reappearance revived memories of lynchings which rankled in many people's minds.

The *New Orleans* floundered up the long Port Jackson inlet, past its countless little bays and sandstone bluffs. Rounding Bennelong Point, George Francis Train beheld the shake roofs of Sydney with the spire of St. James etched against the sky. The city had not grown as Melbourne had since the gold rush began, but it was crowded. Lodgings ashore were almost impossible to find, and the hotels proved unbelievably dirty. Train thought that Californians were more disliked here than down in Melbourne.[30] In spite of the prejudice, however, he noticed a restaurant named "California," and "California hats" spun lazily from strings in front of open-shuttered shops.[31] At a masquerade ball, men dressed as Californians mingled with the more conventional Henry VIII's and Bayards,[32] but the upper classes all complained, as they did in Melbourne, that Australia was no longer the place for them: the cabbage-tree-hat boys had usurped everything; master and servant had changed places. One man said it had become unthinkable to ask an applicant for service to furnish "a character." Employers took what they could get, and paid bloody well for it. No place in the world, Train was told, were working people so rude to "gentlemen."[33] A digger fresh from the mines might accost an Irish servant girl at an upstairs window of her master's house, propose marriage, and take her away at once.

True, some rich had become richer. Shopkeepers enjoyed more trade than ever, shippers filled their vessels, and the theaters were packed. Even stockmen were getting more for their meat, and they received fabulous prices for their land when gold was discovered on it. But no one seemed happy. Wealth, they said, was not everything. Gentry were proud of their stations and believed themselves worthy of respect. They disliked being jostled by common people. Ladies of quality resented seeing their inferiors in the shops purchase gowns that only the wellborn were traditionally able to buy. Australia was becoming Americanized!

George Francis Train signed the guest book at Government House and was invited to dine. He found gracious Governor-General FitzRoy to be a smiling, bowing aristocrat, unperturbed by Australia's changes. He had his horses and his dogs, and if Dr. Lang and his democratic ilk changed Australia or even wanted to make it an independent republic, that was their business. Nor did he fear the Californians as revolutionaries. Quite the contrary, he had found them entirely law-abiding.[34]

FitzRoy introduced Train to the tall, herculean W. C. Wentworth. Train admired the weather-beaten man's giant intellect and likened him to America's Thomas Hart Benton, but found him something of an enigma. Wentworth had won his struggle for the rights of "emancipists" and now was preparing to go home to England seeking approval for a new constitution that would guarantee Australians title to the crown land and what he called self-government. On the surface this seemed truly democratic, and Wentworth went one step further by saying publicly that Britain should remember her American colonies and "if they [the Australians] were not prepared to levy war against the Queen, they better submit to be the laughing stock of Europe."[35]

So far so good, but here was the enigma. Wentworth, with his apparently radical pronouncements, was called "the American constitution hater." To him local self-government meant government by the well-to-do. To hold office, a man must be a substantial property owner—certainly very un-American. "Suppose," Train mused, "a legislator in the United States must possess $50,000?"[36] That kind of plutocratic democracy, championed now by Wentworth, had been opposed by Benjamin Franklin sixty-six years ago; yet Franklin was a millionaire!

Train also met another prominent politician, John Bayley Darvall, Esq., who disagreed with Wentworth, his party, and his proposed constitution. Darvall was a Yorkshire man who admired the American form of government, knew its history, and was outspoken against Wentworth's proposed nonelective Senate—like the House of Lords, eh, what! Thus the man from the frontier was the conservative, the man from the Old Country a liberal.

Train thought that he had seen progress in America, but he had never seen anything like the quick growth of Australia. The country was now producing 40 percent of the world's gold output and her population almost tripled in the decade.[37] With such an exploding society many cautious businessmen might be expected to fail. Had John Fairfax weathered the golden cyclone?

He had indeed! The journalist was just back from a trip to England. His *Herald*, still considered conservative, had changed as Australia changed. Instead of fighting the inevitable, as Wentworth did, Fairfax rode the crest of the new order and prospered with it. He had lauded Hargraves, approved the latter's rewards, and attended dinners in his honor. The *Herald's* circulation and advertising had multiplied, wealth rolled in, and Fairfax, on his trip "home," had paid the debts he left in England sixteen years ago.

Another archconservative was Captain Robert Towns. How

had that close-figuring pessimist fared? Train went to see him. The old trader had become richer than ever—and still complained, no doubt, that he lost £1,000 every year. He had taken an active part in reorganizing the Bank of New South Wales, increasing its capital and equipping it to meet the growing needs of the colony, but he still pinched every farthing. At Towns's wharf, Train saw twelve or fifteen old whaleboats laid up in line; "Rotten-row," Towns called them. He had picked them up at auctions and held them for a rainy day. Seamen's wages, he said, were bound to drop and then he would sell out for a fine profit—if depreciation did not eat their heads off![38]

What had happened to the radical newspapers which had fostered all these democratic changes? Train discovered that they, like so many pioneers everywhere, had failed to prosper. The *People's Advocate* was still printed, but with little success. The *Empire*, now deeply in debt, could not survive long.

The new order these newspapers had helped create was progressing without them to new goals of prosperity and reform. The change had come in Sydney without violence, but when Train returned to Melbourne, conditions there appeared more uncertain than ever. Both the Irish diggers and those loud-talking Americans in the back country might well be fomenting trouble. Opposition to Lieutenant Governor La Trobe was becoming louder daily. Diggers complained that he showed too much sympathy for the pastoralists who held all the land. Pastoralists complained that he failed to suppress the eager diggers. George Francis Train said that the Lieutenant Governor was unable to make the necessary adjustment between a sheep country with 50,000 to 75,000 inhabitants and a mining economy with four times that population. Moreover there were, by this time, some 10,000 Americans in the colony determined to become identified with it. Like it or not, these "democrats" were apt to be heard.[39]

The announcement from London that a new governor had been appointed was greeted with rejoicing.

Rebels and Redcoats

The new governor of Victoria, Sir Charles Hotham, arrived in Melbourne on June 21, 1854. He and Lady Hotham landed amid cheers from a crowd that expected his administration to be as progressive as the new and novel steamboat that brought them. He was a small man, forty-eight years old, who spoke quietly with nervous quickness, making inferiors feel at ease, but they erred if they mistook this manner for leniency in discipline. He was jut-jawed, had a firm mouth trained to give orders, and he already ranked high in the British Navy, retiring eventually as a rear admiral.[1]

Sir Charles was not altogether pleased with his Australian assignment and would have preferred naval service in the Black Sea, where Her Majesty was fighting Russia. However, he accepted the post with correct soldierly obedience, and he determined to straighten out Victoria's social and economic problems. He settled in "Toorak," the tree-surrounded Government House, with its sentry box at the door, and immediately decided to eliminate the colony's financial deficit left him by Lieutenant Governor La Trobe.

Sir Charles noticed at once an apparent discrepancy between the number of diggers in the gold regions and the amount of license fees received by government, and he estimated that he could balance the budget by merely enforcing the licensing system. On July 22, with crisp military finality, he threatened to dismiss all gold commissioners whose districts were in arrears. Later, with his wife, he coached back to the diggings to inspect conditions for himself. The rainy season had come. Creeks that in summer were dry gullies, now ran bank-full with muddy, red water. Occasional white frosts followed a day or two of blue skies, then the rains poured down again without slackening for a week.

At Ballarat, Victoria's largest mining community, the diggers received Sir Charles on August 26 with cheers. They fervently believed the new broom would sweep away the old abuses and right their wrongs. Enthusiastic miners even copied the gallantry of Sir Walter Raleigh by carrying Lady Hotham across a mud puddle. Sir Charles thanked them in a short speech and promised not to neglect their interests.[2] Then he drove another seventy-five miles north through the hilly eucalyptus forests to Bendigo.

On his return to Melbourne Sir Charles pronounced the miners to be peaceable fellows, although he admitted that the influence of more women would undoubtedly have a stabilizing effect on them.[3] Some diggers, he had learned, evaded purchase of licenses by various schemes. Occasionally two men bought one license and carried it alternately, each working every other day. Also, a man with no license felt reasonably safe working the first ten days of each month, when the inspectors were too busy selling licenses to visit the mines. No wonder the system had failed.

Sir Charles blamed the police for inefficiency. He reminded them of his threat to dismiss those officials whose collections were in arrears and insisted that they show more vigilance. Members of his government warned him of the danger of excess stringency. Sir Charles would not listen. After all, he had handled other headstrong fellows in Her Majesty's Navy. Thus, on September 13, 1854, he gave an order for the police to check for licenses "not less than twice a week,"[4] instead of monthly as in the past. Surely, that would stop the worst evasions.

For more than a fortnight no hint of violence followed this order, but Hotham's edict of September 13 may be considered the beginning of his trouble. The diggers' next complaint did not concern licenses, although licenses were at the bottom of it. Violence started at Ballarat on October 6, when James Scobie, a Scotsman, met an old mate named Peter Martin and caroused with him from five in the afternoon until midnight; then they staggered off toward Scobie's tent. On the way they saw a light in the barroom of the Eureka Hotel, the largest public house in Ballarat. The hotel was operated by James F. Bentley, an ex-convict from Norfolk Island via Van Diemen's Land—about as bad antecedents as an Australian could have. He had received a license as recently as last July. Scobie and Martin decided to drink a nightcap at the Eureka. Knocking for admittance, they were told by a determined voice to go away.

Scobie replied by kicking the door with such force that some cracked glass fell out. Through the gap he saw the barkeeper counting his day's receipts. Scobie shouted a few thick-tongued and uncomplimentary remarks. The landlord's wife, attracted by the sound of breaking glass, appeared in a fury, screaming angrily. Scobie called her what she probably was, and his mate dragged him away into the night.

About fifty yards from the hotel the two staggering revelers were overtaken by five persons—hotel man Bentley carrying a shovel, his irate wife, the pub's roustabout, two old cronies of Bentley's, one an ex-convict. Mrs. Bentley pointed to the Scotsman who had called her an ugly name. The ex-convict knocked Scobie down and, with the roustabout, began kicking him. The constable threw down Martin, who managed to crawl away some hundred yards to Scobie's tent and there awakened the Scotsman's partner. Together they went back to the scene of the fracas and found Scobie's dead body. His attackers had fled.[5]

By morning the whole camp bubbled with righteous indignation. Bentley was generally disliked, and his Eureka Hotel had a bad name for cheating patrons and throwing them out after their money was spent. At the inquest into Scobie's death, the diggers became thoroughly incensed when the coroner's jury exculpated the Bentley gang. The diggers' rage increased when they learned that the coroner and one of the gold commissioners—a hated license seller—had been drinking together at the Eureka Hotel until midnight the day of the murder. Moreover, though one member of the jury was a personal friend of Bentley's, an objection to seating him had been ignored.[6]

To protest such high-handed proceedings, an Irish digger, whose claim joined the Scotsman's, organized his mates. The man's name was Peter Lalor. He was an educated chap who had studied at Trinity College, Dublin. Heavyset and full-bearded but with clean-shaven upper lip like many Irishmen, his eyes were steady and his tongue was fluent. Also, like many Irishmen, he thoroughly disliked British rule and descanted continually on the wrongs suffered by his people. Lalor's father had been a member of the House of Commons, where he supported Daniel O'Connell in the long and eloquent struggle for Irish reform. One of Peter Lalor's brothers had taken part in the Young Ireland movement of 1848 [7] which ended in the conviction of Meagher, O'Brien, MacManus, and O'Donohue. Peter himself claimed that he came to Australia in 1852 to get away from politics. But revolt, turmoil, and crusades for liberty throbbed in his blood. No Lalor ever ran from a fight, and three of Peter's brothers served in America's Civil War, though not on the same side. The biased decision of the coroner's jury determined Peter to espouse the diggers' cause.

On the day following the announcement of the unfair verdict, a number of diggers called on the authorities and, after submitting evidence they had collected, appealed for the arrest of Bentley, his cronies, and Mrs. Bentley. All of them were duly apprehended. At a preliminary hearing on October 12, however, the judge, who happened to have a financial interest in the Eureka Hotel, honorably discharged all three of them.

A routine abstract of the hearing was sent to Melbourne, where the Attorney General reviewed the evidence, pronounced it sufficient for a trial, and so notified Sir Charles Hotham, who immediately ordered the arrest of Bentley, his wife, and his associates. The timing of this just action by the Governor is important, for the diggers knew nothing about his order. All they knew was that the guilty Eureka Hotel people had been freed by corrupt officials in Ballarat and something must be done. They called a mass meeting "to have the case brought before other and more competent authorities."[8] Thus the first step toward revolution was taken to correct a wrong already corrected. But, like the colonists in America after repeal of the Stamp Act, the diggers were now thoroughly incensed.

On October 17 some three to five thousand diggers assembled at the spot near the Eureka Hotel where Scobie had been killed. The meeting began in an orderly fashion, with English immigrants shouting all the Chartist slogans[9] they had learned at home—pleas for universal suffrage, a secret ballot, an end to property qualifications for members of Parliament, and for electoral districts that would give the mining areas fair representation. Irishmen voiced their ancient protests against English tyranny, repeating American revolutionary clichés. Specific resolutions were passed condemning the verdict of the local magistrates in the Scobie-Bentley case, and a fund was raised to prosecute these delinquent officials. The assembly elected an executive committee of seven, one of them being the fluent-tongued Peter Lalor.

So far the diggers had not violated British precedent, and no legal objections could be raised against their meeting, but the local magistrates watched with apprehension. To protect their reputations and their stations, they notified the police and the military that the assemblage was irresponsible and that it planned to attack and destroy the Eureka Hotel. This precaution was understandable, though perhaps unwise. Redcoats and "Joes" were as obnoxious to Australian diggers as redcoats and Tories had been to American "rebels" eighty years earlier. Many heretofore peaceable men became enraged when mounted police came to spy on their meeting and guard a den of iniquity like the Eureka Hotel.

After the meeting adjourned, a crowd loitered in front of the Eureka. There was no leader, just an idle throng watching and waiting. Dangerous mobs often stand in this uncertain manner. The police rode around them. Somebody threw a rock. A window broke. The tinkle of glass started a barrage of sticks and stones. Waving shirts and coats frightened the police horses. Rioters surged into the hotel, snatching bottles from behind the bar, handing them out the windows. Men in the street knocked the bottles' necks together in colonial style and drank the contents. The redcoats arrived and with drawn sabers forced the mob from the hotel, but were themselves driven out by a fire that started in the bowling alley. Soon thereafter the Eureka Hotel roared up in flames.[10]

In this crisis Hotham became the victim of his naval training. Insubordination must be punished forthwith. He surmised that La Trobe, his predecessor, had been too lenient with recalcitrant diggers, had failed to suppress their mass demonstrations with sufficient finality. He, Hotham, would show the rascals who ruled. Leaders of the riot—whoever they were—must be arrested. A trial with due publicity would ensue! He ordered 450 additional police, soldiers, and artillery to Ballarat.

The task of identifying possible leaders of the mob who deserved arrest proved difficult. Several men were apprehended, but the local justice of the peace freed the first ones brought before him on the grounds of uncertain identity. Obviously, the justice and the community sympathized with the rioters. Hotham ordered a change of venue for the remainder. Let them be tried in Melbourne, away from understanding friends.[11]

Down in the city these accused leaders were duly indicted—all but one, an American named Carey.* This was the first hint that any Yankees were behind the disturbance, and Carey's release caused some grumbling in Melbourne where many townsmen, remembering the San Francisco lynchings, did not believe that such foreigners deserved favor. Sir Charles said he exonerated this man because other Americans had distinguished themselves for good conduct at the Eureka fire—a questionable statement because several Americans did participate in the riot. The real reason for Carey's exoneration was probably a petition submitted to the Governor by the United States consul general, James M. Tarleton.[12] Certainly it was good politics for Sir Charles to maintain friendly relations with the prosperous Americans, like Train, who lived in Melbourne or Geelong where they were connected with the import trade. Such people might be very valuable to Her Majesty while the Crimean War lasted.

It is possible, too, that Tarleton hoped to influence others besides Sir Charles Hotham. He knew that there were several thousand Americans back at the diggings,† and that Califor-

---

* C. H. Currey, *The Irish at Eureka* (Sydney, 1954), p. 49. According to the Melbourne *Argus* (Oct. 30, 1854), his name was John Kelly.

† L. G. Churchward, "The American Contribution to the Victorian Gold Rush," *Victorian Historical Magazine*, XIX (June, 1942), 90, estimated that 55 percent of the Americans in Victoria were at the diggings. However, they may have numbered less than 3 percent of the population there. See also C. H.

nians, who had a bad reputation for taking the law into their own hands, were prominent among them. An oft-tried means of controlling incorrigible youth is to call the bad boys "good," and give them responsibility. Perhaps Tarleton had this in mind when he published in the Melbourne newspapers a letter "To American citizens resident throughout the Gold-Fields of this Colony" congratulating them for not participating in the disorders of a foreign nation.[13]

Back in Ballarat an unfortunate incident now occurred which stretched to the snapping point an already tense relationship between government and diggers. One of the "Joes" smarting under Sir Charles's order for more efficiency displayed the stupid officiousness characteristic of disciplined underlings. He arrested the crippled servant of the beloved Father Patrick, or Patricius, Smyth for being on the Ballarat goldfield without a license. In vain the cripple explained that he was not a digger and had come at his master's request to inquire about a sick man. The trooper ordered him to headquarters and, when the unfortunate fellow was slow in going, he cuffed and jostled him. At first the mob watched in silence, then began to hoot. At the police station Assistant Commissioner James Johnstone could not logically fine a cripple for lacking a license to dig; hence, to uphold his stupid subordinate's act, Johnstone fined Father Smyth's servant for resisting arrest.

Catholic miners, including most of the Irish, considered this police action a direct attack on both their religion and Father Smyth. They called a mass meeting, this time in the Roman Catholic chapel on Bakery Hill on October 25. Once more Peter Lalor was present and he took a prominent part in framing the resolutions requesting the Governor to investigate this latest affront, and also to look into the outrageous "honourable discharge" of Bentley et al. This of course had already been done, and Lalor may or may not have known it. In any event these resolutions, whether pertinent or not, were designed to inflame

Currey, *The Irish at Eureka* (Sydney, 1954), p. 5, and N. O. P. Pyke, "Foreign Immigration to the Gold Fields" (unpublished M.A. thesis, University of Sydney, 1946), p. 191.

popular opinion as well as to rectify a wrong, and the double-barreled charge had extra revolutionary shocking power for the battle ahead.

The emotionally disturbed people were still burning with righteous indignation, when dispatches from Melbourne announced that the Eureka rioters had been indicted there. Obviously, those few were to be punished for an act of the whole community. To protest this injustice, the leading Ballarat diggers urged workers from neighboring camps to meet with them on October 29, 1854. Hundreds came and stood in rapt attention listening to speakers on a platform adorned with the national flags of England, Scotland, and Ireland as well as the banners of France and the United States. A German band played patriotic tunes. Armed sentries were posted to watch for the approach of police or soldiers.[14]

From this meeting the Ballarat Reform League came into being, although not officially organized until early in November. Its exact purpose is still controversial. Certainly, it stood for the Chartist principles of suffrage and parliamentary representation. In addition, it favored abolition of the licensing system and the opening of crown land to settlement. The *Ballarat Times*, whose editor, Henry Seekamp, sympathized with the movement, pronounced the league the germ of Australian independence and, as we shall see, suffered for his bold statement. Another of the league's sympathizers, at a mass meeting ten days later, denied that immediate separation from Britain was planned provided equal rights could be obtained for the whole community.[15]

More important than the Reform League's ultimate aim was the fact that several foreign radicals joined the movement. In addition to Irish Peter Lalor, there was a long-legged German named Frederick Vern, a man with a peculiar flat face, big mouth, and bright, furtive eyes "like an [Australian] opossum." He had been a soldier of fortune in Peru and Mexico, so he said, and he could quote revolutionary slogans in a Hanoverian brogue. Besides, he was a lion among the ladies, or thought so.

Another foreigner who joined the league was Raffaello Carboni, a small, frail-framed Italian youth with red hair, mustache, and pointed beard. He had failed in the sheep business, hoped to succeed as a writer, and took notes constantly, stuffing them into his pockets. He had studied Rousseau's revolutionary doctrines and received a wound in Italy's vain war for freedom from Austria. Diggers called him "Basta Cosi" ("That's Enough"), an exclamation he was wont to shout on occasion.[16]

As yet no Californian seemed to be participating in the league, but an American named James McGill who had military aspirations watched it closely. The league's purpose differed in the minds of its members and, as during the American Revolution, some favored independence, others did not. Much might depend on the manner in which the authorities acted. In this crisis James McGill saw an opportunity for himself.

Governor Hotham, that inflexible military man, smelled treason even when acts were contaminated only with democracy. Stubborn as George III, he budged not an inch in favor of either the diggers or the police authorities. The law was plain. The wheels of government might grind out justice exceedingly slow but they must not be disturbed. Before ruling on the crippled servant's fine, the Attorney General continued the investigation already begun in the Bentley case and ended by condemning the action of both judge and constable. The former was removed from office, and prosecution was recommended for the latter. Things seemed to be going favorably for the diggers now, with only the case of Father Smyth's servant to be settled. On November 20, however, the government, hewing to the disciplinary line, sentenced to jail three of the members of the Eureka mob who had been brought to Melbourne for trial.[17]

This rebuff on the threshold of victory incensed the Ballarat Reform League leaders who determined to be as obdurate as the officers of the Crown. They sent three delegates to Melbourne to *demand* that Hotham release the convicted men. Lynch courts in California had *demanded* prisoners held by the civil authorities, but that was not the British way. To Hotham the word "demand" from an organization he considered tainted with treason was more than he could overlook. Such an affront to the Crown must be resisted and punished by every means at his disposal, and he was probably pleased when he read in the powerful Melbourne *Argus* that editor Edward Wilson, who had consistently taken the diggers' side in the dispute, agreed now with him that the malcontents were wrong. He explained the diggers' unpardonable utterance by saying that "the ringleaders were principally composed of foreigners"[18]—those damned Californians, perhaps.

Sir Charles must have been pleased with this influential newspaper's sympathy for his position, but he received other information that boded evil. He was keeping himself posted on the progress of events by secret communications from the Bentley clique, who reported that the league planned to enforce its *demands* by kidnaping three "Joes" and holding them as hostages. Whether these reports were true or false cannot now be determined, but Sir Charles dispatched two columns of the military to Ballarat. One was a troop of horse from Geelong, the other a battalion of the 12th Regiment in three-horse carts out of Melbourne.

With these soldiers on the march, Hotham received the league's delegates. He remained dignified, cold, and unremitting. He told them in no uncertain terms that reforms were under way, but that the league must retract its "demand."

Some twenty-four hours later, in the evening of November 28, the forty troopers from Geelong cantered into Ballarat and were greeted with a shower of sticks and stones. An hour behind them the battalion from Melbourne, commanded by Captain H. C. Wise, arrived. In the dark the column of carts passed the outlet of a long, crooked digging which cut back into a hill 120 feet deep. The excavation was the headquarters for a tough lot of Tipperary boys who called themselves Young Ireland. They hated England, and with threats and shillelaghs kept all diggers except their own gang away from their area. These rowdies watched the redcoats trundle by in their carts. When the last wagon approached, the Irishmen ran out, upset the vehicle, and pounced on the startled redcoats, snatched their weapons, and dragged them back in the cut as prisoners. During the hassle a drummer boy was shot in the thigh, and the civilian driver, who happened to be an American working on contract, was badly mauled.[19]

The incident terminated in a few moments. Captain Wise at the head of the column seemed uncertain about what had happened, was not sure how many of the townsmen were against him or how to retaliate in the dark. The situation was faintly reminiscent of the Concord Bridge affair in the American Revolution. He pitched camp, posted sentries, and prepared for trouble as soon as daylight enabled men to shoot.

During the night Captain Wise's squad of battered redcoats who had been captured straggled into camp. Six of them were hospitalized and one died,[20] but at dawn the expected rebel attack did not come. Instead the Captain saw, near his camp, great placards headed: "DOWN WITH DESPOTISM! WHO SO BASE AS TO BE A SLAVE!"—both American Revolution slogans.

These placards called the citizens to a mass meeting that day near the chapel on Bakery Hill. Ostensibly this was to hear the report from the delegates who had waited on Hotham, but many knew that plans for armed resistance would probably be made. Indeed, the belligerent rumors had already reached Melbourne, and Bishop James A. Goold drove all night across the tree-studded downs, hoping to reach his Irish parishioners in time to restrain them.

The citizens assembled before a platform decorated with the flags of many nations. Among them stood a new one of blue silk with a white cross. Stars at each corner and one in the center represented the five Australian colonies. The flag differed from the earlier Anti-Transportation League banner which had decorated many political platforms and had flown from the mastheads of Australian vessels in San Francisco.[21]

The new banner had unusual significance today. A challenge to the British ensign floating above Captain Wise's tented troops on the far side of camp, it might become the flag of a new and independent nation. Below the platform a gigantic crowd gathered—a multitude larger than the Mount Alexander meeting of 1851, and much more experienced in revolution. The November day was hot, for summer had come. A sly-grog seller passed a black bottle along the line of dignitaries seated on the platform. Timothy Hayes, a quiet-mannered Irishman, called the assemblage to order. He was a working partner of Peter Lalor's and a close friend of Father Smyth's. Bishop Goold had, no doubt, conferred with Hayes prior to the meeting.

One by one the chosen speakers addressed the assembly, reiterating the diggers' wrongs in Chartist language, adding Young Ireland's protests against tyranny in the moving phrases of O'Connell's oratory. Appropriate references were made to American revolutionists' complaints against "taxation without representation" and the marching of redcoats into a peaceful district.

In this impassioned assembly, Peter Lalor delivered his first public address and felt the thrill of power an orator knows and never forgets. Finally, the chairman of the three delegates who had been sent to Melbourne made his report, stating that Sir Charles refused to countenance a "demand."

Young Frederick Vern leaped to his long legs. The bright eyes in his flat face danced with excitement. In fluent though broken English he offered a resolution enjoining all miners to publicly destroy their licenses and pledge themselves to protect from arrest anyone of their number who did so.

This was an appeal for organized resistance to Her Majesty's law, and the second part of the resolution was obviously treason. Chairman Hayes probably remembered his talk with Bishop Goold. Certainly he realized the threat of the nearby troops, and he called the meeting's attention to the motion's gravity and asked the assembly to consider what they would do if one of them was taken to jail for failing to have a license. "Will a thousand of you die to defend a digger without a license?"

A deafening chorus replied, "Aye!"

"Will two thousand die?"

Again the chorus roared, "Aye!"

"Will four thousand die?"

Once more the response was overwhelming, and Timothy Hayes was moved to recite:

> On to the field, our doom is sealed
> To conquer or be slaves;
> The sun shall see our country free,
> Or set upon our graves.[22]

A bonfire was kindled, and amid defiant volleys some five hundred miners tossed their licenses into the flames. Bishop Goold had evidently failed to calm the Irish blood. True, a few men were not yet ready for this insubordination to government, but mass emotion is always volatile and minority opinion might become infected.

At this point the petty government officials committed another of their blunders. Perhaps they were acting under Hotham's orders, for the Governor was keeping in touch by code with the progress of events. At any rate, Captain Wise, whose battalion still suffered from the Tipperary boys' mauling, and Gold Commissioner Rede, whose "Joes" had been insulted repeatedly by the diggers, determined that "sedition must be put down by force."[23] To show their authority, the two men decided to send an officer to the diggings on the morrow and demand licenses, well knowing that many had been burned. All diggers found without them would be clapped into jail. If there must be war, let it begin now!

This offensive task was given to Assistant Commissioner Johnstone, who had already earned digger hatred by his treatment of Father Smyth's servant. Johnstone called first on Irishmen at the Gravel Pits, met resistance, and sent for more police. It was a stormy day, with a hot wind whipping yellow dust from hundreds of miners' dumps and flapping the calico sails that ventilated deep shafts. Men's tempers were on edge. Many diggers came to the surface seeking relief.[24] Timothy Hayes stood at the windlass of his pit. He heard the distant cry of "Joe," and sent word to Peter Lalor who was working in the shaft 140 feet below. Lalor jumped into the bucket, was reeled to the surface, and strode through the swirling dust toward the commotion. At another shaft the frail, red-headed Raffaello Carboni was taking a rest. To him the cry of "Joe" aroused a lifelong hatred of Austrian oppressors. Shouting "Basta Cosi" through his bristling mustache and pointed beard, he started toward the disturbance. So did the long-legged, excitable German, Frederick Vern, but no American spoke up. Perhaps Consul General Tarleton had intimidated them. Perhaps not!

At police headquarters Resident Gold Commissioner Robert Rede heard the uproar, donned his gold-lace cap of authority, and joined his "Joes." Furiously indignant, the self-righteous young autocrat insisted that his word was law, the actions of his men must be obeyed.

Vern shouted, in his thick accent, some revolutionary taunt. Police slapped him on neck and shoulder, telling him that he was under arrest. Instantly the mob leaped, like a pack of mad dogs, on the officers. Bricks and stones began to fly. A revolver boomed. Vern escaped and later displayed his hat with a bullet hole in the crown—from his own gun, scoffers said. Commissioner Rede, more self-righteous than ever and trying not to flinch under the shower of stones, read the Riot Act, an old English statute which made every man present guilty of felony if he did not leave immediately.

Rede followed this pronouncement by calling for the nearby redcoats who came, eager for revenge. They helped him arrest a few men, but many of the diggers escaped to yesterday's meeting place on Bakery Hill, where they armed themselves with pikes and guns. The military made no further effort to pursue or disband them.

The embattled diggers were thoroughly aroused now, but they had no military organization, no leader. Peter Lalor rose to the occasion. The stocky Irishman mounted a stump and called on the mob to form companies, pikemen in one place, riflemen in another, pistoleers in a third, men with cutlasses in a fourth—"quite in American military style,"[25] one observer said. Those swashbuckling Americans who had recently defeated poor little Mexico had a bad reputation for militarism but, as yet, had taken no noticeable part in the Australian revolt.

A Canadian named Ross and a color guard upholding the Southern Cross banner started back over the gully to the Eureka area, a spot made sacred since the burning of the hotel. The armed diggers followed, marching two abreast. If license collectors wanted to oppose them, now was the time.

The "Joes" did not appear and the insurgents had the field to themselves. Their leaders met in the back room of a nearby store to choose a commander in chief. Vern wanted the position. After all, he claimed to have had military experience in Mexico and Peru, and he could recite the revolutionary slogans which fired fighting men's hearts. Little Carboni, however, opposed the tall man's ambition, saying that the leader should be a British subject. Carboni nominated Peter Lalor, and the Irishman was elected, only one voice dissenting. Under its new leader the "army" marched back to Bakery Hill, where the Southern Cross flag was hoisted to the top of an eighty-foot pole. Let Captain Wise and his redcoats see it without using telescopes.[26]

Under this brilliant standard Peter Lalor stood with a shotgun in his left hand, the stock on his foot. He raised his right hand for attention and called: "It is my duty now to swear you in, and to take, with you, the oath to be faithful to the Southern Cross. I order all persons who do not intend to take the oath to leave the meeting at once. Let all divisions under arms fall in, in their order, around the flagstaff."

There was a shuffle of a thousand feet, the groping of undrilled men to find places in semimilitary arrangement—and it was finally accomplished. The poetic Carboni was impressed by the rough clothes of the men, by their shaggy beards and tousled hair, but he noticed, too, the intense stare in all their eyes, as though magnetized by the silken flag and by the purpose it signified. He said later that he thought these men felt something akin to the spirit of the Crusaders to Palestine.

Lalor knelt before them, with head uncovered. He raised his right hand pointed at the flag and said in clear and measured tones: "We swear by the Southern Cross to stand truly by each other, and fight to defend our rights and liberties."[27]

The exact meaning of this oath and the purpose of those who took it has been questioned by historians. Undoubtedly many diggers planned separation from Britain, but it is questionable whether the majority of them did so. The American Revolution began with only about one-third of the people favoring independence, and this Australian group may have been divided similarly. Peter Lalor was quoted as saying the next day that he planned independence, but this is hearsay. He did not put it in writing. On the night of the oath he did write his sweetheart, saying that they had taken up arms "in self defense. . . . Should I fall," he continued, "shed but a single tear on the grave of one who has died in the cause of honour and liberty, and then forget me until we meet in heaven."[28] This can be interpreted as either planned revolution or merely armed protest, but, as during the American Revolution, opinions and majorities might change.

No "Joes" appeared to contest the assembly, so the Ballarat Reform League decided to send two delegates to the police camp and *demand* release of prisoners arrested that morning, and also to *demand* a pledge from Commissioner Rede that there would be no more "license hunting." Red-headed Carboni was one of these delegates, and Father Smyth went along to introduce them and make the meeting as peaceable as possible, but Rede was obdurate. He objected, as Hotham had, to the "demand." However, he did consent to release two prisoners on Father Smyth's surety. Carboni said later, at a hearing when he and others were endeavoring to clear their records of treason, that he had begged Commissioner Rede to believe that the diggers did not plan revolution; they had armed only to stop further license hunting. Rede replied that the license was "a mere catchword of the day," a mere cloak to cover a democratic revolution.[29]

Commissioner Rede was undoubtedly expressing the opinion of his superior, Sir Charles, and they were not alone in suspecting that a revolution had begun. The alarm spread to Melbourne, where the gold-rush boom had burst. Men were out of work. A surplus of goods could not be sold. New residences built for prospective immigrants stood empty. A warehouse, constructed at a cost of £40,000 and renting during the boom years for £50,000 a year, could not now be sold for £300.[30]

To address these discontented Melbourne people, the Ballarat Reform League sent several speakers who had taken part in the Bakery Hill license-burning assembly. Presumably, the financial depression had hurt American merchants and shippers. Some of them, even the well-known George Francis Train, might be desperate. Certainly, that unpredictable chap was always eager for new adventures. In counting rooms, in the

Exchange, at mass meetings, and to any street-corner crowd that would listen these agitators pointed out the similarity between the diggers' complaints and those of Americans in colonial times. Fred Vern was particularly vociferous, shouting his familiar revolutionary slogans and begging support of the diggers' cause in the fight for liberty.

To counteract this propaganda, Consul Tarleton did his utmost to keep the Americans neutral and to placate Sir Charles. He cautioned his countrymen against participating in the internal affairs of a nation not their own, complimented them for not being implicated in the Eureka fire, and pointed out that Britain like America, was famous for the freedom its government allowed her citizens.

Consul Tarleton also reminded Sir Charles that, although "foreigners" were allegedly stirring up the revolt, a chief sufferer at Eureka had been an American who owned an interest in the bowling alley that had burned. Furthermore, Tarleton called Sir Charles's attention to the fact that an American teamster working for the British government had been one of the casualties when the 12th Regiment was attacked. In addition, Tarleton probably continued to hint about the importance of remaining friendly with American shipping interests during these critical days of the Crimean War.

Consul Tarleton succeeded only partly in holding back the Americans. Train and most of his friends remained noncommittal, but one group—either more belligerent than the rest or mortified by being called cowards, afraid to fight for the principles of their country—expressed sympathy for the rebels. However, these Americans resolved not to be "foremost in an open outbreak against the government."[31]

This was too equivocal for ambitious James McGill, who organized what he called the Independent Californian Rangers' Revolver Brigade. He was an inconspicuous chap, short in stature and quite young, probably about twenty-one. The place of his birth is unknown, but he had the manners of a gentleman, spoke correct English, and had evidently attended a military academy in the United States. He habitually used the noticeable American expression, "What's up?" Obviously he craved mili-

tary glory, and he tried to repeat Vern's bombastic words. His
brigade, armed with Colt six-shooters and Mexican machetes,
did not formally join the diggers' army but remained independent, as the brigade's name implied. Charles Ferguson enlisted in this questionable organization. George Francis Train
said that McGill came to him to purchase $80,000 worth of
Colt revolvers and, as part of the deal, offered him the presi-
dency of a proposed republic.[32] Perhaps McGill did, but it must
be remembered that Train told this story years later, and that
he was one of those fluent talkers who always have statistics on
the tip of the tongue and untrustworthy generalizations in mind.

With the colony thus staggering on the brink of revolution,
the diggers constructed a low barrier of boards, sandbags, and
trusses of hay, thereby enclosing on three sides an acre of land
at the Eureka Lead. The rebels, themselves, did not agree on
the purpose of this stockade, but they did admit that it would
hardly hold a flock of sheep. This was, of course, hindsight
testimony given by men attempting to free themselves from a
charge of treason. If not built for military defense, why was it
built at all?

In any event, the digger army marched from its various camps
to the stockade on December 1, 1854. The diggers numbered
a bit more than eight hundred, and half of them were probably
Irish. A German blacksmith who claimed to have served in the
Mexican wars set up a forge and pounded out rough-edged
pikes "making money as fast as any Yankee." The crude weapons
sold well to sentimental Irishmen who knew through popular
legends that pikes had served against British tyranny at Vinegar
Hill in the Rebellion of 1798.[33]

Into this encampment of ragged troopers marched the Independent Californian Rangers' Revolver Brigade, 200 strong.[34] At
the column's head rode bantam-sized James McGill, a self-styled
Napoleon with a page holding his charger's bridle. This chivalric
footman, named Smith, had come from America as an employee
of the Adams Express Company. The Revolver Brigade was
still "independent," but tall, gangling Vern, with sword drag-
ging the ground, welcomed its members as fellow comrades-at-
arms and boasted about his own 500 riflemen assembling on

the nearby hills. In addition, 400 more "patriots" were known to be marching from the Creswick diggings four abreast behind a Hanoverian band playing the "Marseillaise." Up at Bendigo a gigantic rally had been held, and at Mount Alexander a mass meeting was addressed by E. N. Emmett, a name to reckon with in Irish revolutionary history. Chartist resolutions were passed. Diggers everywhere seemed to be eager for action. The Melbourne *Argus* admonished its readers: "Let the intelligent minds of the colony well consider who and what have made two thousand British subjects swear allegiance on their bended knees to a flag of their own choosing, and which absorbs nationalities,—'The Southern Cross.' " [35]

18

The Shot Not Heard
Round the World

To suppress the threatened revolution in Ballarat, Governor Hotham reinforced the soldiers there by sending the remaining battalions of the 12th and 40th regiments from Melbourne with two fieldpieces and two howitzers, the latter manned by marines from frigates in the harbor.[1] If an Australian Paul Revere galloped ahead to arouse the countryside, his name is forgotten.

The last of these soldiers marched out of the city on December 1, 1854. Prior to their arrival at the diggings, a dispatch printed in the Melbourne *Argus* described the precarious situation in Ballarat by saying that two armed camps faced each other. On one side stood the government forces with cavalry in white caps and red shirts, on the other "2,000 men, the bone and sinew of the colony, under arms of every description, from the Irish pike of the last century to the revolver of yesterday—from the rifle of Manton to the cheap Birmingham fowling piece,—from the djerid of the Arab and the cutlass of 'Jack Tar' to the plowshare and the reaping hook."

This report mentioned neither American insurgents nor James McGill, but it added drama that did not exist and, like so much chromatic journalism, did more to aggravate violence than allay it. As a matter of fact, the rebels, although brave enough individually, were unprepared to fight anyone, especially trained British redcoats. Everybody seemed to be giving orders and nobody heeded them. Obviously, the command's unity had broken down.

The insurgent army had divided into two groups, one favoring peaceful negotiations, the other urging armed resistance. The ostensible commander in chief, Peter Lalor, felt that the time had come for compromise, and that his personal future lay in parliamentary debate. With him, also desiring peace, was Carboni who may have remembered the futility of fighting giant Austria. In opposition, McGill and Vern, both subordinate commanders, were shouting for war and holding suspiciously secret meetings, evidently planning a revolution within the revolution. Noting the dissatisfaction, Peter Lalor—according to his testimony when defending himself later—went to Vern and offered him the supreme command. The German declined, and Lalor turned to McGill but was rebuffed again. The potato was getting too hot for anyone to hold!

In the midst of this confusion the 400 patriots from Creswick trudged in, lame, dirty, soaked to the skin by a thunderstorm that swept over them, and half-drunk on the grog they had brought for the ten-mile march. At the Eureka Stockade they found no billets, no arms, not even necessary rations. That night they slept on the hard ground, huddling around big fires. Nights were chilly after hot December days. Before morning these rebels decided that they had been duped by demagogues and straggled homeward, very hungry and tired.[2] Their grumbling departure broke the morale of many of the home boys, most of whom had heard enough oratory and wanted to return to work.

Many of the local volunteers also began to leave the stockade during the morning of December 2. The "army" was evaporating rapidly, but a military faction among those who remained began drilling under a self-proclaimed veteran of Waterloo who shouted in a martial manner: "Shoulder pikes," and "Ground arms." He explained how to execute another command, which he called "Receive cavalry," by saying, "Poke your pike into the guts of the horses and draw them out from under their tails."[3]

Fire-eating Vern, swollen with oratory, found some relief by haranguing McGill's Independent Californian Rangers' Revolver Brigade, promising to lead it to victory or death. People recalled later that a "Declaration of Independence," patterned after America's, was circulated. Carboni said that no one would take responsibility for this document.[4] (Its existence has been questioned.)

At noon, as men became hungry, more of the rebels straggled away hunting food. A Dr. Kenworthy appeared, asking for McGill. Carboni stopped and questioned the stranger. The physician said that he wanted to offer his services as surgeon in case of war. Carboni considered the fellow an affable chap, a little too affable, especially when Kenworthy, learning that Carboni was Italian, began expatiating on the glories of Mazzini and the heroism of an American soldier of fortune named Captain Forbes, who had fought in Rome in 1848.[5] Obviously, the man wanted something. Was he a Benedict Arnold?

Later the physician found McGill and talked quietly with him. What he said is unknown, but he may well have brought a message from Consul Tarleton, telling the American youth to quit the fight at once. In any event, fiery little McGill detailed about one-third of his Revolver Brigade, including the incorrigible Charles Ferguson, to remain as sentries at the stockade. With the majority of his men McGill marched out of the enclosure, telling those he left behind that he intended to intercept the contingent of soldiers with their howitzers coming up the road from Melbourne. But instead of marching east he wheeled north to Creswick, explaining later that he went there to get a cannon.

Discipline had now become so weak that rebel soldiers came and went much as they pleased. Lalor was still titular commander in chief, but he exercised no apparent authority. In this disorganized situation Carboni and his fellows of the "peace wing" received disturbing information. Some rebels had begun to requisition food and arms from stores without authority, paying for them with slips of paper signed with an "X." One of these scripts read: "Received from Ballarat store 1 pistol for the Comtee X. Hugh McCarty—Hurrah for the People." Another said: "The Reform Lege Comete, 4 drenks, fower chillings, 4 Pies, for fower of thee neight watch troops X P."[6]

When Carboni learned that men of this caliber were "pressing" supplies, he feared that radical leaders had mutinied and taken over the command. He hunted for Lalor and found him asleep in his tent, so exhausted he could not be aroused. Thoroughly dismayed, Carboni started back to his own quarters. A sentry stopped him, and Carboni discovered that he did not know the correct password, which happened to be the Irish revolutionary slogan "Vinegar Hill." Yes, there was no doubt now, wild Irishmen other than Lalor were in charge. Sullen knots of them stood around the camp, talking excitedly, complaining about inaction, threatening to attack, come night, the nearby camp of redcoats. Other diggers demurred, called for new leadership. In the confusion more men skulked away. That night only about 150 remained in the stockade, and some of them were the American sentries left by McGill.[7]

Apparently the insurrection was withering from lack of organization, strong leadership, and intelligent planning. In another twenty-four hours it might have died a natural death and been buried along with the Red Ribbon Movement in La Trobe's administration. At that point, Britain's top colonial executives, with practical wisdom, might well have righted the diggers' wrongs. However, history does not always work that way. Captain Wise and his battalion still smarted from the memory of the mauling given them by the Tipperary boys. Spies in the stockade reported the diminishing number of defenders. Obviously, the diggers were no match now for 250 drilled horse and foot, together with 100 armed police. The military knew, too, that reinforcements were on the way from Melbourne— the reinforcements McGill had gone to stop. Why wait for them to share the glory of a victory that could be won immediately?

Before daybreak on December 3, 1854, the military advanced, no drums beating, no fifes. According to British precedent, the commander's first duty was to read the Riot Act; then, in case the rebels failed to disperse, he would attack. However, this was reckoning without the rebels. In the dawn's early light a Californian Rangers' Brigade sentry spied the approaching troops and called the captain of the guard. He came running, saw the redcoats, and shouted to his off-duty detail: "Californian Rangers to the front." The Americans scrambled to the barricade and began to shoot. For them this was Lexington and

Concord once more! The bombardment aroused Vern's riflemen from their bivouac. They reached for their guns and shouldered their way into the American ranks. All semblance of order disappeared. Lalor, in his tent, heard the shooting and ran to the stockade.

The soldiers, in the meantime, halted at the first fire and prepared to charge. A reporter for the Melbourne *Argus* said that they fired two rounds of blank cartridges, then fixed bayonets and advanced. An unlikely story, for bullets soon began to riddle the stockade boards, kicking up dirt, sand, and splinters. Diggers collapsed, their wide-awakes and cabbage-tree hats rolling across the area. Carboni, still in his tent, heard the firing, ran out, and saw a Canadian writhing on the ground with a shot in his groin. Beside the injured man sprawled Edward Thonen, the Prussian chess expert who sold lemonade in the stockade. He had been killed by a bullet through his mouth. Also among the dead lay the German pike maker.[8]

Day was breaking now, and the redcoats in their high Napoleonic kepis were coming forward inexorably, no break in their long ranks, no hesitation. Vern tripped over his sword and bumped into one of the Americans, Charlie Ferguson, who asked why Vern was running. "To stop the rest," Vern shouted over his shoulder as he scampered away to be seen no more in the fight. An American seaman ran to the well and slid down the rope into the darkness. A bullet hit Lalor in the arm and sent him spinning. A comrade pulled off his necktie and wound it around Lalor's arm above the wound, but Lalor soon fainted from loss of blood. Friends carried him to a depression, then covered it with loose boards so that he could not be seen. A moment later redcoats bounded over the barricade, plunging their bayonets into prostrate figures, snatching fagots from campfires, burning tents and their contents. With a wild hurrah, they hauled down the Southern Cross flag and danced around the staff as though it were a Maypole.

The fight lasted only ten or fifteen minutes. Three or four soldiers and police had been killed, eleven privates and two officers severely wounded—one of them, Captain Wise, fatally. The diggers' loss[9] is not known, but it was much greater. Fifty men were carried out of the smoking ruins. More than half of these were Irish—the nationality that undoubtedly predominated in the revolt. Five could not be identified, but no American of record was killed. Nearly all the wounds seemed to be on the head, neck, and upper chest—parts of the body exposed above the barricade, but some of the dead showed bayonet thrusts evidently received after death.[10]

As soon as the soldiers and police left the charred area, friends lifted Lalor from his hiding place and carried him into the bush. Vern escaped the colony, well disguised, on a Sydney vessel. He sent back a message deploring the fact that fate denied him a warrior's death, a patriot's grave, and decreed that he should languish in banishment. "Victoria," he wrote, "thy future is bright. I confidently predict a Bunker's Hill . . . as the issue of your next insurrection." He was still in New South Wales—still languishing, no doubt—in 1861.[11]

More than one hundred prisoners had been taken and, after being robbed by the redcoats, were herded into a log jail so small they could not sit down.[12] How many of them had belonged to McGill's Californians was not known, and the authorities feared that many dangerous rebels still roamed the nearby hills.

Next day, December 4, seemed quiet. Some diggers returned to work, while men suspected of being their leaders were arrested one by one. Many more, besides Lalor, undoubtedly skulked in the bush, and McGill with two-thirds of his brigade was still somewhere among the eucalyptus trees. The bombastic correspondent for the Melbourne *Argus* informed his paper that the digger force was not broken, and he declared that intelligent people in Ballarat would rally in hundreds to maintain order.

After dark that night a nervous picket at police headquarters began to fire. Citizens believed that the revolt had commenced again, but by midnight quiet was restored. Rumors said that a woman, a child, and three innocent men on the road had been shot. Other rumors declared this a false story to stir up hatred of the "Joes."

At dawn, December 5, shooting began again but stopped in a few minutes. The cause of the bombardment remains a mystery. Later in the day Major General Sir Robert Nickle arrived with the redcoats McGill had set off to ambush. The General did not know that the female figure in the stagecoach he had seen back at the Moorabool crossing, twelve miles east of town, was James McGill escaping to his American friends at Port Phillip. In Ballarat, Sir Robert declared martial law and restored peace, albeit the peace of death and dictators.[13]

While order came in this manner to Ballarat, uncertainty and fear of the mob shook the coast towns. At Geelong, a mass meeting petitioned Hotham to placate the diggers and set aside the licensing system. The assembly had barely dispersed when word came that the rebels who had left the Eureka stockade prior to the fight were marching down the road to plunder coastal villages. Rich residents hid their valuables, even buried some of their jewels. Sympathizers of the diggers maintained that no raid was threatened, that all the looting and "pressing" which had occurred was the work of government spies done to discredit the diggers' cause. Everyone seemed confused.

In Melbourne, the peppery editor of the *Argus* who had consistently taken the diggers' part, blaming all violence on foreigners, announced that the respectable leaders of the Ballarat Reform League had withdrawn from it. Editor Wilson was unwilling to admit, in his paper, that Britishers would be guilty of revolution. "This is still an English colony," he wrote, "with English laws, English habits, and English sympathies! If we do fight, let the encounter be an English one, conducted upon English principles, and in an English spirit!"

These reassuring words, voiced the day after the battle, failed to calm the fear in Melbourne that the rebels were coming. As in Geelong, the people hid their jewelry, and guards were placed at the banks. The excitement came to a climax when the mayor called for a mass meeting on December 6 to discuss the emergency. The day was hot and gusty, an irritating day like the one that followed the license burning at Ballarat when armed diggers defied the military. Red dust whirled along the streets, powdering the shoulders of men's frock coats and the bonnets of women who ventured out. Shopkeepers and businessmen assembled, as did 3,000 laborers, many of them diggers from the creeks. A few temperate civic leaders tried to bring dignity to the meeting, but hecklers began heckling hecklers, and in the confusion and gusts of red dust, parliamentary order became difficult to maintain. Many cried for the dismissal of Colonial Secretary John Foster—an ironic demand because Foster, born and educated in Ireland, was duty bound to obey Hotham's orders, even though he never approved them.[14] Other hecklers demanded that all rebels be pardoned, all prisoners released.

Officials made conciliatory speeches, appealed to the people to support the flag of Old England—of "home"—rather than that of the Southern Cross. A member of the Legislative Council, John O'Shanassy, who, like editor Wilson, had sided with the diggers, realized now that the insurrection had gone too far. Hoping to quell the turbulent Irish, he used an old subterfuge for attracting a mob's attention. He shouted revolutionary slogans, said that he agreed with the crowd's complaints and also sympathized with the struggle for Irish autonomy which had cost the "martyrs" banishment to Australia. He even went so far as to say that he was a personal friend of Smith O'Brien's, and differed from him only in the methods of obtaining the ends sought. Then, after this opening wedge into the Irish heart, he pleaded for all classes of his fellow colonists to restore "peace to our adopted country." Shouts, perhaps from men planted in the noisy assembly, seemed to approve this speech and "His Honour the Mayor" dissolved the assembly, but he failed to reckon with Irish ebullience. As soon as the mayor vacated the platform, a new chairman reconvened the meeting, which promptly passed a resolution for the dismissal of Foster—symbol of the Hotham policy.

This and other resolutions were too mild to satisfy part of the mob, and when the second meeting adjourned, a thousand dissatisfied participants with clenched fists and swinging clubs marched down Swanton Street, determined to show contempt for the government. Spying two troopers, the mob pursued them in full cry—a "fox hunt" in the streets of Melbourne. The unfortunate men darted into the shelter of a residence, and the ugly-tempered crowd surrounded the house. Down at the jail, turnkeys feared that an attempt might be made to liberate all prisoners.

Terror of a general riot gripped the city. Property owners

worried, although no serious looting occurred. Bankers, merchants, and landlords sent a written declaration to Governor Hotham expressing their loyalty to the Queen and their willingness to serve as a constabulary to maintain order. Editor Wilson, completely out of sympathy with the violence that had developed from the cause his paper originally championed, printed an editorial urging every responsible person to join the proposed corps.[15]

Back in Ballarat, Irish friends secreted Peter Lalor in Father Smyth's presbytery, where his arm was amputated. However, he dared not hide here long because the government offered a reward of £400 for his arrest, so he was hauled, under a concealing load of brushwood, to a friend's house in distant Geelong.[16]

With peace restored in Ballarat by martial law, and with the jail dangerously overcrowded, preliminary trials began on December 5 and lasted for a week. One hundred and fifty-six diggers had been arrested, among them several members of the Independent Californian Rangers' Brigade. Henry Seekamp, editor of the *Ballarat Times*, which had served as the voice of the disaffected diggers, was also in custody.[17]

American Consul Tarleton exerted himself to have all Americans released, although he showed little concern for a Southern Negro named John Joseph. Among the first to be tried was the incorrigible Charles Ferguson. He defended himself by claiming to be a Methodist minister who had visited the Eureka Stockade out of curiosity and had been caught there. The crowd listening to the case knew Ferguson to be a man who was not above selling a spot of sly-grog on occasion, but all remained dutifully silent. The prosecution failed to break the prisoner's story and he was released. With cheers and laughter the crowd carried him on their shoulders to the nearest pub. George Francis Train, who had already smuggled McGill into one of his ships, took friendly custody of the counterfeit minister and kept him out of further mischief.[18]

Obviously, sympathy for the rebels was still running high, and Governor Hotham might have profited by heeding it. But he acted as he had previously: Let the rebels be tried in Melbourne! Accordingly, thirteen prisoners were loaded into carts and hauled to the capital for trial on charges of treason. Among them was Carboni, shackled to black John Joseph, the sole American still held in custody. John was a simple-minded Negro whose kindly humor had endeared him to the diggers,[19] some of whom resented the fact that John's color seemed to prevent Consul Tarleton from protecting him. What sort of democracy was the United States? Other Australians, prejudiced by renewed reports of California lynchings, complained against pardoning any Americans. However, the Irish, always vociferous, defended the pardons and releases, calling attention to the hospitable receptions given MacManus, Meagher, O'Donohue, and Mitchel in the United States.

At the treason trial in Melbourne, the Negro's case came first on the docket—a serious mistake on the part of the Crown. Kindhearted John Joseph, when ordered to sit in the culprit's box, showed no sign of worry, amused the spectators by scratching his head, grimacing, and whistling before answering a question. The dignified judges in their long curled wigs kept straight faces, but the onlookers could not. The idea of convicting so artless and likable a fellow for treason amused everyone in the courtroom and convulsed the thousands congregated outside. John Joseph might be guilty of disturbing the peace, of waging war on the British Empire, but how could an American Negro be a traitor to the Queen? Amid great laughter and cheering he was dismissed and carried away on the shoulders of the crowd, much as Ferguson had been. Two men applauded so boisterously they were sentenced to a week in jail for contempt of court. A British-born Negro was quoted as saying that a sorry day had come for liberty in Her Majesty's dominions when it had to be upheld by a black man from slaveholding America.[20]

The second culprit was also promptly acquitted. This displeased Hotham. Traitors must not escape the law in such a manner! He ordered the remaining prisoners to be tried by a different court, thus postponing further trials for more than three weeks. But when these cases were called, Hotham was again frustrated. The first two men to be tried, Timothy Hayes and Raffaello Carboni, were acquitted. This should have taught

Hotham a lesson. Although he received hundreds of letters urging him to abandon further prosecutions, he remained obdurate. The law was plain, and he knew the difference between black and white. Furious at the verdicts, he wrote: "If juries would not do their duty, I could discover no reason why I should not do mine."[21]

So the cases dragged on, the jury persisting in acquittals— an excellent example of Australian, perhaps of British, recognition that popular will is common law. In each case the jury agreed that the diggers had been subjected to arbitrary rule, and that if these men had been goaded to take up arms to maintain their rights, they were not traitors. After the tenth acquittal, Hotham gave up, and the Crown filed a *nolle prosequi* for the eleventh man.[22]

Thus the people's will triumphed and Australian democracy is said to have been born in the Eureka Stockade. An imposing monument marks its site. At the time, Karl Marx badly misjudged the insurrection by proclaiming the fight "a concrete manifestation [of] the general revolutionary movement in Victoria."[23] He overlooked the fact that these workers were small, independent capitalists striking for individual rights. Instead of presaging communism, the discovery of gold in California and Australia gave capitalism a tremendous boost. Britain's economy, which had been faltering, revived with spectacular suddenness. The United States, which had recently acquired vast territories stretching from the Rocky Mountains to the Pacific, began its age of overland expansion.

Between 1850 and 1875, the world's supply of gold increased more than it had done during the three and a half centuries since Columbus discovered America. Most of this gold came from California and Australia. The rush to California had commenced three years ahead of Australia's, but by 1853 Australia was outproducing California by millions of dollars. Even more important, Australia continued to produce gold in great quantities. The supply seemed almost inexhaustible, as an American engineer named Herbert Hoover learned when he laid the basis of his mining fortune there at the turn of the twentieth century.[24]

In view of the amazing opportunities in Australia, it is not surprising that the population trebled within a decade after the first rush, nor is it remarkable that these new citizens insisted on political recognition and pointed to the fight at Ballarat as the heroic beginning of a new order. Like Bunker Hill, the actual fight was a mere token demonstration and, also like Bunker Hill, it was a defeat, but both episodes became symbols of a new nationalism with tremendous emotional value. The embattled farmers at Concord Bridge fired a "shot heard round the world," starting two centuries of democratic revolutions. If the shot fired by embattled diggers at the Eureka Stockade has not been heard beyond the borders of Australia, that is because the continent down under lacked a Ralph Waldo Emerson. However, the Australian shot (even if fired by a trigger-happy Californian of the Rangers' Revolver Brigade) brought into being a new nation that has led the world in social reform.

Diggers and those who came with them in such overwhelming numbers changed Australia from a land of big estates to a nation of the "common man." The digger influx initiated the Australian ballot—that safeguard of true democracy. Few people realize that Australians also have led other countries in adopting the eight-hour day, the forty-hour week, minimum wages, unemployment compensation, sickness benefits, compulsory arbitration, and that great innovation, a labor party[25]—all basic to the dawn of a new democratic era.

The average Australian, from grade school to the grave, cherishes the name "Eureka Stockade."* In recent years some historians have questioned the stockade's significance, pointing out that Chartists and cabbage-tree-hat boys began agitating for reform even before the California gold rush threatened to create a labor shortage. The reforms, these historians say, would probably have developed without a rebellion, and the same writers add strength to their case by showing that Australia's revolutionary social legislation, which has set a world pattern, was not

---

* The name "Eureka Stockade" was being used more than a hundred years after the fight by an Australian communist minority, much as the name "Minute Men" has been adopted by a fringe minority in California to excuse their revolutionary collection of arms.

enacted until the 1880's, a full generation after the diggers' fight. In like manner, revisionists in the United States have pointed out that efforts to achieve the fundamental goals of the Declaration of Independence and the Constitution started long before the American Revolution, and that many of the desired ends were not attained until half a century later—some of them not even then! In spite of these qualifications, the Revolution remains a turning point in American history, as does the Eureka Stockade for most Australians. Perhaps the full force of the great social changes down under did come a generation later, but it must always be noted that the first parliament in the colony of Victoria, at its session in 1855, immediately after the rebellion, voted to adopt the "Australian ballot," which the United States began using in 1888.

The Australian gold rush, inspired in California, had another aspect worthy of notice. Aside from the social reforms that grew with Australia's development, the Ballarat rebellion certainly taught Great Britain one more important lesson in colonial administration. Instead of liquidating the "traitors" with Latin-American finality, all were permitted to continue exercising such talents as they possessed. Noisy Vern was not silenced but, to his own dismay, discovered that people no longer cared to listen to his revolutionary clichés. Frail, inconspicuous Carboni was allowed to write, and publish, the book he had long planned. He also stood for election to the Local Court at Ballarat—and won.[26] Peter Lalor, with his gift for oratory, his statesmanship, and the everlasting appeal of his patriotic gestures with the stub of the arm he lost at the stockade, began a long political career. First he represented his district in the Legislative Council, then in the Assembly, where he served as speaker for seven years. He was twice chosen for the high office of minister to the Crown, and he could have been knighted had he desired that honor. For a rebel, who had escaped from Her Majesty's soldiers by hiding under a pile of boards, to rise so high in Her Majesty's service is surely remarkable. Perhaps it was this new tolerance, this adaptability and understanding, instead of the impatient dogmatism of George III and the King's Party, which eventually made Great Britain so expert in colonial administration.

Notes

(All abbreviated titles are given in full in the Sources.)

CHAPTER 1

[1] *A Century of Journalism* (Sydney, 1931), p. 55.
[2] *Hobart Daily Courier*, May 5, 19, 1849.
[3] Charles Bateson, *Gold Fleet for California* (Sydney, 1963), pp. 23, 28.
[4] L. G. Churchward, "Australia and America" (unpublished M.A. thesis, University of Melbourne, 1941), p. 13.
[5] C. Hartley Grattan, *The United States and the Southwest Pacific* (Cambridge, Mass., 1961), p. 84; [E. Lucett], *Rovings in the Pacific* (London, 1851), p. 292.
[6] Lucett, *op. cit.*, p. 45; G. C. Mundy, *Our Antipodes* (London, 1855), p. 10.
[7] *Sydney Morning Herald*, Dec. 11, 23, 1848; Mundy, *op. cit.*, p. 426.
[8] *Sydney Morning Herald*, Dec. 23, 1848.
[9] *Ibid.*
[10] *Ibid.*, June 10, 1849; William Jackson Barry, *Past & Present and Men of the Times* (Wellington, N.Z., 1897), p. 80.
[11] Robert Towns, MS, Nov. 1, 1849 (Journal and letters in the Mitchell Library, Sydney).
[12] *Sydney Morning Herald*, Dec. 26, 1849.
[13] Towns, MS, June 28, 1849; Churchward, *op. cit.*, p. 64.
[14] Towns, MS, Jan. 11, 20, 1849; *Sydney Morning Herald*, Jan. 11, 1849.
[15] The first available copy of this weekly, dated January 6, 1849, claims to be the sixth issue, although the paper presumably started on January 1, 1849. The printer obviously was confused.
[16] *People's Advocate*, Jan. 6, March 24, 1848.
[17] *Sydney Morning Herald*, Jan. 15, 1849, quoting the London *Times*, Sept. 16, 1848.
[18] Bateson, *op. cit.*, p. 162.
[19] *Sydney Morning Herald*, Jan. 11, 1849.
[20] *Alta California*, Suppl., March 29, 1849.

CHAPTER 2

[1] R. Edmond Malone, *Three Years' Cruise in the Australian Colonies* (London, 1854), p. 140.
[2] *Sydney Morning Herald*, Jan. 6, 1849.
[3] *Alta California*, Suppl., March 29, 1849.
[4] William Tecumseh Sherman, *Memoirs* (New York, 1875), I, 65.
[5] Stockton *Placer Times*, April 28, 1849.

[6] James M'Eachern letter from San Francisco dated May 16, 1849, printed in the Hobart *Colonial Times*, Dec. 25, 1849.

[7] *Alta California*, July 2, 1849.

[8] Charles Bateson, *Gold Fleet for California* (Sydney, 1963), p. 42.

[9] *Sydney Morning Herald*, Aug. 30, 1849.

[10] *Ibid.*, Feb. 3, 1849.

[11] *Ibid.*, Feb. 1, 1849; *South Australian Register*, Feb. 28, 1849.

[12] *Sydney Morning Herald*, Jan. 8, 29, Feb. 1, 1849.

[13] *Ibid.*, Feb. 10, 1849; *Hobart Town Advertiser*, Feb. 16, 1849.

[14] *Hobart Daily Courier*, Oct. 20, 1849; L. G. Churchward, "Australia and America" (unpublished M.A. thesis, University of Melbourne, 1941), p. 64.

[15] Edward Hammond Hargraves, *Australia & Its Goldfields* (London, 1855), p. 70.

[16] *Hobart Town Advertiser*, Jan. 13, 1849.

[17] *Sydney Morning Herald*, Jan. 6, 1849.

[18] *Alta California*, May 24, 31, 1849.

[19] *Ibid.*, May 4, 1849.

[20] *Sydney Morning Herald*, March 13, 1849.

[21] *Hobart Town Advertiser*, April 3, 1849.

[22] *Sydney Morning Herald*, March 13, 1849.

[23] *Ibid.*, Feb. 3, 1849; Churchward, *op. cit.*, p. 63.

[24] *Sydney Morning Herald*, April 3, 1849.

[25] Hobart *Colonial Times*, May 15, 1849; *Hobart Daily Courier*, May 16, 1849.

[26] *Sydney Morning Herald*, June 9, 1849.

[27] Bateson, *op. cit.*, p. 156.

[28] Robert Towns, MS, June 16, 18, 1849 (Journal and letters in the Mitchell Library, Sydney).

CHAPTER 3

[1] Captain Harry O'May, MS (in Captain O'May's possession, Hobart, Tasmania).

[2] *Sydney Morning Herald*, Jan. 18, 1849; *Hobart Town Guardian*, Feb. 7, 1849; J. H. Cullen, *Young Ireland in Exile* (Dublin, 1928), p. 63.

[3] "My Trip to Australia," *Frank Leslie's New Family Magazine*, II (April, 1858), 305.

[4] G. C. Mundy, *Our Antipodes* (London, 1855), p. 506.

[5] John Mitchel, *Jail Journal* (Dublin, 1913), p. 254; Mundy, *op. cit.*, pp. 474, 484, 500; "My Trip to Australia," p. 305.

[6] Johnson Dean, *On Sea and Land* (Hobart, *ca.* 1905), p. 105; "My Trip to Australia," p. 305.

[7] William Dillon, *Life of John Mitchel* (London, 1888), I, 321; Clive Turnbull, *The Charm of Hobart* (Sydney, 1949), p. 8.

[8] "My Trip to Australia," p. 305.

[9] *Hobart Town Guardian*, July 23, 1849; J. E. Bicheno, "Confidential Report on the Colonial Press," *Tasmanian Historical Research Association Papers and Proceedings*, III (Aug., 1954), 88-89; Dean, *op. cit.*, p. 104; Mitchel, *op. cit.*, p. 264; Mundy, *op. cit.*, p. 482; Turnbull, *op. cit.*, pp. 8-12; James Wood, *The Tasmanian Royal Kalendar* (Launceston, 1849), p. 83.

[10] *Hobart Town Advertiser*, May 12, 1848; Melbourne *Argus*, July 7, 1851; *Hobart Daily Courier*, June 2, 1852.

[11] *Hobart Town Advertiser*, June 6, 1848; Mundy, *op. cit.*, p. 494; "My Trip to Australia," p. 306.

[12] Mitchel, *op. cit.*, p. 437.

[13] *Hobart Britannia*, Jan. 4, May 17, 1849; *Hobart Daily Courier*, May 19, 1849.

14 L. G. Churchward, "Australia and America" (unpublished M.A. thesis, University of Melbourne, 1941), p. 67; Dean, *op. cit.*, p. 51.

15 *Hobart Britannia*, Jan. 18, 1849.

16 *Ibid.*, Jan. 4, 18, 1849.

17 *Hobart Town Guardian*, Jan. 31, 1849.

18 *Hobart Daily Courier*, Jan. 10, 1849.

19 Charles Bateson, *Gold Fleet for California* (Sydney, 1963), pp. 56-61; Mundy, *op. cit.*, p. 518.

20 Hobart *Colonial Times*, Oct. 22, 1850.

21 *Hobart Daily Courier*, May 5, 1849, quoting London *Times*, Jan. 3, 1848.

22 Hobart *Colonial Times*, Jan. 25, 1850.

23 *Ibid.*, April 27, May 1, June 19, 1849; *Hobart Daily Courier*, May 1, 2, 9, June 6, 1849; *Hobart Town Guardian*, May 2, 1849.

24 *Hobart Britannia*, May 17, 1849.

25 *Hobart Town Advertiser*, May 15, 1849; *Hobart Britannia*, May 17, 1849; *Hobart Daily Courier*, May 19, 1849; Hobart *Colonial Times*, June 8, 22, 1849.

26 *Hobart Daily Courier*, May 19, 1849.

27 *Sydney Morning Herald*, May 28, 1849; Hobart *Colonial Times*, June 12, 15, 1849.

28 *Sydney Morning Herald*, June 8, 1849.

29 *Hobart Daily Courier*, June 23, 1849.

30 *Ibid.*, July 14, 1849; Mary Floyd Williams (ed.), *Papers of the San Francisco Committee of Vigilance of 1851* (Berkeley, 1919), p. 248.

31 Hobart *Colonial Times*, June 8, 1849; *Hobart Town Guardian*, July 7, 1849; *Hobart Daily Courier*, June 26, 30, 1849; Jan. 23, 1850.

32 *Hobart Daily Courier*, June 30, 1849; *Hobart Britannia*, July 5, 1849; *Hobart Town Advertiser*, Aug. 7, 1849.

CHAPTER 4

1 Rodman W. Paul, *California Gold* (Cambridge, Mass., 1947), p. 22.

2 *South Australian Register*, Jan. 3, 1849.

3 *Ibid.*, Jan. 20, 31, Feb. 3, 1849.

4 *Ibid.*, Jan. 31, 1849.

5 *Ibid.*, April 18, May 9, 1849; Peter Freuchen, *Book of the Seven Seas* (New York, [1957]), p. 153.

6 Charles Bateson, *Gold Fleet for California* (Sydney, 1963), p. 130.

7 John Sherer, *The Gold-Finder of Australia* (London, 1853), p. 339; *Australian Encyclopaedia* (East Lansing, Mich., 1958), VI, 36.

8 L. G. Churchward, "Australia and America" (unpublished M.A. thesis, University of Melbourne, 1941), p. 63.

9 *Hobart Town Guardian*, June 13, 1849.

10 *Alta California*, Sept. 20, 1849; Churchward, *op. cit.*, p. 63; L. G. Churchward, "Australian-American Relations during the Gold Rush," *Historical Studies of Australia and New Zealand*, II (1940), 15; Bateson, *op. cit.*, p. 160.

11 *Hobart Town Guardian*, June 13, 1849, quoting the *Melbourne Herald*.

12 Robert Towns, MS, June 27, 1849 (Journal and letters in the Mitchell Library, Sydney).

13 *Sydney Morning Herald*, June 22, July 5, 1849.

14 Edward Hammond Hargraves, *Australia & Its Goldfields* (London, 1855), p. 72.

15 *Sydney Morning Herald*, June 28, 1849; *Hobart Daily Courier*, July 7, 1849, quoting *Sydney Morning Herald*.

16 Hobart *Colonial Times*, July 3, 1849; *Hobart Daily Courier*, July 4, 1849.

17 *Ibid.*, July 21, 1849.

18 *Sydney Morning Herald*, July 6, 1849.

[19] Hobart *Colonial Times*, Aug. 14, 1849.

[20] The quarrel is summarized in Hobart *Colonial Times*, Aug. 14, 1849. See also *Hobart Britannia*, Aug. 9, 1849.

[21] *Hobart Daily Courier*, Aug. 22, 1849.

[22] Hobart *Colonial Times*, Aug. 3, 1849.

[23] *Sydney Morning Herald*, Jan. 19, 1850.

[24] "My Trip to Australia," *Frank Leslie's New Family Magazine*, II (April, 1858), 291-292.

[25] *Hobart Daily Courier*, July 7, Oct. 27, 1849; Hobart *Colonial Times*, July 17, 1849.

[26] *Sydney Morning Herald*, July 11, 17, 1849.

[27] *Ibid.*, Aug. 1, 1849.

[28] Aug. 28, 1849.

[29] P. 89.

[30] For announcements of these books about the gold rush see *Sydney Morning Herald*, July 28, Suppl., Sept. 10, Oct. 22, 1849; *People's Advocate*, Aug. 4, 1849; *Hobart Britannia*, Dec. 13, 1849. Henry Vizetelly, *Glances Back through Seventy Years* (London, 1893), I, 343-347, describes the hoax.

[31] *South Australian Register*, April 18, 1849; *Hobart Daily Courier*, July 14, 1849.

[32] Hobart *Colonial Times*, Feb. 12, 1850; Bateson, *op. cit.*, p. 158.

[33] *Hobart Daily Courier*, July 6, 1849; *Sydney Morning Herald*, Aug. 22, 1849.

[34] *Hobart Daily Courier*, July 11, 1849; *Stockton Times*, April 6, 1850.

[35] *Sydney Morning Herald*, July 5, 1849; *South Australian Register*, July 11, 1849.

[36] "My Trip to Australia," p. 298.

[37] F. Lancelott, *Australia As It Is* (London, 1852), I, 265; G. C. Mundy, *Our Antipodes* (London, 1855), p. 123; Roger Therry, *Reminiscences* (London, 1863), p. 264.

[38] Thomas Archer, *Recollections of a Rambling Life* (Yokohama, 1897); *Australian Encyclopaedia*, I, 228.

[39] Archer, *op. cit.*, p. 192.

[40] Lancelott, *op. cit.*, p. 278.

[41] Archer, *op. cit.*, pp. 161-163.

[42] *Sydney Morning Herald*, May 28, 1849; Archer, *op. cit.*, pp. 161-163.

[43] Archer, *op. cit.*, p. 163.

[44] Simpson Davison, *The Discovery and Geognosy of Gold Deposits in Australia* (London, 1860), p. 62.

[45] Archer, *op. cit.*, p. 167; Geoffrey Blainey, *The Rush That Never Ended* (Melbourne, 1963), p. 13; also see picture used as frontispiece in Hargraves, *op. cit.*

[46] Frank Clune, "Pool of the Two-tailed Fish," in *Land of My Birth* (Sydney, 1949), p. 36; Davison, *op. cit.*, p. 51; *Australian Encyclopaedia*, IV, 430.

[47] Davison, *op. cit.*, pp. 2, 15.

[48] Mundy, *op. cit.*, p. 109.

[49] *Sydney Morning Herald*, April 3, 1849.

[50] Davison, *op. cit.*, p. 30.

CHAPTER 5

[1] The account that follows is from Thomas Archer, *Recollections of a Rambling Life* (Yokohama, 1897), especially pp. 164-167.

[2] *Ibid.*, p. 169.

3 Simpson Davison, *The Discovery and Geognosy of Gold Deposits in Australia* (London, 1860), p. 3.

4 Archer, *op. cit.*, pp. 172-173.

5 *Ibid.*, p. 183.

6 *Ibid.*, p. 181.

7 *Alta California*, Nov. 1, 1849.

8 Hobart *Colonial Times*, Jan. 18, 1850.

9 Bayard Taylor, *Eldorado* (New York, 1857), p. 203; Theo A. Barry and B. A. Patten, *Men and Memories of San Francisco* (San Francisco, 1873), p. 161. Note that one Australian, in a letter dated October 3, 1849, thought the name was given by Americans. The name appeared later in the Australian diggings.

10 *Alta California*, Sept. 20, 1849; Hobart *Colonial Times*, Jan. 22, 1850.

11 *Alta California*, Aug. 31, 1849; John Sherer, *The Gold-Finder of Australia* (London, 1853), p. 70; Taylor, *op. cit.*, p. 113.

12 Barry and Patten, *op. cit.*, p. 67.

13 Archer, *op. cit.*, p. 191.

14 *Alta California*, Dec. 17, 1849.

15 Taylor, *op. cit.*, p. 208, says the first mail in three months came on the last day of October, 1849.

16 Sherer, *op. cit.*, p. 70; Taylor, *op. cit.*, p. 55.

17 Archer, *op. cit.*, p. 185.

18 Hobart *Colonial Times*, Feb. 12, 1850.

19 Robert Glass Cleland, *A History of California: The American Period* (New York, 1922), p. 287; Taylor, *op. cit.*, p. 113.

20 Stockton *Placer Times*, Feb. 9, 1850.

21 Hobart *Colonial Times*, Sept. 21, 1850.

22 *Ibid.*, Jan. 18, 1850.

23 *Ibid.*, Jan. 25, 1850; *Hobart Daily Courier*, Jan. 26, 1850.

24 Hobart *Colonial Times*, Feb. 12, 1850.

25 *Ibid.*, Sept. 21, 1849; Barry and Patten, *op. cit.*, p. 21.

26 *Hobart Daily Courier*, Oct. 20, 1849; Peter H. Burnett, *An Old California Pioneer* (Oakland, Calif., 1946), p. 180; Taylor, *op. cit.*, p. 109.

27 *Hobart Daily Courier*, Jan. 26, 1850.

28 Hobart *Colonial Times*, Sept. 21, 1849.

29 Letter dated Sept. 29, 1849, published in Hobart *Colonial Times*, Suppl., Jan. 20, 1850; *Alta California*, Aug. 31, 1849; Taylor, *op. cit.*, p. 109.

30 Barry and Patten, *op. cit.*, p. 24.

31 Hobart *Colonial Times*, Jan. 29, 1850.

32 Theodore H. Hittell, *History of California* (San Francisco, 1897), III, 311.

33 Taylor, *op. cit.*, p. 121; Barry and Patten, *op. cit.*, p. 158.

34 William Henry Ellison, *A Self-governing Dominion: California, 1849-1860* (Berkeley, 1950), pp. 6-12.

35 *Hobart Daily Courier*, Feb. 2, 1850; G. C. Mundy, *Our Antipodes* (London, 1855), p. 530.

36 Hobart *Colonial Times*, Oct. 26, 1849.

37 *Ibid.*, Jan. 25, 29, 1850.

CHAPTER 6

1 Hobart *Colonial Times*, Sept. 21, 1849.

2 *Alta California*, Aug. 2, 1849, reports the first overland immigrants in Sacramento; see also Peter H. Burnett, *Recollections* (London and New York, 1880), p. 335.

3 Letter of Sept. 9, 1849, in Hobart *Colonial Times*, Jan. 4, 1850; Owen Coch-

ran Coy, *In the Diggings in 'Forty-nine* (Los Angeles, 1948), p. 43; Bayard Taylor, *Eldorado* (New York, 1857), p. 77.

[4] Edward Hammond Hargraves, *Australia & Its Goldfields* (London, 1855), p. 77.

[5] *Stockton Times*, May 18, 1850.

[6] Hargraves, *op. cit.*, p. 78.

[7] Louis Becke (ed.), *Old Convict Days* (New York, 1899), p. 37.

[8] Three letters from the discouraged diggers in California printed in Hobart *Colonial Times*, Jan. 18, 25, 1850; *Hobart Daily Courier*, Feb. 13, 1850.

[9] This account is from Hargraves, *op. cit.*, p. 79 ff.

[10] *Alta California*, Dec. 1, 1849; Thomas Archer, *Recollections of a Rambling Life* (Yokohama, 1897), pp. 186, 192; F. Lancelott, *Australia As It Is* (London, 1852), I, 278.

[11] Burnett, *op. cit.*, p. 361.

[12] Robert Glass Cleland (ed.), *Apron Full of Gold* (San Marino, Calif., 1949), p. 33; William Tecumseh Sherman, *Memoirs* (New York, 1875), I, 67.

[13] Archer, *op. cit.*, p. 192.

[14] Taylor, *op. cit.*, pp. 208, 212; Owen Cochran Coy, *Pictorial History of California* (Berkeley, 1925), pl. 169.

[15] Hobart *Colonial Times*, Jan. 18, 1850.

[16] Archer, *op. cit.*, pp. 193-195.

[17] *Ibid.*, p. 207.

[18] Taylor, *op. cit.*, p. 87.

[19] Simpson Davison, *The Discovery and Geognosy of Gold Deposits in Australia* (London, 1860), p. 40; Hargraves, *op. cit.*, p. 88.

[20] Archer, *op. cit.*, pp. 209-210.

[21] *Ibid.*, pp. 222, 228-229, 247-248.

[22] Davison, *op. cit.*, p. 53; Lancelott, *op. cit.*, p. 278.

[23] Hargraves, *op. cit.*, p. 95.

[24] Coy, *In the Diggings in 'Forty-nine*, pp. 42, 55.

[25] *Alta California*, Jan. 2, 1850; Stockton *Placer Times*, Jan. 9, 19, 1850; *Hobart Daily Courier*, Feb. 20, 1850; Archer, *op. cit.*, p. 227.

CHAPTER 7

[1] *Sydney Morning Herald*, July 18, 1849.

[2] Robert Towns, MS, Aug. 10, 1849 (Journal and letters in Mitchell Library, Sydney); *Sydney Morning Herald*, Aug. 4, 6, 15, 1849; Charles Bateson, *Gold Fleet for California* (Sydney, 1963), p. 97.

[3] Hobart *Colonial Times*, Aug. 28, 1849.

[4] *Ibid.*, Oct. 5, 1849.

[5] *Hobart Daily Courier*, Sept. 22, 1849, extracted from Adelaide *Mercury*, Sept. 8, 1849.

[6] *Sydney Morning Herald*, Aug. 20, 22, Sept. 12, 1849.

[7] *Ibid.*, Aug. 27, 1849.

[8] Towns, MS, Sept. 3, 1849.

[9] *Ibid.*, Aug. 23, 1849; *Australian Encyclopaedia* (East Lansing, Mich., 1958), III, 36; Frank Clune, *Wild Colonial Boys* (Sydney, 1948), p. 117.

[10] Towns, MS, Aug. 23, 24, 1849.

[11] *Australian Encyclopaedia*, III, 36.

[12] *Sydney Morning Herald*, Aug. 30, 1849.

[13] Towns, MS, Aug. 23, 1849.

[14] *Sydney Morning Herald*, Sept. 10, 1849.

[15] *Ibid.*, Aug. 31, 1849.

16 *Ibid.*, Aug. 29, 30, 1849.
17 *Ibid.*, Sept. 10, 1849; Bateson, *op. cit.*, p. 126.
18 Towns, MS, July 27, 28, Sept. 11, 12, 1849.
19 *Ibid.*, Aug. 29, Sept. 25, Oct. 5, Nov. 1, 1849.
20 *Sydney Morning Herald*, Sept. 13, 1849; *People's Advocate*, Sept. 15, 1849; *Hobart Daily Courier*, Sept. 19, 1849.
21 Hobart *Colonial Times*, June 28, 1849; March 29, 1850; *Alta California*, Nov. 29, 1849; Bayard Taylor, *Eldorado* (New York, 1857), p. 70.
22 Bateson, *op. cit.*, p. 98.
23 *Hobart Britannia*, Oct. 23, 1849; *Sydney Morning Herald*, Oct. 26, 1849; *People's Advocate*, Oct. 27, 1849; *Hobart Daily Courier*, Nov. 14, 1849; Jan. 2, 1850.
24 *Hobart Daily Courier*, Nov. 14, 1849.
25 A. Campbell, *Rough and Smooth* (Quebec, 1856), p. 13.
26 Hobart *Colonial Times*, Oct. 19, 1849.
27 *Sydney Morning Herald*, Dec. 19, 1849.
28 Towns, MS, Oct. 5, 6, 1849; Theo A. Barry and B. A. Patten, *Men and Memories of San Francisco* (San Francisco, 1873), p. 92.
29 Towns, MS, Oct. 6, 1849; Hobart *Colonial Times*, Oct. 26, 1849.
30 Towns, MS, Aug. 23, 24, 27, Sept. 10, Oct. 5, 1849; *Sydney Morning Herald*, Oct. 3, 1849.
31 *Hobart Daily Courier*, Sept. 26, Oct. 31, 1849.
32 Hobart *Colonial Times*, Oct. 26, 1849; *Alta California*, Jan. 16, 1850.
33 *Sydney Morning Herald*, Nov. 14, 1849.
34 *Alta California*, April 11, 1849; Bateson, *op. cit.*, p. 67.
35 *Hobart Town Guardian*, Oct. 17, 1849; Hobart *Colonial Times*, Oct. 26, 1849.

CHAPTER 8

1 *Sydney Morning Herald*, March 5, 1850.
2 Hobart *Colonial Times*, Oct. 26, 1849.
3 *Sydney Morning Herald*, Oct. 4, 1849.
4 *Ibid.*, Feb. 7, 1850, reprinted in Hobart *Colonial Times*, March 1, 1850.
5 Robert Towns, MS, Oct. 17, 26, Dec. 1, 1849; Jan. 5, 15, 1850 (Journal and letters in Mitchell Library, Sydney).
6 *Ibid.*, Nov. 1, 1849.
7 *Sydney Morning Herald*, Nov. 2, 13, 30, 1849; April 2, 1850; Frederic P. Maude and C. E. Pollock, *A Compendium of the Law of Merchant Shipping* (London, 1853).
8 *Sydney Morning Herald*, April 2, 1850; Hobart *Colonial Times*, May 14, 1850.
9 *Sydney Morning Herald*, April 2, June 11, Nov. 3, 1850.
10 Towns, MS, Nov. 10, 1849; Charles Bateson, *Gold Fleet for California* (Sydney, 1963), p. 49; James T. Ryan, *Reminiscences of Australia* (Sydney, 1894), p. 131.
11 *Sydney Morning Herald*, Nov. 15, 1849; Hobart *Colonial Times*, Dec. 18, 1849.
12 *Hobart Town Guardian*, Nov. 8, 17, 1849; *Sydney Morning Herald*, Nov. 15, Dec. 21, 1849; *Hobart Daily Courier*, Nov. 17, 1849.
13 *Sydney Morning Herald*, Nov. 17, 1849; Bateson, *op. cit.*, p. 108.
14 *Sydney Morning Herald*, Nov. 22, 1849.
15 Hobart *Colonial Times*, Dec. 18, 1849; Jan. 15, 1850; *Hobart Daily Courier*, Jan. 2, 1850.
16 *South Australian Register*, Dec. 8, 12, 1849.

[17] *People's Advocate*, Dec. 22, 1849; *Sydney Morning Herald*, Dec. 20, 1849; G. C. Mundy, *Our Antipodes* (London, 1855), p. 195.

[18] *Sydney Morning Herald*, Dec. 18, 1849.

[19] *Ibid.*, Dec. 28, 1849.

[20] Bateson, *op. cit.*, p. 157.

[21] *Sydney Morning Herald*, Feb. 28, 1850.

[22] *Ibid.*, March 2, 1850.

[23] *Hobart Daily Courier*, March 20, 1850, reprinted from *People's Advocate*, n.d.

[24] *Sydney Morning Herald*, Sept. 26, 1850.

[25] *Hobart Town Advertiser*, Dec. 29, 1849.

[26] *Alta California*, May 24, Dec. 14, 1849.

[27] *Hobart Daily Courier*, Sept. 4, 1850; *Hobart Town Advertiser*, Dec. 25, 1849.

[28] Hobart *Colonial Times*, Oct. 2, 1849, reprinted from *Messenger*, June 16, 1849; *Hobart Daily Courier*, Jan. 30, 1850.

[29] *Hobart Daily Courier*, Oct. 20, 1849; Felix Paul Wierzbicki, *What I Saw in California* (Launceston, 1850), p. 159.

[30] *Sydney Morning Herald*, April 11, 1850.

[31] *Ibid.*, Jan. 18, 1850; Willard B. Farwell, "Cape Horn and Cooperative Mining in '49," *Century Magazine*, XLII (Aug., 1891), 593.

[32] Bateson, *op. cit.*, pp. 122-123; statistics extracted from New South Wales Legislative Council V. & P. (1850), Vol. I.

CHAPTER 9

[1] *Stockton Times*, March 16, 30, May 11, 1850; *Sacramento Transcript*, April 1, 1850; Stockton *Placer Times*, May 17, 1850; "Gold Rush Days: Vital Statistics Copied from Early Newspapers of Stockton, California, 1850-1855" (mimeographed by San Joaquin Genealogical Society of Stockton), p. [1].

[2] *Sydney Morning Herald*, May 20, 1850; George Coffin, *A Pioneer Voyage to California* (Privately printed, 1908), p. 87; Frederick Gerstaecker, *Narrative of a Journey* (London, 1853), II, 42; Rodman W. Paul, *California Gold* (Cambridge, Mass., 1947), p. 23; Bayard Taylor, *Eldorado* (New York, 1857), p. 305.

[3] *Hobart Daily Courier*, March 20, 1850; John Sherer, *The Gold-Finder of Australia* (London, 1853), p. 96.

[4] *Alta California*, Jan. 24, 1850; *Sydney Morning Herald*, June 10, 1850.

[5] *Alta California*, Dec. 29, 1849; Jan. 24, 1850; L. G. Churchward, "Australia and America" (unpublished M.A. thesis, University of Melbourne, 1941), p. 68; Thomas Archer, *Recollections of a Rambling Life* (Yokohama, 1897), p. 226.

[6] Hobart *Colonial Times*, Jan. 4, 1850; Theo A. Barry and B. A. Patten, *Men and Memories of San Francisco* (San Francisco, 1873), pp. 153, 155-156.

[7] Simpson Davison, *The Discovery and Geognosy of Gold Deposits in Australia* (London, 1860), p. 43.

[8] *Ibid.*, p. 42.

[9] Newspaper Cuttings, V, from *Town and Country*, n.d. (Mitchell Library, Sydney); Enoch William Rudder, *Incidents Connected with the Discovery of Gold* (Sydney, 1861), pp. 9, 36.

[10] Rudder, *op. cit.*, p. 35; Sydney *Empire*, Dec. 28, 1860.

[11] Peter H. Burnett, *Recollections* (London and New York, 1880), p. 304.

[12] Davison, *op. cit.*, p. 43.

[13] *Sydney Morning Herald*, March 2, 1850; Taylor, *op. cit.*, p. 214.

[14] *Sacramento Daily Placer Times*, Dec. 29, 1849; Jan. 19, Feb. 23, March 2, 1850; Taylor, *op. cit.*, pp. 219, 226, 276.

15 Frank Marryat, *Mountains and Molehills* (London, 1855), p. 225; Taylor, *op. cit.*, pp. 223, 272.

16 Stephen J. Field, *Personal Reminiscences* (privately printed, 1893), pp. 17, 21.

17 Rudder, *op. cit.*, p. 34.

18 *Ibid.*, pp. 12, 34.

19 Davison, *op. cit.*, p. 187.

20 Joseph Henry Jackson, *Anybody's Gold* (New York, 1941), p. 413.

21 Letter from W. M. Curtayne in *Sydney Morning Herald*, Sept. 30, 1850, describing pack trip on upper Yuba. See also Rudder, *op. cit.*, p. 35; Hubert Howe Bancroft, *History of California* (San Francisco, 1888), VI, 362.

22 Archer, *op. cit.*, p. 226; Rudder, *op. cit.*, p. 35.

23 *Hobart Daily Courier*, Oct. 16, 1850; Theodore H. Hittell, *History of California* (San Francisco, 1897), III, 281-282. Note that Archer, *op. cit.*, pp. 225-226, is the only one who states specifically that the Australians went back to Sonora, whereas Rudder, *op. cit.*, p. 35, says only that he walked 120 miles with them.

24 Davison, *op. cit.*, p. 50.

25 William W. Earnest, MS (privately owned, Naperville, Ill.), p. [49]; Archer, *op. cit.*, pp. 247-248; Rudder, *op. cit.*, p. 36.

26 Davison, *op. cit.*, p. 52.

27 *Marysville Herald*, Aug. 6, 1850; *Sacramento Daily Placer Times*, Sept. 8, 1849.

28 *Sydney Morning Herald*, July 9, 22, 1850; Hobart *Colonial Times*, July 15, 1850; Coffin, *op. cit.*, p. 87; Marryat, *op. cit.*, pp. 24, 37, 39.

29 *Alta California*, Oct. 12, 1850; Rudder, *op. cit.*, p. 37.

30 Davison, *op. cit.*, p. 38.

31 John Elphinstone Erskine, *A Short Account of the Late Discoveries of Gold in Australia* (London, 1852), p. 78; Rudder, *op. cit.*, pp. 34-36. See also Rudder's MS (Fisher Library, Sydney).

CHAPTER 10

1 Letters in Edward Deas Thomson Papers (Mitchell Library, Sydney); *Sydney Morning Herald*, Jan. 7, 1851; Simpson Davison, *The Discovery and Geognosy of Gold Deposits in Australia* (London, 1860), p. 35.

2 *Sydney Morning Herald*, May 17, 1851; Newspaper Cuttings, V, from *Sydney Morning Herald*, Feb. 4, 1906; F. Lancelott, *Australia As It Is* (London, 1852), I, 276; R. Edmond Malone, *Three Years' Cruise* (London, 1854), p. 170.

3 H. John Carlsson Taussig, MS (privately owned, Bathurst); L. G. Churchward, "Australia and America" (unpublished M.A. thesis, University of Melbourne, 1941), pp. 11-24; Roger Therry, *Reminiscences* (London, 1863), pp. 364-365.

4 Hobart *Colonial Times*, Feb. 12, 22, March 22, 1850; *Hobart Daily Courier*, Feb. 16, 20, Aug. 31, 1850; Jan. 19, 1851.

5 *Sydney Morning Herald*, Jan. 15, March 5, 1850. The pamphlet was entitled *California and Its Resources*.

6 Hobart *Colonial Times*, Feb. 12, 15, 1850; *Hobart Daily Courier*, Feb. 13, 1850.

7 Churchward, *op. cit.*, p. 70; Hobart *Colonial Times*, Feb. 19, 22, 26, 1850; March 28, 1851.

8 Hobart *Colonial Times*, Feb. 12, 1850; *Hobart Daily Courier*, March 27, 30, 1850.

[9] Launceston *Cornwall Chronicle*, Feb. 13, 1850; *Hobart Daily Courier*, Feb. 16, 1850; Hobart *Colonial Times*, Feb. 19, 1850.

[10] *Sydney Morning Herald*, Jan. 7, 15, 1850; *Hobart Daily Courier*, May 18, 1850; Churchward, *op. cit.*, p. 71.

[11] Colonial Secretary Records, Denison Period, accession nos. 1830, 1833 (Tasmanian Archives, Hobart); *Hobart Daily Courier*, Aug. 14, 1850.

[12] Charles Bateson, *Gold Fleet for California* (Sydney, 1963), p. 129.

[13] *Sydney Morning Herald*, Oct. 21, 28, Dec. 7, 1850.

[14] *Hobart Daily Courier*, April 13, 1850.

[15] Johnson Dean, *On Sea and Land* (Hobart, ca. 1905), pp. 9-14.

[16] *Alta California*, Nov. 15, 1850; Bateson, *op. cit.*, p. 113; Frederick Gerstaecker, *Narrative of a Journey round the World* (London, 1853), II, 287.

[17] Dean, *op. cit.*, p. 19.

[18] *Hobart Daily Courier*, Sept. 4, 1850; Hobart *Colonial Times*, Dec. 17, 1850.

[19] Dean, *op. cit.*, pp. 48-52.

[20] Robert Towns, MS, letters to Mackey and Captain Pierce, March 20, May 22, June 11, 1850 (Journal and letters, Mitchell Library, Sydney); Hobart *Colonial Times*, Feb. 13, March 29, 1850.

[21] Towns, MS, March 20, May 10, June 10, 11, July 9, 1850.

[22] *Ibid.*, Aug. 28, 1850; *Sydney Morning Herald*, Aug. 30, 1850; Bayard Taylor, *Eldorado* (New York, 1857), pp. 305-306.

[23] *Hobart Daily Courier*, April 13, 1850, May 18, July 31, 1850.

[24] *Ibid.*, July 13, 1850; Hobart *Colonial Times*, July 16, Sept. 27, 1850; *Sydney Morning Herald*, Sept. 7, 1850.

[25] Hobart *Colonial Times*, Feb. 22, 26, 1850.

[26] *Hobart Daily Courier*, Feb. 16, 1850.

[27] Enoch William Rudder, *Incidents Connected with the Discovery of Gold* (Sydney, 1861), p. 38.

CHAPTER 11

[1] R. Edmond Malone, *Three Years' Cruise* (London, 1854), p. 149; G. C. Mundy, *Our Antipodes* (London, 1855), pp. 58, 62.

[2] *Sydney Morning Herald*, May 15, 1851; Sydney *Empire*, Dec. 28, 1860.

[3] H. John Carlsson Taussig, MS (privately owned, Bathurst).

[4] Edward Hammond Hargraves, *Australia & Its Goldfields* (London, 1855), p. 111; Mundy, *op. cit.*, p. 94.

[5] Mundy, *op. cit.*, pp. 91, 94, 121-122; *Australian Encyclopaedia* (East Lansing, Mich., 1958), I, 454-455.

[6] David Mackenzie, *The Gold Digger* (London, 1852), pp. 21-23.

[7] Mundy, *op. cit.*, p. 144.

[8] Frank Clune, *Wild Colonial Boys* (Sydney, 1948), p. 115; Simpson Davison, *The Discovery and Geognosy of Gold Deposits in Australia* (London, 1860), p. 84; W. R. Glasson, *Lewis Ponds Creek* (Sydney, n.d.), p. 23.

[9] Glasson, *loc. cit.*; W. R. Glasson, *Australia's First Goldfield* (Sydney, 1944), pp. 7, 10; Charles L. Barrett (ed.), *Gold in Australia* (London, 1951), p. 5.

[10] Clune, *op. cit.*, pp. 39, 138, 145; Glasson, *Australia's First Goldfield*, p. 11; Glasson, *Lewis Ponds Creek*, p. 20.

[11] Newspaper Cuttings, V (Mitchell Library, Sydney); Glasson, *Lewis Ponds Creek*, p. 15; George French Angas, *Views of the Gold Regions of Australia* (London, 1851).

[12] Hargraves, *op. cit.*, p. 115.

[13] Enoch William Rudder, *Incidents Connected with the Discovery of Gold*

(Sydney, 1861), p. 21; Glasson, *Lewis Ponds Creek*, pp. 15, 20; Geoffrey Blainey, *The Rush That Never Ended* (Melbourne, 1963), p. 16.

14 Hargraves, *op. cit.*, p. 117.

15 *Sydney Morning Herald*, March 22, 1851; Davison, *op. cit.*, p. 460; Rudder, *op. cit.*, pp. 16-17.

16 *Bell's Life in Sydney*, April 12, 1851; Mundy, *op. cit.*, p. 616. L. G. Churchward, "Australia and America" (unpublished M.A. thesis, University of Melbourne, 1941), p. 72, says that 800 gold seekers left in May.

17 Rudder, *op. cit.*, p. 37.

18 *Sydney Morning Herald*, March 26, 1851.

19 *Ibid.*, March 15, 1851; *People's Advocate*, March 22, 29, 1851.

20 George Francis Train, *My Life* (New York, 1902), p. 143, and *Young America Abroad* (London, 1857), p. 404; Mundy, *op. cit.*, p. 56; P. Just, *Australia* (Dundee, 1859), p. 127; Davison, *op. cit.*, p. 362.

21 Davison, *op. cit.*, p. 355.

22 Hargraves, *op. cit.*, p. 119.

CHAPTER 12

1 H. J. C. Taussig, MS (privately owned, Bathurst); *Sydney Morning Herald*, April 29, 1851; W. R. Glasson, *Australia's First Goldfield* (Sydney, 1944), p. 6; Enoch William Rudder, *Incidents Connected with the Discovery of Gold* (Sydney, 1861), p. 38.

2 Geoffrey Blainey, *The Rush That Never Ended* (Melbourne, 1963), p. 18; Frank Clune, *Wild Colonial Boys* (Sydney, 1948), p. 55.

3 Glasson, *op. cit.*, p. 9; Rudder, *op. cit.*, p. 21.

4 F. Lancelott, *Australia As It Is* (London, 1852), I, 284.

5 *Bell's Life in Sydney*, May 10, 1851; *Sydney Morning Herald*, May 14, 26, 1851; *People's Advocate*, May 17, 1851.

6 *Sydney Morning Herald*, May 16, 30, 1851; Louis Becke (ed.), *Old Convict Days* (New York, 1899), p. 212.

7 *Sydney Morning Herald*, May 20, 1851.

8 R. S. Anderson, *Australian Gold Fields*, ed. George Mackaness (Sydney, 1956), p. 12; Charles L. Barrett (ed.), *Gold in Australia* (London, 1951), p. 3.

9 Rudder, *op. cit.*, p. 38.

10 *Sydney Morning Herald*, May 24, 1851; *Hobart Daily Courier*, June 11, 21, 1852; Frederick Gerstaecker, *Narrative of a Journey round the World* (London, 1853), II, 105.

11 Sydney *Empire*, May 19, 1851; *Sydney Morning Herald*, May 23, 1851; *Hobart Daily Courier*, June 11, 1851; *Alta California*, Aug. 17, 1851.

12 *People's Advocate*, May 17, 24, 1851; *Sydney Morning Herald*, May 26, 28, 1851; *Alta California*, Aug. 17, 1851.

13 *People's Advocate*, May 24, 1851; *Sydney Morning Herald*, May 24, 28, 30, 1851; Gerstaecker, *op. cit.*, II, 267; Barrett, *op. cit.*, p. 9; G. C. Mundy, *Our Antipodes* (London, 1855), p. 562.

14 *Bathurst Free Press*, May 28, 1851; *Sydney Morning Herald*, May 21, 28, 29, 31, June 7, 1851; *Hobart Daily Courier*, June 4, 7, 25, 1851; *Alta California*, Aug. 17, 1851; Becke, *op. cit.*, p. 156; John Elphinstone Erskine, *A Short Account of the Late Discoveries of Gold in Australia* (London, 1852), p. 35; Mundy, *op. cit.*, pp. 567-568, 606; C. Rudston Read, *What I Heard, Saw, and Did at the Australian Gold Fields* (London, 1853), p. 6.

15 Sydney *Empire*, June 10, 1851; *Sydney Morning Herald*, May 28, June 16, 1851; W. R. Glasson, *Lewis Ponds Creek* (Sydney, n.d.), p. 16.

16 Letter from U.S. Consul to Daniel Webster, Aug. 8, 1851, in Dispatches

from U.S. Consuls, 1836-1906 (microfilm, University of California, Santa Barbara); *Sydney Morning Herald*, June 21, 23, 1851; Frank Clune, "Pool of the Two-tailed Fish," in *Land of My Birth* (Sydney, 1949), p. 60; George W. Peck, *Melbourne, and the Chincha Islands* (New York, 1854), p. 76.

[17] *Hobart Daily Courier*, June 14, 1851; *Sydney Morning Herald*, June 16, 20, 1851; Hobart *Colonial Times*, July 1, 1851; James T. Ryan, *Reminiscences of Australia* (Sydney, 1894), p. 144; Lancelott, *op. cit.*, p. 301.

[18] *Sydney Morning Herald*, May 30, June 9, 1851; *Hobart Daily Courier*, June 25, 1851; William Thomas Pyke, *Australian Heroes and Adventurers* (Melbourne, n.d.), p. 157.

[19] *Sydney Morning Herald*, May 28, 1851; *Hobart Daily Courier*, June 4, 1851; Geoffrey Blainey, *The Rush That Never Ended* (Melbourne, 1963), p. 21.

[20] Lancelott, *op. cit.*, p. 302; Becke, *op. cit.*, p. 155.

CHAPTER 13

[1] According to the *Sydney Morning Herald*, June 20, 1851, hoarfrost was already covering the ground.

[2] *Hobart Daily Courier*, July 30, 1851; Charles L. Barrett (ed.), *Gold in Australia* (London, 1951), p. 18; F. Lancelott, *Australia As It Is* (London, 1852), I, 305; R. S. Anderson, *Australian Gold Fields*, ed. George Mackaness (Sydney, 1956), p. 13; John Elphinstone Erskine, *A Short Account of the Late Discoveries of Gold in Australia* (London, 1852), p. 41.

[3] G. C. Mundy, *Our Antipodes* (London, 1855), p. 576.

[4] *Sydney Morning Herald*, July 23, 1851.

[5] *Ibid.*, May 8, 1851; *Bell's Life in Sydney*, May 10, 1851.

[6] *Sydney Morning Herald*, May 12, 1851; *Stockton Times*, March 12, 1851.

[7] *Sydney Morning Herald*, July 1, 2, 1851; *Hobart Daily Courier*, Nov. 8, 1851; Hubert Howe Bancroft, *Popular Tribunals* (San Francisco, 1887), I, 181.

[8] Frank Soulé, John H. Gihon, and James Nisbet, *The Annals of San Francisco* (New York, 1855), p. 315; Amelia Ransome Neville, *The Fantastic City* (Boston, 1932), pp. 73-74; George Stewart, *Committee of Vigilance* (Boston, 1964), p. 23.

[9] Robert Towns, MS, June 12, 1850 (Journal and letters in Mitchell Library, Sydney); *Sydney Morning Herald*, July 1, 1851; *Alta California*, Aug. 6, 7, 9, 10, 11, 1851; Mary Floyd Williams (ed.), *Papers of the San Francisco Committee of Vigilance of 1851* (Berkeley, 1919), pp. 74 ff., 134.

[10] *Alta California*, Aug. 25, 1851; Williams, *op. cit.*, pp. 184, 361, 478-479; Theo A. Barry and B. A. Patten, *Men and Memories of San Francisco* (San Francisco, 1873), p. 162.

[11] Quoted in Hobart *Colonial Times*, June 17, 20, 1851, and Melbourne *Argus*, July 12, 1851, from *Sydney Morning Herald*, July 1, 1851; Thomas M'Combie, *Australian Sketches* (London, 1861), p. 12.

[12] Williams, *op. cit.*, pp. 250, 479.

[13] Dispatches from U.S. Consuls, 1836-1906 (microfilm, University of California, Santa Barbara). The Chief Constable's letter of July 24 is in the U.S. Consul's Report of September 6, 1851.

[14] Melbourne *Argus*, July 16, 1851; Lancelott, *op. cit.*, p. 120. A different account of this discovery may be found in Geoffrey Blainey, *The Rush That Never Ended* (Melbourne, 1963), p. 28, and *Australian Encyclopaedia* (East Lansing, Mich., 1958), III, 402.

[15] Charles Bateson, *Gold Fleet for California* (Sydney, 1963), p. 121; Williams, *op. cit.*, p. 57.

[16] Dispatches from U.S. Consuls, 1836-1906, Aug. 20, 1851.

17 *Alta California*, June 11, 14, 1851; Soulé, Gihon, and Nisbet, *op. cit.*, p. 350.
18 Williams, *op. cit.*, pp. 16, 53, 54, 132.
19 *Ibid.*, p. 103.
20 *Alta California*, June 14, 1851.
21 Barry and Patten, *op. cit.*, pp. 239-242; Williams, *op. cit.*, p. 23.
22 George Coffin, *A Pioneer Voyage to California* (privately printed, 1908), p. 125; James Augustin Brown Scherer, *"The Lion of the Vigilantes": William T. Coleman* (Indianapolis, 1939), pp. 111, 571; Soulé, Gihon, and Nisbet, *op. cit.*, p. 570.
23 Williams, *op. cit.*, p. 23; Soulé, Gihon, and Nisbet, *op. cit.*, p. 571.
24 Soulé, Gihon, and Nisbet, *loc. cit.*; Barry and Patten, *op. cit.*, pp. 239-242.
25 *Alta California*, July 6, 1851; Bancroft, *op. cit.*, p. 361; Williams, *op. cit.*, pp. 222-223.
26 Barry and Patten, *op. cit.*, pp. 113-119.
27 Williams, *op. cit.*, p. 224.
28 *Ibid.*, pp. 225, 550.
29 *Alta California*, Aug. 19, 26, 1851; Soulé, Gihon, and Nisbet, *op. cit.*, p. 321.

CHAPTER 14

1 Letter dated April 2, in *Sydney Morning Herald*, July 1, 1851; *ibid.*, July 12, Aug. 20, 21, 1851; *Tasmanian Colonist*, July 21, 1851; *Alta California*, June 15, 16, Aug. 4, 1851.
2 Sydney *Empire*, Aug. 20, Oct. 22, 1851.
3 Geoffrey Blainey, *The Rush That Never Ended* (Melbourne, 1963), pp. 32, 34; Samuel L. Clemens, *Following the Equator* (New York, 1897), I, 237; Samuel Mossman and Thomas Banister, *Australia Visited and Revisited* (London, 1853), p. 31; R. S. Anderson, *Australian Gold Fields*, ed. G. Mackaness (Sydney, 1956), p. 41; Rodman W. Paul, *California Gold* (Cambridge, Mass., 1947), p. 118; *Australian Encyclopaedia* (East Lansing, Mich., 1958), IV, 321; *Encyclopaedia Britannica* (Chicago, 1961), IV, 597.
4 L. G. Churchward, "Australia and America" (unpublished M.A. thesis, University of Melbourne, 1941), p. 81; Mrs. Charles Clacy, *A Lady's Visit to the Gold Diggings of Australia in 1852-53* (London, 1853), p. 11; E. Scott (ed.), *Lord Robert Cecil's Goldfields Diary* (Melbourne, 1935), p. 13; Charles L. Barrett (ed.), *Gold in Australia* (London, 1951), p. 23; Anderson, *op. cit.*, p. 16; Mrs. A. Campbell, *Rough and Smooth* (Quebec, 1856), p. 121; Simpson Davison, *The Discovery and Geognosy of Gold Deposits in Australia* (London, 1860), p. 71; John Sherer, *The Gold-Finder of Australia* (London, 1853), p. 251; Paul, *op. cit.*, pp. 21, 25.
5 Hobart *Colonial Times*, June 17, 1851; *Hobart Daily Courier*, June 18, 1851; Melbourne *Argus*, Sept. 12, 1851.
6 Clacy, *op. cit.*, p. 168; R. M. Crawford and G. F. James, "The Gold Rushes," in C. Hartley Grattan (ed.), *Australia* (Berkeley and Los Angeles, 1947), p. 49; *Australian Encyclopaedia*, III, 415.
7 Mary Floyd Williams (ed.), *Papers of the San Francisco Committee of Vigilance of 1851* (Berkeley, 1919), pp. 224, 263.
8 *Alta California*, July 12, 14, 1851; Melbourne *Argus*, Sept. 12, 1851; Hubert Howe Bancroft, *Popular Tribunals* (San Francisco, 1887), I, 296; Frank Meriweather Smith (ed.), *San Francisco Vigilance Committee* (San Francisco, 1883), p. 13; Frank Soulé, John H. Gihon, and James Nisbet, *The Annals of San Francisco* (New York, 1855), p. 581; Williams, *op. cit.*, p. 263.
9 *Alta California*, Aug. 6, 18, 29, 1851.
10 *Ibid.*, Aug. 18, 25, 1851; *Sydney Morning Herald*, Oct. 20, 1851; Hobart

Colonial Times, Oct. 24, 1851; Williams, *op. cit.*, p. 234.

[11] *Alta California*, Aug. 12, 1851; George Stewart, *Committee of Vigilance* (Boston, 1964), p. 132; Williams, *op. cit.*, pp. 232, 303, 454.

[12] *Alta California*, Aug. 18, 1851; Bancroft, *op. cit.*, p. 359; Williams, *op. cit.*, pp. 456-458, 536.

[13] *Alta California*, Aug. 11, 25, 1851; *Hobart Daily Courier*, Nov. 12, 1851; George Coffin, *A Pioneer Voyage to California* (privately printed, 1908), p. 125; Stewart, *op. cit.*, p. 282.

[14] *Alta California*, Aug. 25, 1851.

[15] *Ibid.*, July 6, 10, Aug. 17, 20, 1851; Stewart, *op. cit.*, p. 299; Williams, *op. cit.*, p. 673.

[16] *Hobart Daily Courier*, Nov. 29, 1851; *Hobart Town Advertiser*, Nov. 28, 1851; *Sydney Morning Herald*, Oct. 25, 1851; *People's Advocate*, Nov. 1, 1851; *Alta California*, Aug. 17, 19, 1851.

[17] *Sydney Morning Herald*, Oct. 20, 1851; Sydney *Empire*, Oct. 22, 1851.

[18] *Alta California*, Aug. 4, 1851; *Sydney Morning Herald*, Aug. 20, 1851.

CHAPTER 15

[1] *Sydney Morning Herald*, Suppl., Dec. 16, 1848; I. G. Anderson, *Port Arthur through the Artist's Eyes* (Hobart, 1948), p. 12; J. H. Cullen, *Young Ireland in Exile* (Dublin, 1928), pp. 26, 91, 113; William Dillon, *Life of John Mitchel* (London, 1888), I, 327; John Mitchel, *Jail Journal* (Dublin, 1913), p. 443.

[2] Cullen, *op. cit.*, pp. 9-11; G. C. Mundy, *Our Antipodes* (London, 1855), p. 475; Mitchel, *op. cit.*, p. 236.

[3] Mitchel, *op. cit.*, p. 269; Mundy, *op. cit.*, p. 476; Mary Floyd Williams (ed.), *Papers of the San Francisco Committee of Vigilance of 1851* (Berkeley, 1919), p. 715.

[4] Letter signed J. H. Cullen, Aug. 5, 1947; Colonial Secretary Records, Denison Period, accession no. 1963 (Tasmanian Archives, Hobart); Anderson, *op. cit.*, p. 12; Cullen, *op. cit.*, p. 16; Mitchel, *op. cit.*, p. 231.

[5] *Bell's Life in Sydney*, Feb. 8, 1851; Dillon, *op. cit.*, p. 332.

[6] Cullen, *op. cit.*, p. 93; R. Edmond Malone, *Three Years' Cruise in the Australian Colonies* (London, 1854), p. 47; Mundy, *op. cit.*, p. 515.

[7] Letter of Governor Denison to Earl Grey, March 22, 1851, in Colonial Secretary Records, Denison Period.

[8] Letter of George Aikens to Governor Denison, June 19, 1851, in *ibid.*; *Alta California*, June 7-12, 1851; Williams, *op. cit.*, p. 459.

[9] *Alta California*, July 3, 1851; Williams, *op. cit.*, p. 28.

[10] *Launceston Examiner*, March 17, 1852; Williams, *op. cit.*, pp. 712-716.

[11] *Launceston Examiner*, Feb. 14, 1852; Cullen, *op. cit.*, pp. 45, 59, 85; Michael Cavanagh (ed.), *Memoirs of Gen. Thomas Francis Meagher* (Worcester, Mass., 1892), p. 307; Mitchel, *op. cit.*, pp. 231, 273-274.

[12] *Launceston Examiner*, Feb. 14, 1852; *Hobart Daily Courier*, Feb. 18, 1852; Cullen, *op. cit.*, pp. 51-57; Dillon, *op. cit.*, II, 6.

[13] *Hobart Town Guardian*, Jan. 7, 1852; Cavanagh, *op. cit.*, p. 341; Cullen, *op. cit.*, pp. 51-55, 82, 85; Malone, *op. cit.*, p. 58.

[14] Cavanagh, *op. cit.*, p. 245; Josiah Marshall Favill, *The Diary of a Young Officer . . . during the War of the Rebellion* (Chicago, 1909), pp. 225, 252, 282; Mitchel, *op. cit.*, p. 444; Henry Villard, *Memoirs* (Boston, 1904), pp. 175, 183-184.

[15] U.S. Consul's Semi-Annual Report, Jan. 1, 1852; Hobart *Colonial Times*, May 14, 1852; *Hobart Town Advertiser*, May 6, 1852; *Hobart Daily Courier*, Sept. 22, 1852.

16 C. Manning Hope Clark (ed.), *Select Documents in Australian History, 1788-1850* (Sydney, 1950), II, 307; Charles D. Ferguson, *The Experiences of a Forty-niner* (Cleveland, 1888), pp. 250, 350; Thomas M'Combie, *Australian Sketches* (London, 1861), p. 65.

17 L. G. Churchward, "Australia and America" (unpublished M.A. thesis, University of Melbourne, 1941), p. 90, quoting Lord Robert Cecil's diary entry of March 25, 1852; E. Scott (ed.), *Lord Robert Cecil's Goldfields Diary* (Melbourne, 1935), pp. 10, 13.

18 *Sydney Morning Herald*, Feb. 12, 1850; William Jackson Barry, *Past & Present* (Wellington, N.Z., 1897), p. 116; Cullen, *op. cit.*, pp. 113, 121; Mundy, *op. cit.*, p. 213. The *Irish Exile* appeared on January 26, 1850.

19 Charles L. Barrett (ed.), *Gold in Australia* (London, 1951), p. 23; Churchward, *op. cit.*, p. 81.

20 Mrs. A. Campbell, *Rough and Smooth* (Quebec, 1856), p. 47; Ferguson, *op. cit.*, p. 239.

21 George Stewart, *Committee of Vigilance* (Boston, 1964), p. 8.

22 Campbell, *op. cit.*, p. 52.

23 Mrs. Charles Clacy, *A Lady's Visit to the Gold Diggings of Australia in 1852-53* (London, 1853), p. 26; John Sherer, *The Gold-Finder of Australia* (London, 1853), p. 253.

24 Malone, *op. cit.*, pp. 150, 190.

25 *Hobart Daily Courier*, Nov. 22, 1853, quoting the *Atlas*, Aug. 20. A search of the *Atlas* in both New York and Boston has failed to verify this reference. See also Cullen, *op. cit.*, p. 121.

26 Dillon, *op. cit.*, II, 128, 284.

27 *Ibid.*, I, 283; II, 233, 268, 307, 313.

28 George Francis Train, *Young America Abroad* (London, 1857), p. 413.

29 Dillon, *op. cit.*, II, 291.

30 *Ibid.*, I, 312, 340.

31 *Ibid.*, p. 323.

32 Train, *op. cit.*, p. 362.

33 Dillon, *op. cit.*, II, 12, 19.

34 Mitchel, *op. cit.*, pp. 305, 318; Williams, *op. cit.*, p. 105; Train, *op. cit.*, p. 362.

35 Mitchel, *op. cit.*, p. 453.

36 *Ibid.*, p. 339.

37 Train, *op. cit.*, p. 362.

38 Dillon, *op. cit.*, II, 26.

39 *Ibid.*, p. 27; Mitchel, *op. cit.*, p. 34.

40 San Francisco *Daily Herald*, Oct. 13, 1853; Dillon, *op. cit.*, II, 29; Mitchel, *op. cit.*, p. 350.

41 Train, *op. cit.*, p. 413.

42 Dillon, *op. cit.*, I, 332.

43 Cullen, *op. cit.*, p. 126; Malone, *op. cit.*, p. 57; *Australian Encyclopaedia* (East Lansing, Mich., 1958), VI, 387.

CHAPTER 16

1 L. G. Churchward, "Australia and America" (unpublished M.A. thesis, University of Melbourne, 1941), pp. 84, 90; N. O. P. Pyke, "Foreign Immigration to the Gold Fields" (unpublished M.A. thesis, University of Sydney, 1946), pp. 77, 191; Geoffrey Serle, "The Causes of Eureka," *Special Eureka Supplement, Historical Studies: Australia and New Zealand* (Dec., 1954), p. 18.

[2] Joseph Claughton, MS (privately owned, Richmond, B.C., Canada); William W. Earnest, Journal (privately owned, Naperville, Ill.), p. [53]; *Alta California*, June 21, 1851; Charles D. Ferguson, *The Experiences of a Forty-niner* (Cleveland, 1888), pp. 215, 218, 219; Robert Samuel Fletcher, *Eureka* (Durham, N.C., 1959), p. 70.

[3] Johnson Dean, *On Sea and Land* (Hobart, ca. 1905), p. 55; Ferguson, *op. cit.*, pp. 221, 232.

[4] Mrs. A. Campbell, *Rough and Smooth* (Quebec, 1856), pp. 44, 45; Mrs. Charles Clacy, *A Lady's Visit to the Gold Diggings* (London, 1853), pp. 22, 23; George W. Peck, *Melbourne, and the Chincha Islands* (New York, 1854), p. 30; George Francis Train, *Young America Abroad* (London, 1857), p. 2.

[5] Clacy, *op. cit.*, p. 26; Frederick Gerstaecker, *Narrative of a Journey round the World* (London, 1853), II, 269; Peck, *op. cit.*, pp. 30, 32, 42, 54, 55, 109; Clive Turnbull, *Bonanza* (Melbourne, 1946), p. 16.

[6] L. G. Churchward, "The American Contribution to the Victorian Gold Rush," *Victorian Historical Magazine*, XIX (June, 1942), 95; Churchward, "Australia and America," p. 21.

[7] Churchward, "The American Contribution," pp. 87, 89.

[8] Claughton, MS, Aug. 14, 1852; *Alta California*, June 18, 1851; Clacy, *op. cit.*, p. 234; Ferguson, *op. cit.*, p. 324; Campbell, *op. cit.*, p. 124; R. Edmond Malone, *Three Years' Cruise in the Australian Colonies* (London, 1854), p. 150; Train, *op. cit.*, p. 387.

[9] *Hobart Daily Courier*, Oct. 3, Nov. 30, 1853; Churchward, "The American Contribution," p. 91; Churchward, "Australia and America," pp. 93, 97; Turnbull, *op. cit.*, p. 10.

[10] Churchward, "Australia and America," pp. 95, 96; C. Stuart Ross, "Two American Types That Left Their Stamp on Victorian History," *Victorian Historical Magazine*, VII (July, 1919), 130; Turnbull, *op. cit.*, pp. 13-14.

[11] Churchward, "Australia and America," p. 105; Ferguson, *op. cit.*, p. 350; Pyke, *op. cit.*, p. 175.

[12] Melbourne *Argus*, March 5, 11, 1852; Hobart *Colonial Times*, Nov. 12, 1852; *Hobart Town Guardian*, March 27, 1852; Campbell, *op. cit.*, p. 45; Train, *op. cit.*, p. 357.

[13] Clacy, *op. cit.*, p. 26; Ferguson, *op. cit.*, p. 26; Peck, *op. cit.*, pp. 105-106; Train, *op. cit.*, p. 370.

[14] Joseph Henry Jackson, *Anybody's Gold* (New York, 1941), pp. 189, 190; Willis Thornton, *The Nine Lives of Citizen Train* (New York, 1948), p. 48; George Francis Train, *My Life* (New York, 1902), p. 167.

[15] *Hobart Daily Courier*, July 1, Sept. 30, Oct. 12, 15, 1853.

[16] Claughton, MS, Aug. 21, 1852; Clacy, *op. cit.*, p. 200; Campbell, *op. cit.*, p. 65; Peck, *op. cit.*, p. 76.

[17] Geoffrey Blainey, *The Rush That Never Ended* (Melbourne, 1963), pp. 32, 45; Clacy, *op. cit.*, pp. 203, 205; Train, *Young America Abroad*, p. 319.

[18] Campbell, *op. cit.*, p. 78; Pyke, *op. cit.*, p. 171; *Australian Encyclopaedia* (East Lansing, Mich., 1958), I, 395; Clacy, *op. cit.*, p. 89.

[19] *Alta California*, Dec. 29, 1849; *Sydney Morning Herald*, June 13, 1851; *Hobart Daily Courier*, April 14, 1852; July 1, 1853; John Elphinstone Erskine, *A Short Account of the Late Discoveries of Gold in Australia* (London, 1852), p. 20; Ferguson, *op. cit.*, pp. 244, 264, 266, 311; F. Lancelott, *Australia As It Is* (London, 1852), I, 299; Train, *Young America Abroad*, pp. 369, 373.

[20] *Hobart Daily Courier*, Aug. 9, 1853; Campbell, *op. cit.*, p. 76.

[21] Clacy, *op. cit.*, p. 168.

[22] C. Manning Hope Clark (ed.), *Select Documents in Australian History, 1788-1850* (Sydney, 1950), II, 55; William Thomas Pyke, *Australian Heroes and Adventurers* (Melbourne, n.d.), p. 34.

23 Raffaello Carboni, *The Eureka Stockade* (Mosman, N.S.W., Australia, 1942), p. xvii; Ferguson, *op. cit.*, p. 275.

24 Campbell, *op. cit.*, p. 100.

25 Melbourne *Argus*, Dec. 1, 1853; Train, *Young America Abroad*, pp. 358, 360.

26 Ferguson, *op. cit.*, p. 254; John Sherer, *The Gold-Finder of Australia* (London, 1853), p. 225.

27 Turnbull, *op. cit.*, p. 23.

28 Peck, *op. cit.*, p. 92.

29 Train, *Young America Abroad*, p. 395.

30 [J. R. Godley, ed.], "Extracts from the Journal of a Visit to New South Wales in 1853" (in unidentified publication in Mitchell Library, Sydney), p. 508; Malone, *op. cit.*, p. 140; Amos S. Pittman, "The California and Australia Gold Rushes," *California Historical Society Quarterly*, XXX (March, 1951), 29-30; Train, *Young America Abroad*, p. 401.

31 *Sydney Morning Herald*, Aug. 8, Oct. 5, 1853.

32 Malone, *op. cit.*, p. 150.

33 Godley, *op. cit.*, pp. 517-518.

34 C. H. Currey, *The Irish at Eureka* (Sydney, 1954), p. 10; Godley, *op. cit.*, p. 500.

35 A. G. L. Shaw, *The Story of Australia* (London, [1954]), p. 128.

36 Train, *Young America Abroad*, p. 390.

37 *Australian Encyclopaedia*, VII, 189; David Swift and Heinz Marcuse, "The Golden Century," *Mining and Geological Journal*, IV (Sept., 1951), 11; Train, *Young America Abroad*, p. 406.

38 Simpson Davison, *The Discovery and Geognosy of Gold Deposits in Australia* (London, 1860), p. 89; *Australian Encyclopaedia*, IV, 4; VIII, 542; Train, *Young America Abroad*, p. 403.

39 Turnbull, *op. cit.*, p. 32.

CHAPTER 17

1 C. H. Currey, *The Irish at Eureka* (Sydney, 1954), p. 29; Charles D. Ferguson, *The Experiences of a Forty-niner* (Cleveland, 1888), p. 299; P. Just, *Australia; or Notes Taken during a Residence in the Colonies* (Dundee, 1859), pp. 134-136.

2 Raffaello Carboni, *The Eureka Stockade* (Mosman, N.S.W., Australia, 1942), p. 19.

3 N. O. P. Pyke, "Foreign Immigration to the Gold Fields" (unpublished M.A. thesis, University of Sydney, 1946), p. 236.

4 Currey, *op. cit.*, p. 30.

5 *Ibid.*, pp. 31-32.

6 *Ibid.*, p. 34.

7 *Ibid.*, p. 3.

8 *Ibid.*, p. 34; C. Manning Hope Clark (ed.), *Select Documents in Australian History, 1851-1900* (Sydney, 1955), II, 57.

9 Carboni, *op. cit.*, p. 24.

10 William Jackson Barry, *Past & Present and Men of the Times* (Wellington, N.Z., 1897), p. 120; Carboni, *op. cit.*, pp. 24-25.

11 Currey, *op. cit.*, p. 37; George Francis Train, *Young America Abroad* (London, 1857), p. 416.

12 Melbourne *Argus*, Oct. 30, 1854; Currey, *op. cit.*, p. 49.

13 Melbourne *Argus*, Oct. 31, 1854.

14 *Ibid.*, Nov. 4, 1854, quoting *Geelong Advertiser*, Nov. 1, 1854.

15 Carboni, *op. cit.*, pp. 37, 41; Clark, *op. cit.*, p. 58; Currey, *op. cit.*, p. 41.

[16] Carboni, *op. cit.*, pp. 52, 71; Pyke, *op. cit.*, p. 248.

[17] Melbourne *Argus*, Dec. 6, 1854; Currey, *op. cit.*, p. 44.

[18] Melbourne *Argus*, Dec. 1, 1854.

[19] *Ibid.*, Dec. 12, 1854; Carboni, *op. cit.*, pp. xviii-xix; Currey, *op. cit.*, p. 50; Train, *op. cit.*, p. 5.

[20] Melbourne *Argus*, Dec. 2, 1854.

[21] *Ibid.*, Dec. 5, 1854; Carboni, *op. cit.*, pp. xviii-xix, 42, 47; Currey, *op. cit.*, pp. 50, 53, 83; *Australian Encyclopaedia* (East Lansing, Mich., 1958), IV, 97.

[22] Carboni, *op. cit.*, p. 47; Currey, *op. cit.*, pp. 51-52.

[23] Currey, *op. cit.*, pp. 54, 84.

[24] Geoffrey Blainey, *The Rush That Never Ended* (Melbourne, 1963), p. 54.

[25] *Ibid.*, p. 57; Just, *op. cit.*, pp. 134-136.

[26] Carboni, *op. cit.*, pp. xviii-xix, 49; Currey, *op. cit.*, p. 58.

[27] Melbourne *Argus*, Dec. 5, 1854; Carboni, *op. cit.*, p. 57; Currey, *op. cit.*, p. 59.

[28] Currey, *loc. cit.*

[29] *Ibid.*, p. 63.

[30] Just, *op. cit.*, p. 128; David Swift and Heinz Marcuse, "The Golden Century," *Mining and Geological Journal*, IV (Sept., 1951), 13.

[31] Ferguson, *op. cit.*, pp. 277, 280; Pyke, *op. cit.*, pp. 241, 249.

[32] Willis Thornton, *The Nine Lives of Citizen Train* (New York, 1948), pp. 52-53; George Francis Train, *My Life* (New York, 1902), pp. 156, 159.

[33] Melbourne *Argus*, Dec. 2, 1854; Carboni, *op. cit.*, p. 66; Currey, *op. cit.*, pp. 63, 64; Ferguson, *op. cit.*, p. 280.

[34] Currey, *op. cit.*, p. 6.

[35] Melbourne *Argus*, Dec. 4, 8, 1854; Carboni, *op. cit.*, pp. 52, 66; Ferguson, *op. cit.*, p. 280.

CHAPTER 18

[1] Melbourne *Argus*, Dec. 2, 1854; C. Manning Hope Clark (ed.), *Select Documents in Australian History, 1788-1850* (Sydney, 1950), II, 62.

[2] Melbourne *Argus*, Dec. 8, 14, 1854; Raffaello Carboni, *The Eureka Stockade* (Mosman, N.S.W., Australia, 1942), p. 68; Geoffrey Blainey, *The Rush That Never Ended* (Melbourne, 1963), p. 55.

[3] Melbourne *Argus*, Dec. 8, 1854; Carboni, *op. cit.*, p. 71.

[4] L. G. Churchward, "The American Contribution to the Victorian Gold Rush," *Victorian Historical Magazine*, XIX (June, 1942), 47; Carboni, *op. cit.*, p. 74.

[5] Carboni, *op. cit.*, p. 71.

[6] Clive Turnbull, *Bonanza* (Melbourne, 1946), p. 27; William Thomas Pyke, *Australian Heroes and Adventurers* (Melbourne, n.d.), p. 41.

[7] Carboni, *op. cit.*, pp. xviii-xix, 75, 80; C. H. Currey, *The Irish at Eureka* (Sydney, 1954), p. 87.

[8] Melbourne *Argus*, Dec. 5, 1854; Carboni, *op. cit.*, p. 82; Currey, *op. cit.*, p. 4; N. O. P. Pyke, "Foreign Immigration to the Gold Fields" (unpublished M.A. thesis, University of Sydney, 1946), p. 253.

[9] Clark, *op. cit.*, p. 62.

[10] Melbourne *Argus*, Dec. 5, 6, 8, 1854; Carboni, *op. cit.*, pp. 82, 114; Currey, *op. cit.*, p. 69; Charles D. Ferguson, *The Experiences of a Forty-niner* (Cleveland, 1888), p. 283.

[11] Carboni, *op. cit.*, p. 81; N. O. P. Pyke, *op. cit.*, p. 267.

[12] Ferguson, *op. cit.*, p. 283.

[13] Melbourne *Argus*, Dec. 5, 6, 8, 1854; Turnbull, *op. cit.*, p. 27.

[14] Melbourne *Argus*, Dec. 4, 6, 1854; Currey, *op. cit.*, p. 75; George Francis Train, *My Life* (New York, 1902), p. 159.

[15] Melbourne *Argus*, Dec. 6, 8, 1854; Carboni, *op. cit.*, pp. xviii-xix; Currey, *op. cit.*, p. 75.

[16] A copy of the reward proclamation is in the Melbourne Public Library. This is reproduced in David Swift and Heinz Marcuse, "The Golden Century," *Mining and Geological Journal*, IV (Sept., 1951), 8. Currey, *op. cit.*, p. 71, places the reward at only £200.

[17] Melbourne *Argus*, Dec. 6, 8, 1854.

[18] *Ibid.*, Dec. 21, 1854; Ferguson, *op. cit.*, p. 291; N. O. P. Pyke, *op. cit.*, pp. 263, 267, 268; Train, *op. cit.*, p. 161.

[19] Carboni, *op. cit.*, p. 105.

[20] Currey, *op. cit.*, pp. 71, 76, 77; N. O. P. Pyke, *op. cit.*, p. 272.

[21] Currey, *op. cit.*, p. 77.

[22] *Ibid.*

[23] *Australian Encyclopaedia* (East Lansing, Mich., 1958), III, 417.

[24] Herbert C. Hoover, *The Memoirs of Herbert Hoover* (New York, 1952), pp. 30-32.

[25] A. G. L. Shaw, *The Story of Australia* (London, [1954]), pp. 278, 280, 283; G. D. H. Cole, "Trade (Labour) Unions," *Encyclopaedia Britannica* (Chicago, 1961), XXII, 384.

[26] Currey, *op. cit.*, p. 81; N. O. P. Pyke, *op. cit.*, p. 272.

Sources

(The following is a list of works used in citations, not a complete bibliography of the field.)

BOOKS AND ARTICLES

A Century of Journalism: The Sydney Morning Herald and Its Record of Australian Life, 1831-1931. Sydney, 1931.

Alexander, Frederick. *Australia and the United States.* Boston, 1941.

Allen, Harry Cranbrook. *Bush and Backwoods: A Comparison of the Frontier in Australia and the United States.* East Lansing, Mich., 1959.

Allen, William Wallace, and Richard Benjamin Avery. *California Gold Book: First Nugget, Its Discovery and Discoverers, and Some of the Results Proceeding Therefrom.* San Francisco, 1893.

Alpha (pseud.). *The Pioneer Prospector, Reminiscences of the Goldfields in the Fifties and Sixties: Victoria, New Zealand, New South Wales.* N.p., n.d. In Fisher Library, Sydney.

Anderson, I. G. *Port Arthur through the Artist's Eyes.* Hobart, 1948.

Anderson, R. S. *Australian Gold Fields: Their Discovery, Progress, and Prospects.* Glasgow, 1853. Reprinted in Sydney in 1956 with introduction, notes, and commentary by George Mackaness.

Angas, George French. *Views of the Gold Regions of Australia Drawn on the Spot.* London, 1851.

Ansted, David T. *The Gold-Seeker's Manual.* London, 1849.

Archer, Thomas. *Recollections of a Rambling Life.* Yokohama, 1897.

Australian Encyclopaedia. East Lansing, Mich., 1958.

Baker, Sidney John. *The Australian Language.* Sydney, 1945.

Bancroft, Hubert Howe. *History of California.* San Francisco, 1888.

———. *Popular Tribunals.* San Francisco, 1887.

Barrett, Charles L. (ed.). *Gold in Australia.* London, 1951.

Barry, Theo A., and B. A. Patten. *Men and Memories of San Francisco, in the "Spring of '50."* San Francisco, 1873.

Barry, William Jackson. *Past & Present and Men of the Times.* Wellington, N. Z., 1897.

———. *Up and Down; or Fifty Years' Colonial Experience in Australia, California, New Zealand, India, China, and the South Pacific; Being the Life History of Capt. W. J. Barry, Written by Himself, 1878.* London, 1879.

Bateson, Charles. *Gold Fleet for California: Forty-Niners from Australia and New Zealand.* Sydney, 1963.

Becke, Louis (ed.). *Old Convict Days.* New York, 1899.

Bicheno, J. E. "Confidential Report on the Colonial Press," *Tasmanian Historical Research Association Papers and Proceedings,* III (Aug., 1954), 88-89.

Blainey, Geoffrey. *Peaks of Lyell.* Melbourne, 1954.

———. *The Rush That Never Ended: A History of Australian Mining.* Melbourne, 1963.

Bonwick, James. *Notes of a Gold Digger and Gold Diggers' Guide.* London, 1942.

Buffum, E. G. *Six Months in the Gold Mines.* Philadelphia, 1850.

Burnett, Peter H. *An Old California Pioneer.* Oakland, Calif., 1946. Reprint of *Recollections and Opinions of an Old Pioneer.* London and New York, 1880.

Caiger, George (ed.). *The Australian Way of Life.* New York, 1953.

Caldwell, Robert. *The Gold Era of Victoria.* London, 1855.

Campbell, Mrs. A. *Rough and Smooth: or, Ho! for an Australian Gold Field.* Quebec, 1856.

Carboni, Raffaello. *The Eureka Stockade. Mosman,* N.S.W., Australia, 1942.

Caughey, John W. *Their Majesties the Mob.* Chicago, 1960.

Cavanagh, Michael (ed.). *Memoirs of Gen. Thomas Francis Meagher.* Worcester, Mass., 1892.

Cecil, R. A. T. C., Third Marquis of Salisbury. *Lord Robert Cecil's Goldfields Diary; with Introduction and Notes by E. Scott.* Melbourne, 1935.

Chambers, Charles H. *A General View of the State of California, Past and Present; with a Glimpse of the Probable Future.* Sydney, 1850.

Churchward, L. G. "The American Contribution to the Victorian Gold Rush," *Victorian Historical Magazine,* XIX (June, 1942), 85-95.

———. "Americans and Other Foreigners at Eureka," *Special Eureka Supplement, Historical Studies: Australia and New Zealand* (Dec., 1954), pp. 43-49.

———. "Australia and America: A Sketch of the Origin and Early Growth of Social and Economic Relations between Australia and the United States of America, 1790-1876." Unpublished M.A. thesis, University of Melbourne, 1941.

———. "Australian-American Relations during the Gold Rush," *Historical Studies of Australia and New Zealand,* II (1940), 11-24.

Clacy, Mrs. Charles. *A Lady's Visit to the Gold Diggings of Australia in 1852-53.* London, 1853.

Clark, C. Manning Hope (ed.). *Select Documents in Australian History, 1788-1850.* Sydney, 1950.

———. *Select Documents in Australian History, 1851-1900.* Sydney, 1955.

Cleland, Robert Glass. *A History of California: The American Period.* New York, 1922.

Cleland, Robert Glass (ed.). *Apron Full of Gold: The Letters of Mary*

Jane Megquier from San Francisco, 1849-1856. San Marino, Calif., 1949.

Clemens, Samuel L. *Following the Equator.* New York, 1897.

Clune, Frank. "Pool of the Two-tailed Fish." In *Land of My Birth.* Sydney, 1949. Pp. 36-63. This story was printed in Melbourne in 1946 as *Golden Goliath.*

——. *Wild Colonial Boys.* Sydney, 1948.

Coffin, George. *A Pioneer Voyage to California and round the World, 1849-1852.* Privately printed, 1908.

Cole, G. D. H. "Trade (Labour) Unions," *Encyclopaedia Britannica* (Chicago, 1961), XXII, 384.

Coleman, William T. "San Francisco Vigilance Committee," *Century Magazine,* XLIII (Nov., 1891), 133-150.

Coy, Owen Cochran. *Gold Days.* Los Angeles, 1929.

——. *In the Diggings in 'Forty-nine.* Los Angeles, 1948.

——. *Pictorial History of California.* Berkeley, 1925.

Craig, William. *My Adventures on the Australian Goldfields.* London, 1903.

Crawford, R. M., and G. F. James. "The Gold Rushes and the Aftermath, 1851-1901." In C. Hartley Grattan (ed.), *Australia.* Pp. 47-64. Berkeley and Los Angeles, 1947.

Cullen, J. H. *Young Ireland in Exile.* Dublin, 1928.

Currey, C. H. *The Irish at Eureka.* Sydney, 1954.

Davis, William Heath. *Seventy-five Years in California.* San Francisco, 1929. An enlarged edition of *Sixty Years in California* (San Francisco, 1889).

Davison, Simpson. *The Discovery and Geognosy of Gold Deposits in Australia.* London, 1860.

Dean, Johnson. *On Sea and Land: A Trip to California in 1850-3 with Chapters on South-Sea Islands, "Port Phillip," and Beautiful Tasmania.* Hobart, *ca.* 1905.

Dillon, William. *Life of John Mitchel.* London, 1888.

Ditmars, Raymond L. *Reptiles of the World. . . .* New York, 1936.

Dow, Hume. "Eureka and the Creative Writer," *Special Eureka Supplement, Historical Studies: Australia and New Zealand* (Dec., 1954), pp. 50-61.

Doyle, E. A. (ed.). *Golden Years, 1851-1951: Published by the Victorian Government To Celebrate the Centenary of the Discovery of Gold in Victoria.* Melbourne, 1951.

Dunbabin, Thomas. *The Making of Australia.* London, 1922.

Dunlop, Eric W. "The Golden Fifties," *Royal Historical Society, Journal and Proceedings,* XXXVII (1951), 23-24.

Earp, G. B. *The Gold Colonies of Australia and Gold Seeker's Manual.* London, 1852.

Ellison, William Henry. *A Self-governing Dominion: California, 1849-1860.* Berkeley, 1950.

Erskine, John Elphinstone. *A Short Account of the Late Discoveries of*

Gold in Australia. London, 1852. Reprinted in Sydney in 1957 with introduction, notes, and commentary by George Mackaness.

Farwell, Willard B. "Cape Horn and Cooperative Mining in '49," *Century Magazine,* XLII (Aug., 1891), 579-594.

Favill, Josiah Marshall. *The Diary of a Young Officer Serving with the Armies of the United States during the War of the Rebellion.* Chicago, 1909.

Feely, John A. "With the *Argus* to Eureka," *Special Eureka Supplement, Historical Studies: Australia and New Zealand* (Dec., 1954), pp. 25-42.

Ferguson, Charles D. *The Experiences of a Forty-niner during Thirty-four Years' Residence in California and Australia.* Cleveland, 1888.

Ferguson, John Alexander. *Bibliography of Australia.* Sydney, 1951.

Field, Stephen J. *Personal Reminiscences of Early Days in California.* Privately printed, 1893.

Fletcher, Robert Samuel. *Eureka: From Cleveland by Ship to California, 1849-1850.* Durham, N. C., 1959.

Freuchen, Peter. *Book of the Seven Seas.* New York, [1957].

Gerstaecker, Frederick. *Narrative of a Journey round the World.* London, 1853.

Gill, S. T. *The Diggers & Diggings of Victoria As They Are in 1855, Drawn on Stone.* Melbourne, 1855.

Glasson, W. R. *Australia's First Goldfield.* Sydney, 1944.

———. *Lewis Ponds Creek.* Sydney, n.d.

———. *Ophir Revisited.* Sydney, 1947.

———. *The Romance of Ophir: The Discovery of Australia's First Payable Gold.* Sydney, 1935.

[Godley, J. R. (ed.)]. "Extracts from the Journal of a Visit to New South Wales in 1853." In unidentified publication in Mitchell Library, Sydney.

Grattan, C. Hartley. *The United States and the Southwest Pacific.* Cambridge, Mass., 1961.

Grattan, C. Hartley (ed.). *Australia.* Berkeley and Los Angeles, 1947.

Hancock, W. K. *Australia.* New York, n.d.

Hargraves, Edward Hammond. *Australia & Its Goldfields.* London, 1855.

———. Letter describing gold discoveries, Sydney *Empire,* Dec. 28, 1860.

Hill, James M. *Historical Summary of Gold, Silver, Copper, Lead, and Zinc Produced in California, 1848 to 1926.* U.S. Bureau of Mines, Economic Paper no. 3. Washington, 1929.

Hittell, Theodore H. *History of California.* San Francisco, 1897.

Hives, Frank. *The Journal of a Jackaroo.* Toronto, 1933.

Hole, R. T. "Australia's First Goldfields." In *Bathurst: The Cradle of the Nation Celebrates the Centenary of Gold.* Bathurst, 1951.

Hoover, Herbert C. *The Memoirs of Herbert Hoover: Years of Adventure, 1874-1920.* New York, 1952.

Howitt, William. *Land, Labour and Gold: or, Two Years in Victoria; with Visits to Sydney and Van Diemen's Land.* London, 1855.

Humphrey, Seth King. *Loafing through the Pacific.* Philadelphia, 1929.

Hurt, Peyton. "The Rise and Fall of the 'Know Nothings' in California," *Quarterly of the California Historical Society,* IX (March, 1930), 16-49, 99-128.

Jack, Tom, and Harry. *Two Years Leave in Australia*. Plymouth, Eng., 1872.

Jackson, Joseph Henry. *Anybody's Gold: The Story of California's Mining Towns*. New York, 1941.

Jameson, R. G. *Australia and Her Gold Regions*. New York, 1852.

Jenkins, Olaf P. (ed.). *The Mother Lode Country*. California Division of Mines, Bulletin 141. San Francisco, 1948.

Just, P. *Australia; or Notes Taken during a Residence in the Colonies from the Gold Discovery in 1851 till 1857*. Dundee, 1859.

Keese, Oliné [Mrs. C. W. Leakey]. *Old Tasmania Days: The Broad Arrow: Being Passages from the History of Maida Gwynuhan*. London, 1887.

Kent, Bruce. "Agitations on the Victorian Gold Fields, 1851-54," *Historical Studies of Australia and New Zealand*, VI, no. 23 (Nov., 1954).

Lancelott, F. *Australia As It Is: Its Settlements, Farms and Gold Fields*. London, 1852.

LeRoy-Beaulieu, Pierre. *Les Nouvelles Sociétés*. Paris, 1901.

Levasseur, E. *La Question de l'Or. Les Mines de California et d'Australie*. Paris, 1858.

Lewis, Oscar. *Sea Routes to the Gold Fields*. New York, 1949.

[Lucett, E.] *Rovings in the Pacific from 1837 to 1849*. London, 1851.

M'Combie, Thomas. *Australian Sketches: The Gold Discovery, Bush Graves, &c., &c*. London, 1861.

McGuire, Paul. *Australia, Her Heritage, Her Future*. New York, 1939.

Mackenzie, David. *The Gold Digger: A Visit to the Gold Fields of Australia in February, 1852*. London, 1852.

Malone, R. Edmond. *Three Years' Cruise in the Australian Colonies*. London, 1854.

Marryat, Frank. *Mountains and Molehills or Recollections of a Burnt Journal*. London, 1855.

Maude, Frederic P., and C. E. Pollock. *A Compendium of the Law of Merchant Shipping*. London, 1853.

Mitchel, John. *Jail Journal*. Dublin, 1913.

Moody, Peter. *New Mount Alexander and Australian Golconda. . . . The Ovens River, or Great South Western Gold Field*. Sydney, 1852.

Moorehead, Alan. *Cooper's Creek. . . .* New York, 1963.

Morrell, W. P. *The Gold Rushes*. New York, 1941.

Mossman, Samuel, and Thomas Banister. *Australia Visited and Revisited: A Narrative of Recent Travels and Old Experiences in Victoria and New South Wales*. London, 1853.

Mundy, G. C. *Our Antipodes: or Residence and Rambles in the Australasian Colonies with a Glimpse of the Gold Fields*. London, 1855.

Murray's Guide to the Gold Diggings. London, 1852. Reprinted in Sydney in 1956 with introduction, notes, and commentary by George Mackaness.

"My Trip to Australia," *Frank Leslie's New Family Magazine*, II (April, 1858), 289-306, 401-414.

Neville, Amelia Ransome. *The Fantastic City: Memoirs of the Social and Romantic Life of Old San Francisco*. Boston, 1932.

O'Keefe, Cornelius. "Rides through Montana," *Harpers New Monthly Magazine*, XXXV (Oct., 1867), 568-585.

Parsons, George F. *The Life and Adventures of James W. Marshall, the Discoverer of Gold in California.* Sacramento, 1870.

Paul, Rodman W. *California Gold.* Cambridge, Mass., 1947.

———. *Mining Frontiers of the Far West, 1848-1880.* New York, 1963.

Peck, George W. *Melbourne, and the Chincha Islands; with Sketches of Lima and a Voyage round the World.* New York, 1854.

Pitt, Leonard. "The Beginnings of Nativism in California," *Pacific Historical Review,* XXX (Feb., 1961), 23-38.

Pittman, Amos S. "The California and Australia Gold Rushes As Seen by Amos S. Pittman with Introduction and Notes by Theressa Gay," *California Historical Society Quarterly,* XXX (March, 1951), 15-37.

Pyke, N. O. P. "Foreign Immigration to the Gold Fields." Unpublished M.A. thesis, University of Sydney, 1946.

Pyke, William Thomas. *Australian Heroes and Adventurers.* Melbourne, n.d. This work appeared in several editions; it was published in London in 1889 and again in 1909.

Raymond, Rossiter W. *Statistics of Mines and Mining in the States and Territories West of the Rocky Mountains.* Washington, D. C., 1870.

Read, C. Rudston. *What I Heard, Saw, and Did at the Australian Gold Fields.* London, 1853.

Richardson, Henry Handel. *Fortunes of Richard Mahoney.* Melbourne, 1951.

Ridgway, Robert H. *Summarized Data of Gold Production.* U.S. Bureau of Mines, Economic Paper no. 6. Washington, 1929.

Ross, B. *California: The Country and Its Resources.* Pamphlet published in Adelaide in 1850 reprinting a San Francisco *News* article.

Ross, C. Stuart. "Two American Types That Left Their Stamp on Victorian History," *Victorian Historical Magazine,* VII (July, 1919), 126-134.

Rudder, Enoch William. *Incidents Connected with the Discovery of Gold in New South Wales, in the Year 1851.* Sydney, 1861.

Ryan, James T. *Reminiscences of Australia.* Sydney, 1894.

San Francisco City Directory. San Francisco, 1850.

Scherer, James Augustin Brown. *"The Lion of the Vigilantes": William T. Coleman and the Life of Old San Francisco.* Indianapolis, 1939.

Scott, E. *See* Cecil, R.A.T.C., Third Marquis of Salisbury.

Serle, Geoffrey. "The Causes of Eureka," *Special Eureka Supplement, Historical Studies: Australia and New Zealand* (Dec., 1954), pp. 15-24.

Serle, Percival. *Dictionary of Australian Biography.* Sydney, 1949.

Shaw, A. G. L. *The Story of Australia.* London, [1954].

Sherer, John. *The Gold-Finder of Australia.* London, 1853.

Sherman, William Tecumseh. *Memoirs of General William T. Sherman. By Himself.* New York, 1875.

Small, J. *The New Zealand and Australian Songster . . . to Which Is Added Extracts from His Diary on the Australian Goldfields.* New Zealand, 1866.

Smith, Frank Meriweather (ed.). *San Francisco Vigilance Committee of '56 with Some Interesting Sketches of Events Succeeding 1848.* San Francisco, 1883.

Soulé, Frank, John H. Gihon, and James Nisbet. *The Annals of San Francisco.* New York, 1855.

Stewart, George. *Committee of Vigilance: Revolution in San Francisco, 1851.* Boston, 1964.

Strezelecki, Paul E. de. *Physical Description of New South Wales and Van Diemen's Land.* London, 1845.

Swift, David, and Heinz Marcuse. "The Golden Century," *Mining and Geological Journal,* IV (Sept., 1951), 5-16.

Taylor, Bayard. *Eldorado, or, Adventures in the Path of Empire.* New York, 1857.

Tennant, Kylie. *Australia: Her Story.* New York, 1953.

——. *The Battlers.* London, 1941.

Therry, Roger. *Reminiscences of Thirty Years' Residence in New South Wales and Victoria.* London, 1863.

Thornton, Willis. *The Nine Lives of Citizen Train.* New York, 1948.

Train, George Francis. *My Life in Many States and in Foreign Lands.* New York, 1902.

——. *Young America Abroad, in Europe, Asia, and Australia.* London, 1857.

Turnbull, Clive. *Bonanza: The Story of George Francis Train.* Melbourne, 1946.

——. *The Charm of Hobart.* Sydney, 1949.

Villard, Henry. *Memoirs of Henry Villard, Journalist and Financier, 1835-1900.* Boston, 1904.

Vizetelly, Henry. *Four Months among the Gold-Finders in Alta California; Being the Diary of an Expedition from San Francisco to the Gold District.* London, 1849.

——. *Glances Back through Seventy Years.* London, 1893.

Walske, R. D. "The Significance of Eureka in Australian History," *Special Eureka Supplement, Historical Studies: Australia and New Zealand* (Dec., 1954), pp. 62-80.

Ward, Russel. *The Australian Legend.* Melbourne, 1958.

Welles, C. M. *Three Years' Wanderings of a Connecticut Yankee.* New York, 1859.

Westgarth, William. *Victoria; Late Australia Felix . . . Being an Account of the Colony and Its Mines.* Edinburgh, 1853.

Wierzbicki, Felix Paul. *What I Saw in California.* Launceston, 1850.

Williams, Mary Floyd. *Fortune, Smile Once More!* Indianapolis, 1946.

——. *History of the San Francisco Committee of Vigilance of 1851.* University of California Publications in History, XII. Berkeley, 1921.

Williams, Mary Floyd (ed.). *Papers of the San Francisco Committee of Vigilance of 1851.* Berkeley, 1919.

Wood, Gordon Leslie (ed.). *Australia: Its Resources and Development.* New York, 1947.

Wood, James. *The Tasmanian Royal Kalendar, Colonial Register, and Almanack.* Launceston, 1849.

Wood, William H. R. *Digest of the Laws of California.* San Francisco, 1857.

NEWSPAPERS

Alta California
Ballaarat [sic] Times
Bathurst Free Press
Bell's Life in Sydney and Sporting Chronicle
Bendigo Advertiser
Daily California Courier
Geelong Advertiser
Hobart Britannia, and Trades' Advocate
Hobart *Colonial Times and Tasmanian*
Hobart Daily Courier
Hobart *Mercury*
Hobart Town Advertiser
Hobart Town Guardian
Launceston *Cornwall Chronicle*
Launceston Examiner
Marysville [California] *Herald*
Melbourne *Argus*
Melbourne Morning Herald
People's Advocate and New South Wales Vindicator
Sacramento Daily Placer Times
Sacramento Daily Union
Sacramento Transcript
San Francisco Daily Evening Picayune
San Francisco Daily Herald
Sonora [California] *Herald*
South Australian Register
Stockton *Journal*
Stockton *Placer Times*
Stockton Times
Sydney *Empire*
Sydney Morning Herald
Sydney Sporting Times
Tasmanian Colonist

MANUSCRIPTS

Brooks & Co. Letter Books, Items 67-73 (Mitchell Library, Sydney).

Claughton, Joseph. Journal of voyage to Australia in 1852 (in possession of Mrs. Isobel Arndt, Richmond, B.C., Canada).

Colonial Secretary Records, Denison Period (Tasmanian Archives, Hobart).

Cullen, J. H. Letter concerning S. O'Brien's secret visits which caused Governor Denison to punish him (Tasmanian Archives, Hobart).

Earnest, William W. Journal of an American prospector who met Thomas Archer in the Mother Lode country (in possession of Mrs. W. C. Wirth, Naperville, Ill.).

General Letter Books, 1844-1857; Letter Books, 1847-1853 (Mitchell Library, Sydney).

"Gold Rush Days: Vital Statistics Copied from Early Newspapers of Stockton, California, 1850-1855." Mimeographed by San Joaquin Genealogical Society of Stockton, 1958.

Governors' Dispatches (Tasmania) 1825-1855 (Tasmanian Archives, Hobart).

Halterman Collection. Early photographs (Mitchell Gallery, Sydney).

New South Wales Legislative Council V. & P. (1850), Vol. I.

Newspaper Cuttings (Mitchell Library, Sydney).

O'Brien, Smith. Letter breaking his parole (Dr. W. L. Crowther Collection, Hobart).

O'May, Captain Harry. Notes on ships leaving Hobart during gold rush (in Captain O'May's possession, Hobart, Tasmania).

Reynolds Letters (Mitchell Library, Sydney).

Rudder, E. W. Notes (Fisher Library, Sydney).

Sydney Chamber of Commerce Minutes, 1851-1852 (Mitchell Library, Sydney).

Sydney Railway Company. Letter Book, September, 1848–April, 1852 (Fisher Library, Sydney).

Sydney Railway Company. Minutes, Vol. I (Fisher Library, Sydney).

Taussig, H. John Carlsson. Notes on discovery of gold on Lewis Ponds Creek (in possession of Mr. H. J. C. Taussig, Bathurst).

Thomson, Edward Deas. Papers (Mitchell Library, Sydney).

Towns, Robert. Journal and letters (Mitchell Library, Sydney).

United States Consuls, Dispatches from, 1836-1906 (microfilm, University of California, Santa Barbara).

United States Consul's Semi-Annual Report, January 1, 1852 (Washington, D.C., 1852).

Acknowledgments

This book is the result of a research fellowship at the University of Sydney under the auspices of the Fulbright program. I am forever grateful to Geoffrey Rossiter, executive officer of the United States Educational Foundation, for his cooperation in this project, and to Mrs. Rossiter for her hospitality during the nine months my wife and I spent in Australia. Mr. Rossiter's assistant executive officer, Robert McCaig, also offered kindly advice in his efforts to orient two strangers in a new land.

At the University of Sydney I am indebted to Dr. Alan Birch for sending me copies of minutes kept by the Sydney Railway Company, and to Dr. A. G. L. Shaw who shared with me his vast knowledge of Australian history. In the university's Fisher Library, E. V. Steel, the librarian, suggested pertinent topics for this research. The university archivist, David S. Macmillan, who had recently unearthed a rare picture of the Hargraves nugget, supplied me with photographs of it and also of reproductions of London sources that I might otherwise have overlooked. In the Mitchell Library in Sydney, Miss Mander Jones was constantly helpful and resourceful, permitting me to study the rarest manuscripts, including the journal of Captain William Bligh, written at the time of the famous mutiny.

Dr. George Mackaness, noted Australian specialist on the gold rush who has edited many publications in that field, hospitably entertained my wife and me, giving us the benefit of his research. Mr. Keast Burke, also of Sydney, gave me a rare little book by Eric Baume entitled *Sydney Duck*, and invited us to his home in the suburbs, where he keeps one of the finest collections of photographs of the Australian diggings. Zellie McLeod, of the *Daily Telegraph*, gave me information available only to a trained newspaper woman, including the addresses of several people named Marshall who claimed to be descendants of the discoverer of gold in California. Dr. A. P. Elkins, vice-chairman of the Aboriginal Commission, was good enough to furnish me letters of introduction which enabled me to meet and know the primitive blackfellows.

At the Australian National University in Canberra, my wife and I were cordially received by Professor W. E. Stanner and Dr. David Hodgkin. Also L. F. Fitzhardinge, "Reader in the Sources of Australian History," liberally furnished me statistics on emigration during the gold rush from Australia to California compiled by David Packer of the university's Department of Demography. Professors Edgar Waters and Russel Ward enthusiastically shared their firsthand knowledge of Australian station life and bush songs. To Dr. P. J. Calvert and his wife Betty we are everlastingly indebted for an insight into early Australian life not found in books, for helping us meet many gracious and well-informed people, and for motor trips through the green hills of New South Wales. Norman Bartlett and his wife Eve, both established Australian authors, proved to be excellent companions and authorities on the gold rush—especially on Australia's part in the California rush. We are also deeply indebted to Professor Arthur Dale Trendall, master of University House at the National University, for introducing us to scholars of the gold rush as well as making available to us comfortable accommodations among many congenial fellow students.

At the University of Melbourne, Professor Norman Harper introduced me to those outstanding scholars of the gold rush, Geoffrey Serle and L. G. Churchward. Professor J. T. A. Burke hospitably guided us to many historic sites in the city. Mr. Ivan J. Thompson and his charming wife Christine escorted us across the countryside from the wildlife sanctuary at Healesville west of the Dandenongs, past the estate of the operatic soprano, Melba, to the faraway sylvan valley where woodchopper James Esmonds made his historic discovery of gold in the summer of 1851—a lush spot, beautified when we were there by the ringing notes of a bellbird in the tall eucalyptus trees.

In the Tasmanian Archives at Hobart, Peter Eldershaw and Miss Elizabeth Patterson produced records that were invaluable to my study. Robert Sharman, who knows the city intimately, took time from his off-duty hours to point out historic buildings. Captain Harry O'May gave me copies of his extensive notes on the gold rush to California and told me many facts about sailing ships which only an experienced mariner could know. Mr. Colin Perkins and his daughter Patricia (now Mrs. Myles McRae of "Selma," Bothwell, Tasmania) generously took my wife and me to meet people who knew the local history of Hobart. Among them was Dr. W. L. Crowther, who showed me the letter Smith O'Brien wrote when breaking his parole. With Dr. and Mrs. Richard Foxton and Mrs. P. C. Piper, we visited the quaint village of New Norfolk.

I wish also to record my appreciation of the hospitality shown us by Sir Edward and Lady Morgan at the Australia Club in Sydney and at their home in North Adelaide. In addition, they took us on a delightful ride across the Mount Lofty Ranges during the rainy season. In Brisbane, Harry and Maud Jones and their daughter Shirley treated us to a splendid motor tour through the green backcountry of Queensland.

In the United States I am indebted to Merle Curti, who encouraged from the beginning my study of this neglected field in American history. Those connoisseurs of rare books, Glen Dawson of Los Angeles and J. E. Reynolds of Van Nuys, generously presented me with rare items concerning the gold rush from Australia. Strohm and Catherine Newell of San Diego, both collectors extraordinary, sent me books and pictures which I found very helpful in this work. John Galvin of Tasmania's Launceston, California's Santa Barbara, and Ireland's Dublin generously offered me microfilming privileges in his extensive library of Australiana. William R. Moran of La Canada, California, world traveler and discerning collector of Australiana, sent me photostats of items I would never have found.

George L. Harding of Berkeley thoughtfully wrote me about articles published on the subject of my research. Mrs. Winifred McAree of Santa Barbara was kind enough to tell me that her sister, Mrs. Isobel Arndt of Richmond, British Columbia, had inherited a journal kept by her grandfather who went to Australia from England, and she helped me get a copy, which has been useful in preparing this book.

I want to thank William Spaulding of the advertising department of Levi Strauss & Company for information on the founding of that firm. In the San Francisco Maritime Museum, Mr. A. Harmon, librarian, and Mrs. Mathilda Dring of the Photographic Section, spent hours checking for me the tonnage of gold-rush vessels and identifying pictures of them. In the University of California's Bancroft Library, Director George P. Hammond, and the head of public services, Barr Tompkins, were generous with their time in showing me valuable material.

At the California State Library in Sacramento, Allan Ottley, California section librarian, was unstinting with his help both in answering questions through the mail and in placing the well-catalogued resources of his library at my disposal on a visit there. Richard H. Dillon, George Stewart, John H. Kemble, and Samuel C. McCulloch, all experts on subjects covered by this study, generously answered anxious inquiries.

On the eastern edge of the tules at Stockton, Mrs. Ernest Smutney helped me at the Public Library with both the early newspapers and microfilms of them. Cornelius Muller, professor of botany at the University of California, Santa Barbara, identified for me the vegetation of the Mother Lode country. At Harvard University Miss Priscilla Parmakian, Mrs. Elise U. Mock, and Mrs. Jean C. Ratche of the Photographic Reference Department hunted for citations concerning the Irish "traitors." I am indebted to Harold Merklen of the New York Public Library and Clifford K. Shipton, director of the American Antiquarian Society, for the same futile search. Kevin H. White, secretary of the Commonwealth of Massachusetts, checked for me the Archives, revealing the true political status of Freeman Cobb which has been incorrectly recorded by the best authorities.

University Librarian Donald C. Davidson at the University of California, Santa Barbara, has given me infinite assistance. In spite of his colossal task of converting a library that shelved fewer than 50,000 books in 1947 to one scheduled to house

735,000 volumes in 1971, he has been unceasingly eager to provide sources for this work. I am also deeply indebted to efficient Martha Peterson, head of Acquisitions, discerning Herbert Linville, head of Government Publications, resourceful Donald E. Fitch and ever-agreeable Dorothy Annable in the Reference Department, as well as the persistent and always pleasant Vivian M. Karschner, who not only located but also borrowed for me rare books on interlibrary loan. In the Department of Special Collections, Christian Brun and Dolores Ritchie were continually helpful in suggesting unique and pertinent material. Luella Howard, with her usual speed and accuracy, typed the entire text, wondering (at least part of the time) how a cabbage-tree hat was made.

And, as in twelve earlier volumes, I want to acknowledge the assistance of my wife Mildred, who sailed the seven seas with me in search of material for this book. Together we combed the libraries and archives of a half-dozen Australian cities, picnicked in the lush eastern forests of Queensland, New South Wales, and Victoria, enjoying the mateship of a hospitable people—even in the dead heart of the continent beyond Alice Springs, while waiting for the billie to boil under great eucalyptus trees on the bank of a dry river. With me she traveled up and down California's Mother Lode, seeking the spots familiar to Australian gold seekers. She typed the citations, and her skilled editorial eyes read the entire manuscript. Her patience and literary judgment help to extract the black sand from the gold that gives this volume whatever value an assayer may determine.

J. M.

Index